Creative and Critical Thinking

W. EDGAR MOORE

CHAIRMAN, DEPARTMENT OF COMPREHENSIVE LOGIC
UNIVERSITY COLLEGE · UNIVERSITY OF FLORIDA

HOUGHTON MIFFLIN COMPANY · BOSTON

New York Atlanta Geneva, Ill. Dallas Palo Alto

Developed from

APPLIED LOGIC

by Winston W. Little, W. Harold Wilson, and W. Edgar Moore

With the Assistance of

The Staff of Comprehensive Logic
University College · University of Florida

Paul T. Thurston

George R. Bentley

Gerald B. Standley

William C. Childers

William E. Kline

Marna V. Brady

Frank Sciadini

Morton Wolfson

Preface

Creative and Critical Thinking is the outgrowth of long experimentation with a course in effective thinking which has been an integral part of the general education program at the University of Florida since 1935. We believe that a course devoted exclusively to the development of effective thinking is as necessary as a basic course in English or mathematics. While students can and do improve their thinking through the study of such courses as English, mathematics, physical science, and social science, the typical instructor is too hard pressed by the demands of subject matter to spare more than an occasional moment for improving thinking. We believe that effective thinking is too complex a process to be adequately treated as an adjunct to a course devoted primarily to other subject matter, and too important in our civilization to be relegated to spare moments. A course devoted exclusively to effective thinking, together with all the attention instructors in other courses can spare, is none too much.

This text was developed from *Applied Logic,* first published in 1955. In *Applied Logic* our purpose was to present a text that would have a real influence on the life of the student by developing intellectual skills he could put to practical use in solving the myriad problems which confront him throughout life. To that end we changed the content and emphases of the traditional logic course. To the formal and material fallacies we added the devices of persuasion commonly used in advertising and propaganda. We attempted to simplify the traditional treatment of deduction and make it more effective in improving both the student's deductive skill and his precision in the interpretation of language. We also tried to make the standard techniques of induction more concrete and specific. In the belief that any realistic approach to induction must embrace the theory of probability, we included an elementary treatment of probability and used it to clarify certain problems in induction. From the behavioral sciences we drew materials relevant to subjective factors in thinking. Our assumption was that insight into such subjective factors as emotion, prejudice, and cultural influence is a necessary part of sound thinking.

Comments from thousands of students encouraged us to believe that our objectives were accomplished to some degree. Consequently we planned to make only minor revisions in *Applied Logic.* But as work on the revision proceeded, we became convinced that the educational needs of college students had changed so much that major revisions were desirable.

The explosion of knowledge, the increasing tendency of technical information to become obsolete, and the growing complexity of our society convinced us that students need more specific instruction in selecting and using information to solve new problems and make decisions in unfamiliar situations.

Preface

In *Creative and Critical Thinking* we have tried to respond to this need by weaving materials from many disciplines into a unified set of procedures for recognizing and defining problems, gathering relevant information, devising and testing solutions to problems, and making decisions. Since critical thinking alone cannot produce new answers, we have emphasized the constant interplay of creative *and* critical thinking in problem solving. We have also added a chapter on aids to creative thinking.

Our staff members, who are experienced academic advisers, now believe that one objective of a course in effective thinking should be to promote academic achievement. Accordingly, to show the student the relevance of college courses to his own life, we have stressed the importance of background information in all kinds of problem solving and decision making.

We agree with the numerous educators who have pointed out that unsolved personal problems seriously hamper educational progress. Furthermore, we have observed a high correlation between unsolved personal problems and poor procedures of thinking. We have therefore tried to show the student how to apply rational procedures of thinking to his own emotionally charged problems. Because we believe that many personal problems stem from confusion over values, we have added two chapters designed to show the student how to use the procedures of effective thinking creatively as well as critically to construct for himself a wholesome and reasonably consistent system of values. Our experience indicates that students can cope with academic life more successfully by using these procedures and viewing their problems in a context of logic.

On the theory that extensive practice is necessary in learning effective procedures of thinking, we have supplied exercises in which the student is required to apply the procedures to a wide variety of problems, including some that freshmen frequently encounter.

In 1965, with the kind permission of Houghton Mifflin Company, a mimeographed version of this text was used by more than three thousand students. We then revised this version in the light of our experience with it.

Grateful acknowledgment is due many people. Fruitful suggestions have been drawn from *Reliable Knowledge,* by Harold A. Larrabee; *Personality: A Biosocial Approach to Origins and Structure,* by Gardner Murphy; and *On Becoming a Person,* by Carl R. Rogers. Both technical advice and encouragement were provided by three administrative officers of the Health Center at the University of Florida, Dr. Samuel P. Martin, Provost, Dr. Darrel J. Mase, Dean of the College of Health Related Professions, and Dr. Peter F. Regan, Head of the Department of Psychiatry (currently Executive Vice President, State University of New York at Buffalo). Special thanks are due to Henry F. Thoma and John W. Poindexter for incomparable editorial supervision. The devoted assistance of Jane Crumrine Moore has been indispensable.

With the exception of some historical material and a few incidents that are public knowledge, the subject matter of illustrations and exercises is fictitious. Any resemblance to actual persons, advertisements, or names of products is coincidental and unintentional.

W. E. M.

Contents

Contents

1 Decision Making

On June 4, 1944, General Dwight D. Eisenhower, Allied Supreme Commander, faced a difficult and fateful decision. Operation Overlord, the invasion of the continent of Europe, had been scheduled to begin on June 5, but unusually foul weather in the English Channel had forced postponement of D day until June 6. On the morning of June 4 the weather was still foul and the forecasts gloomy. General Eisenhower then had to decide whether to postpone D day again. The greatest invasion force ever assembled was poised and ready for the attack. The fate of hundreds of thousands of men and the course of the entire war could depend on his decision.

Operation Overlord had been planned on the assumption that D day would be scheduled when certain meteorological conditions would prevail. A late-rising moon was necessary so that paratroopers could jump under cover of darkness yet have moonlight shortly afterwards in order to carry out their essential missions. A low tide at dawn was necessary to expose the underwater obstacles the Germans had erected on the beaches. A calm sea was vital for the small craft that would ferry the troops to shore. Once the beachheads had been established, calm seas for several days after D day were necessary for the landing of hundreds of thousands of troops and mountains of supplies.

It was reasonable to assume that bad weather on D day could turn Overlord into a catastrophe. Clouds over Normandy would prevent bombers and paratroopers from finding their targets. Rough seas would swamp the small landing craft and prevent the landing of materiel. Once set in motion, Overlord could not be stopped without tremendous cost. All these factors argued for postponement.

On the other hand, postponement could also mean catastrophe. If D day were postponed again, it would have to be postponed for nearly a month, for moon and tide would not be favorable again until July. Great pains had been taken to mislead the Germans into thinking that the invasion would come in the area of Calais. It seemed unlikely that the real plans could be kept secret another month, for nearly two hundred thousand men had been briefed for the Normandy invasion before the first postponement was forced by the weather.

As often happens when momentous decisions must be made, General Eisenhower was caught between Scylla and Charybdis. If he acted without sufficient information, he could make a dreadful mistake. He did not have sufficient information, for he could not know with certainty how dangerous a postponement would be. On the other hand, if he waited too long to get the information he needed, he would be caught in the pitfall of *decision by indecision, i.e.,* delaying a decision until it is made by time or events. The longer he waited the more he would know about the weather; but if he waited too long, it would be too late to issue the necessary orders.

As the hours of June 4 ticked away, General Eisenhower waited and watched the weather reports. At 9:30 P.M. he assembled his senior staff officers to hear the latest forecasts. The meteorologists reported an unexpected development: a new weather front was moving toward the English Channel. They predicted that the weather would be barely passable on the morning of June 6 and would worsen soon thereafter. But they could not be sure that their predictions would prove true.

Now the fateful decision was up to General Eisenhower. His information was still insufficient, but he knew that he had only a few more minutes left in which to issue the necessary orders. He made his momentous decision: D day would be June 6.[1] He had followed the rules of effective thinking: he had gathered all the information he could, he had weighed it carefully, and he had avoided decision by indecision.

You may never have to make a decision so fateful for so many people as General Eisenhower's. But the complex and rapidly changing society in which you live will force you to make many difficult decisions as fateful for you as General Eisenhower's was for the world. The decisions you make will be vital to your success, your happiness, and even your health. And you, like General Eisenhower, will be forced to choose between the perils of decision by indecision and making decisions without sufficient information. How well your decisions turn out will depend in part on the procedures of thinking you use.

---

[1] For details of this decision, see Cornelius Ryan, *The Longest Day* (New York: Simon and Schuster, 1959); Omar N. Bradley, *A Soldier's Story* (New York: Holt, 1951); Dwight D. Eisenhower, *Crusade in Europe* (New York: Doubleday, 1948).

The importance of procedures in thinking is amply illustrated by the history of science. Prior to the seventeenth century science had made relatively little progress. In the last three centuries, however, a number of procedures of thinking have gradually evolved that are now known as the scientific method. The use of these procedures has been responsible to a large degree for the fantastic success of modern science in discovering the secrets of the universe as well as solutions of technological problems. It now seems credible that any problem that can be taken to the laboratory can eventually be solved.

Outside the context of the laboratory, however, most of us repeatedly commit the same blunders in thinking that seriously retarded science until the development of effective procedures. Consequently, progress in solving most human problems has lagged far behind progress in science. Human problems cannot, of course, be taken to the laboratory and subjected to rigorous controls, and some of the procedures of the scientific method do not apply to these problems. Nevertheless, a large body of evidence gives us ample reason to believe that effective procedures in thinking can be of great value in solving human and personal problems.

This textbook presents a comprehensive set of procedures of thinking designed to be helpful not only to the scientist but also to the layman struggling with personal problems involving strong feelings. These procedures are based directly on the philosophy and methods of science; but other elements, particularly from the behavioral sciences, have been added to make the procedures useful in a wide range of situations.

1. Creative and Critical Thinking

The procedures described in this text require two distinctly different kinds of thinking, *creative thinking* and *critical thinking*. Creative thinking may be defined as the formulation of possible solutions to a problem or explanations of a phenomenon, and critical thinking as the testing and evaluation of these solutions or explanations.

Creative thinking and critical thinking are as essential to effective thinking as a good offense and defense are to a winning football team. Both are essential in all areas of human activity. To put a new product on the market, the manufacturer must first "create" the idea for the new product. But if he has good business sense, he will not market the product until it has been thoroughly "criticized" by testing and evaluation. In solving a crime, a good detective "creates" possible explanations and then tests them with all the evidence he can get. If he fails to "create" the right explanations, he cannot possibly solve the crime. If he is careless in "criticizing" the explanations he has created, his "solution" of the crime may be the wrong one. In diagnosing an illness, the physician first "creates" possible diagnoses that seem to fit the symptoms and then "criticizes" these by further examination of the patient or by laboratory tests. His final diagnosis cannot be right unless the possible diagnoses he has "created" include the right one. Even when his possible diagnoses do include the right one, he may still make a mistake if he is careless in "criticizing" his possible diagnoses.

The methods of modern science are both creative and critical. In trying to explain a phenomenon a well-trained scientist first tries to "create" many tentative explanations. Then he subjects each possible explanation to rigorous tests. Often all the explanations he has "created" fail to pass the tests, but in the process he has acquired more information about the phenomenon under investigation. He then proceeds to "create" and "criticize" other possible explanations until he finds one that withstands rigorous testing.

Outside the context of the laboratory, however, scientists and laymen alike tend to be careless about both creative and critical aspects of thinking. When our feelings are aroused we are likely to act first and think only after it is too late. We tend to seize upon the first course of action that occurs to us without bothering to criticize it or to find better courses of action. The blunders we make are the natural consequences of our failure to create and criticize.

Create and *criticize*, then, are the twin watchwords of the effective thinker.

2. Phases of Decision Making

The general procedure for applying creative and critical thinking to any problem can be described as a cycle with five phases. This cycle need not and should not be followed rigidly in the sense that each phase must be completed before the next is begun. In practice you may go back to an earlier phase or work on several phases simultaneously. But if you are to have any real assurance that your ultimate decision is sound, all phases must be completed. The details of each phase will vary with the problem, but the general principles apply to all situations.

The details of each phase are too complex to permit more than a brief description of the cycle at this point. Even so, you should begin immediately to practice using the cycle with your own problems. Merely reading or talking about effective thinking is not enough. Only by practice can you acquire the skills you need.

Phase 1. Recognizing and Defining the Problem. A typical process of decision making begins with recognition of a problem. In this book the word *problem* is used in a broad sense. The "problem" may be how to deal with a threat to safety or psychological well-being, or how to take advantage of an opportunity, or to discover what happened, or to predict what is going to happen, or to find the cause of some phenomenon, or to find the answer to a philosophical question, or to decide whether to believe something you have read or heard.

Many problems are never solved because they are not recognized soon enough or not recognized at all. For example, some freshmen fail in college because they do not recognize soon enough that their academic work is unsatisfactory or that they are in an unsuitable curriculum.

Once a problem has been recognized, it should be carefully defined. If you do not correctly define your problem, you are not likely to solve it. You may solve some problem, but not the one you should have been trying to solve. Suppose, for example, that near the middle of your first term in college an instructor tells you that you are likely to fail his course. You may react in characteristically human fashion by resenting this instructor who is thwarting your wishes, and you may without realizing it define your problem to be getting even with this instructor. You may succeed in solving *this* problem, only to realize too late that the real problem was how to pass the course.

In many situations defining the problem will be the most difficult phase: once you have correctly defined the problem, the rest will be relatively easy. Often you will start with the wrong definition. The thinking you do in the last four phases can help you realize that your original definition was wrong. In this event you should start over at the beginning of the cycle. Sometimes you will find it helpful to use the entire five-phase cycle to define the problem.

Three general rules should be observed in defining a problem. *The definition should not be too broad.* The definition of a problem sets the guidelines for the succeeding phases of the cycle. If the definition is too broad, the guidelines will probably be too broad and the investigation may flounder aimlessly. Suppose a medical research worker defines his problem as to determine the total physiological and emotional effects of anesthetics used in surgery. His investigation will lead him in so many directions that he may become hopelessly confused. Such large problems should be broken down into smaller ones and solved one at a time.

On the other hand, *the definition should not be so narrow as to exclude a possible solution.* Suppose the medical research worker defines his problem to be determining which anesthetic causes the least nausea after surgery. If he treats his problem as part of a larger problem — to determine which anesthetic is best — his definition may be satisfactory. But if he forgets that anesthetics may have other harmful effects besides nausea and that some of these effects may not appear until long after surgery, then his definition is too narrow.

Finally, *the definition should not in itself be a conclusion.* Suppose a medical research worker notices that patients who have been given a certain anesthetic are emotionally depressed. If he defines his problem as to learn why the anesthetic causes depression, his definition is in itself a conclusion — that the anesthetic does cause the depression. His first problem should be to determine *whether* the anesthetic causes the depression.

Phase 2. Gathering Information. Once you have defined your problem, you can begin to gather information about it. The information may be of many kinds. The detective may call his information "clues"; the doctor may call his "symptoms"; the scientist, "data"; the layman, "facts." Adequate and accurate information is essential to sound decisions. The more information you have on which to base your decision, the more likely it is to be sound.

Phase 3. Forming Tentative Conclusions. The next phase is to form tentative conclusions. This you can begin to do as soon as you have enough information to suggest tentative conclusions, but you must remember that your conclusions at this stage are only tentative. The objective in this phase is to form as many tentative conclusions as possible. The more you form, the more likely you are to include a sound one. Furthermore, forming several tentative conclusions is the best safeguard against the danger of accepting or acting on a conclusion without adequate evidence.

In this phase your thinking must be primarily creative. You should give your imagination complete freedom and postpone critical thinking until the next phase. If you try to find the flaws in tentative conclusions while forming them, you will inhibit your imagination and you may choke off a sound conclusion before it can be born. In this phase it is desirable to give attention to every idea that comes to mind. Sometimes ideas you might impatiently reject as wild or irrelevant turn out to be solutions of problems or important clues to solutions. For example, men first noted centuries ago that malaria epidemics are frequently accompanied by plagues of mosquitoes, but it was not until the nineteenth century that Dr. Ross investigated the connection and found how malaria is transmitted.

Phase 4. Testing Tentative Conclusions. The objective of the fourth phase is to "criticize" all tentative conclusions by testing them for *reliability.*

All tentative conclusions involve some kind of inference, *i.e.*, a process of reasoning by which a conclusion is derived from evidence. Suppose you are eligible for the draft and you read this statement in a magazine: "All men now being drafted are being trained for duty in a foreign war." If you conclude that you will be drafted and sent to duty in a foreign war, your conclusion is the result of an inference in which you combined two pieces of evidence, the statement in the magazine and the fact that you are eligible for the draft. If you immediately charge down to a recruiting office to volunteer so that you can choose your branch of the service, you have violated a cardinal rule of effective thinking by forming only one tentative conclusion and acting on it without testing it for reliability. Although your conclusion could prove to be true, it is not *reliable.* A conclusion is reliable only when it is *known* to be true. In order to know that a conclusion is true you must know that (1) the evidence used is in itself reliable, *i.e.*, known to be true; (2)

all inferences involved are flawless. Your conclusion fails to meet either test: the statement in the magazine may not be true; furthermore, your inference is full of holes.

Throughout history man has been notoriously careless in testing his conclusions. Consequently he has made countless blunders and accumulated a vast amount of misinformation which has led to more blunders. Ideally, *all* conclusions should be tested for reliability. If you test some but not others, you may be protecting your cherished beliefs by testing only the tentative conclusions that displease you.

Phase 5. Evaluation and Decision. The objective of the fifth phase of the cycle is to decide whether the degree of reliability of your tentative conclusions, as measured in Phase 4, is sufficient. When you begin testing tentative conclusions by appropriate methods, you will soon discover that absolutely reliable conclusions are rare. Usually there will be some weakness either in the evidence or in the inferences, or in both. In practical matters the best we can hope for is a high degree of reliability. If we delayed decision making until we reached absolute reliability, we would dwell forever in the limbo of decision by indecision.

The minimum degree of reliability you should have before accepting or acting on a conclusion varies with the circumstances. A juror in a murder case who believes that convicting an innocent defendant of murder would be a tragic error should demand the high degree of reliability known as *true beyond reasonable doubt.* A housewife trying to decide which is the better of two boxes of cereal can afford to settle for a much lower degree of reliability, since little is at stake. The purchasing agent of a college cafeteria trying to make the same decision should demand a higher degree of reliability than the housewife because more is at stake.

When evaluation of your tentative conclusions shows that none of them is sufficiently reliable, you should repeat the whole cycle. Each time you repeat the cycle you are likely to discover new information, which may suggest new and more promising tentative conclusions. The process should be repeated until you have a conclusion with a degree of reliability sufficient for your purpose.

But how do we know when the degree of reliability is sufficient for our purpose? This question is not easy to answer, and much of this book is devoted to examining it.

Phases of Decision Making

1. Recognizing and Defining the Problem
2. Gathering Information
3. Forming Tentative Conclusions
4. Testing Tentative Conclusions
5. Evaluation and Decision

---

3. The Personal Point of View

Every phase of decision making is strongly affected by the fact that each of us sees himself and the world from his own unique point of view. This personal point of view can be described as a triad of components.

Frame of Reference. One of these components is the frame of reference, *i.e.,* the organized body of accumulated knowledge and experience with which one interprets new experience and guides his behavior. One's frame of reference embraces his whole realm of experience, including the physical world and how to get along in it, and other people and how to get along with them.

The frame of reference limits *perception, i.e.,* the process by which we give meaning to sensory stimuli. We do not "see" automobiles or "hear" music; we "see" light waves and "hear" sound waves; we *perceive* automobiles and music. Perception can occur only in terms of information in the frame of reference. An African native with no knowledge of automobiles might perceive a red sports car as a strange red dragon, and flee for his life. He could not possibly perceive it to be a sports car. If it were possible to keep a human being in complete isolation from birth to age eighteen and then to put him suddenly in a college classroom, he could perceive little of his situation because his frame of reference would not contain the necessary information. Even though his sensory organs were perfect, he would for practical purposes be deaf, dumb, and blind. In all probability he would be terrified. You can realize how essential your frame of reference is to perception by recalling experiences you now understand that you could not understand as a child because you lacked the necessary knowledge.

The frame of reference also limits the ability to recognize a problem. People often fail to recognize serious problems because their frames of reference do not include the necessary knowledge. The man who has just bought his first boat and whose frame of reference does not include any knowledge of Coast Guard regulations or the knowledge that gasoline fumes are heavier than air might be unable to perceive the significance of gasoline spilled on the hatch covering the engine. If he starts his engine without thoroughly airing the engine compartment, he has failed to recognize a serious problem. His frame of reference is inadequate for the particular situation. His next problem may be more easily recognized.

Likewise, the frame of reference limits ability to interpret or use evidence in solving any kind of problem. For example, before identification by fingerprinting was developed, police were handicapped in gathering evidence. The evidence was frequently there — the police simply lacked the knowledge to use it.

The frame of reference also limits the acquisition of new knowledge, for knowledge is necessary to acquire knowledge. Even the most intelligent student who knows no chemistry would be helpless at first in a rigorous course in organic chemistry. Many a college freshman has falsely concluded that he is not bright enough for college because his frame of reference is not yet adequate for the demands of his courses.

False information in one's frame of reference can be worse than no information at all. A witch doctor will have little chance of stopping an epidemic of typhoid fever as long as he believes that typhoid is caused by evil spirits. There would be no science of astrophysics today if astronomers had continued to believe, as they did in the Middle Ages, that the earth is the center of the universe.

A rich and accurate frame of reference is absolutely essential to effective thinking. Stocking it with the information you will need poses a continuing problem of selection, for a vast amount of information is available. The library of a large university may contain more than a million bound volumes and hundreds of current newspapers and magazines. Assuming that the bound volumes average 200,000 words each and that a student reads 500 words a minute for twelve hours a day, 360 days a year, in his four college years he could read less than three one-hundredths of 1 per cent of the bound volumes alone! Since you can read only a tiny fraction of the books available to you, whenever you read a particular book you prevent yourself from reading some other. Likewise,

when you select one experience you automatically exclude other experiences. You cannot afford to stock your frame of reference with trivia.

The information in your frame of reference has much to do with the kind of person you are and will become. Clearly, therefore, you should select your knowledge according to the kind of person you want to become. If you wish to succeed in your career, you should, of course, acquire the necessary technical knowledge. If you wish to be successful as a human being, as well as an expert in some specialized field, it is logical to include in your frame of reference at least the fundamentals of what is known as a "general" or "liberal" education. One fundamental is a basic knowledge of social science. The society and culture in which you live exert powerful forces on what you think and how you behave. If you are content to be tossed about by these forces like a small boat at sea without a rudder, you need not know much about these forces. You make your own decisions and steer your own course only to the extent that you understand how these forces affect you.

Since we live in the twentieth century, we need a basic knowledge of the physical and biological sciences. At no time in man's history have the findings of science been more relevant to the decisions we must make. Background knowledge of the physical and biological aspects of our environment is essential to sound decisions. Political leaders today must make many vital decisions involving science, and in a democracy they must have the support of a majority of the voters. The mistaken notions of voters ignorant of science could influence politicians to make decisions that might endanger the nation's natural resources, its health, or even its security.

Still another of the fundamentals is a knowledge of the humanities. Through a study of philosophy you can acquaint yourself with the most important value systems man has devised and thereby gain the perspective necessary for intelligent selection of the values you use to guide your life. Literature provides a vast casebook of human behavior through which you can sample and evaluate experience without going through it yourself.

Language skill is also fundamental. It is essential not only in acquiring knowledge but also in using it. As we shall see in Chapter 18, many of our errors are caused by the misuse of language.

Values. Another major component of the personal point of view is one's system of *values, i.e.,* the standards by which he runs his life. Whether or not he realizes it, the soldier who decides to advance into heavy enemy fire instead of retreating has based his decision on a *value judgment, i.e.,* a conclusion about the worth of an object, experience, idea, or action in terms of human needs. As we shall see in later chapters, especially 14 and 35, value judgments are involved in most, if not all, decisions we make.

The Self-Concept. The third major component is the *self-concept, i.e.,* one's picture of the kind of person he is. The motivation for most thinking stems from a basic need to develop and maintain a satisfactory self-concept. To a person living alone in a wilderness all his life, the self-concept presumably would be less important than physical safety and comfort. But in a complex society, where the necessities of life are usually acquired without great difficulty, maintaining a satisfactory self-concept becomes for most people the focal point of endeavor. To maintain it most people will go without food or sleep. If necessary, they will even risk life itself.

4. Objectivity

How effective our thinking is depends in part on how objective we are, *i.e.,* on the degree to which we can view ourselves and the world without distortion. Because each of us can observe reality only through the lens of his personal point of view, absolute objectivity is impossible. A person may be reasonably objective in one area and highly prejudiced in another, partly because his frame of reference may be adequate and accurate in one area but distorted in another.

The self-concept can be a powerful stimulus to a search for truth. Viewing oneself as a lover of truth may provide the motivation for great effort in both creative and critical thinking. Unfortunately, a threat to the self-concept can also be a powerful stimulus to self-deception. The student threatened by low grades can all too easily deceive himself into believing that grades are not important. Or he can deceive himself into believing that low grades are not really his own fault by convincing himself that the instructor is unfair, that his courses are too hard, or that there is too much noise in his dormitory. Such self-deception eases the pain of the threat for the moment, but distorts his view of reality.

When a person deceives himself in order to protect his self-concept, he reduces the effectiveness of his thinking not only in the immediate situation but in the future as well. For when one deceives himself he is likely to be embedding errors in his frame of reference so that his concept of reality becomes distorted. He begins to see the world not as it is but as he would like it to be. Further self-deception then becomes necessary in order to protect this distorted view. The more distorted one's view of reality, the more difficult it is to deal directly and constructively with threats to the self-concept.

Because self-concept, frame of reference, and value system are interdependent, one defends his personal point of view as a whole. Thus, a threat to an important idea in one's frame of reference can be as much a threat to the self-concept as a personal insult. In fact, we can formulate a kind of psychological Ohm's law: *the resistance to a new idea is directly proportional to the threat of the new idea to the self-concept.* When the threat to the self-concept is strong, the reaction can be violent.

The history of science is full of examples of this kind of resistance. Galileo's astronomical treatise, the *Dialogue on the Two Chief Systems of the World,* published in 1632, was a skillful and devastating attack on the Ptolemaic concepts of astronomy accepted by most scholars and scientists of the time. Thus not only the frames of reference but also the self-concepts of these authorities were seriously threatened. They reacted violently.

Pope Urban was persuaded by the enraged Aristotelians that Simplicio, the scholastic who is the butt of the whole dialogue, was intended for himself; and, bitterly wounded in his vanity by this supposed insult, he ordered Galileo to appear before the Inquisition. Though he was never formally imprisoned, he was threatened with torture; and, forced to "abjure, curse, and detest the aforesaid errors," he was banished to a country estate in 1633. His *Dialogue* and Kepler were placed on the Index, from which, with Copernicus, they were not withdrawn till 1835.[2]

The progress of modern science is due in large part to the fact that scientists have learned to be more objective while working within the context of the laboratory than either scientists or laymen have learned to be in wrestling with problems outside the laboratory. Objectivity in interpreting reality is just as important in human affairs as in science. If we perceive reality as we wish it to be instead of as it is, we are as handicapped in coping with it as would be a physicist who persisted in believing the phlogiston theory.

The procedures of thinking presented in this text are designed to promote objectivity. But procedures alone are not sufficient. If they were, it would be reasonable to assume that scientists would be significantly more objective outside the laboratory than laymen. The truth appears to be that they are not. As

James Bryant Conant puts it, once the scientific investigator leaves his laboratory "he can indulge his fancy all he pleases . . . free from the imposed discipline of his calling . . . my own observations lead me to conclude that as human beings scientific investigators are statistically distributed over the whole spectrum of human folly and wisdom much as other men."[3]

Procedures of thinking, like any tool, can be misused. They can be properly used to detect and correct distortions in our views of reality, or misused to defend and protect distortions. If you apply your critical skill to ideas you dislike, and fail to apply it with equal care to ideas you like, your critical skill becomes a barrier that hides the truth from you.

The problem of preventing the self-concept from distorting one's view of reality is discussed in later chapters. Meantime two essentials for objectivity should be kept in mind. The clue to one of them comes from the history of science. Objectivity in science has been achieved in part through a value judgment that establishes a counter-threat to the self-concept of the laboratory worker who lets himself reach the conclusions he wants to reach without adequate evidence. As Dr. Conant has pointed out, the traditions and methods of science create an environment that is hostile to wishful thinking.

Let him deviate from the rigorous role of impartial experimenter or observer at his peril; he knows all too well what a fool So-and-so made of himself by blindly sticking to a set of observations or a theory now clearly recognized to be in error.[4]

Thus one essential is to picture yourself as a person who tries to know the truth, no matter how unpleasant or threatening it may be.

The second essential is to develop a kind of objectivity about your own feelings. Many people mistakenly try to be objective by

[2] John Herman Randall, Jr., *The Making of the Modern Mind* (Boston: Houghton Mifflin, 1940), p. 235.

[3] James B. Conant, *On Understanding Science* (New York: Mentor, 1951), p. 23.
[4] *Ibid.,* p. 23.

eliminating their feelings. As we will see later, much of our thinking takes place below the conscious level. When we try to eliminate our feelings, we merely drive them underground, where they continue to exert powerful and often disruptive influences on our thinking.

A much better way is to be tolerant and open to our feelings so that they come easily to the surface. When we know what they are, we can deal with them much more effectively. When we are trying to make a decision about what has happened or is happening in the world of reality outside us, our feelings are irrelevant and should not be permitted to affect our decisions. But when we are trying to decide how outside reality affects us personally, our feelings are quite relevant. And to conceal them from ourselves violates the principles of effective thinking as much as concealing evidence about outside reality. The second element in objectivity, then, is to be open to our feelings, to exclude them when they are not relevant, to include them when they are, and to know the difference.

5. Improving Thinking

It should now be clear that perfection in thinking is unattainable, and a satisfactory solution to every problem is too much to expect. Thus the student who tries to learn how to solve every problem and make the right decision every time is as unrealistic as the baseball player who tries to learn how to hit a home run every time at bat. Man does not usually strive for a goal once he believes it is unattainable. He may continue to dream about it, but he will not strive for it.

You are therefore urged to strive for *effective* thinking rather than *perfect* thinking. In this book we shall consider thinking effective when it meets two criteria: (1) when sound procedures are followed reasonably well, and (2) when the information used is as complete and accurate as can reasonably be expected.

Effective thinking, like playing a musical instrument, requires practice. Opportunities for practice are provided in the numerous exercises in this book. You should give them careful attention. You should also practice the procedures of effective thinking in making simple decisions. Otherwise you may fail to use these procedures when the issue is important. The rewards for learning to think effectively are great. There are many new frontiers left to conquer, but they are intellectual rather than geographical. Learning to think effectively is important enough to be your central purpose in college.

Suggested Supplementary Reading

James B. Conant, *On Understanding Science* (New York: Mentor Books, 1951).

Harold A. Larrabee, *Reliable Knowledge*, rev. ed. (Boston: Houghton Mifflin Company, 1964), pp. 1–45.

EXERCISE 1

1. It is 8:30 P.M. of the first day of classes in the fall semester at Wysacki University. Joe Smythe, a beginning freshman, has been studying his chemistry assignment since 7:30 P.M. Curious to know how much he has left to study, he looks quickly at the rest of the assignment. He discovers that, at the rate he has been covering the assignment, he will need six more hours to complete it. He has three other assignments to prepare for tomorrow. What phase of the decision-making cycle has Joe reached?

recognition of problem

2–5. *Below are four definitions of Smythe's immediate problem. In the line below each definition, state the rule or rules, if any, for defining problems that this definition violates.*

2. To prepare his parents for the fact that he is going to flunk chemistry. *conclusion*

definition is too broad

3. To find a method of completing his chemistry assignment in four hours.

definition is too narrow

4. To learn how to make every minute count in all of his activities. *broad*

definition should not be a conclusion

5. To estimate the average amount of study time per week all of his assignments will require. *close to problem*

definition should not be a conclusion

6. Joe estimates that at his present rate of study his assignments will require sixty hours each week. Classes and labs require twenty-two hours. What phase of the decision-making cycle is Smythe working on? *gathering information*

7. Smythe should now *form tentative conclusions*

8. List three tentative conclusions Smythe might form.

divide time Alot 2 hrs.
a. *complete other assignments*

b. *do all chem don't do others*

drop chemistry
c. *do a little of the other three*

11

9. Which of these tentative conclusions should Smythe act on? _____ b _____

10. Suppose Smythe now defines his problem to be to find out why it takes him so long to complete his assignments. Form a tentative conclusion that would be likely to threaten Smythe's self-concept.

he should not waste time

11–14. *Consider the following statements:*

1. The average student at Wysacki is expected to study at least two hours per week per credit.
2. Smythe is a beginning freshman.
3. Smythe's courses total fourteen credits.
4. Smythe is average among Wysacki students.

11. Write the numbers of the statements that can be combined to make an inference.

_1, 3, 4_

12. Write a conclusion that can be inferred from these four statements.

he must spend 28 hrs. in study

13. Is this conclusion reliable? _____ no _____

14. If not, why not?

it may be he can spend less according to the type of courses he has

15. During his senior year in high school Joe decided to study engineering in college because he had heard that graduates in engineering receive relatively high starting salaries. State below the value judgment apparently involved in Joe's decision.

Joe is interested in the materialistic aspect

16. What is your opinion of this value judgment?

It is a selfish judgement

17. Mary Smythe is having trouble removing stains from her cotton sports slacks. She forms the tentative conclusion that a mixture of ammonia and chlorine bleach will work better than either chemical alone. In deciding whether to act on this tentative conclusion, what knowledge should Mary have in her frame of reference?

should have knowledge of how each works alone

2 The Hypothetical Syllogism

If the hundreds of decisions we must make every day were as complex and difficult as General Eisenhower's, most of us would never finish breakfast. The fact that most of us do finish breakfast and do manage to make the decisions required of us is due to our ability to organize our experience and use it in decision making by a mental process known as *deductive inference.*

Each of us has in his frame of reference innumerable *propositions, i.e.,* sentences that state a relationship between two objects, actions, ideas, or qualities. These propositions cover one's whole range of knowledge and experience, from traffic laws to value judgments. In many of our decisions we simply connect the immediate situation with one of these propositions and derive a decision by deductive inference. Suppose you are searching for a parking place. You see enough space for your car near the corner ahead, but when you get there you see that the space is next to a fire hydrant. You must now decide whether to park by the hydrant.

You have now completed Phase 1 by defining your problem.

In a situation like this, Phase 2 of the cycle (gathering information) consists simply of searching your frame of reference for a proposition that fits. Suppose the proposition you find is this: I do not park by fire hydrants. Phase 3 (forming tentative conclusions) is almost automatic, for the connection between proposition and situation is obvious. In such situations most of us leap to a decision without bothering to complete Phases 4 and 5, and sometimes these decisions lead to disaster.

On or about June 3, 1944, Field Marshal Erwin Rommel, commander in chief of the main German forces defending the coast of France, made a seemingly simple decision that was to have major consequences for Operation Overlord. He wanted to go to Germany to try to persuade Hitler to strengthen the forces guarding the French coast. The trip would take several days. Presumably he wanted to be at his post when the expected invasion came, for he believed that the fate of Germany would be settled during the first twenty-four hours of the invasion. His problem was when to go.

We can only speculate, of course, about what went through his mind as he made his decision. But he probably had the following propositions available for Phase 2 (gathering information).

1. On June 3 the weather was bad.
2. The official German meteorologists predicted that the weather would be even worse between June 4 and June 6.
3. An increased volume of radio messages from the British to the French resistance forces had been noted.
4. Both Rommel and the German high command believed that if the weather was bad, the Allies would not launch their invasion for two more days.
5. The German high command believed that several days before the invasion the volume of radio messages from the British to the French resistance forces would increase.

General Rommel may have combined Propositions 2 and 4 and concluded by deductive reasoning that the Allies would not launch their attack before June 7. In any case he decided to leave for Germany on June 4. Consequently he was not at his post during the critical hours of D day. If he had been, the Germans might have been quicker to react to the invasion, and the outcome could have been quite different. At least as far as his military duties were concerned, Rommel seems to have made a disastrous decision.

In order to learn how deductive reasoning can lead us into error, let us examine a highly useful pattern of deduction called the hypothetical syllogism, which will be used extensively in this text.

1. The Hypothetical Proposition

A distinctive feature of the hypothetical syllogism is its major premise, which is a hypothetical proposition (when a proposition is used in deductive reasoning it is called a premise). A hypothetical proposition consists of two parts, the *antecedent* and the *consequent*. The antecedent states a condition or situation that precedes or causes or is accompanied by another condition or situation described in the consequent.

Proposition 4 in Rommel's information can be stated as a hypothetical proposition.

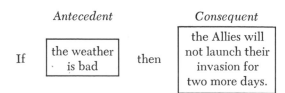

It is important to understand that a hypothetical proposition makes no claim that either the antecedent or the consequent is true. The hypothetical proposition states a relationship between antecedent and consequent: that the consequent is true *if* the antecedent is true. If Rommel had stood on a cliff on the coast of Normandy and observed that the weather was bad and that the Allies were launching their invasion at that very moment, then his observations would have proved the proposition to be false, because the asserted relationship between antecedent and consequent did not in fact exist.

2. Structure of the Hypothetical Syllogism

A hypothetical syllogism consists of a major premise in hypothetical form, a *minor* premise,[1] and a conclusion presumably inferred from the two premises. The minor premise is usually a simple or factual statement to the effect that something is true or not true. It must declare that some specific situation, object, or idea meets or fails to meet the conditions described either in the antecedent or in the consequent. It may or may not repeat the words used in the ante-

[1] Called the "unconditional" premise in many texts.

cedent or consequent, but it must establish something about its subject (not necessarily the grammatical subject) definitely, not hypothetically.

Typical everyday decisions begin with the minor premise, which describes the situation about which a decision must be made. The major premise states a law, policy, or procedure for dealing with it. For example, when the traffic officer observes your car parked by a fire hydrant, his observation starts his reasoning and forms his minor premise. The law he is obliged to enforce forms his major premise. His deductive reasoning can be fully stated in the hypothetical syllogism below.

	Antecedent		*Consequent*
Major Premise: If	a car is parked by a fire hydrant	then	I must give it a ticket.

Minor Premise: This car is parked by a fire hydrant.

Conclusion: I must give it a ticket.

The officer may not consciously think of his major premise, but it is part of his reasoning nonetheless.

In a hypothetical syllogism the conclusion is derived by *deductive inference*. In the example above the inference is the recognition that, since the minor premise states that the conditions described in the antecedent of the major premise are true in this specific situation, then the conditions described in the consequent of the major premise must also be true in this specific situation.

3. Validity

In Phase 4 of the cycle, the procedure for testing tentative conclusions varies with the nature of the inference. When the inference is deductive, the tentative conclusion should be tested for *validity*. A deductive inference is *valid* when the premises are so related that the conclusion must be true if the premises are true. Testing deductive inferences for validity is relatively easy, for the rules of validity are precise.

Hypothetical syllogisms take four forms, depending on how the minor premise is related to the antecedent or consequent of the major premise.

4. Affirming the Antecedent

The minor premise may *affirm* the antecedent, *i.e.*, it may declare that conditions described in the antecedent of the major premise are true in the particular situation involved.

	Antecedent		*Consequent*
Major Premise: If	it rains	then	there will be clouds.

Minor Premise: It is raining.

Conclusion: There are clouds.

Here the minor premise affirms the antecedent, for it states that the condition described by the antecedent is true now. The conclusion is valid, for the major premise declares that there are always clouds when it rains, and it is raining now. Unless one of the premises is false, there must be clouds in the sky.

Affirming the antecedent is a *valid* form, that is, it yields a valid conclusion. But not just any conclusion will do. Given the premises above, you are not entitled to conclude that the sky is free of clouds or that it is raining in Cambodia. The only valid conclusion you can reach is that there are clouds. When the minor premise affirms the antecedent, the conclusion, to be valid, must declare that the conditions of the consequent are true of the specific subject of the minor premise.

5. Denying the Antecedent

The minor premise may *deny* the antecedent by declaring that the conditions stated in the antecedent are not true in the particular situation involved.

Antecedent   Consequent

Major Premise: If | it rains | then | there are clouds. |

Minor Premise: It is not raining.

Many people would be tempted to conclude from this evidence that there are no clouds. But this argument would be invalid, for the hypothetical premise does not declare that clouds come *only* when it rains. It describes what happens if it rains, but states nothing about what happens if it does not rain. We can not determine from these premises whether there are clouds or not. Any definite conclusion about clouds would be invalid.

Denying the antecedent is thus an *invalid* form. Showing in the minor premise that the antecedent is not true of a particular situation proves nothing about whether the consequent is true of the situation. There may be — in fact, there often are — other conditions under which the consequent may be true in addition to those described by the antecedent.

Probably it was a logical fallacy of this type that encouraged the Communists to attack South Korea in June, 1950. The United States Secretary of State, Dean Acheson, had proclaimed that the United States would defend from attack all areas east of a line he drew in the Eastern Pacific. Korea was west of the imaginary line. The Communists apparently reasoned:

> If an area is east of the line, then the United States will defend it from attack. But South Korea is not east of the line. Therefore, the United States will not defend South Korea from attack.

6. Affirming the Consequent

The minor premise may affirm the consequent by stating that the conditions described by the consequent are true. Suppose you get a letter from a friend saying

he is seriously ill, but that if he can obtain a scarce serum, he will recover. You later receive a card from him saying that he is well. Can you conclude that he got the serum?

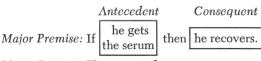

Antecedent   Consequent

Major Premise: If | he gets the serum | then | he recovers. |

Minor Premise: He recovered.

This form tempts the careless thinker to conclude that your friend got the serum. But such a conclusion is invalid, for the major premise does not declare that getting the serum is the *only* condition under which he can recover. There may be other conditions. Hence affirming the consequent is an *invalid* form.

7. Denying the Consequent

Suppose, instead of a card from your sick friend, you get a telegram saying that he died of his illness. You wonder whether he got the serum. A hypothetical syllogism will tell you.

Major Premise: If he had gotten the serum, then he would have recovered.

Minor Premise: He did not recover.

Conclusion: He did not get the serum.

Since the minor premise flatly contradicts the consequent of the major premise, you can validly conclude that the antecedent is also false — your friend did not get the serum. Should you learn later that he did get the serum and died anyway, blame the premise, not the inference.

Denying the consequent is a *valid* form. Assuming that the hypothetical premise is true, any situation that does not fit the consequent cannot fit the antecedent. But note again that only one conclusion will do. You cannot conclude from the premises that your friend got the serum too late, or that it hastened his death. To be valid, the conclusion must declare that the conditions described by the antecedent are not true of the specific situation. Nothing else will do.

The minor premise need not be negative to deny an antecedent or consequent. The minor premise below is a positive statement, but it denies the consequent by stating that the conditions described by the consequent are not true.

	Antecedent		Consequent
Major Premise: If	one is diligent	then	he will not fail.

Minor Premise: Smythe failed.

Given these premises, you can validly conclude that Smythe is not diligent.

The rules for validity of hypothetical syllogisms are summarized below.

If the minor premise	The conclusion is
Affirms the antecedent	valid if it affirms the consequent
Denies the antecedent	invalid
Affirms the consequent	invalid
Denies the consequent	valid if it denies the antecedent

8. Uncertain Relationship Between Premises

It is not enough for a minor premise to *seem* to affirm an antecedent or deny a consequent. For the syllogism to be valid, one of these relationships must be stated clearly and unequivocally.

	Antecedent		Consequent
Major Premise: If	it rains	then	the game will be postponed.

Minor Premise: The Weather Bureau predicts rain.

Any conclusion inferred from these premises is invalid, for the minor premise only appears to affirm the antecedent. Saying that the Weather Bureau predicts rain is not the equivalent of saying that there will certainly be rain. This fallacy will be called an *uncertain relationship between premises.* The words do not have to be the same, but the relationship must be clear from a reasonable interpretation of the premises. If information not stated in the premises is needed in order to establish the relationship, the syllogism should be ruled invalid.

9. Non Sequitur

In the two valid forms of the hypothetical syllogism, affirming the antecedent and denying the consequent, we noted that not just any conclusion is valid. We must still check the conclusion to make sure that it follows from the premises before we can be sure it is valid. The only valid conclusion following an affirmed antecedent states that the consequent is true. The only valid conclusion following a denied consequent states that the antecedent is not true. A conclusion cannot go even a hair's breadth beyond the evidence in the premises and still be valid. Consider the following example.

If one has an accident while violating the law, then he is legally responsible. You were violating the law by exceeding the speed limit when you had your accident. Therefore, you are legally and morally responsible.

The form of this syllogism is valid, for the premises would yield a valid conclusion that you are legally responsible. But the above conclusion goes beyond the antecedent by adding the element of moral responsibility. This conclusion is thus invalid because it does not necessarily follow from the premises given.

We call this fallacy (*i.e.,* error in reasoning) a *non sequitur.* In a *non sequitur* the fault is in the conclusion. In the other fallacies in hypothetical syllogisms (affirmed consequent, denied antecedent, and uncertain relationship) the fault is in the premises.

It is the essence of validity that the conclusion go only as far as the evidence justifies. A conclusion that does not go as far as the evidence is still valid. Suppose that the hypothetical premise in the example above had read: "If one has an accident while violating the law, he is both legally and morally responsible." Given the same minor premise, the conclusion "You are legally responsible" would be valid, even though the element of moral responsibility is not included. In short, a valid conclusion need not state everything that necessarily follows, but it must never state anything else.

10. Validity and Reliability

In the preceding chapter we noted that a conclusion is completely reliable only when the evidence used is known to be true and the inferences have no possible loopholes. The careful thinker must never forget that *validity has nothing to do with the truth or falsity of the evidence.* It is not necessary to know that a proposition is true in order to use it as a premise. A premise may be merely an assumption, *i.e.,* a proposition that may or may not be thought true. For example, to deal with a specific action of a Communist government, the State Department must make an assumption about the intent or significance of the Communist action before deciding how to deal with it. The student deciding what courses to take next term must make assumptions about the grades he will make this term. Even though his assumptions may prove to be false, he cannot avoid using them.

A valid conclusion can be inferred from premises believed to be false.

Premises: { If one is a descendant of British parents, one is British. All Americans are descendants of British parents.

Inference:

Conclusion: All Americans are British.

The conclusion in this example is valid, for there is no loophole in the inference; if the premises are true, the conclusion must be true. Yet the conclusion directly contradicts what we believe about Americans. We can reject the conclusion as unproved, not because the inference is invalid but because the minor premise is unreliable.

The fact that a conclusion is invalid does not mean that it is necessarily false. The fact that the conclusion is invalid means only that the premises are not sufficient to prove the conclusion true. Thus we may have the following combinations of premises, inferences, and conclusions.

Premises	Inference	Conclusion
Known to be true	valid	known to be true
Known to be true	invalid	in doubt
One or more known to be false	valid	in doubt
One or more known to be false	invalid	in doubt
One or more in doubt	valid	in doubt
One or more in doubt	invalid	in doubt

When we have tested a conclusion and found it valid, we have eliminated doubt about the soundness of the inference, but *we have done nothing to demonstrate the truth of the premises.* Before we can complete Phase 5 of decision making, therefore, we must evaluate the reliability of the premises themselves. The propositions we use as premises can be evaluated for reliability by deductive reasoning from other premises. We can in turn evaluate these premises by deductive reasoning from still other premises, and so on. Ultimately, however, we must reach a premise which we must either assume to be true without sufficient proof or which we must evaluate by methods other than deductive reasoning. We consider these methods, as well as other problems in evaluating conclusions for reliability, in the chapters that follow.

Now let us return to Field Marshal Rommel's decision. Whether the results of a decision are good or bad can be judged only in terms of values. If Rommel believed that it was his supreme duty to be at the front when the invasion began, then his decision was disastrous. Whether his thinking was effective, however, must be judged in a different way. As we noted in Chapter 1, thinking is effective when sound procedures are followed reasonably well and the information used is as complete and accurate as can reasonably be expected.

Rommel may have combined Propositions 2 and 4 to get the following syllogism.

Major Premise: If the weather is bad, then the Allies will not launch their attack for two more days.

Minor Premise: The official German meteorologists predict that the weather will be bad at least until June 7.

Conclusion: The Allies will not launch their invasion before June 8.

If Rommel failed to test his conclusion and to discover that the relationship between the premises is uncertain, then his critical thinking was at fault. Some military historians believe, however, that the fault lay in the German weather forecast rather than in Rommel's thinking. It is entirely possible that Rommel realized that his conclusion was not reliable but acted on it even so because the official weather forecast was the most reliable information he could obtain. Like General Eisenhower, he was threatened with decision by indecision. He would have been justified in believing that if he postponed his trip to Germany long enough he would not make it. It is interesting to note in this connection that Allied meteorologists had weather stations that gave them data not available to the Germans and were able to detect the changing weather sooner than the Germans.

It is also possible that Rommel's creative thinking was at fault. As we noted in Chapter 1, forming several tentative conclusions is the best safeguard against accepting or acting on a conclusion without adequate evidence. Propositions 3 and 5 in the list available to Rommel can be combined into a hypothetical syllogism with this conclusion: "The invasion will come within several days." The conclusion is not valid, of course, because the minor premise affirms the consequent. Even so, this conclusion was worth considering.

Perhaps Rommel accurately judged the reliability of his conclusion but was careless with Phase 5 (evaluation and decision) in acting on a conclusion that was insufficiently reliable for the circumstances. It is also possible that Rommel's decision was influenced by subjective factors. He was tired. His wife's birthday was June 6. Perhaps he wanted to believe that the invasion would not come for a few days and let his wish attach a higher degree of reliability to his conclusion than was justified.

11. Logical Shorthand

Since we will be analyzing many hypothetical propositions and premises, we can save trouble by adopting a shorthand for writing propositions and premises. From symbolic logic let us borrow the symbols in the box below and substitute them for the structure words in propositions and premises.

Structure Words	Symbol
If . . . then . . .	$\supset$
Therefore . . .	$\therefore$

Note that antecedent and consequent are identified by structure words rather than by position in the sentence. In the following proposition the antecedent is stated last.

No student is a failure *if* he is improving his thinking.

In using the horseshoe symbol to stand for the structure words *if* and *then,* the antecedent of a hypothetical proposition must be written to the left of the symbol. Otherwise the meaning will be changed. *The hypothetical relationship is not reversible.*

It is not recommended that the symbols *p* and *q,* used in symbolic logic to stand for antecedent and consequent respectively, be used at this point. Our emphasis will be on meaning, and meaning tends to be submerged when symbols are used for antecedents and consequents. But to save writing, antecedents and consequents can be abbreviated if care is taken to preserve their exact meaning.

The use of our logical shorthand is illustrated below (the example is invalid).

Full Statement

If Communist governments could be trusted, then the cold war could be eased.

But Communist governments cannot be trusted.

Therefore, the cold war cannot be eased.

Shorthand Statement

Communist govts.   cold war
could be trusted $\supset$ could be eased

Communist govts. can't be trusted

∴ Cold war can't be eased

EXERCISE 2A

1–7. *These items refer to the syllogism below.*

If Jones studied faithfully, then he passed the course.
Jones passed the course.
Therefore, Jones studied faithfully.

1. Write below the antecedent of the major premise.

If Jones studied faithfully

2. Write below the consequent.

then he passed the course

3. What is the relationship between the minor premise and the major premise?

affirms the consequent

4. What is the relationship between the conclusion and the major premise?

affirms the antecedent

5. Is the conclusion valid? *no*

6. If not, why not? *he may have passed due to other conditions*

7. Write the syllogism in logical shorthand.

Jones studied faithfully ⊃ he passed course
Jones passed course
∴ Jones studied faithfully

8–15. a. *In Line A show the relationship between the premises by writing the appropriate number from Key List A.*
   b. *In Line B write V if the conclusion is valid or I if it is invalid.*
   c. *If you write I in Line B, indicate the fallacy by writing in Line C the appropriate number from Key List C.*

KEY LIST A	KEY LIST C
1. *The antecedent is affirmed.*	1. *Denied antecedent*
2. *The antecedent is denied.*	2. *Affirmed consequent*
3. *The consequent is affirmed.*	3. *Uncertain relationship*
4. *The consequent is denied.*	4. *Non sequitur*
5. *The relationship is uncertain.*	

8. If the victim was murdered, then there would be water in his lungs.
There is no water in his lungs.
Therefore, the victim was not murdered.

8A _____ 4 _____   8B _____ V _____   8C _____

9. If a student is late to Dr. Wiltmore's class, then he is marked absent.
John was marked absent today.
Therefore, he must have been late to class.

9A _____ 3 _____   9B _____ I _____   9C _____ 3 _____

10. If the temperature is below 80 degrees, then Carol will refuse to go swimming.
The temperature is 75 degrees this afternoon.
Therefore, Carol will not go swimming this afternoon.

10A _____ 1 _____   10B _____ V _____   10C _____

11. If our sentries remain alert at their posts, then the enemy cannot infiltrate our lines.
Enemy troops have infiltrated our lines.
Therefore, our sentries must have fallen asleep at their posts.

11A _____ 4 _____   11B _____ I _____   11C _____ 4 _____

12. If a chapter is assigned, then questions on it will be included in the examination.
There were two questions on Chapter 5 in the exam.
Therefore, Chapter 5 was assigned.

12A _____ 3 _____   12B _____ I _____   12C _____ 2 _____

13. If one is to be successful in business, then he has to be clever.
Mr. Higgins was entirely unsuccessful in business.
Therefore, he must not have been a clever man.

13A _____ 2 _____   13B _____ I _____   13C _____ 1 _____

14. If the ship can maintain a speed of twenty knots, then it can outrun the storm.
The *South Seas* can easily maintain a constant speed of twenty knots.
Therefore, the *South Seas* will reach port on time.

14A _____ 1 _____   14B _____ I _____   14C _____ 4 _____

15. If killing is evil, then capital punishment should be abolished.
The prisoner was found guilty of first-degree murder.
Therefore, he should not be executed.

15A _____ 5 _____   15B _____ I _____   15C _____ 3 _____

EXERCISE 2B

1–7. *These items refer to the syllogism below.*

If Bill has a poor teacher, then he will never learn the subtleties of his profession. His teacher is Mr. Cowan, who is considered the foremost authority in his field. Bill no doubt will learn the subtleties of his profession.

1. Write below the antecedent of the major premise.

If Bill has a poor teacher

2. Write below the consequent.

then he will never learn the subtleties of his profession

3. What is the relationship between the minor premise and the major premise?

uncertain
denies antecedant

4. What is the relationship between the conclusion and the major premise?

denies consequent

5. Is the conclusion valid? *no*

6. If not, why not?

other conditions

7. Write the syllogism in logical shorthand.

Bill has poor teacher ⊃ he will never learn subtleties of profession
Mr. Cowan, his teacher is foremost authority in field
∴ Bill will learn the subtleties of profess.

8–17. *If the following premises yield a valid conclusion, write the conclusion in the line provided. If the premises do not yield a valid conclusion, write the name of the fallacy.*

8. To be eligible for medical school, a student must have excellent grades. Mary was accepted by the top medical school in the country.

∴ Mary had excellent grades

9. If we pick up intelligible radio signals from outer space, then we will know that other intelligent beings exist out there.
We have not picked up any intelligible signals from outer space.

invalid

10. If the wrecked car had been speeding, then it would have overturned.
The car skidded off the road but did not overturn.

∴ _the car was not speeding_

11. When a poem is interesting it is not unpopular among people of good taste.
The distinguished Great Poems Society judged Myrick's poem technically flawless.

invalid due to uncertain relationship

12. When a woman believes such gossip, then she must be quite suggestible.
The woman next door believes every bit of it.

∴ _the woman next door is suggestible_

13. To think effectively one must have a rich frame of reference.
John is a college graduate.

invalid due to uncertain relationship

14. If at times emotions interfere with objectivity in thinking, then one cannot know the whole truth about reality.
It is clearly impossible to know the whole truth about reality.

invalid

15. If the seller neglects to get the contract notarized, it is not binding.
My lawyer informs me that the contract is not binding.

invalid

16. In order to win the election, Jones must carry the large cities.
But he has lost every large city.

∴ _he cannot win the election_

17. Even though it might involve great sacrifice, if one is able to obtain a college education he will never regret it.
A large number of high school graduates are unable to get a college education.

invalid

3 Reliability and Probability

If General Eisenhower had delayed his decision about D day until he had a conclusion derived by valid inference from reliable premises, Operation Overlord would never have been completed. His problems with reliability can be seen in the syllogism below.

Major Premise: The weather ⊃ D day should
forecasts are   be June 6.
favorable

Minor Premise: Allied meteorologists predict that the weather will be favorable for a brief period.

Conclusion: D day should be June 6.

The major premise states a decision Eisenhower presumably made before the evening of June 4. As he was doubtless well aware, however, he could not be certain that this decision was right. Thus the major premise as stated is less than absolutely reliable. Furthermore, the minor premise does not clearly affirm the antecedent. The great majority of decisions we must make are like General Eisenhower's in that we must base them on conclusions that are not completely reliable. For practical purposes, therefore, the fourth phase of the decision-making cycle (testing tentative conclusions) must include a method of assessing the degree of reliability of tentative conclusions.

The concept of probability can be very useful for this purpose, since it provides a convenient way of expressing the degree of reliability demonstrated for a conclusion. The word *probable* involves an intricate concept of the nature of evidence. As we use the term *probability* here, we shall mean by it *the degree of likelihood that a proposition is true, based on the evidence in hand.* There is more in this definition than meets the eye, and we must explore its implications carefully. We can thus learn to assess the reliability of a tentative conclusion more accurately.

Our definition of probability has two important parts. Let us consider the second part first — "based on the evidence in hand." Suppose we toss a silver dollar behind the sofa where we cannot see it, and we hear the characteristic ringing noise a coin makes only when it is settling on a hard surface.

For all practical purposes it is a fact that the dollar is resting heads up or tails up, but which? Without crawling behind the sofa and looking, what evidence do we have in hand? Let us assume that we tossed the coin without skill or intention to make it fall in any certain way, and that the dollar is balanced. These two assumptions constitute our "evidence in hand."

With this evidence, what is the *degree of likelihood* for the proposition, "The coin fell heads up"? The two assumptions constituting our evidence in hand give us no reason whatever for thinking that the dollar is any more likely to fall heads up than tails up. Our proposition, then, is equally likely to be true or false. In point of fact, of course, it is either true or false, and if we could only see the coin we would know which. But in that case we would be using different "evidence in hand."

1. Assumptions of Theoretical Probability

The probability of an event can be calculated only in terms of fundamental assumptions. Measuring the probability in tossing coins and similar situations is often called *theoretical* probability because the measurement is based on an assumption about the relative likelihood of the individual events. Actually, such an assumption is only a theory, *i.e.,* an assumption for which we do not have complete proof. In effect, because we cannot think of any reason why a balanced coin tossed without skill or intention should be more likely to fall one way than another, we assume that there is no reason. Extensive experience with coins indicates that this particular assumption is sound.

To cite another example, suppose three persons are sitting around a table on which there is a deck of cards. What is the probability that the top card in the deck is the ace of spades? The answer will differ according to each person's knowledge of the deck. Suppose the first person has just come into the room and knows nothing about the deck except that it appears to be a standard one. On the basis of his evidence in hand, he can assume only that the deck is standard and that the ace of spades is as likely as any other of the fifty-two cards to be on top. Thus to him there is one chance in fifty-two that the ace of spades is on top. Suppose that the second person has been playing with the deck and knows that all twenty-six black cards are on top, but does not know which of these is the ace of spades. On the basis of his evidence in hand, he can assume that the ace of spades is as likely to be on top as any of the twenty-six black cards, and that the chances are one in twenty-six that it is on top. Suppose, further, that the third person saw the top card placed on the deck and knows that it is the ace of spades. He needs no theoretical probability.

Thus theoretical probability can be measured only in terms of assumptions, and will be no more reliable than the assumptions themselves. As with all propositions, the more evidence we have in hand, the more specific the assumptions can be. Given the necessary assumptions, theoretical probability can be expressed in definite mathematical terms.

2. The Master Formula

Theoretical probability is usually expressed in terms of the following formula:

$$\text{theoretical probability} = \frac{\text{number of favorable possibilities}}{\text{total possibilities}}$$

In tossing our silver dollar, the total possibilities are two: heads up and tails up. By "favorable possibilities" we do not necessarily mean possibilities to be desired, but rather the possibilities whose theoretical probability we are trying to calculate. In calculating the probability that the dollar fell heads up, there is only one favorable possibility, heads up, and the theoretical probability would therefore be expressed by the fraction $\frac{1}{2}$. When we draw a card from a

standard deck, the total possibilities are the number of cards in the deck, fifty-two. If we are calculating the probability of drawing the ace of spades, there is only one "favorable" possibility, the ace of spades itself. Thus the probability of drawing this card would be expressed by the fraction $\frac{1}{52}$.

3. Single Events

The theoretical probability for any single event, such as tossing *one* coin or drawing *one* card, is computed by filling in the master fraction: favorable possibilities divided by total possibilities.

What is the probability, for example, of drawing an ace purely by chance from a standard deck? The total possibilities are the fifty-two cards. The favorable possibilities are the four aces. Thus the probability is $\frac{4}{52}$, or $\frac{1}{13}$.

What is the probability of rolling an even number with one die? The total possibilities are the six sides of the die. The favorable possibilities are the three sides with an even number of dots. Thus the probability is $\frac{3}{6}$, or $\frac{1}{2}$.

4. Independent Related Events

Suppose that we toss two coins together. What happens to one coin has no effect on the other; hence the events are *independent*. When we try to compute the probability of tossing two heads with two coins, we have *related* events, because we are considering the combined behavior of the two coins.

In computing the probability that two or more related events will occur together, the rule of multiplication applies: *the probability that two or more related events will occur together is the product of the fractions expressing the probability of each event.*

For example, what is the probability that both a penny and a nickel will fall heads up? You will find computing the probability of related events like this example easier if you visualize what must happen. First visualize tossing the penny and count the total possi-

bilities. There are two: heads up and tails up. Now write this as the denominator of a fraction, as shown below.

(Total possibilities: heads up and tails up) $\overline{2}$

Now ask yourself how many of these total possibilities are favorable, *i.e.*, meet the requirements of the problem. In this case only one (heads up) will do. Now write in *1* as the numerator of the fraction. Thus the probability that the penny will fall heads up is $\frac{1}{2}$. Now repeat the procedure for the nickel. There are two possibilities, heads up and tails up, only one of which will do. Thus the probability that the nickel will fall heads up is also $\frac{1}{2}$. Note that the two events are related, because both must happen if the requirements of the problem are to be satisfied. The next step in the procedure, then, is to multiply the two fractions.

1st Event (Penny Heads Up)		2nd Event (Nickel Heads Up)		Both Events
$\frac{1}{2}$	$\times$	$\frac{1}{2}$	$=$	$\frac{1}{4}$

Now test your understanding so far by computing the probability of guessing the correct answers on the first two questions of an objective test purely by chance. Assume that each question has five answers, only one of which is correct. Fill in the blanks below, and then check the answer at the end of this chapter.

1st Question Right		2nd Question Right		Both Questions Right
No. right answers: ⎯⎯ Total possible answers:	$\times$	No. right answers: ⎯⎯ Total possible answers:	$=$	⎯⎯

5. Dependent Related Events

Suppose we have a bag containing three white marbles and two black ones. If we draw a marble from the bag, restore it to the bag, and then draw again, we have independent related events such as we have been studying. If, however, we draw a marble from the bag, lay it aside, and then draw again, the contents of the bag change each time a marble is withdrawn. Such events are *dependent, i.e.,* the theoretical probability of each event is affected by one or more prior events. In computing the probability of dependent events, the rule of dependency applies: *when the events are dependent, the fraction expressing the probability of each event must be adjusted for the effect of previous events.*

For example, let us compute the probability that two marbles drawn by chance from the bag described above will be black. First, let us write the probability fraction for the first marble drawn. The total possibilities are five (three white and two black), of which two are favorable, *i.e.,* black. Thus the probability that the first marble drawn will be black is $\frac{2}{5}$.

Now visualize the contents of the bag as you make the second draw. One marble has been removed, so that the total possibilities are four. In adjusting the number of favorable possibilities in dependent related events we must make some kind of assumption about what happened in the first event. If the first marble drawn was white, then two black marbles remain, but if the first marble drawn was black, only one black marble remains. *In adjusting the numerator in dependent events, always assume that the first event was favorable.* This assumption is necessary because the probability fraction written for the first event is the probability that it is favorable. Thus the numerator in the second fraction is 1 (*i.e.,* one black marble left), and the probability that the second marble drawn will be black is $\frac{1}{4}$. Since both events must occur, the two fractions are multiplied, as shown below.

1st Event (Black Marble)		2nd Event (Black Marble)		Both Events
$\frac{2}{5}$	$\times$	$\frac{1}{4}$	$=$	$\frac{2}{20}$

You can easily demonstrate for yourself why the fractions for related events must be multiplied. Suppose there are sixteen candidates for homecoming queen at Wysacki, one of whom is Dianne. Unwilling to make the value judgment themselves, the judges decide to choose the queen purely by chance. Since there are sixteen possibilities, one and only one of which is favorable, the probability that Dianne will be chosen is $\frac{1}{16}$. Now suppose that the judges decide to draw the names of the sixteen candidates from a hat. To prolong the suspense, they decide that the last name drawn will be the winner. They first draw out eight names. The probability that Dianne will survive this draw is $\frac{8}{16}$, or $\frac{1}{2}$. Now the judges draw four more names and discard them. The probability that Dianne will survive this draw is $\frac{4}{8}$, or $\frac{1}{2}$. Now there are four candidates left. The judges draw out and discard two of the remaining names. The probability that Dianne will again survive is $\frac{2}{4}$, or $\frac{1}{2}$. With only two names left, the probability that Dianne will be the last one drawn is $\frac{1}{2}$. Note that to be drawn last, Dianne must survive four draws, in each of which the probability that she will survive is $\frac{1}{2}$. Thus the probability that she will survive all four draws is $\frac{1}{2} \times \frac{1}{2} \times \frac{1}{2} \times \frac{1}{2}$, or $\frac{1}{16}$. In other words, she has half of a half of a half of a half of a chance of being chosen.

Now test your understanding by computing the probability of this problem. Suppose you have seven cigars, three of which contain small charges of black powder that will explode when the cigar is smoked. What is the probability that you can select purely by chance two cigars that are not explosive? Fill in the blanks below, and then check the answer at the end of this chapter.

1st Event		2nd Event		Both Events
Non-explosive cigars: $\dfrac{4}{}$ Total cigars: $\dfrac{}{7}$	$\times$	Non-explosive cigars: $\dfrac{3}{}$ Total cigars: $\dfrac{}{6}$	$=$	$\dfrac{2}{7}$

Now try another problem. Suppose a mail order catalog offers slacks in three colors, red, yellow, and blue, but specifies that the customer cannot choose the color. On a different page the catalog offers sweaters in the same colors, but with no choice. Suppose you would like to order a sweater and a pair of slacks, but you abhor the combination of red slacks and a yellow sweater. What is the probability that you would get this particular combination? Write out the fractions before peeking at the answer at the end of the chapter.

Now try a subtle problem using the same situation. What is the probability that slacks and sweater will be of the same color?

We shall examine procedures for computing more complex problems in probability in Chapter 9.

6. "True" Probability

Now let us examine some of the implications of the concepts we have discussed. Computing the probability of events is actually a kind of inference in which the assumptions are the evidence in hand and the computation is the inference. As with all other kinds of inference, we cannot be certain that the probability we compute for an event is the "true" probability unless we are certain that the evidence in hand is complete and accurate and that the computation is accurate. Thus conclusions we draw about the probability of events, like other conclusions, vary in reliability.

Organized gambling flourishes in part because many gamblers do not understand probability and make errors in their inferences about the probability of winning. For example, the gambler who infers that when two coins are tossed two heads are as likely to turn up as a head and a tail has made an error in inference, and he is likely to pay dearly for it.

Conclusions about the probabilities of events can also be wrong because the evidence in hand is incomplete or inaccurate. In theoretical probability, the evidence in hand is an assumption that one possibility is as likely as another. The theoretical probability of guessing by chance alone the right answer to an objective question with five choices is $\frac{1}{5}$. The assumption is that each choice is as likely to be the right one as any other. When we infer that the probability of rolling a "twelve" with a pair of dice is $\frac{1}{36}$, we are assuming that each face of a die is as likely to be on top as any other face. Unfortunately, especially for amateur gamblers, the assumptions of theoretical probability are not always true. Dice and roulette wheels have been known to be loaded, and card sharks have been known to stack the deck. Thus even though the computations are accurate, theoretical probabilities are not always true probabilities.

7. Empirical Probability

Empirical probability differs from theoretical probability only in the kind of evidence involved. In theoretical probability the evidence in hand is a theory or theories about the likelihood of events, such as the theory that a coin is as likely to fall heads up as tails up. In empirical probability, the evidence in hand is past experience with the events in question. For example, if you toss a coin ten times and it falls heads up eight of the ten times, the theoretical probability that it will fall heads up the next time is still $\frac{1}{2}$, on the assumption that heads up is as likely as tails up. If, however, you use only your experience with the ten tosses as your evidence in hand, the empirical probability that on the next toss the coin will fall heads up is $\frac{8}{10}$. Note that the rules and the methods of computation in theoretical and empirical probability are the same. It is the evidence in hand that is different.

Many decisions must be based on empirical probability. Consider, for example, some of the decisions the promoter of a football bowl game must make. Suppose the bowl game is a new one, to be played in a stadium seating 100,000, and a week before the game only 10,000 tickets have been sold. Bad weather is likely to reduce the sale of tickets drastically. The promoter can, for a price, purchase rain insurance. To decide intelligently whether to buy the insurance, he cannot avoid estimating the probability that enough rain will fall at a time that will seriously reduce the sale of tickets.

Computation of the probabilities of events like rain, illness, accidents, and victories in elections must be based on empirical assumptions, *i.e.*, assumptions based on past experience. Empirical assumptions may be less reliable than theoretical assumptions. In the first place, past experience is rarely either complete or accurate. The most reliable experience the promoter could use would be the records of the United States Weather Bureau, founded in 1891. Accurate records of rainfall going back another hundred years might show a quite different probability. In the second place, some factor in the total situation may change and thereby change the probability that an event will occur. Many meteorologists believe, for example, that the large amount of carbon dioxide being released into the atmosphere from automobile exhausts and other sources is changing the climate of the world.

In making decisions it is often helpful to compute the probabilities even though the necessary empirical assumptions are little better than reasoned guesses. For example, suppose that near the middle of your first term in college you are incapacitated for two weeks by illness. Your problem is to decide whether to drop out for the remainder of the term. Suppose further that if you drop out now you can start afresh next term, but if you finish this term you must pass all four of your courses to stay in school. The danger that completing the term will put you out of school is certainly a relevant fac-

tor in your decision. But how great is this danger? You can make an intuitive guess, or you can make a reasoned guess by estimating the probability that you will pass each course and then multiplying the fractions for each course. The result is still a guess, but it is likely to be more reliable than a mere intuitive guess because the procedure forces you to take into account some of the separate factors involved.

People who are ignorant of the theory of probability tend to overestimate the likelihood of related events. For example, students asked to estimate the probability that their favorite football teams will win every game tend to rate the probability much higher if they merely make a single guess than if they estimate the probability of each game and multiply the fractions. Even when it is not practical to compute probabilities, it is helpful to remember the rule that the probability that two or more independent events will occur together is the product of the fractions expressing the probability of each event. The lower the probability of each event, the greater will be the difference between the probability of the single event and the probability of the combined events. For example, if the probability that you will pass each course is $1/2$, the probability that you will pass all four is $1/16$; but if the probability that you will pass each course is only $1/4$, the probability that you will pass all four is only $1/256$.

8. Degrees of Reliability

The concepts of probability are useful in assessing the degree of reliability of most conclusions. Near the beginning of this chapter *probability* was defined as the degree of likelihood that a proposition is true, based on the evidence in hand. In many cases the probability, as defined above, that a statement is true is also an assessment of the reliability of the statement. Suppose, for example, that you overhear a person you do not know make the following statement.

Joe Smythe guessed right on all ten five-choice objective questions on his zymology test, and he didn't know anything about the questions.

How can you assess the reliability of this statement? You can begin by computing the theoretical probability of guessing right on ten five-choice questions purely by chance. Assuming that each question has only one right answer, the probability is $(\frac{1}{5})^{10}$ or $\frac{1}{9,765,625}$. Using only theoretical probability as the evidence in hand, you would have to rate the reliability of the statement very low.

Now suppose you know Smythe well, and he tells you the statement is true. If you believe Smythe tells the truth 99 per cent of the time, then on the basis of this empirical evidence alone, the probability that the statement is true is $\frac{99}{100}$. Other empirical evidence might also be considered, such as the tendency of students to exaggerate their ignorance when bragging about their luck on tests. There is also the possibility that the test was so poorly written that some of the choices would be obvious even to an ignoramus. In a situation like this you cannot compute precisely the probability that the statement is true. The best you can do is make a reasoned guess that the probability is less than $\frac{99}{100}$. Whatever you guess, however, the probability that the statement is true is also an assessment of its reliability.

The language of probability can be used to express the degrees of our ignorance about a proposition. For example, consider this proposition: The Cambodia Tigers will defeat the Pakistan Lions in the Olympics. If we know nothing whatever about Cambodia and Pakistan or the Tigers and the Lions, we have no evidence in hand. On this basis, therefore, we should infer that the proposition is as likely to be true as false, and its probability is $\frac{1}{2}$. Now if we look in an atlas and learn that Pakistan has a much larger population than Cambodia, we have a little evidence in hand, since teams of larger nations tend to win more often than teams of smaller ones. On this evidence in hand, we might infer that the probability of this proposition is about $\frac{4}{10}$. Now suppose that we learn that the Cambodia Tigers have not been defeated in twenty years and that the Pakistan team has been organized only recently. Even with this evidence we can make only a reasoned guess about the "true" probability that Cambodia will win, but we should certainly increase our estimate. Although these probability estimates differ sharply, they were all reasonably good inferences: the differences are accounted for by the evidence in hand.

The language of probability is useful in expressing the degree of reliability of propositions and conclusions. In exercises to follow, we will refer to nine different degrees of reliability.

1. *Certain.* Reserved for propositions and conclusions about which there can be no possible doubt, as in closed systems of thought such as Euclid's geometry. In exercises to follow, you will sometimes be instructed to assume that the premises are true. When conclusions drawn from these premises are valid, the syllogism should be considered a closed system and the conclusion rated *certain.* Probability: 1.

2. *True beyond reasonable doubt.* All reasonable doubt eliminated. Suppose when you look in the yard for the morning paper you find a paper folded in the usual way and in the place where the newsboy usually leaves it. The dateline on the paper reads "Saturday." You turn on the radio and hear the announcer finish a commercial about a sale at a supermarket which "will continue through today, Saturday." There is still room for doubt. The newspaper and the radio could have combined to perpetrate a hoax by convincing you that it is Saturday when

it is really Friday. But such a doubt is not reasonable.

Since we cannot define a reasonable doubt precisely, we cannot attach a precise probability fraction to this level of reliability. For convenience, however, let us assign it the range from $999/1000$ up to but not including 1.

3. *Highly probable*. The evidence is strong but does not eliminate all reasonable doubt. Probability range: $9/10$ to $998/1000$, inclusive.

4. *Probable*. The weight of the evidence is favorable but not as strong as 3. Probability range: $501/1000$ to $899/1000$, inclusive.

5. *Indifferent*. Our ignorance is complete, or the evidence we have is as strong for as against. Probability: $1/2$.

6. *Improbable*. The weight of the evidence is negative in about the same degree as 4 above (probable) is positive. Probability range: $499/1000$ to $101/1000$, inclusive.

7. *Highly improbable*. The weight of the evidence is negative in about the same degree as 3 (highly probable) is positive. Probability range: $1/10$ to $2/1000$, inclusive.

8. *False beyond reasonable doubt*. The weight of the evidence is sufficient to eliminate any reasonable doubt that the proposition is false. Probability range: $1/1000$ down to but not including 0.

9. *Certainly false*. Reserved for closed systems in which there is no possibility that the proposition could be true. Probability: 0.

ANSWERS TO SELF-CHECK QUESTIONS

Page 27. Two questions right: $1/5 \times 1/5 = 1/25$

Page 28. Two non-explosive cigars: $4/7 \times 3/6 = 12/42$ or $2/7$

Page 29. Red slacks and yellow sweater: $1/3 \times 1/3 = 1/9$. (Since you have no knowledge of the colors in stock, you have no reason for thinking that one color is more likely than another.)

Slacks and sweater of matching color: $3/3 \times 1/3 = 1/3$. (Since the problem does not state which color, all three colors are favorable. Thus it does not matter what color the slacks are, provided the sweater is of the same color.)

EXERCISE 3

Where any kind of computation is required, write your complete computation in the space provided.

1–7. *These items refer to an objective test. Each question on the test has four choices, one and only one of which is correct.*

1. What is the probability that choice three is the correct answer to question one?

_____1/4_____

2. What assumption was involved in your answer to the question above?

each has a chance
that one is the correct answer

3. What is the probability that you can guess correctly the first two questions purely by chance?

_____1/16_____

4–7: Compute the probabilities of the events described. Assume that only chance is involved.

4. Guess the first question right and the second question wrong.   ____3/16____

5. Guess both of the first two questions wrong.   ____9/16____

6. Guess the first three questions right.   ____1/64____

7. Guess the first question right, the second wrong, and the third right.

_____3/64_____

8–14. *These items refer to the following set of questions from a test in bacteriology in which each term matches one and only one definition.*

Term	Names bacteria which:
Psychrophilic	1. Grow well at 9 degrees centigrade
Heterotrophic	2. Grow utilizing light as energy source
Chemosynthetic	3. Grow in an inorganic medium
Autotrophic	4. Grow only with organic compounds in the medium
Photosynthetic	5. Grow utilizing chemical bond energy

8–12: Compute the probabilities on the assumption that only chance is involved.

8. Guess the first question right. _____1/5_____

9. Guess the first two questions right. _____1/25 or 1/20_____

10. Guess the first three questions right. _____1/125 or 1/60_____

11. Guess the first four questions right. _____1/625 or 1/120_____

12. Guess all five questions right. _____1/3125 or 1/120_____

13. Suppose that all you know about the subject is that Choice 2 is not the correct answer to the first question. What is the probability that you can guess the first question right?

_____1/4_____

14. Assume that you have already correctly answered the first question. What is the probability that you can guess correctly the remaining four? _____1/256_____

$1/4 \times 1/4 \times 1/4 \times 1/4$

15. Suppose you can fly home for Thanksgiving by two routes. If you go by Continental Airlines you must change planes in St. Louis, and during the past year the flight to St. Louis made the connection to your destination two out of three times. If you go by Alpha Airlines you must change planes both in Indianapolis and Evansville. The flight to Indianapolis made the connection to Evansville eight times out of ten during the past year, and the flight to Evansville made the connection there seven times out of ten. On the basis of this information alone, which route should you take?

2/3 or 56/100   Continental Airlines

16. What assumptions were involved in your decision above?

only routes taken; assume second is independent events

4 Evaluating Evidence

In preceding chapters we noted that the function of critical thinking is to evaluate the reliability of conclusions. In practice, the question of the reliability of a conclusion is not whether it is true or false, but the extent to which it has been demonstrated to be true or false. In judging the reliability of a conclusion we must consider the reliability of the evidence on which the inferences are based as well as the inferences themselves. No matter how skillful or careful we are in the interpretation of evidence, we are likely to go astray unless the evidence itself is reliable. Let us turn, then, to the problems of judging evidence. We will find that the practical question of the reliability of evidence, as with conclusions, is not whether it is true but how much confidence we are justified in placing in it.

The basic ingredient in evidence is what the scientist calls *observations, i.e.,* verbalized perceptions. Whenever the scientist weighs something or takes its temperature, and records his data, he is making an observation. When a witness testifies in court that he saw the defendant leave the scene of a crime, he is reporting an observation he claims to have made.

An observation begins with *sensation,* a complex process in which sensory stimuli are received by the sense organs and transmitted to the brain. If you look at the vapor trail of a jet plane, the light waves from the sky are received by the retinas of your eyes and transmitted to the brain. The image produced is a sensation. The next stage is *perception,* the interpretation of sensations by the brain in terms of experience stored in the frame of reference. You *sense* the visual stimuli in the sky — you *perceive* the vapor trail of a jet plane. Before perceptions can be used in reasoning they must be symbolized. To feed his perceptions into a computer the scientist must express them in words or symbols. To use your perceptions in reasoning you must express them in words or other symbols.

If you have been assuming that your own observations are always reliable, it is time to disillusion yourself, for errors may creep into all three stages in observation. Sensations may be inaccurate because of imperfections in sensory equipment. For example, a person afflicted with myopia or astigmatism may not sense what a person with normal vision does. To one who is color blind, rainbows may look drab and sunsets dull. Some persons are unable to sense the harmonics and overtones of musical instruments.

We also make innumerable errors in perception. Sensations can be interpreted only in terms of the frame of reference. When your frame of reference does not contain the knowledge necessary to perceive something for what it is, you are likely to perceive it to be something it resembles. If your frame of reference contains no knowledge of the vapor trails of jet planes, you would probably perceive the vapor trail to be a straight and narrow cloud. Furthermore, perceptions are often shaped by what we are looking for or thinking about. We perceive the sparkle of dew in the grass to be the dime we are looking for. We perceive the backfire of an automobile to be a gunshot. Deer hunting has become dangerous because eager hunters sometimes perceive the movement of another hunter in the underbrush as that of a deer, and fire away.

The verbalization of perceptions is subject to error because language is not an absolutely accurate vehicle for communicating perceptions. If the language you use in describing a perception is vague, or ambiguous, or inaccurate, then your observation will not be sharp and accurate, no matter how accurate your perception was.

Many of the problems of evaluating observations can be seen in a trial at law, where the testimony of witnesses may constitute all or most of the evidence. When a witness testifies that he saw the defendant leaving the scene of the crime carrying a smoking revolver, the jury should not naively accept this observation as truth without considering two questions: (1) Was the witness lying? (2) Was the witness capable of making the observation he claimed he made? Over the

years our courts have evolved an elaborate code to guard against false or improper testimony. The code governs such matters as the kinds of testimony that may be admitted in evidence, who may give testimony, in what circumstances, and at what stage in the proceedings, and how the testimony of a witness may be attacked. The judge acts as referee in enforcing these rules of evidence. A questionable decision on whether a given bit of evidence may be admitted for consideration may be made the basis of an appeal for a new trial. So elaborate have these rules become, and so encrusted with qualifications and exceptions, that ten heavy volumes are required to cover them.[1] Even a superficial study of the rules of evidence will show that the courts have long been concerned with the problems of evaluation we shall discuss in this chapter.

As a rule, courts will not admit *hearsay evidence, i.e.,* testimony based on what the witness heard others say. Experience has shown this kind of evidence to be generally unreliable. The person who made the statement may have been mistaken, and he is not available for cross-examination. Moreover the witness may be lying, and his observations of the other person's statements are subject to the usual errors of perception and language.

The principal weapon against the unreliable witness, and particularly the witness who is lying, is cross-examination. Any inconsistency, even on a minor point, that the cross-examiner can bring out lowers the reliability of the evidence. Only a very clever witness can fabricate testimony without being caught by a skillful cross-examiner.

In evaluating the reliability of evidence it is essential to distinguish observations from inferences. It is this distinction newspaper

[1] The student interested in a non-technical description of legal proof should read Ernest Mortenson, *You Be the Judge* (New York: Longmans, Green, 1940), pp. 343–399.

editors have in mind when they urge cub reporters to "get the facts." In 1944 Chicago was plagued by a series of incendiary fires in apartment houses on the south side of the city. In one of these fires, in which several persons lost their lives, firemen found mattresses burning at the foot of both the front and rear stairways in the building. The cub reporter would be stating a fact should he write: "Firemen found mattresses burning at the foot of both the front and rear stairways of the building." But he would be bringing in something else should he write: "The fire was started by an arsonist who tried to murder the inhabitants of the building by blocking both exits with burning mattresses." In this latter statement the reporter would be making an inference about the origin of the fire and the motive of the person starting it. The reliability of propositions that state both observation and inference must be judged by the standards of both. Henceforth, in discussing evidence of any kind let us reserve the word *fact* for a proposition that has been demonstrated to be true beyond reasonable doubt.

The degree to which we are justified in being confident that an observation is true depends upon the conditions in which the observation was made and the ability of the observer. Before accepting any observation as fact you should ask six questions, any one of which may be grounds for reasonable doubt about its reliability. You should ask these questions about your own observations as well as those of others.

1. Physical Conditions

The first question is whether the physical conditions under which the observation was made were favorable. When one is sitting in the grandstand well to one side of home plate, one's location is not as favorable for calling balls and strikes as the umpire's. The coach at a football game is not in a good position to observe some aspects of the action, and he therefore stations an observer in the pressbox high above the field. The farther you are from an accident the less reliable your perceptions of it will be. One should not expect his perceptions to be reliable when conditions make accurate perception difficult.

Attorneys often use cross-examination to show that a reliable observation was unlikely under the prevailing conditions. According to a famous story, Abraham Lincoln won his first defense at a murder trial by this technique. The prosecution's case rested mainly on testimony of a witness who swore that he saw the defendant fire the fatal shot and run away. In cross-examining this witness, Lincoln led him to testify to a number of details: that he was standing twenty feet or more from the defendant at the time of the shooting, that the shooting occurred in heavy timber, that he could see how the pistol was pointed, that the shooting occurred at night, that the nearest lights were candles three quarters of a mile away, that he saw the shooting by moonlight. Then Lincoln dramatically produced an almanac, offered it in evidence, and read from it that the moon did not rise until several hours after the shooting. Under the strain, the witness broke down and confessed that he had fired the fatal shot himself.[2]

2. Sensory Acuity

The second question is whether the observer had the sensory acuity necessary for the observation. What one individual sees sharply at a hundred feet another will see only as a blur. What one individual hears distinctly another will not hear at all. When unusual sensory acuity was necessary for an

---

[2] For an account of this and other cases in which cross-examination played a vital part, see Francis L. Wellman, *The Art of Cross-Examination* (New York: Macmillan, 1925).

observation, the attorney usually asks his own witness questions designed to convince the jury that the witness did have the necessary sharpness of vision or hearing.

In scientific procedure, where accurate measurement is essential, elaborate instruments and techniques for measurement have been designed to aid the senses. The laboratory technician who estimated temperature and weight by feel, or length by sight, would not last long in his job. In evaluating the reliability of scientific investigations where accurate measurements of weight, length, volume, and the like are essential, the accuracy of the instruments used should be considered as well as the sensory acuity of the observer.

3. Technical Knowledge

The third question is whether the observer had the necessary knowledge to make the observation he claims to have made. As we noted in Chapter 1, perception is limited by the frame of reference. A person with 20–20 vision watching a football game under perfect physical conditions cannot determine whether the linemen are charging properly unless his frame of reference includes the necessary technical knowledge of football.

As our world becomes increasingly complex, we must depend more and more upon experts for observations we are not capable of making ourselves. The layman cannot determine whether a tumor is cancerous; he must depend on a pathologist. Courts of law rely increasingly on expert witnesses as crime detection becomes more and more technical. Physicians, psychiatrists, ballistics experts, fingerprint experts, and handwriting experts are frequently called to give testimony. Without their assistance, the average layman sitting on the jury would be unable to determine whether the defendant is insane, whether the fatal bullet came from the defendant's gun, whether the ransom note was written by the defendant, or whether the prints left at the scene of the crime are those of the defendant or his brother-in-law.

4. Degree of Objectivity

The fourth question is whether the observer is objective. We noted in Chapter 1 that certain subjective factors decrease our objectivity. The same factors affect our observations.

The accuracy of observations is affected adversely by *prejudice*. What we perceive is affected by what we look for. In a fight between two students, the fraternity brother of one may perceive that the other landed all the dirty blows.

The accuracy of observations is also affected adversely by *emotion*. To a person who is afraid, the snake looks bigger than it is; in rough, open water the skiff seems smaller than it is; an innocent gesture by an antagonist becomes the motion of reaching for a gun. Under emotional stress a person is more susceptible to suggestion. If the stress is strong enough, he may become subject to hallucinations and delusions.

What we happen to be paying *attention* to also affects what we observe. We rarely perceive all the elements in a situation. We tend to perceive only those we are interested in or which attract our attention. All of us, walking into a dormitory room, would probably perceive a blazing wastebasket, but once the fire is extinguished the occupant of the room and the housing official would probably not perceive the same elements in the situation.

5. Effects of Memory

A fifth question is whether the observer is likely to remember his observation accurately. We should never forget that memory is selective: we tend to remember some things and forget others.

The personal point of view is a strong factor in this selectivity. We tend to remember instances that seem to support the self-concept and to forget instances that threaten the self-concept. As Nietzsche put it: "My memory says that I did it, my pride says that I could not have done it, and in the end, my memory yields." Thus we tend to forget evidence that would force a revision in the self-concept or frame of reference. We usually forget what we feel no need to remember. We quickly forget the telephone number we do not expect to use again. The student quickly forgets the material he crammed for an examination, especially if he does not expect to use it again. For this reason, your college education will be more valuable in the long run if you try to find a purpose in your life for each course you take.

Other things being equal, we remember best the instances we have encountered most frequently. Propagandists and advertisers take advantage of this tendency. When you go to the drugstore to buy toothpaste, you are likely to ask for the brand you remember best because you have heard it most.

Other things being equal, we are likely to remember best the instances we have encountered most recently. Political propagandists sometimes use this principle of recency by reserving for the day before election some argument particularly damning to the opposition in the hope that the undecided voter will go to the polls with this argument fresh in mind.

Other things being equal, we remember best those instances that were most vivid. For this reason advertisers and propagandists take great pains to make their ideas vivid and dramatic. But vividness has nothing to do with reliability.

We should never forget another human tendency — to imagine that we remember what we have forgotten or never perceived. Because both perception and memory are selective, we can rarely recall accurately all details of an episode. When we try to recall them our imagination tends to fill in the gaps.

The witness to an accident, unable to recall important details, supplies them from his imagination. He remembers what *should* have happened in terms of his dominant impression of the episode, even when it did not happen that way. This tendency is in part responsible for the conflicting testimony often obtained from witnesses.

This is why we remember the past as "the good old days" — the "old-oaken-bucket" delusion. We remember the coolness of the well water and forget such painful details as hauling up the heavy bucket.

6. Corroboration

The sixth question is whether the observation has been sufficiently corroborated by other observers. The chance of error in observation is so great that, even though an observation seems to meet all the tests we have so far discussed, it usually should not be accepted as true beyond reasonable doubt until it has been corroborated by other observers.

In general, when the observations of two or more persons correspond, two principles apply: (1) the higher the reliability of each observer, judged by the criteria discussed above, the higher the reliability of the observation; (2) within limits, the larger the number of observers, the higher the reliability. These principles, though useful, must be applied with caution. An unknown factor in the situation or a common error in the frames of reference of the observers could make a thousand seemingly reliable observers wrong, whereas one seemingly unreliable observer could be right.

7. Degree of Accuracy Required

When using observations in making decisions we must often consider the degree of accuracy required. In some situations a rough approximation is sufficient. For example, suppose the witness in a jury trial testifies that he observed the defendant put fifty drops of poison in food later eaten by the decedent. Suppose, further, that ten drops of this poison is lethal. In this situation, whether the defendant actually put forty-five or fifty-five drops of poison in the food is of little consequence, since the issue at stake is whether the amount put in the food was lethal.

In other situations, observations may be misleading unless completely accurate. For example, the Greeks believed the following hypothetical premise.

> The earth moves $\supset$ a closer star would
> through space   show parallax with
>   respect to a more
>   distant star.[3]

They assumed that they would perceive parallax if it were present. But because their technical equipment for stellar observation was inadequate, the Greeks were unable to observe parallax between stars of different distances from the earth. Thus they validly concluded that the earth does not move through space. For this and other reasons, Ptolemy's geocentric theory prevailed for centuries. Even after Copernicus advanced the heliocentric theory in the sixteenth century, the great Danish astronomer Tycho Brahe rejected the idea that the earth moves, because he was unable to measure any parallax of the stars in spite of the fact that his instruments were capable of measuring angles to within one minute of arc. It was not until 1838, over two hundred years after Galileo first used the telescope for astro-

nomical purposes, that the telescope and its accessories were sufficiently refined to enable Bessel to measure stellar parallax. The angle he measured was about one seven-thousandth of a degree!

8. Evidence from Authorities

Each of us must frequently make decisions requiring highly specialized knowledge that we do not ourselves have. In such matters we are forced to use as evidence the opinions of authorities. These opinions usually involve both observations and inferences that we cannot evaluate because we do not have the necessary technical or specialized knowledge.

As citizens we cannot ourselves go to Washington to conduct personal investigations of the affairs of government; we must depend on reports and commentaries in the newspapers and on radio and television. In more complicated affairs we must frequently rely on interpretations by commentators. Newspapers, in their effort to be objective, do not tell the whole truth. When one political personage falsely accuses another of being a Communist, the newspaper, trying to be objective, reports merely that so-and-so says so-and-so is a Communist. It does not point out to its readers that the speaker has no great reputation for veracity and has no way of knowing whether the accused person is or is not a Communist. Yet, without this information, the reader has little chance of evaluating the statement correctly. Newspaper columnists and radio and television commentators flourish because they supply the interpretation for which the public feels a need.

When we do not ourselves have the technical or specialized knowledge necessary to evaluate the opinions of authorities, we must in effect evaluate the authorities themselves. When the issue is important we should concern ourselves not only with the general reliability of an authority but also with his reliability on the specific issue at stake. You

---

[3] If one holds a pencil at arm's length and observes it by closing first one eye and then the other, the pencil appears to move against the background of objects behind it. The closer the pencil is held to the eye the greater the apparent movement, which is called parallax. In this case the parallax could be measured as the angle at the pencil subtended by the distance between the observer's two eyes. If the parallax angle and the distance between the two eyes are known, it is a relatively simple matter to calculate the distance from the eyes to the pencil.

should cultivate the habit of asking yourself three questions about an authority before you accept his opinion.

1. *How much does he know about the specific question at issue?* We are likely to assume that, because a man has achieved renown as an authority in one field, he must be a person of superior intelligence and therefore competent in other fields as well. But the world's greatest authority on nuclear physics may be the world's poorest authority on politics. Granted that he had to be a person of superior intellect to become a great authority in any field, he probably had to concentrate his effort on physics, to the neglect of other matters. When we consult an authority, it is his competence in the field in question that matters. While there is no completely reliable rule for determining competence, there are a number of helpful clues. Membership in learned or professional societies may be a clue. A surgeon who is a Fellow of the American College of Surgeons is not necessarily a better surgeon than one who is not, but recognition by such a group is an indication that he probably is. Other clues are degrees held and the institutions granting them. A Ph.D. degree from a reputable institution is not an absolute guarantee of competence in the specific field of the degree, but it is strong evidence of such competence. Remember, however, that a Ph.D. in zymology does not qualify its holder as an authority in English literature. A librarian can usually assist you in looking up clues to an authority's competence.

2. *Is he objective about the matter in question?* Courts of law long ago recognized that the testimony of a witness is less reliable if he has a pecuniary or emotional interest in the matter on which he is testifying. If personal interest may make factual testimony unreliable, it may have an even more adverse effect on the reliability of opinions, and authorities are not exempt from this influence. In important matters it is well to try to discover the authority's own peculiar interest, if any, and discount his opinion accordingly. Civilian and military authorities may differ, for example, on how much money is needed for national defense. One should not infer that either deliberately gives a false opinion in order to promote his own interests. The point is that as human beings they tend to see what they want to see. When the salesman tells you that the car he sells is the best in its field, he is not necessarily lying; he may just be blinded by enthusiasm, or he may be right. We should be careful not to overlook emotional interests, which are frequently more powerful than pecuniary ones. For example, an authority who gains renown for an opinion or a conclusion tends to develop an emotional attachment to it that will not allow him to give it up easily.

3. *Finally, what do other authorities conclude about the matter?* Suppose your doctor tells you that the pain in your leg is caused by osteomyelitis and that surgery is necessary. Without extensive medical knowledge you cannot yourself evaluate the reliability of the doctor's observations of your leg and of the x-rays taken of it. Nor can you as a layman evaluate the inferences involved in the diagnosis. You should, of course, consult other physicians — not, as many people do, to find one who will give you a more palatable diagnosis, but to help you determine the reliability of the original diagnosis. Experts sometimes reach different conclusions from the same evidence. When they do, our best criterion of reliability is a majority opinion of qualified authorities. Clearly, a common conclusion reached independently by three medical specialists is a sounder basis for decision than the conclusion of only one.

In general, the fact that we must often base decisions on the observations or opinions of authorities does not mean that we should accept their views uncritically, for authorities are not infallible. The history of science, for example, shows that many theories once considered incontrovertible have now been demonstrated to be false beyond reasonable doubt. Many propositions we now accept as true beyond reasonable doubt will eventually meet the same fate. Authorities, as well as laymen, sometimes reason from unreliable premises, and sometimes make unreliable inferences. A conclusion based on an affirmed consequent or a denied antecedent is invalid, whether the inference is made by a layman or an authority.

When the subject is not too technical and the authority states the evidence on which he based his conclusion, you should test it by the appropriate criteria described in later chapters, especially 6, 7, 12, 16, and 17. If you read carefully what the authority says, you will often find that he is claiming only that his conclusion is probably true — not that it is fact. Sometimes, when the authority claims that his conclusion is highly probable or true beyond reasonable doubt, a critical examination may reveal weaknesses in evidence or inference that make his conclusion less reliable than he seems to believe.

Suggested Supplementary Reading

HAROLD A. LARRABEE, *Reliable Knowledge,* rev. ed. (Boston: Houghton Mifflin Company, 1964), pp. 99–124.

EXERCISE 4

1–5. *Classify the italicized passages according to the key list below.*

KEY LIST
A. *Sensation*   B. *Perception*   C. *Observation*   D. *Inference*

1. As Jill walked by a clump of shrubbery on her way to class she *heard a noise* she could not identify.

                                        _____A_____

2. Then she heard the noise again and *realized that it was made by a rattlesnake.*

                                        _____B_____

3. With some agitation she said to a student walking ahead of her, "*I heard a rattlesnake in those bushes.*"

                             ___C or D___

4. At that moment *she saw a squirrel scamper out of the bushes.*   _____C_____

5. Then she noticed that the ground beneath the bushes was covered with dry leaves. "*The noise I heard must have been made by that squirrel rattling the leaves,*" she said.

                                        _____D_____

6. Describe an instance of erroneous perception from your own experience.

_____

_____

7–14. *Use Key List A below to indicate all grounds on which there is reason to question the italicized observation. Assume that the observers are not deliberately lying. Use Key List B to rate the reliability of the observation. Exclude your personal opinion of the issue and base your judgment solely on the criteria in Key List A.*

KEY LIST A
1. *Physical conditions were not favorable.*
2. *The observer lacked the necessary sensory acuity.*
3. *The observer lacked the necessary technical knowledge.*
4. *The observer was not objective.*
5. *The observer is not likely to have remembered the observation.*
6. *There is insufficient corroboration.*
7. *The observation is not sufficiently accurate.*

KEY LIST B
1. *Certainly true*
2. *True beyond reasonable doubt*
3. *Highly probable*
4. *Probable*
5. *Indifferent*
6. *Improbable*
7. *Highly improbable*
8. *False beyond reasonable doubt*
9. *Certainly false*

7. Spectator, who was sitting in the end zone, speaking of a play which occurred at mid-field: *"I clearly saw Smythe,* who was playing left tackle, *deliberately break the arm of our quarterback* during that pileup."

A 1, 3, 4 B 6

8. American child, aged twelve, who has never been in a foreign country: "I saw the man yesterday when he came into the room. *He was a Korean, about forty years old."*

A 3, 5 B 7

9. Ph.D. in physics: *"The painting which was sold to the plaintiff is not a genuine Rembrandt."*

A 3, 6 B 6

10. Man who wears hearing aid: "I was sitting on my front porch, and the defendant was sitting in his car at the curb. *I heard him whisper to his companion, 'Here's where we get easy dough.'"*

A 1, 2, 5 B 8

11. Mechanic: "When I lubricated the defendant's car about a month ago, *I noticed that the tire on the left front wheel was not new."*

A 5, 7 B 2

12. Housewife: "I was looking out of my window, across the street from the defendant's house. I happened to be watching his window. I could see clearly because the sun was shining. *I saw him put a .32 automatic in his pocket.* I never have approved of his doings."

A 1, 3, 4, 5 B

13. Medical examiner, testifying in murder trial in which the defendant could not have been at the scene of the crime earlier than 11:00 P.M.: *"My examination showed that the deceased was shot sometime between 10:30 P.M. and midnight."*

A 3, 7 B

14. Unidentified radio commentator: *"The Demopublican convention was a farce from beginning to end.* The platform and candidates were picked in advance by the bosses, and the delegates were mere puppets on a stage, moved by strings pulled by the bosses."

A 4, 6 B 5

5 Forming Hypotheses

At about 6:00 P.M. on November 1, 1955, William Albert Scraggs, inspector for the Civil Aeronautics Board, answered his telephone and heard his chief say: "United Airlines Flight 629 has crashed west of Denver. I am putting you in charge of the investigation — find out why the plane crashed."[1]

Information given Scraggs by his chief included the following propositions.

1. All forty-four persons aboard were killed.
2. Flight 629 left Denver twenty-two minutes late.
3. The crash occurred within eleven minutes after take-off.
4. The plane was a DC 6B.

Note that no two of these propositions can be combined into a valid syllogism. Each of them is an observation about a particular plane or a particular group of passengers. Any one of them might serve as a minor premise, but none will do as a major premise. Nor can Scraggs extract from his frame of reference any premise with which one or more of these propositions can be combined to tell him why Flight 629 crashed. While

[1] The character Scraggs and his role in the investigation are fictitious. Details of the crash are taken from newspaper and magazine reports.

deductive inferences will prove useful in the investigation, they will not suffice. For Scraggs' problem is new in the sense that its solution cannot be derived from premises he already has. Inductive inferences are necessary in situations like this.

1. Inductive Inferences

In all except the simplest of decisions, we are likely to use both deductive and inductive inferences and to shift quickly from one to the other. An understanding of the nature of both types is essential to effective thinking because the methods of testing are very different. When a deductive inference is valid, the conclusion must be true if the premises are true, for the conclusion is inherent, though not stated, in the premises. For example, when the insurance agent explains that he must charge a higher rate to insure your car because you are under twenty-five years of age and all drivers under twenty-five must pay a higher rate because they have more accidents, he is making a deductive inference. If you wish to disagree with the agent, it is useless to challenge his inference, for it is valid. If there is a weakness in his argument, it is in the premises, for a valid deductive inference does not go beyond the evidence stated in the premises.

An inductive inference, on the other hand, *goes beyond the evidence to a statement of something that has not been verified by observation.* Officials of the insurance company made an inductive inference when they put together thousands of facts about accidents and the ages of the drivers involved and concluded that younger drivers should be charged higher premiums because they are more likely to have accidents. They went beyond the evidence by drawing a conclusion about drivers in the future on the basis of drivers in the past. If you wish to disagree, you could challenge the evidence itself, though in this case you would probably find that the evidence had been carefully collected. Or you could challenge the inference on the ground that the accident rate for the past will not necessarily continue into the future.

Thus the weakness in a conclusion derived by valid deductive inference lies in the premises, while the weakness in a conclusion derived by inductive inference may lie in either evidence or inference or both. It does not follow, however, that conclusions derived from deductive inference are more reliable, for most of the premises we use in deduction have been derived by inductive inference. In this and the following chapters we study three types of inductive inferences: hypotheses, generalizations, and causal theories. All of these have one characteristic in common — they go beyond the evidence in hand. Because inductive inferences do go beyond the evidence in hand, they are our primary tool in solving new problems, finding new solutions to old problems, and developing new premises.

2. The Nature of Hypotheses

The type of inductive inference most likely to be useful to Scraggs at this point produces *hypotheses.* The term *hypothesis* is often used in a general sense to refer to any theory or unproved assumption. But in this book we use *hypothesis* in a more restricted sense to refer to a *tentative conclusion that relates and explains a group of different items of information.*

Let us clarify our definition with examples. Suppose you return to your room and observe that (1) the door is open, (2) the table is overturned, and (3) the drawers of your chest are open and the contents in disorder. Your observations give you a set of three different propositions. They are not necessarily related. You could have pulled out the drawers and stirred up their contents as you dressed hurriedly; your roommate could have turned over the table in a mad dash to class; an official of the housing office could have left the door open.

If, however, you did not yourself leave the drawers pulled out, you would probably be disturbed by your observations. Almost before entering the room you would make a guess to account for them. Depending on your experience, you might make any or all of the following guesses: "I have been robbed"; "My roommate has had one of his periodic tussles"; "Someone has a grudge against me." These guesses are hypotheses. Each of them relates and explains the three different items of information by ascribing them to a common cause. For example, the hypothesis "I have been robbed" explains why the door was left open, the table overturned, and the drawers left in disorder, for it is reasonable to suppose that a robber might do all these things in his haste to find valuables and escape. All three hypotheses are derived by inductive inference, for they go beyond observation and supply an explanation not subject to your own observation.

The decision-making cycle with the hypothesis as the basic type of tentative conclusion is highly useful in a wide variety of situations. It is used by historians reconstructing the past, by doctors making diagnoses, by detectives investigating crimes, by lawyers pleading cases, by newspaper reporters piecing together stories, by military strategists interpreting intelligence reports, by economists predicting future market conditions, by counselors helping students solve their problems, and by students solving their problems. It is used in combination with other techniques by scientists unraveling the secrets of the universe.

In using hypotheses you should begin Phase 3 (forming tentative conclusions) as soon as a few items of information have been gathered. For there is a reciprocal relationship between hypotheses and information: information is the substance from which hypotheses are formed, and forming hypotheses guides the search for further information.

A hypothesis adds meaning to a group of propositions that the individual propositions do not have. For example, consider Joe Smythe's semester grade report shown below.

Course	Credits	Grade
English 1	3	C
Social Sciences 1	3	A
Mathematics 1	3	D
Chemistry 1	3	D
Engineering Graphics 1	3	F

Different people would form different hypotheses about these grades according to their frames of reference. Joe's parents might form the hypothesis that Joe did not study much during the semester. Joe's rival for the affections of a certain co-ed might form the hypothesis that Joe is not very bright. A well trained counselor might form two hypotheses: (1) Joe plans to become an engineer, and (2) engineering is not a suitable career for Joe. Note that all these hypotheses, though formed from different points of view, add meaning to the grades. Any particular meaning might not be true, of course, but meaning has been added nevertheless.

By adding meaning to the propositions in hand, a hypothesis serves as a guide to what information is relevant. Suppose your problem is to find out why Joe made poor grades in three courses. Without one or more hypotheses you would have no basis for deciding what kind of information to seek. You might gather vast quantities of data about Joe, such as his weight, height, or taste in food, without including any information of use in solving your problem. On the other hand, suppose you formed the hypothesis that Joe made bad grades in these courses because he was not really interested in engineering. This hypothesis gives you a clear sense of direction in seeking more information. Even if the hypothesis eventually proves to be wrong, your investigation of it is likely to turn up useful information.

Now let us return to the case of Flight 629. Scraggs had hardly hung up his telephone before he had formed the following hypotheses to guide his investigation.

A. The crash was caused by a storm.
B. The crash was caused by engine failure.
C. The crash was caused by fire aboard the plane.
D. The crash was caused by structural failure.

Forming hypotheses is the essence of creative thinking. In a sense it is like guessing what picture a jigsaw puzzle will make before you put it together. When you have taken only a few pieces from the box your imagination has few clues to help; on the other hand, your imagination is virtually unlimited because the picture could be of almost anything. Later, as you begin to assemble some of the pieces, your imagination has more clues, but it is more limited because fewer pictures will fit the pieces you have assembled. Even when you have many of the pieces assembled your imagination must fill in the gaps.

At this stage in his investigation Scraggs had only a few clues to help his imagination fill in the picture of what caused Flight 629 to crash. Proposition 1 makes his investigation important, but does little to suggest what caused the crash. Propositions 2 and 3 suggest that the plane might have been delayed in Denver by some kind of mechanical trouble, which might later have caused the crash. Proposition 4 would be helpful only if other planes of the type had crashed before. Because he had few clues, Scraggs' imagination was almost unrestricted, for the only causes of the crash eliminated by the evidence so far in hand are those connected with the take-off.

3. Guidelines for Forming Hypotheses

Three general guidelines should be followed in forming hypotheses.

1. *The hypotheses should solve or help to solve the problem as defined.* Since Scraggs' problem is to discover why the plane crashed, he would be wasting his time forming hypotheses about the effects of the crash on the families of the passengers or about the cost to the airline.

2. *The more hypotheses formed, the better.* We must be extremely careful not to limit ourselves to one hypothesis, for if we do, the probability is high that we will exclude the very information that will provide the key to the problem. Also, if we begin with only one hypothesis, we are likely to develop a liking for it and unconsciously search only for evidence to support it. We must avoid trying to establish any particular hypothesis. Darwin remarked that it was so easy to pass over facts contrary to a favorite hypothesis that he found it necessary to write them down, or he was almost sure to forget them. The preventive is to form several hypotheses. The more we form, the more likely we are to form the correct one.

3. *Extra effort should be made to form unpalatable hypotheses.* The psychological Ohm's law is especially applicable to hypothesis formation: we tend to restrain the imagination in forming hypotheses that threaten the self-concept in any way. If Scraggs believed that his knowledge of airplane engines was inadequate for this investigation, he would have been far less likely to form the hypothesis that the crash of Flight 629 was caused by engine failure.

4. Adding and Testing Consequents

Although you can begin testing a single hypothesis as soon as you have formed one, it is generally better procedure to form a number of hypotheses before you begin extensive testing. If you complete the cycle with a single hypothesis you risk becoming attached to it. Furthermore, especially in complex investigations, you can usually save time by testing a number of hypotheses simultaneously. Since hypotheses go beyond the evidence in hand, and *valid* conclusions never do, hypotheses cannot be tested for validity. We test hypotheses by asking ourselves what else would be true if the hypothesis is true.

The first step is to complete a hypothetical proposition by using the hypothesis in question as the antecedent and then adding a consequent that might have been, or was, or might be, or is, or will be true if the hypothesis is true. Shown below are Scraggs' first four hypotheses, to each of which a consequent has been added.

Hypothesis		*Consequent Added*
A. The crash was caused by a storm	⊃	weather reports would show bad flying weather in the area of the crash.
B. The crash was caused by engine failure	⊃	one or more engines may have been running badly when Flight 629 took off from Denver.
C. The crash was caused by fire	⊃	the wreckage would show signs of fire.
D. The crash was caused by structural failure	⊃	evidence might be found in the wreckage of the plane.

The second step is to test the consequents by any practicable means. Note that the consequents themselves point like the needle of a compass to sources of relevant information. Note also that Scraggs can save time and trouble by testing several hypotheses simultaneously: he can test Consequents A and B by calling the airport, and C and D by inspecting the wreckage.

Scraggs' call to the airport yielded the information in the following propositions.

5. Flying conditions in the area of the crash were excellent.
6. All engines were functioning normally at take-off.

The next step is to assess the significance of the evidence gathered by testing consequents. The significance of such evidence can be seen by completing a hypothetical syllogism, using the evidence gathered as the minor premise. Consider Proposition 5 in relation to Hypothesis A.

The crash was caused ⊃ weather reports would
by a storm   show bad flying
                          weather in the area of
                          the crash.

Weather reports show that flying conditions were excellent.

∴ The crash was not caused by a storm.

The syllogism above shows that Proposition 5 is a *diverging proposition*, i.e., *a proposition that reduces the probability that a hypothesis is true* by denying a consequent that would be or might be true if the hypothesis is true. In Scraggs' frame of reference the consequent of the above syllogism would have to be true if the hypothesis is true. Since he now believed that this consequent was clearly denied, he discarded Hypothesis A.

Now consider Proposition 6 in relation to Hypothesis B.

The crash was caused ⊃ one or more engines
by engine failure   may have been
                          running badly when
                          Flight 629 took off
                          from Denver.

All engines were functioning normally at take-off.

Proposition 6 is also a diverging proposition, but it is not as significant as Proposition 5. Since the consequent is qualified by the word *may*, we would be guilty of *non sequitur* if we concluded that the plane crash was not caused by engine failure. Even so, the proposition does reduce the probability that the hypothesis is true.

The next morning Scraggs was on the scene of the crash testing Consequents C and D. A quick inspection of the wreckage yielded two surprising facts.

7. Wreckage from the plane showed no signs of fire.
8. Debris from the plane was widely scattered.

Proposition 7 clearly diverges from Hypothesis C. Proposition 8 diverges from Hypothesis D, for in plane crashes caused by structural failure the debris is not normally as widely scattered as the debris from Flight 629. Thus, as often happens in complex investigations, Scraggs has partially tested his original four hypotheses and found no supporting evidence for any of them. Even so he has made progress, for Proposition 8 suggests a new hypothesis.

E. The crash was caused by an explosion aboard the plane.

Proposition 8 not only suggests Hypothesis E but also provides a *converging* proposition, *i.e., a proposition that increases the probability that a hypothesis is true by affirming a consequent that would be or might be true if the hypothesis is true.* The significance of a converging proposition can be seen by putting it into a hypothetical syllogism.

The crash was caused ⊃ debris from the plane
by an explosion   would be widely
aboard the plane   scattered.

Debris from the plane was widely scattered.

∴ The crash was caused by an explosion aboard
the plane.

If you studied Chapter 2 thoroughly, you should have already noted that this conclusion is invalid because the consequent is affirmed. Even so, Proposition 8 increases the probability that Hypothesis E is true by eliminating all possible causes of the crash that would not result in widely scattered debris. Another consequent with which to test Hypothesis E is obvious: someone may have seen the explosion. Eyewitnesses were quickly found, all of whom agreed that the plane exploded in mid-air. What began as a hypothesis had now become an observation.

In adding and testing consequents three general guidelines should be followed.

1. *Consequents should bear on the truth or falsity of the hypothesis being tested.* Consider Hypothesis E, to which a consequent has been added.

The crash was caused ⊃ the airline is liable for
by an explosion   damages.
aboard the plane

This consequent does not bear on the truth or falsity of the hypothesis in question, because it cannot be determined whether or not the airline is liable for damages until the cause of the crash is known.

2. *The consequents should be worth testing.* Whether or not a consequent is worth the time and expense of testing depends on its significance to the truth or falsity of the hypothesis and the importance of the issue. Scraggs would soon have to consider this guideline.

3. *When there is doubt that the consequent would certainly be true if the hypothesis is true, the consequent should be appropriately qualified.* The consequents added to Hypotheses B and D are qualified by the words *may have been* and *might*, respectively. Failure to so qualify a consequent

may lead us to attach too much significance to it.

5. Priorities in Testing Hypotheses

The order in which you test hypotheses is sometimes important. Three principles are useful in deciding which hypothesis to test first.

One of these is the principle of *urgency*. Sometimes you should test first the hypothesis that, if true, would require the most immediate attention. Suppose you smell smoke in your house and these hypotheses occur to you: (1) your house is on fire, and (2) your neighbor is burning trash. A prudent man would test first the hypothesis that his house is on fire.

If no hypothesis in your list would require immediate attention, then the principle of *economy* should prevail, and you should begin with the hypothesis that can be tested with the least expenditure of time or money. If your car stops dead in front of a filling station, you could test the hypothesis that your ignition system has burned out, but it would be both easier and quicker to test first the hypothesis that you have run out of gasoline.

A third principle is *bias*. When you have strong feelings about some of the hypotheses in your list, you would be well advised to check first the ones you like least. If you permit yourself to give priority to the one you like best, you may unconsciously search for evidence to support it, and not test it fairly.

6. Repeating the Cycle

In complex investigations it is sometimes necessary to repeat the five-phase cycle many times before a satisfactory solution can be found. Each repetition of the cycle usually produces new information that suggests new or revised hypotheses and narrows the investigation by eliminating some hypotheses.

At this point Scraggs repeated the cycle. He returned to Phase 1 and redefined his problem: to find the cause of the explosion aboard Flight 629. To guide his search for additional information he skipped to Phase 3 and formed two more specific versions of Hypothesis E.

F. A fuel tank exploded.
G. Gasoline fumes seeped into a compartment of the plane and exploded.

Scraggs added the same consequent to both hypotheses: evidence would be found in the wreckage. He then proceeded with a closer inspection of the wreckage, and added a new and startling proposition to his information.

9. Debris from the plane was scattered over six square miles.

In Scraggs' frame of reference Proposition 9 diverged strongly from Hypothesis F because he did not believe that the explosion of a fuel tank would scatter debris so widely.

To test Hypothesis G he added this consequent: the debris from a particular compartment would be more widely scattered than other debris. Scraggs now had to consider the second guideline for adding and testing consequents. To test this consequent conclusively would require collecting and assembling much of the debris. Would testing this consequent be worth the enormous cost? While he pondered this question, Scraggs continued to examine the wreckage and added a new proposition.

10. Some of the wreckage had an acrid odor like burned-out fireworks.

This proposition suggested a revision of Hypothesis G, as well as a consequent by which to test it.

H. The explosion was $\supset$ residue from the caused by high explosives *might be* explosives in a found in the debris. compartment of the plane

Note that Scraggs has observed the third guideline for adding and testing consequents. At this point he could not be certain that residue from high explosives could be found, because the debris was so widely scattered. He therefore qualified his consequent with *might be*. If he had not done so, and if he also failed to find any residue from high explosives, he might have rejected the hypothesis.

To test this consequent he continued to examine bits of the wreckage and added another proposition.

11. There was a grayish residue on some bits of debris.

Scraggs thought the residue was from high explosives, but to be certain he had it examined by an explosives expert. The expert's report provided Proposition 12.

12. The grayish residue in question was from dynamite.

Proposition 12 both suggested and strongly converged on a new hypothesis concerning the cause of the crash.

I. The crash was caused by an explosion of dynamite aboard the plane.

Although Scraggs has added and tested many consequents, note that he has not yet completed Phase 4 (testing tentative conclusions), for an essential part of this phase is an assessment of the degree of reliability demonstrated for his hypotheses. On the basis of the evidence in Propositions 1–12, Scraggs judged Hypothesis I to be highly probable.

Scraggs now proceeded to Phase 5, the function of which is to decide whether the reliability of any tentative conclusion, as judged in Phase 4, is sufficient in the circumstances. For Scraggs the question was whether he should now make a formal report to his chief. He decided that the degree "highly probable" was sufficient, and made his report. The problem now belonged to officials of the Civil Aeronautics Board, who had to judge for themselves the degree of reliability of Hypothesis I and decide whether it was sufficient to justify calling in the Federal Bureau of Investigation. They too judged Hypothesis I to be highly probable and decided that this degree of reliability was sufficient.

Procedures for judging the reliability of hypotheses are discussed in the next chapter, in which the case of Flight 629 is continued. You should not read it until you have completed the following exercise, in which you can put to work what you have learned about forming hypotheses, and adding and testing consequents.

EXERCISE 5

This exercise continues the case of Flight 629. Complete each item before reading beyond it.

1–2. Write two hypotheses to account for a dynamite explosion aboard Flight 629.

(1) _dynamite had been planted as bomb_

(2) _dynamite was the plane's cargo_

3. Write a third hypothesis, one that would be unpalatable to the president of the airline.

faulty engine caused cargo to explode

4–8. *These items refer to the following hypotheses.*

J. Neither passengers nor crew were aware that dynamite was aboard the plane.
K. The dynamite came aboard the plane in a passenger's baggage.

4. Criticize Hypothesis J in terms of the guidelines for forming hypotheses.

doesn't help to solve problem

5. Criticize Hypothesis K in the same terms. _acceptable_

too limited; threatens self-concept

6. Criticize the following as a consequent of Hypothesis K: The baggage would have been put aboard in Denver. _related to problem_

should use might have been

7. Criticize this consequent in the same terms: Collecting the fragments of the plane and fitting them into a mock-up would show that the explosion occurred in the compartment where baggage from Denver was carried.

should use might show

8. Criticize this consequent in the same terms: The passenger may have intended to blow open a bank vault.

may have would lead to non sequitur

9–11. *These items refer to the following new propositions.*

13. A crew of forty men collected fragments from the plane and took them to Denver, where experts fitted them into a mock-up of the plane.

14. The general manager of engineering of United Air Lines examined the mock-up and said that the center of the explosion was in Pit 4, where baggage was carried.

9. Which of these propositions is itself a hypothesis? _____ *14*

10. What is the effect of Proposition 13 on the reliability of Proposition 14?

converging   proposition

11. On which hypothesis (J or K) does Proposition 14 converge? _____ *K*

12–13. *These items refer to Proposition 15 below.*

15. Two hundred FBI agents searched the area of the crash and found a piece of an Eveready battery and a cog from a clock that might have been used as a timing device.

12. What revision in Hypothesis K does Proposition 15 suggest?

the dynamite came aboard as bomb

13. Write a hypothesis to explain Proposition 15 that would make it irrelevant to Hypothesis K.

a person could be carrying an alarm clock and flashlight

The following propositions were brought to light by FBI agents who investigated the lives of the victims of the crash and their relatives.

16. Mrs. Daisy E. King boarded Flight 629 in Denver.
17. Mrs. King was going to Alaska to visit a married daughter.
18. Mrs. King's baggage weighed eighty-seven pounds, thirty-seven pounds over the limit.
19. Mrs. King was taken to the airport by John Gilbert Graham, her son by a former marriage.
20. At the airport Graham bought six air travel insurance policies on his mother.

14. Add an appropriate consequent to Hypothesis L below.

L. Graham put a bomb in Mrs. King's baggage ⊃ *Graham would collect insurance*

15. Which of the propositions above converge on Hypothesis L? _____ *20*

16. Write a hypothesis that accounts for all the evidence so far presented without involving Mrs. King or John Graham in a crime.

bomb could have come aboard in someone else's luggage

increases the probabi[...]
is true from $\frac{1}{52}$ to [...]
that of Flight 629, h[...]
of converging prop[...]
sessed precisely. Us[...]
do is to make a rea[...]
knowledge in your fr[...]
no two persons hav[...]
reference, some disa[...]
pected.

As we noted in Cha[...]
of a converging prop[...]
into focus by using it [...]
and the minor prem[...]
syllogism, the antece[...]
hypothesis in question[...]
come thoroughly fan[...]
thetical syllogism you[...]
simply by constructing[...]
sition in which the a[...]
verging proposition an[...]
statement that the hy[...]
true. Consider Propos[...]
Hypothesis M.

Converging Proposition
In the opinion of
experts the crash was
caused by an explosion
aboard the plane

The reliability of the [...]
tion thus formed is a n[...]
icance of the converg[...]
tually Proposition 3 con[...]
three rival hypotheses.[...]
bility of all three riva[...]
likely that some other h[...]
explanation, but it doe[...]
the relative reliability o[...]
The number as well [...]
converging propositions[...]
effect of converging pr[...]
tive to the extent that [...]
not overlap. It is ordin[...]
of a single proposition th[...]
high degree of reliabili[...]

6 Testing Hypotheses

Two weeks after the crash of Flight 629 the FBI accused John Gilbert Graham of murder. The FBI's accusation can be expressed as Hypothesis M.

M. The crash of Flight 629 was caused by a bomb placed in the baggage of Mrs. Daisy E. King by John Gilbert Graham.

Was Hypothesis M sufficiently reliable to justify this accusation? Let us examine the evidence and judge for ourselves.

1. Rival Hypotheses

Judging the reliability of a hypothesis involves a problem unlike any we have so far encountered. Since a hypothesis is derived by inductive inference, it necessarily goes beyond the evidence in hand. Consider some of the evidence for Hypothesis M.

1. About eleven minutes after take-off, Flight 629 exploded in mid-air and crashed.
2. All forty-four persons aboard were killed.
3. In the opinion of experts the crash was caused by an explosion aboard the plane.
4. A grayish residue was found on fragments from the inside of the plane.
5. Experts identified the residue as the byproduct of an explosion of dynamite.
6. FBI agents who searched the area of the crash found a part of a battery and a cog from a clock, both of which could have been used in a timing device for a bomb.
7. Mrs. King was taken to the Denver airport by John Gilbert Graham, her son by a former marriage.

Hypothesis M goes beyond the evidence in these propositions, which contain no direct evidence that Graham put a bomb in Mrs. King's baggage. Yet Hypothesis M puts these propositions into a picture that explains them. It explains why the plane crashed, why a grayish residue was found on fragments from the inside of the plane, why part of a battery and a cog from a clock were found in the area of the crash, and how Graham could have put the bomb in his mother's baggage. The question at issue is whether Hypothesis M is the *true* explanation of the evidence now in hand. Perhaps there are other hypotheses that would explain the evidence as well or better.

This question leads us to one of two essential steps in judging the reliability of a hypothesis — forming as many *rival hypotheses* as possible to explain the relevant facts. Hypotheses are rivals when only one can be true. Hypotheses M, and N on the next page

below are riva
only one can b

N. The bomb
put in an
ployee wh(

Hypotheses ar
they differ. H
Hypothesis M
true, for M–1 i:

M-1. The cras
a time
placed ir
King by
Mrs. Kin

Rival hypotl
of testing hyp
main issue. S
FBI at this poi:
of murder, as i
sible should be
of Flight 629
murder. If we
Propositions 1–
rival for M anc

O. The crash
time bomb
senger oth(
other than
airline.

We now have
and O.
The second
relative reliab:
formed. It is n
to perform ea
steps must be
If we could l
and O are the
and if the evid
probability of
point we do r
justify assumin
eses are possib

that the hypothesis in question is false. The reliability of the resulting proposition is the measure of the significance of the diverging proposition.

Diverging Proposition	Null Hypothesis
The explosion occurred in Pit 4 ⊃	it is *not true* that the bomb that destroyed the plane was put in an engine compartment by an employee who was angry with the airline.

The significance of Proposition 11 can now be seen to be high, for it seems highly improbable that the bomb was moved from an engine compartment to Pit 4.

A hazard in interpreting diverging propositions should be carefully avoided. Hypothesis N, like many hypotheses, is composed of several subhypotheses: (1) the plane was destroyed by a bomb, (2) the bomb was placed aboard the plane by an employee who was angry with the airline, and (3) the employee placed the bomb in an engine compartment. Proposition 11 virtually demolishes the third subhypothesis, for it is difficult to think of any way the explosion could have occurred in Pit 4 if the bomb had been placed in an engine compartment. Proposition 11 does not diverge at all from the subhypothesis that an angry employee placed the bomb aboard the plane, for he could have put it in Pit 4. It would therefore be a mistake to abandon this subhypothesis because of Proposition 11. When a proposition diverges mainly from a subhypothesis, the other subhypotheses should be salvaged by excising the questionable element.

N-1. The bomb that destroyed the plane was put aboard by an employee who was angry with the airline.

The number as well as the significance of diverging propositions must be considered, for the effect of diverging propositions, like

that of converging ones, may be cumulative. Consider Propositions 12 and 13, which diverge from Hypothesis O.

12. The FBI investigated the lives of all passengers boarding the plane in Denver and, except for Mrs. King, found nothing to incriminate them or their relatives.
13. Pit 4 contained only mail and baggage put aboard in Denver.

These propositions in combination reduce the reliability of Hypothesis O to a low level. Proposition 12 tends to eliminate all the passengers who boarded the plane in Denver except Mrs. King, and Proposition 13 tends to eliminate all the others. Note that the same proposition may converge on one hypothesis and diverge from another. Proposition 13 diverges from Hypothesis O and converges on Hypothesis M.

4. Criteria

If we could be certain that we had formed all possible rival hypotheses, and if we could be certain that all except one of these is false, then we could be certain that the remaining hypothesis is true. Obviously these conditions can never be completely fulfilled. Our inability to think of another hypothesis which explains the relevant facts does not prove that there is none. In situations like the case of Flight 629 there is no way to know the number of possible hypotheses. Consider Hypothesis O. We could form many specific versions of O for the thirty-nine passengers aboard, for their relatives and acquaintances, and even for people not connected with the passengers. Since we cannot completely fulfill these conditions, the measure of the reliability of a hypothesis must be how close we can come to forming all possible rival hypotheses and eliminating all except one.

It should be noted that in assessing the reliability of a hypothesis creative thinking is as important as critical thinking, for creative thinking is required to form rival hypotheses. A person who lacks skill in creative thinking might accept Hypothesis M with less evidence because he cannot think of rivals.

Assessing the reliability of all conclusions involves human judgment. Assessing the reliability of hypotheses is particularly subject to influence from the personal point of view. For example, a loyal employee of the airline would be likely to rate Hypothesis M higher than would a relative of a passenger: if M is true, the airline is blameless; if N–1 is true, the airline may be liable for heavy damages. Thus individuals can be expected to differ in rating the reliability of hypotheses. Careful attention to the following criteria will increase your objectivity and thereby improve the soundness of your decisions.

1. *The number and significance of converging propositions.* Propositions converging on a hypothesis raise its reliability and lower the reliability of its rivals. Suppose the evidence supporting Hypotheses M, N–1, and O is equal in significance. Assuming that these three are the only possible hypotheses, the probability of each would be ⅓. A converging proposition that raises the reliability of Hypothesis M to ½ would lower the reliability of the others to ¼. Furthermore, the greater the number and significance of converging propositions the more difficult it is to form rival hypotheses. Propositions 11 (The explosion occurred in Pit 4) and 13 (Pit 4 contained only mail and baggage put aboard in Denver) limit the suspects to those who could have put a bomb in baggage or mail put aboard in Denver. Thus the number and significance of converging propositions is an indirect indicator of how close we have come to forming all possible rival hypotheses.

2. *The number and significance of diverging propositions.* Diverging propositions not only lower the reliability of the propositions from which they diverge but also raise the reliability of rival hypotheses in proportion to their total significance.

3. *The reliability of evidence.* Any doubt about the reliability of a converging or diverging proposition reduces its significance. The reliability of propositions must be judged by the appropriate criteria. Most of the propositions listed above are observations and should be judged by the criteria discussed in Chapter 4. Proposition 3 (In the opinion of experts the crash was caused by an explosion aboard the plane) states a hypothesis; its reliability should be judged by the criteria we are now discussing.

Note that doubt about the reliability of a proposition affects the reliability of a hypothesis in proportion to the significance of the proposition. Consider Proposition 14 in relation to Hypothesis M.

14. In the opinion of a chemist the dynamite was manufactured by Du Pont.

If we learned that Proposition 14 is false, the effect on Hypothesis M would be negligible, for the maker of the dynamite is not significant. In contrast, if we learned that Proposition 13 (Pit 4 contained only baggage and mail put aboard in Denver) is false, the effect would be much greater, for this proposition is an important strand in the evidence supporting Hypothesis M.

4. *Completeness of the evidence.* As we have noted, a hypothesis may be composed of subhypotheses. These subhypotheses may be like links in a chain in that the hypothesis as a whole is no stronger than the weakest subhypothesis. Thus the evidence cannot be considered complete unless all subhypotheses are adequately supported. Hypothesis M is a case in point, as it is composed of three subhypotheses: (1) the crash was caused by a bomb, (2) the bomb was in the baggage of Mrs. Daisy E. King, and (3) the bomb was placed in Mrs. King's baggage by John Gilbert Graham. On the basis of the evidence now in hand, the first sub-

hypothesis can be rated true beyond reasonable doubt. It has neither rival hypotheses nor diverging propositions, and the converging propositions are numerous and significant. In contrast, the third element should not be rated higher than probable. It has two rival hypotheses (N–1 and O), and the total significance of its converging propositions is low. Thus at this point Hypothesis M as a whole should not be rated higher than probable.

5. *Unexplained evidence.* Hypotheses should be formed to account for all possibly relevant items of evidence, because a proposition carelessly ignored as irrelevant may be the key to the problem. Once the truth has been established beyond reasonable doubt it is easy enough to determine whether a proposition is relevant. Until then, however, there is no positive test for relevance, for a proposition is relevant or irrelevant only in terms of a hypothesis. Consider Proposition 15.

15. Flight 629 waited twelve minutes in Denver for a late passenger.

The only way to test this proposition for relevance is to form and test a hypothesis to which it is relevant. One such hypothesis is that someone delayed the passenger in order to get an opportunity to put a bomb in his baggage. The FBI investigated the late passenger and added another proposition.

16. No evidence was found to connect the late passenger with the bomb.

6. *Thoroughness of the investigation.* The more thorough the investigation the more likely it is that all relevant evidence has come to light. More than two hundred FBI agents investigated all aspects of the crash of Flight 629. It is unlikely that significant evidence remained undiscovered. The thoroughness of the investigation is the primary criterion in judging the significance of propositions

stating that no evidence of something was found. Proposition 16 is a case in point. If the investigation of the late passenger had been cursory, this proposition would have had little significance. As it happened, however, the investigation of the late passenger was thorough enough to make it unlikely that he was connected with the bomb.

7. *Possibility of unformed rival hypotheses.* Any doubt that all possible rival hypotheses have been formed reduces the reliability of at least one rival. For illustration, assume that we estimate the probabilities that Hypotheses M, N–1, and O are true to be $\frac{3}{4}$, $\frac{3}{16}$, and $\frac{1}{16}$, respectively (note that these fractions total one). If there is reasonable doubt that these three are the only possible rivals, we must reduce the reliability of at least one rival to make room for this doubt, for the total probability of two or more rival hypotheses cannot exceed one. The number and significance of both converging and diverging propositions, the completeness of the evidence, unexplained evidence, and the thoroughness of the investigation are all indicators of whether all possible rival hypotheses have been formed. In the case of Flight 629, all these indicators are positive. The probability is very high that one of the three rival hypotheses, M, N–1, and O, is true.

8. *Reliability of rival hypotheses.* The reliability of any hypothesis should be judged in terms of its rivals. It would be theoretically possible to prove a hypothesis to be true beyond reasonable doubt without a single converging proposition, if we could prove beyond reasonable doubt that we had formed and eliminated all possible rivals. By the same token, no rival hypothesis should be rated true beyond reasonable doubt as long as a single rival remains with a rating higher than false beyond reasonable doubt. On the basis of the evidence presented so far, including that in the previous chapter,

Hypothesis M is weak only with respect to the completeness of the evidence implicating Graham. Unfortunately for Graham's longevity, there was more evidence.

17. Mrs. King was the only Denver resident who boarded Flight 629 in Denver.
18. According to his wife, Graham said that he had surreptitiously placed a "Christmas present" in Mrs. King's baggage.
19. According to an employee of an electrical supply company in Denver, Graham bought a timing device a few days before the crash.
20. According to a merchant who knew Graham when he was a boy, Graham bought twenty sticks of dynamite three days before the crash.
21. Graham had no legitimate reason for having dynamite.
22. Graham had an impressive criminal record.
23. Graham lied about a number of details when he was being questioned by the FBI.

All these propositions converge on Hypothesis M and only on M. Even though the investigation was thorough, no propositions that diverged from M came to light. No unexplained items of information remained. There was no reason to question the reliability of the propositions converging on M. There are no propositions that converge on rivals N–1 and O that do not also converge on M. We are now justified in rating Hypotheses N–1 and O false beyond reasonable doubt and Hypothesis M true beyond reasonable doubt.

Some people object to rating any hypothesis true beyond reasonable doubt when the evidence is circumstantial rather than direct. Many experienced lawyers, however, believe that circumstantial evidence is often more reliable than direct evidence. As one veteran lawyer explains it, witnesses can err in identifying the criminal, or they may lie about an identification because they have strong motives for seeing the defendant convicted

or acquitted. When witnesses do decide to lie, they seem to prefer a big lie to a little one. An intelligent witness may be afraid to lie about details, lest he be charged with perjury, for he may not know how much is known about the details. An unintelligent witness may tell a big lie and still tell the truth about details because he does not realize their significance. Thus, this lawyer feels, testimony about circumstances is generally more reliable than testimony about the crime itself.

5. Evaluation and Decision

A few months later Graham was tried for murder in the first degree. The primary problem facing the jury was to decide for itself the degree of reliability of the State's hypothesis by completing Phase 4. Presumably the jury completed Phase 5 (evaluation and decision) deductively. The law in effect provides two major premises: (1) If the evidence is judged sufficient to remove any reasonable doubt that the State's hypothesis is true, then the defendant must be found guilty; (2) if there is a reasonable doubt, the defendant must be acquitted. The jury judged the State's hypothesis to be true beyond reasonable doubt and found Graham guilty. The sentence was death. Graham's attorney appealed the verdict to the Supreme Court of Colorado, which upheld the verdict and ordered the execution of the sentence. The Court's opinion contained the following paragraphs.

We have painstakingly examined and studied the entire record in this case, and from it we are impelled to the conclusion that the verdict of the jury was based not upon conflicting evidence, but upon uncontradicted, competent testimony; properly admitted exhibits, and the confessions, oral and written, of the defendant. No other verdict than guilty of murder in the first degree could have been returned with due regard to the evidence before the jury, and defendant must suffer the penalty provided by law, he having been accorded every constitutional guaranty. Nowhere in the reports of criminal cases have we found a counterpart to this case, and we doubt if anything approaching it can be found in fiction.

Finding no error in the record, the judgment is affirmed and it is ordered that the sentence be executed during the week ending January 12, 1957.[1]

Phase 5 is often more complex than in the Graham case. We must often act in situations in which our hypotheses have only a low degree of reliability and in which there are many actions we can take. We shall discuss procedures for dealing with such situations in Chapters 13 and 14.

[1] *Pacific Reporter,* 2nd series (St. Paul: West, 1957), Vol. 302, p. 748.

EXERCISE 6

This exercise is based on the trial of Bruno Richard Hauptmann for the kidnapping and murder of the Lindbergh baby, whose body was found in the woods behind the Lindbergh home after a ransom of $50,000 had been paid. Suppose you are foreman of the jury. According to the instructions of the judge, Hauptmann is guilty of murder in the first degree if he participated in the crime, even though he may not have killed the child himself. The State's hypothesis is that Hauptmann did participate in the crime. The jury's problem is deciding whether the evidence presented in the trial is sufficient to justify rating the State's hypothesis true beyond reasonable doubt. The following evidence has been introduced by the prosecution.

1. A wood technologist testified that a ladder found under the nursery window was made by a skilled carpenter (which Hauptmann was).
2. The technologist testified further that wood in the ladder was dressed by a plane found in Hauptmann's garage.
3. He testified further that a piece of wood in the ladder was cut from a board in the floor of Hauptmann's attic.
4. Another expert testified that nails in the ladder were made by the same machine as nails in a box in Hauptmann's garage.

1. Which of the above propositions converges most significantly on the hypothesis that Hauptmann made the ladder?

_____ 3

2. Write a rival for the above hypothesis that also explains Propositions 1–4.

Hauptmann might have had an apprentice with access to his tools

3. Rate the reliability of your rival hypothesis, using the terminology defined at the end of Chapter 3.

_____ indifferent

4. Write a rival hypothesis that explains Propositions 1–4 without involving Hauptmann in the crime.

His ladder may have been stolen

5. According to which criteria is the evidence (Propositions 1–4 only) weak with respect to the State's hypothesis?

evidence isn't complete

EXERCISE 6

Additional evidence introduced by the prosecution included the following:

5. Prints of feet wrapped in some kind of cloth were found on the ground near the foot of the ladder. Hauptmann's feet were small enough to have made these prints.
6. A rung on the ladder was broken.
7. Marks on the ground indicated that the kidnapper might have injured his leg.
8. Hauptmann was walking with a cane some weeks after the crime.

6. How significant is the combination of Propositions 5–8 for the subhypothesis that Hauptmann used the ladder in the crime?

taken together the significance is high

7. Write a rival for the State's hypothesis that explains Propositions 1–8 without involving Hauptmann in the crime.

Hauptmann's ladder was stolen after he was injured by a man of the same foot size

As the trial progressed, additional evidence was introduced.

9. The ransom notes were apparently written by a German.
10. Hauptmann was born and reared in Germany.
11. Paper found in Hauptmann's home was identical to paper used in the ransom notes.
12. Handwriting in the ransom notes appeared to be disguised. A sample of Hauptmann's handwriting appeared to be disguised in the same way.
13. The following words misspelled in the ransom notes were similarly misspelled in Hauptmann's diary: "tit" for "did," "ouer" for "our," "note" for "not," and "boad" for "boat."
14. Two handwriting experts testified that Hauptmann wrote the ransom notes.
15. A handwriting expert introduced by the defense testified that Hauptmann did not write the ransom notes.

8. Which propositions in this group diverge from the subhypothesis that Hauptmann wrote the ransom notes?

15

9. Is the testimony in Proposition 15 more reliable than in 14?   *no*

10. Rate the reliability of the subhypothesis that Hauptmann wrote the ransom notes.

probable

11. What effect would rating this subhypothesis false beyond reasonable doubt have on the State's hypothesis?

the State's hypothesis would be less reliable; but doesn't destroy it.

12. What effect would rating this subhypothesis true beyond reasonable doubt have on the State's hypothesis?

the State's hypothesis would be true

Evidence presented by the defense included the following proposition.

16. The baby's nurse committed suicide a few weeks after the kidnapping.

13. Write a hypothesis to which Proposition 16 is relevant that is a rival for the State's hypothesis.

The nurse killed the baby

14. Write a subhypothesis to which this proposition is relevant that would converge on the State's hypothesis.

the nurse was Hauptmann's girlfriend and accomplice

15. Write a hypothesis explaining this proposition that makes it irrelevant to the case.

She was depressed over the baby's death

Still further evidence presented included the following.

17. Dr. J. F. Condon, who acted as intermediary, testified that he sat on a bench in a cemetery and talked with a man who presented the baby's nightgown as evidence that he was the kidnapper.
18. Dr. Condon testified that at a later meeting in the cemetery he gave this man $50,000 in bills, the serial numbers of which had been recorded.
19. Dr. Condon identified Hauptmann as the man he met in the cemetery.
20. A taxi driver testified that Hauptmann was the man who gave him a dollar to deliver a note to Dr. Condon.
21. Lindbergh testified that Hauptmann's voice was that of the man in the cemetery.

22. Dr. Condon testified that he gave his address and a privately listed telephone number to the man in the cemetery.
23. This address and telephone number were found scribbled on the back of a closet in Hauptmann's house.
24. Hauptmann said he found the address and number in a newspaper ad.
25. The address and number had not been published either in a newspaper or in the telephone directory.
26. Nearly $15,000 of the ransom money was found under a board in Hauptmann's garage.
27. After the ransom money was delivered, Hauptmann lost about $9,000 in the stock market, bought a new car, went on expensive trips, and quit his job (Federal agents estimated that about $35,000 was spent in these and other ways).
28. Hauptmann testified that a man named Fisch gave him the money.
29. Hauptmann testified that he loaned Fisch $2,000.

16. Which of the propositions in this group (17–29) converge on a subhypothesis that Hauptmann was the man in the cemetery?

all except 21

17. Which of the propositions in this group diverge from this subhypothesis?

21

18. Which of the propositions in this group are least reliable in terms of the criteria for observations?

21, 28, 20, 19

Other evidence included the following.

30. Hauptmann worked near the Lindbergh home shortly before the kidnapping.
31. While on the witness stand Hauptmann seemed reluctant to answer questions.
32. Hauptmann denied his guilt.
33. Hauptmann had a criminal record in Germany.

19. Write a rival for the State's hypothesis that explains all evidence presented without involving Hauptmann in the crime.

Hauptmann has an identical twin

20. With respect to which criteria is the State's hypothesis now weak?

still circumstantial evidence

21. Rate the reliability of the State's hypothesis. *highly probable*

22. Rate the reliability of this hypothesis: No one but Hauptmann was involved in the crime.

highly probable

7 Generalizations

In Chapters 5 and 6 we discussed the use of one type of inductive inference, the hypothesis, in the decision-making cycle. Now let us turn to a second type, the generalization. The term *generalization* is commonly used in a number of senses. In this book, however, we use it in a limited sense to refer only to *an inference made about a group of instances without observing all instances in the group.* The term *instances* is used here to refer to things of a kind. Instances may be objects, people, ideas, or actions that have some factor in common. For example, automobiles, freshmen at Wysacki University, political philosophies, and felonies are groups of instances.

Generalizations should not be confused with *enumerations.* If you taste every apple in a crate and then conclude that all these apples are sour, you have made an enumeration, *i.e.,* a conclusion based on *all* instances in the group. But if you taste only a few apples and then conclude that all or most apples in the crate are sour, you have made a generalization, for you have made an inductive leap from the apples tasted to those not tasted.

1. The Function of Generalizations

Generalizations are indispensable in thinking. Without them our personal points of view would be extremely meager. Generalizations enable us, in effect, to multiply our knowledge. Figuratively speaking, they enable us to extend our knowledge from the red hot stoves that have burned us to all hot objects there are and will be. Without generalizations innumerable decisions we make by deductive inference would have to be made some other way, for most of the premises we use about people, places, actions, things, ideas, and values are generalizations. Without generalizations modern science would be impossible.

Generalizations make it much easier to gather the information necessary for making some kinds of decisions. Consider the television producer who must decide whether to continue a certain show. To make the right decision he should find out approximately how many people watch the show. The cost of an enumeration would be prohibitive; he is therefore likely to use a generalization based on data provided by a rating service.

Generalizations have yet another indispensable function in thinking, for they enable us to predict the future from the past. When an insurance company sets its rates for automobile accident policies it is making a prediction about the cost of accidents in the year to come. Even if the company makes an enumeration of the cost of past accidents involving its own policy holders, any prediction about future costs is a generalization, for it involves an inductive leap from past conditions and policy holders to future conditions and policy holders.

2. Hasty Generalizations

The same inductive leap that enables us to make generalizations can easily lead us into the fallacy of *hasty generalization,* i.e., *making a generalization and accepting it as truth without testing it for reliability.* Suppose an instructor finds that the first student he questions in class is unprepared and concludes without further thought that the class as a whole is unprepared. His conclusion is a generalization, for it is derived by an inductive leap from the one student observed to the class as a whole. It is a *hasty* generalization because he has made no effort to determine whether the one student observed is typical of the whole class.

Hasty generalization is a tempting fallacy because of our human tendency to do things the easy way. It is usually much easier to make a generalization than to test it: it is easier to make a generalization based on one student than to question a number of students and judge how typical they are. Our love of the dramatic adds to the temptation: it is much more dramatic to condemn a whole class than to generalize that half the class is unprepared. Our tendency to protect our personal points of view can make hasty generalizations irresistible. When we want to believe a generalization, we embrace it like a long lost brother and forget about testing it.

The hazards should not make us hesitate to form generalizations. Failure to form generalizations can be as bad as making hasty generalizations. If you get food poisoning twice after eating in a certain restaurant, you would be foolish to eat there again before forming and testing the generalization that the food served in this restaurant is unsafe. The point is that we should never accept a generalization as truth until we have tested it for reliability.

The five-phase cycle of decision making applies to making and testing generalizations as well as to other forms of inference. The five phases should not be followed in rigid sequence, but each phase should be completed.

3. Defining the Problem

In Phase 1 the purpose of the generalization should be clearly defined, because the purpose affects the procedures in the other four phases. Two guidelines should be followed.

1. *The definition should indicate whether the generalization is to be descriptive or predictive.* In a *descriptive* generalization the inductive leap is restricted to the time span of the sample; in a *predictive* generalization the leap extends to the future. A generalization about current Wysacki freshmen is descriptive; one about future Wysacki freshmen is predictive.

2. *The definition should accurately limit the group about which the generalization is to be made.* When the generalization is to be descriptive, the definition should describe precisely the group to be included. A generalization about the opinions of Wysacki freshmen and a generalization about all Wysacki students would require significantly different procedures. When the generalization is to be predictive, the definition should describe the time span as well as the group to be covered.

4. Selecting the Sample

The objective of Phase 2 (gathering information) is to select and observe a sample of the instances that will be representative of the entire group. Because of the expense of observing instances, it is often desirable to observe the smallest sample that will yield the necessary level of reliability. For example, sampling voter opinion is an expensive process, and the political pollster could easily spend more money on a sample than his generalization will earn. So he naturally wishes to use a small sample. But if he is prudent he will take pains to make his sample representative of the total group of voters.

The great danger in taking a sample is that it may be *loaded, i.e.,* that the manner of selection will include a disproportionate number of instances of one kind. A spectacular illustration of the danger in loaded samples can be seen in the *Literary Digest's* prediction of the presidential election of 1936. Until then the *Digest* had an enviable record for accuracy. Its method of polling was to send sample ballots to persons listed in telephone books and city directories all over the country. The last issue of the *Digest* before the election listed a total of 2,266,566 ballots, approximately 4.6 per cent of the number of votes actually cast — a very large sample for political polls. Tabulations indicated a total of 370 electoral votes for Alfred M. Landon and only 161 for Franklin D. Roosevelt. The actual results, however, gave Roosevelt 523 electoral votes and Landon only 8. The *Digest* never recovered from the blow to its prestige, and within a few months it ceased publication.

Apparently the *Digest* sample was loaded in two ways. By sending ballots mainly to people listed in telephone books and city directories, the *Digest* unwittingly introduced a strong socio-economic bias into its sample. Furthermore, the *Digest* counted only the ballots that were returned. Experience indicates that ballots or questionnaires that are returned voluntarily very likely constitute a loaded sample. Returning a questionnaire requires effort; therefore, those with an interest in the outcome are more likely to return the questionnaire.

Whether a sample is loaded or not depends in part on the purpose of the generalization. A sample may be loaded because instances irrelevant to the purpose are included in the sample. Suppose a television producer's problem is to estimate the number of housewives who view a certain soap opera at 10:00 A.M., Monday through Friday. A sample that includes business men and children is loaded by irrelevant instances. Since the purpose of the *Digest* sample was to predict an election, all classes of voters were relevant. The sample was loaded because the lower socio-economic classes were not adequately represented in the sample.

Three types of samples are commonly used to reduce the likelihood of loading and other errors.

1. *Random sample.* One method of reducing the probability of loading is to select the sample at *random, i.e.,* in such a way that *nothing but chance determines the instances selected.* Selecting a purely random sample is not as easy as one might suppose. If a television rating service selected every tenth person passing the corner of Main and First Streets during school hours, the sample would obviously be loaded: the number of children would be disproportionately small. How close a sample comes to being random depends in part on the purpose of the sample. A sample composed of every tenth name on an alphabetic roster of registered voters would presumably be close to random for predicting an election; but it would be heavily loaded for the purpose of rating the popularity of television programs, since it would exclude all people below voting age.

A sample chosen haphazardly is not necessarily random. Suppose an instructor wishes to examine a sample of ten students in his class to determine how well the class as a whole has prepared an assignment. If he selects his sample by letting his eyes roam the class, his sample is haphazard, but it is not necessarily random. Elements in his personal point of view could easily influence the selection. If he is annoyed with the class, he could select the students least likely to be prepared without realizing his bias. One method of selecting a random sample would be to assign each student a number and then select the sample by numbers. Statisticians have found, however, that even the selection of numbers can be influenced by the personal point of view. One method of avoiding this kind of bias is to use a book of random numbers selected by chance by a computer.

2. *Stratified sample.* Another method of reducing the probability of loading is to *identify the relevant strata in the group and select a random sample from each stratum in proportion to the number of instances in each stratum.* To the television rating services the relevant strata are determined by the characteristics of people that could influence their preferences in programs, such as age, sex, region, and educational level. To take a stratified sample, three steps are necessary: (1) identify the strata that could load the sample, (2) ascertain the number of instances in each stratum, and (3) select at random the same proportion from each stratum.

3. *Time-lapse sample.* In many situations samples become unreliable because of changes in the relevant characteristics of the group. Political polls are a case in point. A reliable sample of voter opinion taken in June may not be reliable in July because many voters may have changed their minds. Several respected political polls went wrong in the 1948 national election because the pollsters stopped taking samples in midsummer and failed to detect the shift in sentiment late in the campaign that resulted in the election of Harry S. Truman.

A *time-lapse sample* consists of two or more samples taken with a significant lapse of time between them and compared for consistency. The time between samples and the number of samples needed vary with the situation. The time lapses need not be identical. In a national election, samples taken every two months could be sufficient before the national conventions; between the conventions and the elections, however, the samples should be taken more frequently to detect the effects of the campaign.

The individual samples within a time-lapse sample may be random or stratified. But since the object is to determine changing trends, each sample in the series should be taken in the same way in order to minimize other variables. If in sampling voter opinion you take one sample on Main Street at noon and another in front of a theater in the evening a month later, any difference in the samples may be due to a difference in loading factors rather than to changing opinions.

Time-lapse samples are essential to predictive generalizations. If you know the college board scores of 99 per cent of current Wysacki freshmen you can make a highly reliable descriptive generalization, but unless you also have a sample of the scores of at least one freshman class from the past you have no basis whatever for a predictive generalization that the scores of future freshman classes will either rise or fall.

5. Forming Generalizations

In the early stages of an investigation it is usually desirable to begin with a small preliminary sample in order to learn more about the characteristics of the group. Otherwise you may waste time and money observing a large number of instances only to find that your method of sampling was unsatisfactory. Suppose you have been commissioned by the *Wysacki Reporter* to survey the opinions of the ten thousand Wysacki students about a new rule, to go into effect next year, requiring seniors to pass a comprehensive examination on all subjects studied in order to graduate. It is now Sunday, and your deadline for completing the survey and writing your story is 1:00 P.M. on Friday.

You could begin by asking twenty students whether they favor the examinations. But if you recorded only the answers to this one question your sample would give you relatively little information to guide you in selecting your next sample. A better method would be to form tentative conclusions about the relevant strata in the group before you take your preliminary sample. It seems reasonable to suppose that class (freshman, sophomore, etc.), sex, major field, and grade averages might affect opinions on the issue under investigation. In interviewing students in your preliminary sample you should, therefore, ascertain and record the data relevant to these strata.

Suppose you obtain the following data by interviewing ten students entering the library Sunday night.[1]

Class	Sex	Grade Average	Major	Favor	Oppose	Undecided
Sr.	F	3.1	liberal arts	x		
Sr.	M	3.3	engineering	x		
Jr.	F	2.5	education		x	
Jr.	M	2.1	business		x	
Soph.	F	3.8	liberal arts	x		
Soph.	M	2.5	engineering		x	
Soph.	M	2.1	business		x	
Fresh.	F	3.4	liberal arts	x		
Fresh.	F	2.3	business		x	
Fresh.	M	3.5	architecture			x

Your next step is to form preliminary generalizations from the data in your sample. Some of the many generalizations you might form are stated below.

A. The majority of Wysacki students oppose the examinations.
B. More underclassmen than seniors oppose the examinations.
C. More men than women oppose the examinations.
D. Students in business and education are more likely to oppose the examinations than those in liberal arts and engineering.
E. Students with low averages are more likely to oppose the examinations.

Your preliminary sample is so small that none of the above generalizations have any significant degree of reliability. Even so, they are useful in guiding your next step.

6. Testing Generalizations

Generalizations based on small, preliminary samples should be tested (Phase 4) by taking a larger sample designed to correct any faults observed in the original sample. Your preliminary sample suggests that Wysacki students are heterogeneous with respect to their opinions of comprehensive examinations. Your sample also suggests that class, sex, major, and grade averages are possible loading factors. Ideally you should now take a stratified sample designed to control these factors. You would need to know the total number of Wysacki students, as well as the number in such strata as men, women, freshmen, engineering students, and

[1] A preliminary sample of only ten would be too small for most purposes. This sample is limited to ten for convenience of illustration.

so forth. Since grade averages range on a continuum, you should divide students into categories such as 3.0 and above, and below 3.0. Additional data needed would include the number of students in such substrata as sophomore female liberal arts students with grade averages above 3.0.

It often happens that generalizations involve a conflict in values between reliability and economy. Your problem is a case in point, for with only five days left to finish your survey and write your story, you would probably not have time to take a stratified sample. Consequently you might have to settle for a relatively small random type sample.

A useful procedure would be to take another sample by interviewing ten students entering the gymnasium on Monday night for a basketball game. If the number of students who oppose the examinations is significantly higher in this sample than in your original one, it is probable that the place you take your sample is a loading factor.

You now have a total sample of twenty. You could test this sample by taking another sample of twenty at a different place and time, such as the cafeteria at noon. The more closely this sample matches your first two samples, the higher the reliability of your total sample of forty. Suppose your total sample of forty shows the following.

Category	Favor	Oppose	Undecided
Seniors	5	0	0
Underclassmen	5	25	5
Men	4	14	2
Women	6	11	3
Grade Averages above 3.0	9	0	1
Grade Averages 3.0 and below	1	25	4

To complete Phase 4 you must assess the reliability of your generalizations. Because generalizations are based on samples, we can never be sure they accurately represent the total group. When absolute accuracy is required, enumerations must be made. The practical problem in testing generalizations, therefore, is to judge how close the sample comes to demonstrating the truth of the generalization. In making this judgment we must consider the length of the inductive leap. If you taste twenty-four of the fifty Winesap apples in a crate and find them sour, and generalize that most of the apples in the crate are sour, your inductive leap is very short. If from this sample you generalize that most Winesap apples from a particular orchard are sour, you have made a longer leap. If you generalize that most apples are sour you have made a tremendous leap. There is no foolproof method for judging the degree to which the sample justifies the leap, but there are a number of helpful criteria.

1. *A generalization is no more reliable than the observations on which it is based.* The observations of instances in the sample should be judged for reliability according to the criteria described in Chapter 4. When the instances are responses to questions, as in your survey of student opinion on comprehensive examinations, the resulting generalizations will not be reliable unless the questions asked are phrased in neutral language. Obviously your question should not be: "You don't want to take comprehensive examinations, do you?" A more neutral question would be: "Do you favor or oppose final comprehensive examinations?"

2. *In general, the more heterogeneous the group, the less reliable is the sample.* You know from experience that a very small sample from a well-shaken bottle of milk will show whether the whole bottle is sour. But an accurate estimate of the size of the stones in a carload of gravel will require samples from several parts of the car, including at least one from the bottom. For when gravel is shaken, as it is in transportation, the smaller stones tend to settle to the bottom. A well-shaken bottle of milk is homogeneous

in sourness but a well-shaken carload of gravel is heterogeneous in size of stones.

People are heterogeneous in many respects. A drug that is beneficial to many people may be poisonous to others. Opinions on such matters as television programs, politics, examinations, and professors often range on a continuum from one extreme to the other.

3. *In general, the larger the number of instances observed, the more reliable is the generalization, because of the tendency of large numbers to follow fixed laws.* You can demonstrate this tendency by tossing pennies. In one experiment, ten tosses produced only three heads, or 40 per cent below expectations. But a hundred tosses yielded fifty-one heads, or 2 per cent above expectations, while a thousand tosses yielded 501 heads, almost exactly the expected result.

4. *In general, the more nearly the number of instances in the sample approaches enumeration, the more reliable is the generalization.* You can demonstrate this criterion for yourself by the principle of dependency in probability. Suppose you wish to generalize about the proportion of freshmen who pass Zymology 101. To keep the arithmetic simple, suppose there are only ten freshmen in the course, of whom half will pass and half fail. The smallest possible sample that would include both a passing and a failing freshman would be two, or 20 per cent of the total. The probability that a random sample of two (20 per cent of the group) would mislead you completely by including no failing freshman is $\frac{5}{10} \times \frac{4}{9}$, or $\frac{2}{9}$. But the probability that a sample of five (50 per cent) would mislead you completely by including no failing freshmen is $\frac{5}{10} \times \frac{4}{9} \times \frac{3}{8} \times \frac{2}{7} \times \frac{1}{6}$, or only $\frac{1}{252}$. A sample of six (60 per cent) would have to include at least one failing freshman. In effect, then, the principle of dependency is an automatic corrective factor, for the less representative a sample is the greater the probability that

increasing it will make it more representative.

5. *In general, a stratified sample of a heterogeneous group is more reliable than a random sample of the same size.* Suppose the five freshmen who pass zymology plan to major in the subject, and that the five who fail do not. If you took a stratified sample of two by selecting at random one major (20 per cent of this stratum) and one non-major (20 per cent of this stratum), the probability that your sample would be perfectly representative is 1. The probability that a random sample would be perfectly representative is only $\frac{5}{9}$. The difference in reliability between random and stratified samples decreases as the difference between strata decreases. Now suppose that four of the passing freshmen are majors and one is a non-major. The probability that a random sample of two would be exactly representative is $\frac{5}{9}$. The probability that a stratified sample would be exactly representative is $\frac{17}{25}$.

6. *In general, the greater the margin for error, the more reliable is the generalization.* Consider Generalization A (The majority of Wysacki students oppose comprehensive examinations) in the light of the evidence in your sample of forty. If we ignore the undecided, those who oppose outnumber those who favor by a ratio of five to two. Since only a majority is required, the sample has a substantial margin for error. In contrast, the margin for error in Generalization C (More men than women oppose the examinations) is small, for the ratio of men to women is only fourteen to eleven.

All criteria considered, none of your preliminary generalizations should be rated higher than probable. Since the Wysacki student body is apparently a heterogeneous group, a stratified sample would have been more reliable. You cannot even be certain that your sample is random, since the places and times you took your partial samples could be loading factors. The number of instances in your total sample is very small both in raw size and in proportion to the total group of ten thousand.

7. Evaluation and Decision

When you have tested and assessed your generalizations for reliability, the decision-making process should shift to Phase 5 (evaluation and decision), in which you decide whether your generalizations are sufficiently reliable for your purpose. If you had time, you should increase your sample, since none of your generalizations deserve a rating higher than probable. But suppose you do not have time. You could write a story presenting your generalizations as truth, or you could abandon the project altogether.

A better decision would be to write your story but make it clear that your generalizations have a low degree of reliability. Procedures for deciding what to do about generalizations rated lower in reliability than true beyond reasonable doubt are discussed in Chapters 13 and 14.

EXERCISE 7

1–11. *You are a counselor at Wysacki University, where 3,000 freshmen enroll each year. A number of entering freshmen have expressed anxiety because they have not made a definite choice of vocation. You define your problem to be to determine whether students who have made a definite choice of vocation when they enter Wysacki are more likely to graduate. You decide to study a sample of the freshman class of six years ago.*

1. How should you select a random sample?

take every 10TH name on a list

2. How should you select a stratified sample?

those whose choice was definite and those whose choice was not definite

3. Would a sample composed of one hundred graduates who entered Wysacki six years ago be satisfactory for your purpose?

no

4. Why or why not?

too small a percentage; does not deal with those entered but did not graduate

5. You begin your investigation by selecting a random sample of 100 from the freshman class of six years ago. Official records reveal the following data.

	Number in Group	Number Graduated
Choice definite	35	15
Choice not definite	65	45

On the basis of this evidence alone, rate the reliability of this generalization: Students who have not made a definite vocational choice when they enter college have a better chance of graduating.

probable

6. You now take a stratified sample of 100 and obtain the following data.

Vocational Choices	Number in Group	Number Graduated
Definite	33	16
Not definite	67	50

Does this sample indicate that your sample was significantly loaded?

no

7. Both samples considered, rate the reliability of this generalization: Freshmen entering Wysacki six years ago were more likely to graduate if they had not made definite vocational choices.

probable

8. On the basis of both samples, rate the reliability of this generalization: Wysacki freshmen have a better chance of graduation if they have not made a definite vocational choice.

improbable

9. Rate the reliability of this generalization: College freshmen have a better chance of graduating if they have not made a definite choice of vocation.

too broad a generalization   *improbable*

10. Would you be justified in reassuring freshmen that not having made a definite choice of vocation will not necessarily reduce their chances of graduation?

no

11. Would you be justified in urging high school students not to make a definite choice of vocation before entering college?

no

12–13. *Write in the blanks the numbers of all statements in the key list below that apply to the samples described in these items. Assume that all observations involved are accurate.*

KEY LIST

1. *The population from which the sample is drawn is relatively heterogeneous.*
2. *There is good reason for believing that the sample is loaded.*
3. *The number of instances in the sample is too small for the degree of accuracy required.* *NATURE of testing*
4. *The instances sampled are too small a percentage of the total group for the degree of accuracy required.* *size of sample*
5. *A time-lapse sample should have been taken.*
6. *The sample is not reliable enough for the decision based on it.*
7. *The sample is larger than necessary.*

12. You manufacture electrical components for rockets. Your contract specifies that you receive $10 for each component and pay a penalty of $1,000 for each one that proves defective. Each component costs you $8 to manufacture. Rigorous testing of a component costs $5 and makes the component unsalable. You subject to rigorous testing a random sample of five components, none of which prove defective. You decide that the quality is satisfactory.

4, 5, 6

13. You subject to rigorous testing every fifth component coming off the assembly line. Only one component per thousand proves defective. You decide that the quality is satisfactory.

7?

8 Statistical Concepts

Many problems of modern life require the analysis of vast amounts of quantitative data. In medicine, testing a new vaccine requires that it be tried on a large number of people and that the results be carefully analyzed. Businessmen have learned that they can increase the reliability of their decisions in such matters as the location of new branches by collecting and analyzing data about population, economic trends, and the like. Educators rely on quantitative data in making all sorts of decisions, from determining the passing mark on a certain test to locating a new school or making changes in curricula. Something of the importance, as well as the amount and variety, of the quantitative data available to us can be seen from thumbing through the *World Almanac*, which contains tables of information on such varied matters as batting averages, raw sugar production, and the earnings of corporations. In short, the solution of many problems, whether personal, educational, economic, medical, or otherwise, is facilitated by making generalizations based on quantitative data.

The primary tool used in making such generalizations is statistics. The importance of statistics in modern life has been greatly increased by computers, which enable statisticians to analyze data with incredible speed. Before the age of computers executives had to make many vital decisions with little evidence because the relevant data could not be collected and analyzed soon enough. With the aid of computers executives can base decisions on the analyses of vast amounts of data.

It is not our purpose to make an extended study of statistical procedures. So important have they become, however, that the educated layman needs to understand at least the basic concepts. Perhaps the most effective means of acquiring an understanding of these concepts is to make a few elementary statistical analyses. In doing so, we shall emphasize only the most important concepts and keep the mathematics as simple as possible.

1. Selecting the Sample

When extreme accuracy is required and when the amount of data involved is relatively small, statisticians work from enumerations rather than samples. But often enumerations are impractical, even with computers, and a carefully selected sample will yield information accurate enough for many purposes. Thus when we studied sampling in

Chapter 7 we were dealing with one of the fundamental problems of statistics. Suppose we wish to analyze the performance of 1,100 students on a logic test in order to judge such matters as the difficulty of the test and the effectiveness of the course. If the test scores were already recorded in the memory circuits of a computer, there would be little advantage in working with only a sample, for a computer could perform the necessary computations on all 1,100 scores in seconds. But since most of us have not yet bought computers, and since absolute accuracy is unnecessary in this situation, let us see how we can reduce the computation at little sacrifice of accuracy by working from a sample. A relatively small but representative sample can be obtained simply by arranging the scores in order, from high to low or vice versa, and then selecting every eleventh score.

2. Frequency Tables

Listed below is a sample of 100 scores from a logic test taken by 1,100 students. The sample was selected from scores arranged in order, but they are listed in Table 1 as they might have looked had they been selected at random from the alphabetical roll.

Table 1

Haphazard Array of a Sample of 100 Scores
on a Logic Test

30	53	13	32	30	43	24	28	23	42
10	48	49	35	32	37	29	38	26	34
14	32	19	24	39	20	40	22	37	33
19	36	19	15	20	28	21	34	33	40
61	6	28	49	37	24	41	38	27	42
54	27	34	31	28	45	30	33	36	25
0	43	21	27	38	34	30	30	43	25
58	23	38	36	17	26	29	29	23	24
20	11	29	17	46	19	33	26	31	18
22	51	25	47	39	23	21	44	35	44

It is easy enough to see from these scores that the lowest is 0 and the highest 61. Be-

yond this, the array looks meaningless, even though only 100 scores are listed. The difficulty of interpreting an array of 10,000 scores in haphazard order can easily be imagined.

After the sample is selected, the next step is to arrange the scores in some kind of systematic order. If we simply arranged them from low to high they would make considerably more sense. But we would still have to count to find the number of scores that are alike. For statistical purposes it would be much better to arrange the scores in a *frequency table* by dividing them into *intervals*[1] and counting the number of scores in each interval. Table 2 below shows the logic scores divided into intervals of twenty.

Table 2

Frequency Table of Logic Scores
with Interval of 20

Scores	Frequency
0–19	14
20–39	65
40–59	20
60–79	1

It can be seen at a glance, however, that this arrangement is too crude, because important details are obscured. We cannot tell with any precision what the average is, and well over half the scores are clustered in one interval. On the other hand, if we arranged the scores in intervals of two, we would have thirty-one intervals, and although such a table would yield more exact analyses, the details would tend to hide significant features. As we shall see, increasing the number of intervals also increases the necessary computation. Statisticians, therefore, usually prefer to use intervals of a size that avoids both extremes. Table 3 on page 79 shows the logic scores in intervals of five, an appropriate arrangement that reveals important details without excessive computation.

[1] Often called *classes*.

Table 3

Frequency Table of Logic Scores
with Interval of 5

Interval	Frequency	Cumulative Frequency
0–4	1	1
5–9	1	2
10–14	4	6
15–19	8	14
20–24	16	30
25–29	17	47
30–34	18	65
35–39	14	79
40–44	10	89
45–49	6	95
50–54	3	98
55–59	1	99
60–64	1	100

In this frequency table the column headed *Interval* is the list of the classes in which we have grouped our scores. In the column headed *Frequency* is listed the number of students making scores in each class or interval. In the column headed *Cumulative Frequency* is a running total of the number of students making scores *within or below* each interval. For example, the sixth line in the table shows that seventeen students made scores between 25 and 29, inclusive, and forty-seven students made scores *in this interval or lower*, that is, between 0 and 29, inclusive.

Once our data have been arranged in a suitable frequency table, we can at a glance make a number of generalizations. We can tell, for example, that the great majority of the students clustered between scores of 20 and 44. We can see also that the students were almost symmetrically and rather widely spread out between scores of 0 and 64. And we can see that the best student did about thirty times as well as the poorest student.

3. Frequency Polygons and Curves

The information contained in a frequency table may be presented in readily under-standable form by drawing a picture. The simplest picture is obtained by piling up blocks to indicate the different frequencies. The frequency table of our logic scores (Table 3), thus pictured, would look like the diagram in Figure 1 on the next page.

The same information can be shown by drawing connecting lines through the mid-points of the tops of the columns of blocks. The picture thus obtained is called a *frequency polygon*. Another type of picture, called a *frequency curve*, is obtained by drawing a smooth curve which follows the frequency polygon closely. By eliminating some of the sharp fluctuations of the polygon, the frequency curve theoretically approximates more nearly the way the distribution would have looked had the number of instances been much larger. Thus the frequency curve is a sort of generalization from the instances actually observed to a much larger group of instances. Figure 2 on page 80 shows a frequency curve sketched over a frequency polygon for the data in Table 3.

4. Averages

Because of its great convenience, the frequency table is basic to many types of statistical analyses. The purpose of many of these is to determine the distinguishing characteristics of the group being studied. For example, a manufacturer of automobiles or air conditioners may need an analysis of the incomes of his potential customers in order to decide in which price range to design his product. A teacher may wish specific information about the aptitude and achievement of his class so that he may fit his assignments and discussions to its needs.

The first step in analyzing the distinguishing characteristics of a group is to locate a starting point or center by which the representative core of the group may be located and from which its boundaries or limits may be measured. The "center" needed for this purpose is some kind of measure of the

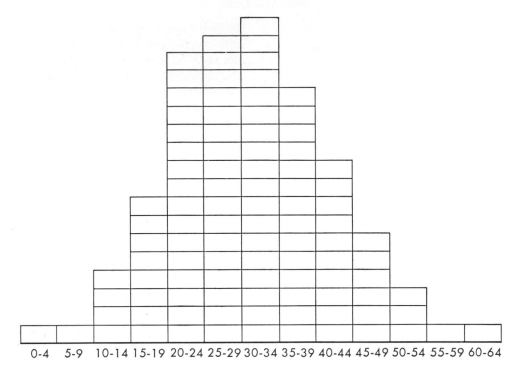

Fig. 1 Column Diagram of Logic Scores

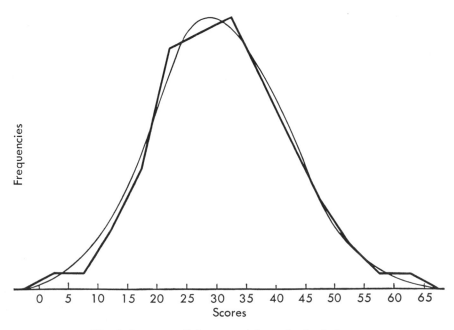

Fig. 2 Frequency Polygon and Curve for Logic Scores

average performance of the group, or, as it is often called, a "measure of central tendency."

One such measure commonly used is the familiar arithmetic average, or *mean*, computed simply by adding all the items and dividing the sum by the number of items. Thus we could get the average of the scores in Table 1 simply by adding the hundred scores and dividing by 100. But this calls for a lot of adding, and we would shudder at the thought of adding 10,000 scores. Consequently statisticians have developed a so-called "short method" of computing the mean from the frequency table, a description of which can be found in any text on statistics.

Even without using this somewhat complicated method, we can save considerable work by taking a *weighted average* from the data shown in Table 3. Since the individual scores in each interval cannot be identified, we must make an assumption about their average value. The most reasonable assumption is that the scores are evenly distributed through the range of the interval. On this assumption the average of the scores in an interval is the *mid-value* of the interval, i.e., halfway between the lowest and highest possible scores in the interval. In determining the mid-value of an interval we must consider the nature of the data. In this distribution we are dealing with test scores in which fractions of less than half, if any, were dropped and fractions of $\frac{1}{2}$ or larger were counted as the next highest number. Thus the interval 5–9 actually includes scores from 4.5 to but not including 9.5. Thus the true mid-value of this interval is the average of the two, or approximately 7.

We cannot get our average, however, merely by adding the mid-values of each interval, for the number of students in the different intervals varies. We must therefore *weight* each interval by multiplying its mid-value by its frequency. Thus for the third interval, 10–14, we would multiply the mid-value, 12, by the frequency in that interval,

4. We would then add the products for the intervals and divide by 100, the total number of scores. Note that an average obtained from a frequency table would probably not coincide exactly with the average obtained by adding the individual scores, for the average of the scores in an interval is not necessarily the mid-value. Usually, however, a weighted average taken from a frequency table is close enough to the mean for practical purposes. The weighted average is another instance of how statistical procedures save work at a small sacrifice in accuracy.

Another common measure of central tendency is the *median,* which is simply the middle number when the numbers have been arranged in order. To get the median of the numbers 1, 4, 2, 6, 9, we must first arrange them in order: 1, 2, 4, 6, 9. The middle number or median in this group is 4. Where there is an even number of items in the group, the median is taken to be the average of the two in the middle. Thus the median of the numbers 1, 2, 4, 6, 8, 9 is 5.

When we are working from a frequency table the median must be approximated. Look at Table 3. Since there are 100 scores in the distribution, the median is the average of the fiftieth and fifty-first scores. A glance at the column headed "cumulative frequency" will show that these two scores occur in the interval 30–34. But the median set at the mid-value of this interval, 32, would be too high, for there are eighteen scores in this interval, and the fiftieth and fifty-first are the third and fourth scores, respectively, in this interval. Statisticians use a more precise method for calculating the median, but for our purpose it is sufficient to estimate that it is low in this interval, or roughly 31. We make this estimate on the assumption that the scores are distributed evenly throughout the interval.

A third measure of central tendency is the *mode,* which is simply the value that occurs most frequently. Thus for the numbers 1, 2, 4, 4, 4, 5, 6, 8, the mode is 4. In working from a frequency table we do not know what the individual scores are. Although statisticians have better methods, for our purpose it is sufficient to guess the mode to be the mid-value of the interval having the highest frequency. Thus in Table 3 we would guess the mode to be the mid-value of the interval 30–34, or 32. (Actually, the mode taken from the individual scores in this table is 30.)

Each of these measures of central tendency has particular advantages, as we shall see in Chapter 10.

5. Percentile Ranks

A statistical measure frequently used in characterizing the performance of an individual on a test is the *percentile rank,* which is often defined as the percentage of the scores which the given score equals or exceeds. Percentile ranks can be computed easily from a frequency table. To get the percentile rank of a score in any interval, simply divide the cumulative frequency of that interval by the total number of scores and multiply by 100. For example, turn back to the distribution in Table 3. To get the percentile rank of a score in the interval 50–54, divide the cumulative frequency for that interval, 98, by the number of scores, 100, which gives .98. Then multiply by 100 (to remove the decimal point), and you get 98. Actually this procedure yields the percentile rank for the top score of the interval, but it is satisfactory for most purposes, especially if the group is large. Note that the percentile ranks would have been more precise if the intervals had been smaller. Thus the fewer intervals, the less precise the percentile rank is.

Percentile ranks have certain advantages over grades and scores in evaluating the performance of an individual on tests and examinations. In the first place, grades and scores tell us little about the performance of an individual with respect to his competition un-

less we know the grades or scores of the other individuals in the group. A grade of A or a score of 90 may mean that the individual is near the top of his group, or it may mean merely that he met a certain standard which most or all of his competitors also met. Percentile ranks, on the other hand, give a specific measure of the individual's competitive position with respect to his group. In the second place, it is difficult to compare an individual's grades or scores on tests in different subjects. A grade of D or a score of 30 on one test may actually represent higher achievement than a grade of A or a score of 90 on another test. On the other hand, where the groups taking the different tests are large and reasonably comparable, percentile ranks give grades and scores a definite meaning in terms of the performance of the group as a whole. Thus, when the groups are reasonably comparable, as would probably be the case with a large freshman class taking two different required courses, the same percentile rank on two different tests would probably represent roughly comparable achievement in the two tests.

6. Measures of Dispersion

Once a center or average has been found, another step in analyzing the characteristics of a group is to determine the *dispersion, i.e.,* the extent to which the group is spread. Wide dispersion indicates heterogeneity in the characteristic being measured. Dispersion is one indication of the worth of a test as a grading device: the more widely scores are spread, the easier it is to separate students by grades.

One measure of dispersion is called the *range,* which is the difference between the lowest and highest figures. Thus the range of our logic scores is 61, since the lowest score is 0 and the highest 61. In working from a frequency table, where we do not know the individual scores, the range is usually taken to be the difference between the mid-values of the lowest and highest intervals. Thus the range for the data in Table 3 is the difference between 2 and 62, or 60, which closely approximates the range computed from the individual scores, which is 61.

For many purposes, however, the range is too crude a measure. In the first place, it may be strongly influenced by a single instance. In the scores of our logic test, had the student who made the lowest score been absent, the range would have been reduced from 61 to 55. Furthermore, for many purposes we are not interested in the extreme cases, whether high or low. Thus, in deciding how much to charge, the manufacturer of a medium-priced air conditioner is not concerned with the extremely poor, who cannot buy the product anyway, nor with the extremely rich, to whom price is not a major factor. Instead, he is concerned with the large central core of potential buyers. For his purposes, some measure of dispersion other than the range would be more suitable.

One measure of dispersion the manufacturer might use, which would leave out of consideration the extremes, is the *10–90 interpercentile range.* It is computed by disregarding 10 per cent of the individual items at each end of the distribution and taking the range of the remainder. For example, consider the following scores: 1, 12, 13, 13, 15, 16, 17, 18, 18, 19. Since there are ten scores, 10 per cent of the scores is one score. Thus we would disregard the lowest score, 1, and the highest score, 19. The 10–90 interpercentile range is simply the difference between the highest and lowest scores remaining, or 18–12, or 6. We can, of course, use other interpercentile ranges, such as the *25–75 interpercentile range.*

Probably the most frequently used measure of dispersion is the *standard deviation,* which is a kind of average of the amounts by which the instances in a group differ from the mean of the group. It is defined technically as *the square root of the arithmetic average of the squares of the deviations from the mean.* Actually this measure is not so complicated as it sounds. The standard deviation, usually symbolized by a small Greek sigma (σ), is computed in Table 4 for a group of ten test scores.

The first step in computing the standard deviation is to determine the mean, since we are trying to measure how much the scores differ from the mean. With only ten scores, it is easy to add the separate scores, which total 90, and divide by 10, the number of

Table 4

Computation of Standard Deviation

Scores	Deviations from Mean	Squares of the Deviations
2	−7	49
4	−5	25
6	−3	9
9	0	0
9	0	0
9	0	0
9	0	0
13	4	16
14	5	25
15	6	36
Sum 90		Sum 160

Mean of scores $= \dfrac{90}{10} = 9$ 　　Mean of Squares of Deviations $= \dfrac{160}{10} = 16$

Standard Deviation (σ) = Square root of 16 = 4.

scores, as shown in the first column of Table 4. Thus the mean is 9.

The second step is to determine how much each score differs, *i.e.*, deviates, from the mean of 9. This is done in the column headed "Deviation from Mean." Since a score of 2 deviates from 9 by −7, −7 is entered in this column for the first score.

The third step is to square these deviations, as shown in the column headed "Squares of the Deviations." The next step is to find the average of all the squared deviations. There are 10 scores, with squared deviations totaling 160. Thus the average of the squared deviations is 16. To get the standard deviation we have only to take the square root of 16, which is 4.

Note that in the example we computed, the standard deviation turned out to be a certain number of score points that represented a unit of measurement of the extent to which all the scores differed from the mean. Actually the standard deviation would be nothing more than an average of the deviations except that the process of squaring the deviations and then taking the square root of the mean of the squares of the deviations results in a figure slightly larger than the straight average would be. This is illustrated by Table 4. Disregarding minus signs, the average of the deviations is 30 divided by 10, or 3, whereas the standard deviation is 4. We shall see more of the significance of standard deviations in Chapter 10.

Suggested Supplementary Reading

W. Allen Wallis and Harry V. Roberts, *Statistics: A New Approach* (Brooklyn: The Free Press of Glencoe, 1956), Chapter 1.

EXERCISE 8

All items in this exercise refer to the following data showing the number of vacuum cleaners sold by thirty salesmen in a ninety-day period.

39	29	28	25	42	40
31	26	25	32	21	27
07	18	16	21	03	21
17	21	26	24	14	16
23	49	31	41	17	11
117	*143*	*126*	*143*	*97*	*115*

1. Compile a frequency table for these sales records, using an interval of five.

Interval	Frequency	Cumulative Frequency
0 - 4	1	1
5 - 9	1	2
10 - 14	2	4
15 - 19	5	9
20 - 24	6	15
25 - 29	7	22
30 - 34	3	25
35 - 39	1	26
40 - 44	3	29
45 - 49	1	30

2. Draw a frequency polygon for the frequency table. Sketch over it a frequency curve.

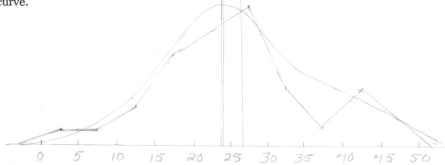

3. What is the mean, computed from the individual sales records? 24.7

4. What is the weighted average, computed from the frequency table?

24.83

5. What is the median, taken from the individual sales records? 24.5

6. Estimate the median from the frequency table. 24.5

7. What is the mode, taken from the individual sales records? 21

8. Estimate the mode from the frequency table. _____27_____

9. Why do the mean, median, and mode computed from the individual records differ from those estimated from the frequency table?

they are exact whereas the others are approximations

10. Draw and label vertical lines on the frequency polygon (Item 2) to show the mean, median, and mode.

11. Estimate the range from the frequency table. _____45_____

12. What is the 10–90 interpercentile range taken from the individual sales records?

_____26_____

13. Would the range or the 10–90 interpercentile range be more truly representative of the salesmen's performance? Why?

eliminates the extremes - 10-90 interpercentile

14. What is the percentile rank of the salesman who sold fourteen vacuum cleaners?

_____13.3%_____

15. Compute the standard deviation for the following records of the ten salesmen in a single district.

Values	Deviations	Squares of Deviations
19	− 6	36
21	− 4	16
22	− 3	9
23	− 2	4
24	− 1	1
25	0	0
26	1	1
27	2	4
30	5	25
33	8	64

$$10\overline{)250}$$
$$25$$

$$\sigma = \underline{\quad 4 \quad}$$

16. If each salesman in the district received a $10 bonus for each vacuum cleaner he sold in excess of one standard deviation above the mean, how much would be the total bonus paid in the district?

_____$50_____

9 Statistics and Probability

1. *Combinations and Permutations*

2. *Alternative Possibilities*

3. *Theoretical Expectation*

4. *The Gambler's Fallacy*

In Chapter 3 we discussed the implications of certain concepts of probability for decision making. We also examined certain elementary procedures for computing probabilities. While it is not our purpose to become deeply involved in mathematics, an examination of several additional concepts of probability is essential for an understanding of the basic concepts and uses of statistics.

1. Combinations and Permutations

In computing some types of probabilities it is necessary to understand the differences between *combinations* and *permutations*. Suppose we toss three coins. The probabilities would be the same whether we toss one coin three times, or three coins one after another, or three coins simultaneously. The possible combinations of heads and tails for three coins are shown in the table below.

Table 5

Combinations of Heads and Tails with Three Coins

1. Three Heads
2. Two Heads and One Tail
3. Two Tails and One Head
4. Three Tails

The probabilities of these combinations are not equal. To understand why not, it is helpful to list all of the *permutations, i.e.,* the different orders in which related events can occur. The fact that the same combination can result from different coins falling heads up or tails up will be easier to see if we identify the individual coins. For convenience in identifying the coins, let us assume that we are tossing a penny, a nickel, and a dime. There are six permutations with respect to the order in which we can toss the three coins: (1) penny, nickel, dime; (2) penny, dime, nickel; (3) nickel, penny, dime; (4) nickel, dime, penny; (5) dime, penny, nickel; (6) dime, nickel, penny. In computing the probabilities of various combinations of heads and tails we can disregard these permutations, for we are not concerned with the order in which the coins are tossed. To avoid confusion over this point, let us assume that our three coins are always tossed in the same order. We cannot, however, ignore another kind of permutation, the order, or pattern, in which the heads and tails occur. All the different patterns are shown in Table 6 on the following page.

Note that, while there are only four combinations possible with three coins, there are eight possible patterns of heads and tails.[1]

---

[1] Patterns 2, 3, and 4 are the permutations for the combination of two heads and one tail; Patterns 5, 6, and 7 are the permutations for the combination of one head and two tails.

Table 6

Patterns of Heads and Tails with Three Coins

	Penny	Nickel	Dime
1.	H	H	H
2.	H	H	T
3.	H	T	H
4.	T	H	H
5.	H	T	T
6.	T	H	T
7.	T	T	H
8.	T	T	T

Examination of the table will show why. Only Pattern 1 produces the combination of three heads. But three patterns (2, 3, and 4) produce the combination of two heads and one tail. These three patterns are different in that a different coin is tails up in each pattern. Note also that each of the eight patterns is equally likely. You can test this statement for yourself by using the procedures described in Chapter 3 to compute the probability for each pattern.

You can learn much about probability simply by studying Table 6. For example, you can compute the probability of getting any given combination of heads and tails simply by counting the patterns. The total number of patterns is the denominator and the number of patterns forming the combination in question is the numerator. The probabilities for each combination of heads and tails are listed in the table below.

Table 7

Combination	Probability
3 Heads	1/8
2 Heads, 1 Tail	3/8
2 Tails, 1 Head	3/8
3 Tails	1/8
	8/8, or 1

Note that the total probabilities of all the combinations is 1.

What is the probability that the nickel will fall tails up and the other two coins heads up? The total possibilities are the eight patterns. There is only one favorable pattern. Thus the probability is $\frac{1}{8}$.

What is the probability that exactly one of the three coins will be tails up? Note that in the preceding problem it was specified which coin would be tails up, whereas in this problem any one of the three coins can be tails up. Thus there are three favorable possibilities (2, 3, 4), and the probability is $\frac{3}{8}$.

What is the probability that at least one of the three coins will fall tails up? All patterns except the first meet the specifications of this problem, so that the probability is $\frac{7}{8}$.

2. Alternative Possibilities

Procedures for solving these more complex problems in probability are worth our attention because they illustrate important principles. One of these principles concerns *alternative possibilities*. Obviously, if you have two or more chances to accomplish a given end, your chances are better than if you have only one chance. But how much better? Suppose you are in a Binomian jail. The jailer hands you a die and offers you a deal: you give him all of your valuables in return for two rolls of the die; if on either roll you get a six he will allow you to escape; otherwise you stay in jail without your valuables.

To compute probabilities in situations with alternative possibilities, a modification must be made in the procedures described in Chapter 3. In the problem above the probabilities would be the same whether you roll one die twice or two dice once. Since the principle involved is easier to see if two dice are rolled, let us assume that you do so. Shown below are the computations for all patterns of sixes and non-sixes possible with two dice.

Table 8

Pattern	First Die		Second Die		Probability
1. Six on both dice	1/6	×	1/6	=	1/36
2. Six on first only	1/6	×	5/6	=	5/36
3. Six on second only	5/6	×	1/6	=	5/36
4. No sixes	5/6	×	5/6	=	25/36
				Total	36/36

A little study of the patterns above will reveal the principle involved in alternative possibilities. Note that Patterns 1, 2, and 3 give you at least one six. The probability of getting at least one six, then, is the total of the probabilities for each of these three patterns: $\frac{1}{36} + \frac{5}{36} + \frac{5}{36} = \frac{11}{36}$. In short, *the procedure for computing problems involving alternative possibilities is to compute the probability for each pattern and then add the probabilities.* This is the only situation in which probability fractions are added: they are added only because the problem has been worked in installments.

Now suppose the jailer has promised you your freedom only if you get exactly one six with two dice. Since he did not specify which die must turn up six, there are two alternative patterns, 2 and 3. Note that both involve a specific order. Since either order will do, the probabilities of both patterns must be added: $\frac{5}{36} + \frac{5}{36}$, or $\frac{10}{36}$. Problems of this kind can be worked, of course, by computing the probability for a specific order and multiplying it by the number of possible orders. For example, the probability of getting exactly one six with three dice would be $\frac{1}{6} \times \frac{5}{6} \times \frac{5}{6} \times 3$, or $\frac{25}{72}$.

The principle of alternative events applies to dependent as well as to independent related events. All the examples above are of independent events. Let us look now at an example of dependent events. Suppose you are one of four players in a card game. To keep the arithmetic simple, assume that you are using only eight cards: the ace, king, queen, jack, ten, nine, eight, and seven of spades. What is the probability that the two cards dealt you will include the ace? This is a problem in alternative events because you have two chances to get the ace. The events are dependent because the probabilities on the second card dealt to you are affected by the first card dealt to you. Shown below are the computations for all possible patterns that include the ace.

Pattern	First Card Dealt			Second Card Dealt		
1.	Ace	1/8	x	Non-ace	7/7	= 7/56
2.	Non-ace	7/8	x	Ace	1/7	= 7/56

Consider Pattern 1. Since there are eight cards in the deck, only one of which is the ace, the probability that the first card you receive will be the ace is $\frac{1}{8}$. With seven cards left in the deck, none of which is the ace, the probability that the second card will not be the ace is $\frac{7}{7}$, or 1.

Now consider Pattern 2, in which the second card you receive is the ace. Note that the probabilities in the two patterns are the same; the only difference is the order in which you receive the ace and the non-ace. Since both patterns satisfy the requirements of the problem, the probabilities of the two patterns must be added. Thus the probability that your two cards will include the ace is $\frac{7}{56} + \frac{7}{56}$, or $\frac{14}{56}$. Problems like this can be worked, of course, by computing the probability for one pattern and multiplying this probability by the number of patterns.

Since the conventional method is to deal one card at a time to each player, you may question the statement that your second card is as likely to be the ace as your first card, on the ground that the ace may be dealt to another player before you receive your second card. But remember that in Chapter 3 we defined *probability* as the degree of likelihood that a proposition is true, based on the evidence in hand. If you can identify the cards and you know that the ace has been dealt to another player, the probability that your second card will be the ace is zero. But if you cannot identify the cards dealt to the other players, you have no evidence in hand to justify a difference in probability. If the ace is dealt to another player, the probability that you will receive it drops to zero. But if the ace is not dealt to another player, the probability that you will receive it increases. In fact, if you are about to receive the last card, and the ace has not yet been dealt, the probability that you will receive it is 1.

Theoretically, if you had unlimited time, energy, pencils, erasers, paper, coffee, and aspirin you could compute any probability by the procedures we have discussed. You would soon discover, however, that the task can be tedious. For example, the total possibilities in answering only five five-choice objective questions are 3,125 (disregarding the order in which the questions are answered). With ten questions the possibilities rise to 9,765,625. If your curiosity extends beyond ten questions, this book will not help you. Incidentally, if you think that luck is a large factor in scores on objective examinations, consider the fact that only one of the 9,765,625 possibilities has all of the answers right.

Mathematicians have devised many short cuts for computing complex probabilities. These are not presented here because our concern is with the concepts rather than the computations. For the student who wishes to go more deeply into the subject there are courses in mathematics and statistics, as well as many useful texts in the library.

Even with these short cuts, many problems would tax the skill and patience of the finest mathematician. Until recently the usefulness of probability theory in decision making has been restricted because the calculations in many problems would cost more than the knowledge was worth. The development of computers, however, has changed this. Because of the speed with which computers can do the arithmetic necessary in statistics and probability, many decisions that once were made by rough guesses are now based on probabilities. Weather forecasting is a case in point. Not long ago weather forecasts predicted rain or no rain. Often there was no rain when rain was predicted, and vice versa, and the public had no way of knowing how much confidence to place in the forecast. Computers have changed this. Meteorologists now feed relevant data on current conditions into a computer, in the memory circuits of which are stored weather data from the past. The computer in effect searches its memory and counts the days when conditions were similar to current ones and the number of such instances in which it rained within a given time. When the weather forecast says "probability of rain 70 per cent," it is really saying that the computer has found that under similar conditions it has rained seventy days out of a hundred. In effect, then, weather forecasts are based on empirical probabilities. This newer method of making and reporting forecasts not only tells the public how much confidence to put in a forecast but also keeps picnickers, fishermen, and the like from becoming too angry when cloudbursts disrupt their pleasures on days when no rain was predicted.

3. Theoretical Expectation

In some instances the theory and methods of computation of probability are useful in measuring the practical value of proposed actions. For example, suppose you are offered a ticket in a charity raffle of an automobile worth $2,000. The ticket costs $1, and 4,000 of them are to be sold. What is the probable worth of a ticket? The answer to this question will take us into the field of theoretical expectation.

We can apply theoretical probability, for we have to assume only that the raffle is honest in order to assign a theoretical value to each ticket. On the basis of the evidence in hand, we can assign each ticket the same value, since each ticket has an equal chance of being the winner. The theoretical value of each ticket, then, will be $1/4000$ of $2,000, or fifty cents. Under these circumstances, if you buy a ticket with the idea of investing fifty cents in a business proposition and donating fifty cents to charity, your reasoning is sound. But if you buy a ticket on the assumption that you are investing a dollar in a business proposition, your thinking is unsound, even though you win the automobile, for on the basis of the evidence in hand, your ticket is worth only fifty cents.

The principles of theoretical expectation apply to any situation where you can make reasonable assumptions about the likelihood of events. But you must be careful in making your assumptions. Suppose, for example, you operate a factory that cans orange juice. An instrument worth $500 has been lost, and you believe it has been "canned" somewhere in a batch of 10,000 cans of juice. You estimate the cost of opening these cans, including destruction of the product, to be 25 cents per can. Assuming that the instrument is in one of the cans and that it is as likely to be in one can as another, what is the probable cost of recovering it by opening cans? You might find it in the first can you open, but to be certain of finding it you would have to be prepared to open all the cans. On the basis of the evidence in hand, the instrument is as likely to be in the last as in the first can. If it is in the first can, the cost is 25 cents. If it is in the last can, the cost is $2,500. The average of the two is a few cents over $1,250. Thus, on the basis of your assumptions, it would be cheaper to buy a new instrument. But before you do so, you had better examine your assumptions. Perhaps there is some method by which you could determine that the instrument is more likely to be in one can than another. Perhaps shaking or weighing the cans would determine the location of the instrument. Then only one can would have to be opened.

The principles of theoretical expectation are also useful in estimating the reliability of samples. Table 9 shows the probabilities for each combination of heads and tails possible when we toss ten coins as a group.

Table 9

Combination	Probability
10 Heads	1/1,024
9 Heads, 1 Tail	10/1,024
8 Heads, 2 Tails	45/1,024
7 Heads, 3 Tails	120/1,024
6 Heads, 4 Tails	210/1,024
5 Heads, 5 Tails	252/1,024
4 Heads, 6 Tails	210/1,024
3 Heads, 7 Tails	120/1,024
2 Heads, 8 Tails	45/1,024
1 Head, 9 Tails	10/1,024
10 Tails	1/1,024

Now suppose we take a sample of ten coins from a very large group of coins lying on a table. If the coins are distributed evenly heads up and tails up, and if we disregard the factor of dependency, the probability that the sample would be exactly representative, *i.e.*, would include exactly 50 per cent heads, is only $252/1024$. Note, however, that as the percentage of heads or tails increases, the probability decreases. We can make two generalizations from this data: (1) it is improbable that a random sample will be exactly representative; and (2) the less representative a random sample is, the less likely it is to occur.

4. The Gambler's Fallacy

A good many people seem to believe that there is something akin to a law of atonement in probability, whereby if a coin tossed 20 times has "misbehaved" by falling heads up only 6 times, it will sooner or later atone for its misbehavior by falling heads up more often than tails up. While coins might do this often enough to give a poor thinker some instances to support his belief in such a law of atonement, there is no sound basis for it.

A coin has no memory, no conscience, no desire to please. The explanation for the fact that coins, dice, and the like do seem to atone for their "misbehavior" is to be found in the tendency for disparities to be swallowed by large numbers. When a coin "misbehaves" by producing only 6 heads in 20 tosses, the disparity seems large; but if the coin "behaves" for the next 980 tosses, the total result would be 496 heads and 504 tails, at which point the disparity is small. No matter how often a coin has fallen heads up, the probability that it will fall heads up on the next toss is still $\frac{1}{2}$ — unless something other than chance is operating.

Suggested Supplementary Reading

DAVID BERGAMINI AND THE EDITORS OF LIFE, *Mathematics* (New York: Time Incorporated, 1963), Chapter 6.

WILLIAM MENDENHALL, *Introduction to Statistics* (Belmont, California: Wadsworth Publishing Company, Inc., 1963).

EXERCISE 9

1–8. *These items pertain to an objective test with three choices for each question, only one of which is right. Compute the probability for Items 1–8 on the assumption that the questions are answered purely by chance, i.e., with no knowledge whatsoever of the subject matter.*

1. Answering the *first two* questions *right*. $\frac{1}{3} \times \frac{1}{3}$ _____ $\frac{1}{9}$

2. Answering the *first* question *right* and the *second wrong*. _____ $\frac{2}{9}$

   $\frac{1}{3} \times \frac{2}{3}$

3. Answering the *first* question *wrong* and the *second right*. _____ $\frac{2}{9}$

   $\frac{2}{3} \times \frac{1}{3}$

4. Answering the *first two* questions *wrong*. _____ $\frac{4}{9}$

   $\frac{2}{3} \times \frac{2}{3}$

5. Answering *exactly one* of the *first two* questions *right*. _____ $\frac{4}{9}$

   $\frac{2}{9} + \frac{2}{9}$

6. Answering *exactly one* of the *first two* questions *wrong*. _____ $\frac{4}{9}$

   $\frac{2}{9} + \frac{2}{9}$

7. Answering *at least one* of the *first two* questions *right*. _____ $\frac{5}{9}$

   $\frac{2}{9} + \frac{1}{9} + \frac{2}{9}$

8. Answering *at least one* of the *first two* questions *wrong*. _____ $\frac{8}{9}$

   $\frac{4}{9} + \frac{2}{9} + \frac{2}{9}$

9–18. *A playful friend has changed the labels on seven cans of the same size on your kitchen shelf. Compute the probability for each item below on the assumption that you select the cans you open purely by chance. The cans contain:*

Tomato juice	Creamed chicken
Prune juice	Beef stew
Orange juice	Lamb stew
Grapefruit juice	

9. The *first* can opened will contain *tomato juice*. _____ $\frac{1}{7}$

10. The *first* can opened will contain *juice*. _____ $\frac{4}{7}$

11. The *first* can opened ·will contain *tomato juice* and the *second* can *lamb stew*.

    $\frac{1}{7} \times \frac{1}{6}$ _____ $\frac{1}{42}$

12. The *first* can opened will contain *juice* and the *second* can *meat*. $\frac{12}{42} = \frac{2}{7}$

    $\frac{4}{7} \times \frac{3}{6}$

13. The *first two* cans opened will contain *citrus juice*. _____ $\frac{1}{21}$

    $\frac{2}{7} \times \frac{1}{6}$

14. *Neither* of the *first two* cans opened will contain *citrus juice*. _____ $\frac{20}{42} = \frac{10}{21}$

    $\frac{5}{7} \times \frac{4}{6}$

15. The *first* can *but not the second* will contain *citrus juice*. _____ $\frac{10}{42} = \frac{5}{21}$

    $\frac{2}{7} \times \frac{5}{6}$

16. *At least one* of the *first two* cans opened will contain *citrus juice.* ⎯⎯⎯⎯ $\frac{22}{42} = \frac{11}{21}$

$\frac{2}{42} + \frac{10}{42} + \frac{10}{42}$

17. *All* of the *first three* cans opened will contain *meat.* ⎯⎯⎯⎯ $\frac{6}{210}$

$\frac{3}{7} \times \frac{2}{6} \times \frac{1}{5}$

18. The *last* can opened will contain *tomato juice.* ⎯⎯⎯⎯ $\frac{720}{5040} = \frac{1}{7}$

$\frac{6}{7} \times \frac{5}{6} \times \frac{4}{5} \times \frac{3}{4} \times \frac{2}{3} \times \frac{1}{2}$

19. Suppose you are testing transistor radios for a consumer organization. You select a random sample of five from a shipment of ten imported radios. Assume that two of the ten radios are defective. What is the probability that none of your sample of five is defective?

$\frac{8}{10} \times \frac{7}{9} \times \frac{6}{8} \times \frac{5}{7} \times \frac{4}{6}$ ⎯⎯⎯⎯ $\frac{2}{9}$

20. What is the probability that your sample of five will be truly representative of the shipment of ten?

$\frac{2}{10} \times \frac{8}{9} \times \frac{7}{8} \times \frac{6}{7} \times \frac{5}{6} \times 5$ ⎯⎯⎯⎯ $\frac{5}{9}$

21. Now suppose you select a random sample of five radios from a shipment of 1,000, 20 per cent of which are defective. Is the probability that your sample will be truly representative of the shipment of 1,000 greater or less than the probability in Item 20 above? $\frac{200}{1000} \times \frac{800}{999} \times \frac{799}{998} \times \frac{798}{997} \times \frac{797}{996}$ ⎯⎯ *greater*

22. Suppose you answer ten true-false questions purely by chance. According to theoretical expectation, how many should you get right?

$\frac{1}{2} \times 10$ ⎯⎯⎯⎯ 5

23. Suppose on a true-false test of 100 items you guess the answers purely by chance. When you check your answers against the key, you find that you guessed the first ten right. What would be the theoretical expectation as to your total score?

$\frac{1}{2} \times 90 = 45 + 10$ ⎯⎯⎯⎯ 55

24. Suppose you wish to invest \$10,000 in common stocks. You have selected ten stocks, each of which you believe has a probability of ⁶⁄₁₀ of going up \$1 per share and a probability of ⁴⁄₁₀ of going down \$1 per share. Would it be safer to invest \$10,000 in one stock or \$1,000 in each of the ten?

⎯⎯⎯⎯ 10 shares

25. Why?

⎯⎯⎯⎯⎯⎯⎯⎯⎯⎯⎯⎯⎯⎯⎯⎯⎯⎯⎯⎯⎯⎯⎯⎯⎯⎯⎯

⎯⎯⎯⎯⎯⎯⎯⎯⎯⎯⎯⎯⎯⎯⎯⎯⎯⎯⎯⎯⎯⎯⎯⎯⎯⎯⎯

10 Reasoning from Generalizations

1. The Normal Probability Curve

2. Inferences from Normal Distributions

3. Inferences from Irregular Distributions

4. Interpreting Averages

5. Hazards in Interpreting Statistics

6. Misuse of Statistics

The probabilities we computed for the combinations of heads and tails possible with ten coins (see Table 9) have other interesting implications. The curve shown below was derived by translating these probabilities into a frequency polygon and then "smoothing" the polygon into a curve by statistical procedures.

1. The Normal Probability Curve

This curve is often called the "normal curve of distribution" because it delineates the distribution we would expect when nothing but chance is affecting the distribution. A normal curve has several distinguishing characteristics. Note that it is symmetrical. From this it follows that mean, median, and mode all fall at the midpoint. The rate at which frequencies decrease on either side of this midpoint can be expressed in standard deviations. The territory defined by the first standard deviation below the mean includes 34.13 per cent of the population. Note further that the rate of decrease in frequencies is not uniform, for the territory defined by the second standard deviation below the

mean includes only 13.59 per cent of the population, while the territory of the third standard deviation below the mean includes only 2.145 per cent. Since a normal curve is symmetrical, the standard deviations above and below the mean include the same percentages. Thus the territory covered between one standard deviation to the left and one standard deviation to the right of the mean includes 68.26 per cent of the population, a large but relatively uniform central

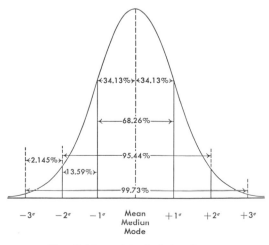

Fig. 3 Normal Probability Curve

core. Two standard deviations on both sides include 95.44 per cent, a larger group but twice as diverse. Three standard deviations on both sides include 99.73 per cent. The remaining .27 per cent (27 out of 10,000) of the population unaccounted for would be included in additional standard deviations.

2. Inferences from Normal Distributions

It is unlikely that any actual distribution would have the exact characteristics of a normal probability curve. But interestingly enough, distributions of all manner of things, from scores on intelligence tests to the wing spread of pigeons, resemble such a curve. The resemblance is so strong that the normal probability curve is useful as a standard of comparison in analyzing empirical distributions.

First let us look at the significance of our three measures of dispersion — range, 10–90 interpercentile range, and standard deviation — in terms of the normal probability curve. Suppose you are planning to manufacture a new automobile, and you have made a survey of the horsepower potential buyers prefer. Your survey shows an approximately normal distribution.

	Horsepower
Range	150
10–90 interpercentile range	40
Mean	175
Standard Deviation	15

The large size of the range compared to the 10–90 interpercentile range tells you that it is hopeless to try to please everybody with one engine. You must therefore content yourself with trying to please a central core of the population.

The mean, together with the 10–90 interpercentile range, tells you that an engine of 175 horsepower will come within 20 horsepower of satisfying the middle 80 per cent of your potential customers. The mean and the standard deviation, together with the characteristics of a normal curve, tell you that an engine of 175 horsepower will come within 15 horsepower of satisfying 68 per cent of your potential customers, and within 30 horsepower of satisfying about 95 per cent. But suppose the standard deviation had been 40 instead of 15. You would then know that your customers' preferences vary widely. An engine of 175 horsepower would then come only within 40 horsepower of satisfying 68 per cent of the market you want to reach, and you had better consider offering different engines.

Thus the size of the standard deviation has a significance of its own. Suppose that the standard deviation on a test of 100 items is 15. If the distribution is normal, 68 per cent of the students would be spread out over a total of two standard deviations, or 30 score points, which is a wide spread for a test of 100 items. But suppose the standard deviation had been only 2. This would mean that 68 per cent of the students are clustered within a range of only 4 score points. One would be justified in suspecting either that the test did not distinguish very well between poor and good students, or that the students taking the test were very much alike in ability, or both. On the other hand, when the standard deviation is relatively large, one is justified in forming a tentative conclusion that the test differentiated among the students rather well, or that the students varied a great deal, or both.

Inferences about the significance of an individual instance can also be drawn by comparison with the normal probability curve. For example, let us suppose that you have taken a college aptitude test given to thousands of college students all over the country. You know that the distribution was approximately normal, the maximum possible score 100, the mean 50, and the standard deviation 15. If your score is 50, you would be exactly in the middle, with half of the students on either side of you. If your score is 65, you would be exactly one standard deviation better than the mean, and you would be as good as or better than approximately 84 per cent of your competition. You might now be said to be at the top of the great middle class. A score of 80 would put you two standard deviations above the mean, and in select company — as good as or better than approximately 98 per cent of the competition. A score of 95 would put you out almost by yourself, as good as or better than 99.865 per cent of the competition. But note that each standard deviation covered the same number of score points, so that it took three times as many points above the mean to get out by yourself as it did to get to the top of the middle class. Thus one moral of standard deviations might be that it is wise to think twice before going into a highly competitive occupation like professional baseball unless your aptitude for it is at least two standard deviations above the mean for the total population eligible by age and sex for that occupation.

Many nationally administered tests are scored in terms of standard deviations and normal distributions. The Scholastic Aptitude Test given by the College Entrance Examination Board is a case in point. Each form of this test is given to a fairly large sample of students, and the mean and the standard deviations of their scores are computed. The mean is then arbitrarily assigned a score of 500. Each hundredth of a standard deviation is assigned a value of one point. Thus, if your score on this test is 497, it is three hundredths of a standard deviation below the mean of the sample group. If your score is 600, it is exactly one standard deviation above the mean.

This system has several advantages. The scores are easily interpreted by anyone with an elementary knowledge of statistics, whereas the raw scores on the test cannot be interpreted without studying the distribution. Furthermore, with this system scores on different forms of the test are readily compared. If raw scores were used, comparison would be much more difficult, since the mean on one form of the test might differ considerably from the mean on another form.

3. Inferences from Irregular Distributions

When a distribution is irregular, *i.e.*, when its characteristics differ significantly from those of a normal distribution, we can draw certain inferences about the population covered, according to the type of irregularity.

Sharp fluctuations in a distribution are usually an indication of an inadequate sample. The frequency polygon below, which has been sketched over a normal probability curve, shows the distribution of heads and tails obtained by shaking ten pennies in a jar and pouring them out thirty-two times. We would not expect the polygon for so small a number of instances to follow the normal probability curve very closely, and indeed this one does not. Polygons plotted for a small number of instances, whether of tossed coins or the weight of cabbage heads, are likely to look jagged, like the one shown in Figure 4.

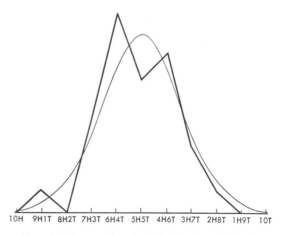

10H 9H1T 8H2T 7H3T 6H4T 5H5T 4H6T 3H7T 2H8T 1H9T 10T

Fig. 4 Polygon Showing Distribution of Heads and Tails in 32 Pourings of 10 Coins

When the number of instances in a distribution is large enough to make a smooth curve, the variations from the normal curve may be due to the operation of some factor other than chance. To introduce an element into the tossing of coins, a drop of solder was affixed to Lincoln's head on ten pennies. These coins were then placed in a jar, shaken well, and poured out 256 times. The frequency polygon in Figure 5, sketched over a normal curve, shows the distribution obtained.

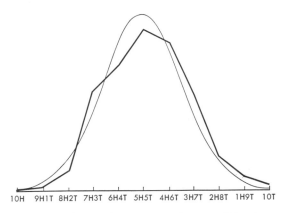

10H 9H1T 8H2T 7H3T 6H4T 5H5T 4H6T 3H7T 2H8T 1H9T 10T

Fig. 5 Polygon Showing Distribution of Heads and Tails in 256 Pourings of 10 "Loaded" Coins

The fact that this polygon follows the normal probability curve more closely than the one in Figure 4 is presumably due to the larger number of instances. All the combinations in which heads and tails are equal or heads are in the majority, with the exception of the combination of seven heads and three tails, fall below the expected frequencies; while all the combinations in which tails are in the majority exceed the expected frequencies. The unexpectedly large frequency for the combination of seven heads and three tails is presumably due to a freak of the distribution, since the number of tails exceeds theoretical expectations everywhere else in the distribution. The excess number of tails could itself be a freak of the distribution, since 256 instances is not a large number, but the presence of solder on the coins provides the most reasonable explanation.

When instances involving dice, coins, and the like deviate significantly and consistently from the theoretical expectations, a search for a factor other than chance is indicated.

The curves for some distributions are *skewed, i.e.,* stretched out on one side or the other. Curves stretched out to the right are said to be *positively skewed,* while those stretched out to the left are *negatively skewed.* The curve in Figure 6 is positively skewed. In this curve the mode, median, and mean are not in the same position, as would be true of a normal probability curve. Both mean and median have been pulled to the right of the mode by a relatively small number of extremely high values.

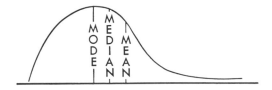

Fig. 6 Positively Skewed Curve

Skewness may be an indication of the operation of some factor other than chance. For example, the salaries of professional baseball players are determined not by chance, but by such factors as the league in which they play and their value to the team. Since there are more minor leagues, in which salaries are relatively low, than major leagues, there are more low salaries than high ones, and the distribution curve would probably look something like the one in Figure 6. Skewness in scores on standardized tests, such as tests of intelligence or college aptitude, usually indicates some factor other than chance in the selection of the individuals taking the test, since standardized tests are designed to yield an approximately normal distribution. Skewness in scores where the test has not been standardized usually indicates that the test is not suited to the abilities or knowledge of the students.

Sometimes distributions are *bimodal, i.e.,* the instances cluster around two centers in-

Fig. 7 Bimodal Distribution

stead of one. A bimodal curve is shown in Figure 7.

If our manufacturer of automobiles should find a bimodal curve in the distribution of customer preferences in horsepower, two different engines or two different models would be indicated. When a teacher finds a bimodal distribution in his class, he has in effect two classes in one, and what would be intelligible to the lower group would probably be dull to the upper group.

4. Interpreting Averages

In normal distributions, mean, median, and mode all have the same significance. In irregular distributions, however, especially where there is strong skewness, each of these measures has a different significance, and it is important to use the measure appropriate for the purpose in hand.

To illustrate, let us take a hypothetical example which will keep the arithmetic simple. Suppose you are considering zymology as a vocation, and you have the following list of salaries of American zymologists.

$ 4,000	$10,000	$12,000	$ 18,000
$ 6,000	$10,000	$14,000	$196,000
$10,000	$12,000	$16,000	

The mean of these salaries is $28,000, the median $12,000, and the mode $10,000. But if the last salary were omitted, the mean would drop to $11,200, the median to $11,000, and the mode would remain $10,000. While this is an exaggerated case, it illustrates the fact that extreme and unusual instances have a much stronger effect on the mean than on either median or mode. If you choose zymology as a profession on the ground that you would probably earn a salary of $28,000, you would be using the wrong average, for you would be using the mean as an indication of the typical salary, whereas you should have used the median or the mode. Assuming that you can become a zymologist but know nothing else about your aptitude for the vocation, the probability of your earning the median salary or more is $6/11$, whereas the probability of your earning as much as the mean salary is only $1/11$.

To summarize the characteristics of the three measures of central tendency, the mean takes all instances into full account. It should be used in situations where every item is equally important to the whole. Computation of honor point averages is an example.

The median and the mode take into account the relative positions and frequencies of the various instances in relation to the whole, but they are not distorted by the extreme instances. They are measures that you would consider with respect to the probable income in a vocation you are contemplating. The median would tell you the "middle income" of those working in the vocation, and the mode would tell you what income is most frequently earned. If the median and mode differ appreciably, the distribution of incomes may be skewed somewhat like the salaries of professional baseball players, and this will be of importance to you. This skewness is likely to reflect keen competition and an extraordinary demand for ability at the high end of the scale, and, as we have said, unless you have evidence that you will be very good in the vocation, your chances of achieving success may be better in some other field.

When the issue is important and the data are available, the frequency distribution and its curve should be studied carefully. Choosing a vocation is one of many situations that demonstrate the importance of gathering and studying all the evidence you can find. To draw conclusions without knowing a great deal about salaries in the given vocation, about your qualifications, and about your probable achievements compared with the achievements of others in that vocation is to run the risk of deceiving yourself disastrously.

5. Hazards in Interpreting Statistics

The basic statistical concepts we have been discussing are invaluable in decision making — provided certain hazards in interpretation are avoided.

A fundamental hazard in all statistical analysis lies in selecting the sample on which the analysis is based. Generalizations based on statistical analyses, like other inferences, are no more reliable than the evidence on which they are based. Since they are based on observations of a sample of the total group, *generalizations are reliable only to the degree that (1) the observations themselves are accurate, and (2) the sample is representative of the total group.*

Careful application of statistical techniques can easily lure us into a false sense of security by causing us to forget that the sample is only a sample and not an accurate enumeration. We then become prone to the fallacy of hasty generalization by extending inferences about the sample to groups not represented in the sample at all.

We are particularly vulnerable to hasty generalization when we attempt to predict the future on the basis of a single sample from the present or the past. No matter how accurate the sample at the time it was taken, it is not necessarily an accurate indication of the future characteristics of the group. This is not to say that we should avoid predicting the future on the basis of samples from the past, for evidence from the past is often the only evidence we can get. *But wherever the passage of time may even remotely affect the situation, time-lapse samples should be used in predictions.*

Insurance companies are making predictions when they base their charges for a given kind of insurance on past experience with the particular kind of risk involved. They protect themselves from some of the hazards of prediction by collecting vast amounts of data. Furthermore, the data are in effect time-lapse samples. Thus their predictions are more reliable because of the tendency of large numbers of instances to remain relatively stable and because time-lapse samples reveal changes in trends. A glance at the vital statistics cited in the *World Almanac* will illustrate this tendency. For example, Table 10, based on some of these figures, gives the death rate per 100,000 population for the principal types of accidental deaths for the years 1960–1963.

This table shows that rates of accidental deaths do change, but they usually change slowly enough for the companies to make necessary adjustments in premium rates. Even so, the companies carry large reserves and in effect pool their resources by insuring one another.

Another hazard lies in applying a generalization to an individual. If, using the data in

Table 10

Accidental Death Rates per 100,000

Type of Accidental Death	1960	1961	1962	1963
All types	52.1	50.4	52.3	53.6
Motor vehicle	21.2	20.8	22.0	23.1
Falls	10.6	10.2	10.5	10.4
Burns	4.2	3.9	4.1	4.3
Drowning	3.6	3.6	3.5	3.4
Railroad	1.3	1.2	1.2	1.1
Firearms	1.3	1.2	1.1	1.2
Poison gases	0.7	0.7	0.7	0.7
Other poisons	0.9	1.0	1.0	1.1

Table 10, you compute the probability that you will die an accidental death within the next twelve months at $53.6/100,000$, the sample you are using is large enough, but you would be assuming that you are as likely to die accidentally as any other of the millions of persons on whom the rate is based. And this is a hazardous assumption, for the probability will be raised or lowered by many factors, such as your age and physical condition, your type of work, how much you ride in automobiles, or how carefully you drive.

Insurance companies must face this problem too. If they charged all applicants the same rate for life insurance, a selective factor would enter, for the old and infirm would tend to take out more insurance than the young and healthy. Insurance companies deal with the problem by dividing the population into strata according to age, sex, occupation, physical condition, and the like, and they vary their rates accordingly.

Even if you had the statistics of the insurance companies available, it would still be difficult to compute your own probability, for there may be great variation among the instances within the several strata. If the death rate for your stratum happened to be two per 100,000, your probability might still range from near zero to near certainty because of your individual characteristics. *The more heterogeneous the group covered by the generalization, the more precarious is the prediction of individual behavior.*

A related hazard is involved in comparing two or more sample groups. Suppose the alumni office at Wysacki announces that its graduates are earning a mean salary of $9,000, while the alumni office at State University announces that its graduates are earning a mean salary of $12,000. It would be extremely hazardous to conclude from this evidence that State alumni earn more than Wysacki alumni. Presumably both averages were derived from samples, and the samples might not be comparable at all. Suppose the Wysacki sample was taken at random and

that every graduate included in the sample was interviewed. Suppose that the State sample was taken from questionnaires voluntarily returned by alumni. This latter sample is highly likely to be loaded, since alumni who are making low salaries are not as likely to return the questionnaires as those who are proud of the fact that they are making high salaries. *Inferences should not be drawn by comparing samples unless you know the samples are representative.*

Another hazard lies in attaching undue significance to small differences in averages, because small differences are likely to be due to chance. It would surely be imprudent to believe, for example, that women are better students than men on the ground that the honor point average of the women at Wysacki was 2.3333 while that of the men was 2.3331.

Both students and faculty are prone to certain hazards in interpreting percentile ranks. It is hazardous to conclude, because you made a percentile rank of 55 in English and 45 in chemistry, that your performance was better in English. It is altogether possible that the group taking chemistry studied harder and learned more than the group taking English, and that the percentile rank of 45 in chemistry actually represents significantly higher achievement than the 55 in English. It should never be forgotten that percentile ranks have meaning only in terms of the group from which they were computed.

Nor is it safe to conclude, since you made percentile ranks of 0 and 5 on your first and second tests in English, and percentile ranks of 45 and 55 on your first and second tests in zymology, that you made more progress in zymology than in English. For differences in percentile rank near the middle of a distribution mean much less than differences of the same magnitude near the extremes. On the logic test for which scores were given in Table 3, raising your score from the interval 0–4 to the interval 5–9 would raise your percentile rank only one point, whereas raising your score from the interval 25–29 to the interval 30–34 would raise your percentile rank eighteen points.

Although standard deviations are somewhat more reliable than percentile ranks (since each standard deviation represents the same spread) they also must be used with caution. It is hazardous to conclude that your performance was better in zymology than in English on the ground that your score in English was only average, whereas your score in zymology was a standard deviation above the mean. For it is altogether possible that the group taking English was so superior in ability and effort to the group taking zymology that your score in English represents higher achievement.

Thus measures of dispersion should be applied to individuals only with great care, for they are meaningless except in terms of the particular group on which they are based.

6. Misuse of Statistics

It has been said that figures never lie, but liars figure. While statistics can be an important tool in discovering the truth and in making sound decisions, statistics can also be misused by propagandists, advertisers, and others to distort the truth and to lead us into making unsound decisions.

One method of using statistics to deceive is to deliberately exaggerate the significance of small differences in averages. A manufacturer of potato peelers might arrange a perfectly fair test of the efficiency of his own and rival brands in which his gadget peeled a few more potatoes per hour. The differ-ence might not be any greater than would occur between two peelers of the same model. But he could make the difference seem much greater by using in his advertising a graph like this:

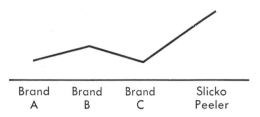

| Brand A | Brand B | Brand C | Slicko Peeler |

Note that this graph does not show how many potatoes any brand peeled. It is well to be suspicious of any graph in which frequencies and quantities are not specifically shown.

Another method is the use of deliberately loaded samples. You should be suspicious of statements like this fictitious one: "Eighty-seven per cent of the doctors interviewed reported that they prescribed 'Painstop.'" This statement could be literally true and yet misleading. Suppose "Painstop" is a brand of aspirin, and that free samples were distributed to one hundred doctors shortly before these doctors were asked whether they ever prescribed "Painstop." Note that the fictitious statement above does not indicate how many doctors were interviewed, or how often they prescribed "Painstop," or how the doctors interviewed were selected.

There are other methods too numerous to describe. Suffice it to say at this point that we should distrust statements based upon statistical evidence unless we are given the information necessary for judging the reliability of the statements.

EXERCISE 10

1–12. *Suppose you find a paper labeled "Distribution of Honor Points Earned by Selected Group of Wysacki Freshmen in Their First Semester," showing the frequency table below.*

Interval	Frequency	Cumulative Frequency
0– 4	1	1
5– 9	4	5
10–14	7	12
15–19	11	23
20–24	16	39
25–29	9	48
30–34	4	52
35–39	2	54
40–44	3	57
45–49	5	62
50–54	8	70
55–59	14	84
60–64	10	94
65–69	5	99
70–74	1	100

1. What is the mean computed from this table?   _36.94_

2. What is the percentile rank for the interval 35–39?   _54%_

3. What is the median?   _32_

4. The standard deviation of the distribution is approximately 19.5. About how many instances fall within one standard deviation on either side of the mean? = _61_

_29 or 32_

5. How many honor points were earned by a freshman who stood one standard deviation above the mean?

_57_

6. Had the distribution been normal, approximately how many freshmen would have fallen within one standard deviation on both sides of the mean?

_68_

7. Approximately what is the 10–90 interpercentile range?   _48_   _52_

8. Describe the distribution (*i.e.*, "approximately normal," "positively skewed," etc).

bimodal

9. Which of the following statements are *probably true* of the distribution? (1) Some factor other than chance entered into the selection of the cases included. (2) The character of the distribution is mainly due to the small number of instances. (3) The group included within the distribution is in effect two groups in one. (4) The group is heterogeneous. (5) The group would be easy to teach. (6) The group does not have a well-defined central core.

1, 3, 6

10. Suppose you plan to enter Wysacki. You make the following assumptions: (a) the frequency table you found accurately represents the performance of all Wysacki freshmen during the semester covered; (b) the distribution is an accurate prediction of the performance of future Wysacki freshmen; (c) you have no knowledge of how you will compare with Wysacki freshmen. On the basis of these assumptions, what is the probability that you will earn not less than twenty nor more than twenty-four honor points?

16/100

11. Which assumptions in the item above are hazardous?

a, b

12. Suppose you know that the rules require a freshman to earn at least thirty honor points to be initiated into a fraternity, and you learn that Smythe was initiated at the end of his first semester. Assuming that Smythe is included in the above distribution, what is the probability that Smythe earned at least forty honor points?

46/100

13–17. *These items concern the three curves shown below.*

| Curve A | Curve B | Curve C |

13. Describe Curve A.   *neg. skewed*

14. Describe Curve B.   *pos. skewed*

15. Describe Curve C.   *normal*

16. In which of the three curves would there be the greatest difference between range and 10–90 interpercentile range?

A

17. How could Curves A, B, and C be used to deceive?

11 Forming Causal Theories

We turn now to perhaps the most important of inductive techniques. People in all walks of life constantly search for the causes of phenomena in order to understand and control their physical and social environment and to repeat desirable experiences and avoid undesirable ones. The student who makes an unexpectedly high grade on a test tries to find the cause, and his professor tries to learn what teaching techniques help students learn more effectively. A thinking citizen tries to learn what causes his community or nation to be a good or a bad place to live in so he can preserve the good qualities and eliminate the bad ones. The social scientist tries to discover the causes of "good" and "bad" social phenomena.

The importance, the problems, and the methods of finding causes are nowhere better illustrated than in the history of medicine. Doctors and patients have searched for the causes of aches and pains, illnesses, disease, aging, and death in order to prevent or at least postpone them. In medicine, as in other sciences, progress was slow until the attitudes and procedures (known collectively as the scientific method) were developed and applied. It was not until the early seventeenth century that William Harvey discovered the circulation of the blood. Since then, physi-

cians and scientists have been adding illustrious chapters to medical history at an ever-increasing rate.

The achievements of medicine, as well as those of other sciences, seem even more notable when we consider the difficulties of finding causes. The very concept of causation is complex and elusive. A given phenomenon such as malaria may have many causes. The cause you select will depend on your point of view and your purpose. The laboratory technician may claim that malaria is caused by the presence of certain parasites in the blood, while the public health officer may insist that malaria is caused by the bite of anopheles mosquitoes. An epidemiologist might attribute malaria to anopheles mosquitoes that bite persons infected with malaria and then transmit the parasites by biting other people. A sanitation engineer might blame bad drainage that leaves pools of stagnant water in which the mosquitoes breed. A climatologist might point to heavy rainfall that provides the water. A social scientist might blame the lack of a social conscience in a community that permits the mosquitoes to thrive. An educator might point to the ignorance of the community. An economist might blame the lack of economic resources needed to rid the community of breeding places for the mosquitoes. Each point of view is at least partially correct, for malaria has been eliminated in many regions by simultaneous attacks on most of these causes.

The cause of a *single event* may be found by procedures we have already discussed. Scraggs found the cause of the crash of Flight 629 by forming and testing hypotheses. If the symptoms of a disease are known, your doctor may diagnose your ailment by a relatively simple deductive inference. If he finds that you have a certain pattern of symptoms and that this pattern is caused only by a certain disease, he can validly infer that you have the disease. The relationships between symptoms and diseases are not always this direct, however, and he may have to use a combination of generalization, hypothesis, and deductive inference. He may start with a generalization, previously made by medical researchers, that certain symptoms are caused by any one of a number of diseases. Each of these diseases then becomes a rival hypothesis. He may eliminate all but one of the rivals by deductive inferences made from laboratory tests.

When we are searching for the causes of *multiple instances* of a phenomenon, such as malaria, cancer, automobile accidents, aging, economic depressions, poverty, or riots, we enter a new realm we refer to as *causal theory*. Causal theory is the most treacherous of all forms of inquiry. Consider the causal theory that malaria is caused by parasites transmitted by the bites of anopheles mosquitoes. Forming this causal theory required two kinds of inductive leap. One was a generalization: All people with malaria have been bitten by anopheles mosquitoes that had previously bitten people with malaria parasites in their blood. The second leap was a special kind of hypothesis: These mosquito bites cause malaria. The hypothesis is a long leap in the dark. Millions of people have scratched billions of mosquito bites, but no one has ever actually seen malaria parasites pass from the bloodstream

of one person into the mosquito and then to the bloodstream of another person. Inferences involving a long leap in the dark need not frighten us if we follow certain procedures. A high quality of both creative and critical thinking will be required, but the rewards are commensurate with the task.

The problems and procedures of causal inquiry are illustrated by a tragic and yet significant chapter in the history of medical research. In 1940, Dr. Theodore Terry, Assistant Professor of Ophthalmology at the Harvard Medical School, examined a baby who was going blind. The immediate cause of the blindness appeared to be a grayish white membrane in the eyes. Dr. Terry had never seen any condition like this, nor was there any mention of it in medical literature. He soon recognized his problem — a new and terrible disease. Within a year five more babies afflicted with this new disease were referred to him. Long and painstaking study under a high-powered microscope revealed the nature of the white membrane in the babies' eyes: the retina was completely detached and restricted; the fibrous strands were matted into a thick, tangled mass. Dr. Terry gave the disease a formidable name — retrolental fibroplasia. Meanwhile hundreds of cases had been reported in the United States and Europe. Dr. Terry and many others dedicated themselves to the problem of stopping the scourge. But first they had to find the cause.

1. Finding Common Factors

We have noted that the kind of information we should search for in Phase 2 varies with the problem. When we are using hypotheses to solve a problem, we seek different facts or observations that can be fitted together into a hypothesis. When we are using generalizations, we seek observations or instances of the same kind. When the problem is to find the cause of multiple instances of a phenomenon, the objective of Phase 2 is to discover the common factors —

i.e., similarities in the instances in which the phenomenon has occurred, or common differences between the instances in which the phenomenon has occurred and those in which it has not occurred, or both. The search for common factors should include those that changed before the appearance of the phenomenon.

When nothing is known about the cause or causes of a phenomenon, Phase 2 must begin with the assembly of information about instances of the phenomenon, unguided by causal theories. When the number of instances is great, it is usually wise to begin with a study of a relatively small sample. Otherwise much effort may be wasted in a fruitless analysis of large quantities of information. Presumably Dr. Terry used as his sample the six cases of retrolental fibroplasia (later called "RLF") that had been referred to him and made an intensive study of the case histories, searching for common factors. The first common factor he found is described in the proposition below.

1. All six babies afflicted with RLF were born prematurely.

2. Types of Causal Theories

In searching for causes we can begin Phase 3 as soon as a common factor is discovered. Proposition 1 above provides enough information to begin Phase 3 by forming a tentative conclusion. When we are seeking the cause of multiple instances of a phenomenon, the tentative conclusions formed are *causal theories*. On the basis of the common antecedents described in Proposition 1, we might form the following causal theory.

A. RLF is caused by premature birth.

Note that this causal theory is like a hypothesis in that it involves an inductive leap from the fact that all six cases of RLF observed were premature babies to a tentative con-clusion that prematurity is the cause of RLF. Note also that Causal Theory A is like a generalization in that it involves the infer-ence that what is true of the six cases so far observed is true of cases not yet observed. It is important to note that with causal theories, as with hypotheses and generaliza-tions, the five-phase cycle should not be used rigidly. As soon as a common factor is dis-covered, a causal theory should be formed about it. Meanwhile the search for other common antecedents should continue.

Causal theories may involve four different relationships between cause and effect.

1. *Necessary Cause.* A necessary cause is a condition that must be present if the effect is to occur. Electricity is a necessary cause of light in a bulb, for the light will not occur without the electricity. In other words, *if A is a necessary cause of B, then B will not occur without A.*

2. *Sufficient Cause.* A sufficient cause is any condition that will bring about the event alone and by itself. If A is a *sufficient* cause of B, *then B will always occur when A oc-curs.* A blown fuse is a *sufficient* cause for the light to go out, for the light will go out whenever the fuse blows. But a blown fuse is not a *necessary* cause for the darkness, since the light will go out for other reasons. The bulb might burn out or the current go off.

3. *Necessary and Sufficient Cause.* A necessary and sufficient cause is any condi-tion that will bring about the event alone and of itself, and without which the event cannot occur. If A is a necessary and sufficient cause of B, then B will occur *when and only when A occurs.* Necessary and sufficient causes are rare. One may be tempted to say, "If and only if the current is turned on will the lights burn"; but other conditions are also necessary, such as the correct voltage for the bulbs, satisfactory wiring, and bulbs in working order.

4. *Contributory Cause.* A contributory cause is a factor that helps to create the total set of conditions necessary or sufficient

for an effect. Exposure is thought to be a contributory cause of the common cold in that it helps create the conditions which cause the cold, but we can have a cold with or without exposure. If A is a contributory cause of B, then *B is more likely to occur when A occurs than when A does not occur.* The contributory cause is more often a problem than either the sufficient or the necessary cause. An error we frequently make is to search for too simple a cause. Many times the real cause is a combination of contributory causes.

3. Guidelines for Causal Theories

Three guidelines should be followed in forming causal theories.

1. *At least in the early stages of an investigation, the statement of a causal theory should contain the words "or connected with."* Causal Theory A, for example, should be revised as shown below.

> A–1. Premature birth, *or something connected with it,* is the cause of RLF.

Adding these words to the statement of the causal theory has two advantages. First, they stimulate creative thinking. Without such a qualifier we are more likely to discard the causal theory as false beyond reasonable doubt instead of searching for common factors connected with premature birth. Second, these qualifying words help to protect us from accepting a false causal theory. For example, a comparison of the death rates of people admitted to hospitals and people not admitted might look like good evidence for the causal theory that being admitted to a hospital is a contributory cause of death — if we fail to realize that many people are already seriously ill when admitted.

2. *The statement of the causal theory should indicate the type of causal relationship.* For example, Causal Theory A–1 is shown below, revised to indicate a specific type of causal relationship.

> A–2. Premature birth, or something connected with it, is a *necessary* cause of RLF.

Stating the type of cause involved clearly indicates the type of testing required.

There is a small advantage in beginning with a necessary or a sufficient relationship. If we begin with the weakest relationship, the contributory cause, we may overlook the possible existence of a stronger relationship. Necessary and sufficient causal theories will often fail to stand up under testing, but they can easily be revised. For example, if we find a baby with RLF who was not born prematurely, we can easily revise Causal Theory A–2 by limiting it to the contributory relationship.

3. *Causal theories should be formed for all possibly relevant common factors.* Failure to do so can be as costly as failure to form hypotheses. For example, Dr. Terry noticed another common antecedent in his first six cases of RLF.

> 2. All six babies had been born in modern, well-equipped hospitals.

Was this common antecedent relevant? Dr. Terry had no way of knowing at first. It was entirely possible that it was the result of a loaded sample, since his cases normally came from modern, well-equipped hospitals. Even so, sound procedures required the forming and testing of causal theories involving hospitals. Even when a causal theory proves to be entirely false, the process of testing it often uncovers clues that lead to the true cause. In short, when a common antecedent has any possibility of being relevant, a causal theory should be formed and tested. Failure to do so may prove costly.

4. Preliminary Testing

Preliminary testing of causal theories should begin as soon as practicable, for, as with hypotheses, testing a causal theory often adds new and significant information. The principles of priority in testing hypotheses discussed in Chapter 5 apply to causal theories too. For example, the causal theory about RLF that probably should have had (and was actually given) the highest priority in testing is shown below.

B. Being born in a modern, well-equipped hospital, or something connected with it, is a contributory cause of RLF.

By 1941 the toll from RLF had risen to several hundred cases a year. If RLF was in some way connected with modern, well-equipped hospitals, it would seem likely that the cause could be discovered and eliminated. Thus on the principle of urgency, Causal Theory B should have been tested first. While the cost of testing a causal theory is sometimes unpredictable, Causal Theory B was a likely candidate for priority on the principle of economy too. The comparison of a fairly large sample of babies born in modern, well-equipped hospitals and those born under other conditions would not have been expensive relative to the importance of stopping the disease. Causal Theory B was also a good candidate for priority in testing on the principle of bias, for doctors could hardly be expected to take pleasure in discovering that modern hospitals could be a causal factor in a terrible scourge.

5. Controls

Two basic procedures for testing causal theories are in use today. One of these involves experiments in which relevant factors are controlled as far as practicable. If we wanted to test the effectiveness of a certain gasoline additive in prolonging engine life, we would set up an experiment in which two engines were run under carefully controlled conditions so that the only difference in their operation was the presence or absence of the additive in the gasoline used. At least one other test should be run to eliminate the possibility that the difference in the

life of the two engines was due to the engines themselves rather than to the additive. Even then, an additional test should be arranged involving cars run on the road under normal conditions.

In dealing with human beings, since laboratory conditions are impossible, the usual procedure is to divide the subjects into two groups. One group, called the *experimental* group, is given the medicine, or coffee, or cake, or whatever is being tested. The other group, called the *control* group, is given a *placebo,* a harmless and inert substance that looks like whatever is being tested. All other relevant conditions are kept as nearly the same as possible for both groups. A test of antihistamines would be of little value if our experimental group were to include only workers in a factory and the control group only people outside the factory. If the factory group were shown to suffer less from allergic reactions than the outsiders, it might be because of the air conditioning in the factory rather than because of the antihistamines. Such a procedure would not control all important relevant factors.

In testing for causation with human beings it is extremely important to control psychological factors. Suppose we are testing a new formula to determine whether it will help to prevent the common cold. If we give the medicine to the experimental group, telling them that it will prevent colds, and give nothing to the control group, we have not controlled an important psychological factor — the experimental group know that they got the formula, and the control group that they did not. Experience has shown that under such conditions the experimental group is likely to report significant reduction in the number, duration, and severity of colds even when the formula contains nothing more powerful than sterile sawdust. For most of us would like to believe that three capsules of something a day would help ward off common colds, and we need less evidence for what we want to believe.

The usual method for controlling psychological factors in such situations is to give the control group a placebo and to administer placebo and formula under identical conditions so that no individual can know which he took.

Since it is seldom possible to control all relevant factors in human beings, it is desirable to run the test with a large sample of individuals, on the assumption that with a large group chance tends to equalize factors that cannot be controlled.

When the medicine or object being tested is intended for diverse groups of people, the sample should obviously be diverse. If we were testing a certain food substance to see whether it increased energy, and we tested it only with postmen, we could not conclude without further testing that it would also increase the energy of college athletes. For we would not have controlled such relevant factors as diet, age, and training. Thus we should be careful in extending conclusions about causal connections to groups not included within the sample tested.

The technique of controls should be applied as far as possible when you try to test any theory of causation about yourself. Suppose you are trying to determine whether caffeine keeps you awake. The truth about caffeine seems to be that its effect varies widely with different individuals. The problem, therefore, is to determine its effect on you. It will not suffice to drink coffee every other night, for this will not control the psychological factors. It will be necessary to devise a way to get coffee with caffeine some nights and without caffeine other nights, without knowing which is which. One method would be to buy jars of the instant types and get someone to remove the labels but identify the jars by symbols known only to himself. You could find out what the symbols meant after you had recorded the results. To get a reliable test, it would be necessary to record a large number of instances in order to offset factors you cannot control, such as diet, emotion, and fatigue.

6. Statistical Procedures

The other basic procedure for testing causal theories is statistical. Statistical procedures are necessary whenever it is impossible to establish satisfactory controls. Statistical procedures are widely used in studies of cause and effect in education. Suppose we wished to learn what causal relationship, if any, exists between studying calculus in college and success in medical school. It would not be practical to work with an experimental group of premedical students who study calculus and a control group who do not. Such an experiment would take too long, and there would be too many uncontrolled variables.

A more practical procedure would be to analyze a sample selected to include dropouts as well as graduates. A relatively large sample should be used in order to offset the fact that it is impossible to control all of the possibly relevant factors. Some criteria would have to be adopted for determining success in medical school, such as grades or the percentages of those graduating. If grades are used as the criterion, measures of central tendency could be computed for those who studied calculus and for those who did not. A comparison of these measures would yield evidence — though not necessarily conclusive — as to whether studying calculus is a contributory cause of success in medical school.

Causal relationships are not necessarily all-or-nothing, and we often need to know the degree of causal relationship between two variables. For example, when a new drug is discovered it is necessary to establish the correct dosage, for many drugs are beneficial in certain quantities and harmful in others. In testing the effects of gasoline additive on the performance of automobiles it is desirable to determine the effects of different amounts of the additive.

When we need to determine the degree of relationship between two or more variables, such as vocabulary and success, a statistical tool known as *correlation* can be extremely useful. Suppose our problem is to determine the degree of relationship between vocabulary and success. Our first step is to find a satisfactory method of measuring both success and vocabulary. Many satisfactory tests of vocabulary are available. To measure success we would have to set up criteria. Income could be one criterion, but we should use others as well, lest we come out with a correlation between vocabulary and income rather than vocabulary and success.

Our next step would be to select an adequate sample. It would not do to select a group of highly successful people with excellent vocabularies and another group of unsuccessful people with poor vocabularies, for our sample would be loaded in favor of a high degree of correlation. On the other hand, if we selected our sample purely at random, a very large sample would be required to provide sufficient range in the two variables to represent the true picture. Thus the most economical method of getting a reliable sample might be to take a stratified sample on the basis of one, but not both, of the variables. It would probably be easier to select a sample on the basis of success, stratified to represent typical vocations and grades of success.

With our sample selected, the next step would be to administer a vocabulary test to as many members of the sample as possible. If a significant number of the individuals in the sample refused to take the test, we should suspect our results of being loaded, on the ground that people with poor vocabularies would be more likely than others to refuse to take the test. In this event we should seek some method of persuading the reluctant ones.

With our data in hand, the next step is to determine the correlation between our variables. A practical method for doing so is to construct a *scatter diagram,* as shown in Figure 8. A study of the diagram will show

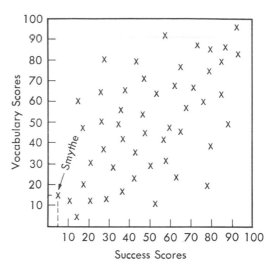

Fig. 8 Supposed Scatter Diagram Showing Moderate Positive Correlation

how it was constructed. The measures of vocabulary and success were arranged in intervals, as in a frequency table except that the number of instances in each interval is not shown. The same principles about the size and number of intervals apply. The x-marks represent the position of each individual with respect to both variables. For an illustration, look at the x-mark identified by the arrow, showing the standing of an individual named Smythe. Note that he is in the interval 0–10 on success and in the interval 10–20 on vocabulary.

The degree of relationship between the two variables shown in a scatter diagram is determined by how closely the x-marks cluster about a diagonal line on the scatter diagram. The degree of this relationship can be measured and expressed precisely by a number known as the *coefficient of correlation,* usually symbolized by the small letter r. A description of methods for doing this can be found in any standard text in statistics. The coefficient of correlation can be roughly estimated by inspecting the scatter diagram.

A *perfect positive* correlation, *i.e.,* one in

which each individual falls exactly on the diagonal running from lower left to upper right and the increases in one variable are directly proportional to increases in the other, is expressed as 1.

A *perfect negative* correlation, in which the relationship is perfect but in reverse, increases in one variable being directly proportional to decreases in the other, is expressed as −1.

Perfect correlations are rare, at least with data involving human beings; most correlations turn out to be fractions between −1 and 0 or between 0 and 1. The scatter diagram in Figure 8 shows a correlation of about .5. Actually the coefficient of correlation for vocabulary and success would vary according to how success is defined. A coefficient of about .5 (plus or minus) between any two variables suggests, but does not prove, that (1) there is a significant causal relationship between the variables, and (2) one variable is not the sole cause of the other.

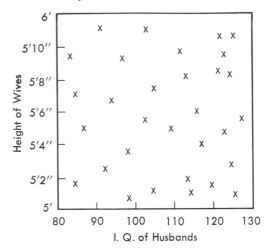

Fig. 10 Scatter Diagram Showing Negligible Correlation

The scatter diagram of Figure 10 shows little or no agreement between the variables. The coefficient is roughly 0.

As with hypotheses, it may be necessary to repeat the cycle many times before a causal theory of sufficient reliability is produced. Sometimes the obstacle is inadequate information in the frame of reference. For example, most of the achievements of medicine in controlling disease were impossible until bacteria and the circulation of the blood were discovered. When several repetitions of the cycle fail to produce a satisfactory causal theory, a general search for knowledge may be necessary. Another obstacle may be the complexity of the phenomena involved. Future discoveries in medicine will be easier because of the knowledge we have accumulated, and, at the same time, more difficult because of the complexity of this knowledge. Medical researchers will of necessity find increasing uses for statistical procedures and computers.

Procedures for judging the reliability of causal theories are discussed in the following chapter, in which the story of RLF is concluded.

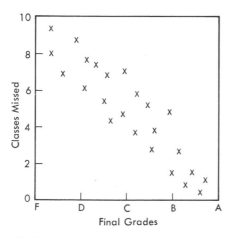

Fig. 9 Scatter Diagram Showing High Negative Correlation

The scatter diagram of Figure 9 shows a coefficient of about −.9. There is strong agreement between the variables, but it is negative.

EXERCISE 11

To preserve the learning value of this exercise, complete each item before reading beyond it.

You are a member of a Peace Corps team stationed at Ambogulia, a remote hamlet in Congolia. Each Saturday morning you go by boat to Corps headquarters at Bungolia, the capital city, and return to Ambogulia Sunday afternoon. On Sunday evening the native chief entertains your team at dinner.

1. On the Sunday night following your first trip to Bungolia you are awakened by a violent attack of coughing and wheezing. You have to sit up the rest of the night in order to breathe. You have never had these symptoms before, but you remember reading in a medical book that coughing and wheezing are symptoms of bronchial asthma. You form the tentative conclusion that you had an attack of bronchial asthma. Is your tentative conclusion (1) a causal theory, (2) a hypothesis, (3) a generalization, or (4) the product of a deductive inference?

_____4_____

2. On the second Sunday night you suffer another attack. You remember reading that bronchial asthma is believed to result from the inhalation or ingestion of certain substances termed *allergens* to which the patient is sensitive. Have you remembered (1) a generalization, (2) a hypothesis, or (3) a causal theory?

_____3_____

3. You define your problem as finding the allergen or allergens causing your asthma. Using only the data given above, list the common factors that may be relevant.

visited same place; chief's entertainment boat ride

4. Write an appropriate causal theory based on the observation that both of your attacks came shortly after dining with the chief.

Dining with chief or something connected with it, is a (sufficient) cause of his attacks

5. On the third Sunday evening you dine with the chief as usual, but you do not have an attack of asthma. Rate the reliability of the theory that dining with the chief is a sufficient cause of your asthma.

improbable

6. Revise the causal theory you wrote for Item 4 to conform to the evidence stated in Item 5.

it is a contributory cause

7. Devise a procedure for testing this revised causal theory.

statistical study of what was eaten

8. On the fourth Sunday night you have a violent attack of asthma following your usual dinner with the chief. Since you must sit up to breathe anyway, you prepare the following table showing as much as you can remember about what you ate or drank on the four previous Sunday nights.

Date	Foods and Beverages	Symptoms
1st Sunday	Rice, boiled lobster, quemolia	Severe
2nd Sunday	Rice, broiled crabs, quemolia	Severe
3rd Sunday	Yams, oysters, water	None
4th Sunday	Rice, fried shrimp, quemolia	Severe

List three common foods and beverages in your table.

(1) rice   (2) seafood   (3) quemolia

9. Which of these are possible necessary causes?   all 3

10. Which are possible sufficient causes?   rice, quemolia

11. On the fifth Sunday evening you drink quemolia (the native fermented beverage) and eat only yams and oysters. That night you have a severe attack. What substance can be eliminated as a necessary cause?   rice

12. On the sixth Sunday evening you eat yams and oysters, and drink only water. That night you sleep peacefully. On the basis of your evidence in hand, which substance is most likely to be the offending allergen?   quemolia

13. Considering the evidence in hand and following the guidelines stated in this chapter, fill in the blanks in this causal theory.

Drinking quemolia is a sufficient cause of my asthma.

14. On the next five Sunday nights you eat nothing but yams and oysters and vary the amount of quemolia you drink. You obtain the data below.

Date	Ounces of Quemolia	Hours Kept Awake by Asthma
7th Sunday	0	0
8th Sunday	3	1
9th Sunday	6	2
10th Sunday	9	4
11th Sunday	12	8

On a separate sheet of paper, construct a scatter diagram for the data.

15. Describe the correlation shown in this scatter diagram (high positive, low negative, etc.).

positive

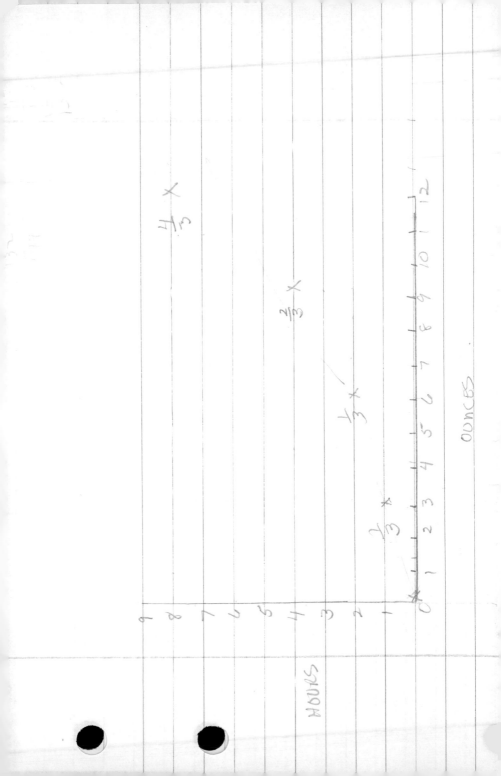

12 Testing Causal Theories

Throughout this book we have emphasized the importance of both creative and critical thinking. If we are not imaginative in forming tentative conclusions, we may miss the truth; if we do not carefully test and evaluate conclusions before accepting them, we may accept falsehood. We should be quick to form tentative generalizations but slow to accept them as truth. The same point and counterpoint are true of causal theory. If we are not quick to notice common factors and form causal theories about them, we may fail to discover the cause. But if we accept causal theories as truth without completing Phase 4, we may be inviting disaster by committing the *post hoc* fallacy.

1. The Post Hoc Fallacy

The name of the *post hoc* fallacy is derived from the Latin expression, *post hoc, ergo propter hoc* (after this, therefore because of this). We commit this fallacy whenever we conclude that one event or condition causes another solely on the ground of temporal priority. The *post hoc* fallacy may be the most expensive of all errors in reasoning. It costs the human race untold amounts of time, money, and discomfort.

The *post hoc* fallacy is the origin of many superstitions. Suppose a superstitious baseball player has been in a batting slump. Then suddenly he breaks out of the slump by hitting two home runs in one game. He would be less than human if he did not want to know the cause of his success so that he could repeat it. He therefore thinks back over the hours since the last game, in which he struck out three times, looking for some factor that was different. He is likely to pounce on the first event or condition he thinks is different and ascribe to it the cause of his two home runs. The different factor could be anything he remembers, such as entering the field through a different gate. The logical fallacy is that the only ground he has for attributing his success to entering a different gate is that this event preceded the home runs. Yet there were probably many other factors with as good or better claim to be the cause of his success. Perhaps something in his personal life that had been causing anxiety had changed for the better. Perhaps he had a relaxing evening and a good night's sleep before his good game. Or perhaps the pitcher was having a bad day.

Subjective factors often lead us into the *post hoc* fallacy. Suppose I have a very bad cold. I see a commercial on television claiming that "Coldstop" tablets will relieve the discomfort of a cold and subtly suggesting that these tablets will cure a cold. Although I have read many times that the medical profession has not found a cure for colds, I am ready to try anything. So I take the cold tablets as directed. Subjective factors will encourage me in committing the *post hoc* fallacy. Since I have disregarded the advice of the medical profession, I would like to believe that I am not a fool. I am therefore likely to think my cold is better the next day, whether it is or not, and to attribute the real or imagined improvement to the pills. Subjective factors, together with the *post hoc* fallacy, may be said to keep medical quacks in business.

The *post hoc* fallacy is responsible for much of the distortion in our frames of reference. Suppose Mr. Smythe has had a hard day at the office. When he reaches home his nerves are frayed and he craves a few minutes of peace and comfort. But his son Joe, aged five, has been lonesome all day and yearns for his father's attention. Joe's efforts to get his father's attention could easily lead to a severe scolding. Joe is then likely to blame the scolding entirely on his own behavior. Especially if the incident is repeated later, it is only natural for Joe to conclude that seeking his father's attention causes scolding. Unable to get attention at home, Joe may try to get it at school and get scolded again. It would be natural for him to compound his error by concluding that seeking attention causes scolding. Joe may retain this false conclusion in his frame of reference long after he has forgotten the incidents that led to it. He may also derive a value judgment from this fallacy: seeking attention is bad.

The *post hoc* fallacy is responsible for many false causal theories. Suppose you do unusually well on a test and then examine your procedures in retrospect to find the factor that was different. And suppose you recall that on the night before this test you went to a movie, whereas usually you studied for tests until very late in the evening. If, with no other evidence, you conclude that going to a movie causes better performance on tests, you have committed the *post hoc*

fallacy. Even on this slender evidence there is nothing wrong with forming a tentative conclusion that going to a movie the night before is a contributory cause of better performance on tests, for this is creative thinking. But if you skip Phase 4 and accept this causal theory as truth, you are guilty of the *post hoc* fallacy.

2. Sources of Doubt

In the preceding chapter we emphasized the use of Phase 4 as a tool for revising causal theories. Let us now consider its use in judging the reliability of causal theories.

Suppose we are testing the causal theory that the use of a dentifrice containing fluorides reduces cavities. Our first task is to *demonstrate that there is a relationship between the phenomenon* (the reduction of cavities) *and the alleged cause* (the use of a dentifrice containing fluorides). We might begin by asking volunteers among Wysacki students to use the dentifrice for a year, according to directions. If these students have significantly fewer cavities this year than previous years, we have demonstrated a relationship between the phenomenon and the alleged cause for *these* students. If we conclude from this evidence that there is a relationship between the phenomenon and the alleged cause for the whole population, we have committed a hasty generalization, for our sample is limited to a single age and occupational group. No such relationship might exist for children, farmers, or astronauts.

Even if we succeed in demonstrating beyond a shadow of doubt that this relationship exists for the entire population, we must still *demonstrate that the relationship is causal.* It is still possible that the real cause of the reduction in cavities was something *connected with* the use of the fluorides rather than the fluorides *per se.* People who deliberately use a toothpaste containing fluorides to reduce cavities may do many other things in connection with the dentifrice, such as more conscientious and regular brushing of teeth, eating less candy, seeing their dentists more often, and so on.

The kind and amount of evidence necessary to demonstrate that the relationship is causal are different for each type of causal relationship. Suppose a carefully controlled experiment with an adequate sample shows that the experimental group (which used a dentifrice containing fluorides, according to directions) had significantly fewer cavities than the control group (who used the same dentifrice without the fluorides). We would be justified in giving a high degree of reliability to the causal theory that the use of a dentifrice containing fluorides is a contributory cause of the reduction in cavities. But on this evidence alone, the reliability of the theory that the use of fluorides is a necessary cause of the reduction in cavities would be very low. There may be many other and better ways of reducing or even eliminating cavities.

In short, to judge the reliability of a causal theory we must judge the degree to which the evidence in hand has eliminated doubts that (1) the relationship between the alleged phenomenon and the alleged cause does indeed exist, and (2) this relationship is the particular type of causal relationship alleged to exist.

3. Types of Evidence

These doubts are reduced by four kinds of evidence.

1. *Agreement.* One kind is derived from John Stuart Mill's classic method of agreement: "If two or more instances of the phenomenon under investigation have *only one circumstance in common,* the circumstance in which alone all the instances agree is the cause (or effect) of the given phenomenon."[1]

[1] John Stuart Mill, *Philosophy of Scientific Method* (New York: Hafner, 1950), p. 214.

The essence of Mill's method of agreement is the *elimination of all except one common antecedent.* A partial analysis of Dr. Terry's first six cases might have revealed the data below.

Case	RLF	Birth	Hospital	Diet
1	Yes	Premature	A	Formula 1
2	Yes	Premature	B	Formula 2
3	Yes	Premature	C	Formula 3
4	Yes	Premature	D	Formula 4
5	Yes	Premature	E	Formula 5
6	Yes	Premature	F	Formula 6

Superficially, the above data seem to meet Mill's rule, for we have two or more cases of the phenomenon under investigation (RLF) and all these instances seem to have only one circumstance in common, premature birth. Actually, this evidence fails to satisfy Mill's rule in two important respects. First, the data suggest two additional common factors: although each baby was born in a different hospital, hospitals have many similarities in procedures and equipment; also, though each baby received a different diet, it is likely that all six formulas had common elements. Second, the data may not include all possibly relevant factors; a more thorough study might reveal many other common antecedents that have not been eliminated. Mill's rule is based on the assumption that the analysis of common antecedents is exhaustive, an assumption rarely true except in closed systems of thought.

In practical situations we can rarely demonstrate that there is only one possibly relevant common factor in an adequate sample of instances of a phenomenon. We cannot be sure that there are no undiscovered common factors even in the relatively few situations where we can find only one. For practical purposes, therefore, let us define *agreement* as the existence of a common factor in at least two instances of a phenomenon. Let us never forget, however, that this form of evidence has little significance when the number of instances is small or when there is more than one common factor.

2. *Difference.* Another type of evidence is derived from Mill's rule of *difference:* "If an instance in which the phenomenon under investigation occurs, and an instance in which it does not occur, have every circumstance in common save one, that one occurring only in the former; the circumstance in which alone the two instances differ is the effect, or the cause, or an indispensable part of the cause, of the phenomenon."[2] Note that Mill's rule of difference requires a comparison of at least one case in which the phenomenon occurred with at least one in which it did not occur. Note further that the essence of the rule is the *elimination of all except one difference* between instances in which the phenomenon occurred and those in which it did not.

In 1941, when the incidence of RLF increased alarmingly, the following data might have been extracted from Dr. Terry's files.

Case	RLF	Birth	Place of Birth
1	Yes	Premature	Hospital A
2	Yes	Premature	Hospital B
3	Yes	Premature	Hospital C
7	No	Premature	Home
8	No	Premature	Home
9	No	Premature	Home

Superficially, the data above seem to prove by Mill's rule that being born in a hospital is the cause, or an indispensable part of the cause, of RLF. For the data show that Cases 1, 2, and 3, in which RLF occurred, differ from Cases 7, 8, and 9, in which RLF did not occur, only in the place of birth. Actually, the data do not satisfy Mill's rule because the rule is based on the assumption that the analysis has been exhaustive, and this one has not been. A more thorough analysis of the cases listed would reveal other differences between cases in which RLF did and did not occur.

It is difficult enough to satisfy the require-

ments of this rule even in laboratory experiments, for there is always the danger that we have not controlled all possibly relevant factors. For practical purposes, therefore, let us define *difference* as a factor that is present in instances in which the phenomenon has occurred and absent when the phenomenon has not occurred. And let us never forget that this form of evidence has little significance when the number of instances is small or there is more than one difference.

3. *Correlation.* A third type of evidence is the degree of *correlation*. It is derived from another of Mill's rules, known as the canon of *concomitant variations:* "Whatever phenomenon varies in any manner whenever another phenomenon varies in some particular manner is either a cause or an effect of that phenomenon, or it is connected with it through some fact of causation."[3]

By 1945 RLF had become the leading cause of blindness among children in the United States. Dr. Terry had died of coronary thrombosis, presumably a casualty in the fight against RLF, and the research he started had been taken over by a committee. A statistical study showed that all victims of the disease so far observed were infants only a few months old. All or nearly all of them were premature. In some hospitals there were no cases of RLF among premature babies, thus eliminating hospital birth as a sufficient cause. In other hospitals 20 per cent of the premature babies developed RLF to some degree. A scatter diagram of data extracted from this statistical study might have looked like the one on page 119.

Superficially this correlation seems to meet Mill's rule, for it shows a variation between two phenomena, the incidence of RLF and the number of days babies were kept in an incubator. But note that Mill's rule contains the word *whenever*. The fact that this scatter diagram shows a concomitant variation does

---

[2] Mill, *op. cit.*, p. 216.

[3] *Ibid.*, p. 227.

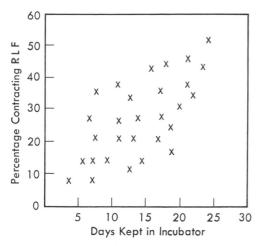

not prove that the incidence of RLF will vary *whenever* the number of days in an incubator varies. Another scatter diagram prepared for another group of babies might show no correlation at all, or even a negative one. Many a medical researcher has been encouraged by a positive correlation only to have the correlation disappear or even reverse itself in later experiments.

Furthermore, a correlation between two variables does not show which causes which. A positive correlation between grades in calculus and success in medical school would not prove that success in calculus causes success in medical school. It might be that success in medical school causes success in calculus, or both might be caused by some other factor.

Finally, even when the sample is adequate, a significant correlation shows only that there is a relationship between the two variables. The relationship may or may not be causal. The scatter diagram above shows only that there may be a relationship between the incidence of RLF and the number of days in an incubator. The real cause may not be incubators *per se* but something connected with their use.

4. *Converging causal theories.* Converging propositions may support causal theories as well as hypotheses. Suppose the head physician at Wysacki has found that all thirty students who became ill with food poisoning ate banana cream pie at an off-campus café. A laboratory analysis of another of these pies showing that it contains organisms known to cause this particular kind of food poisoning, would converge strongly on the causal theory that eating the banana pie caused the illness of the thirty students. Note, however, that this evidence converges on rather than proves the causal theory. It is still possible that the organisms were not in the pies eaten by the students.

4. Criteria

As with other types of inductive inferences, there are no foolproof methods of assessing the reliability of causal theories. The judgment of the most careful investigator is influenced by his personal point of view. Insufficient or false information in his frame of reference may keep him from correctly interpreting the evidence. His self-concept and his values may induce him to favor one causal theory and resist another. Lack of skill in creative thinking may prevent his forming the one true causal theory. Individuals can therefore be expected to differ in their judgments of the reliability of causal theories. Careful attention to the following criteria will increase both your objectivity and your skill.

1. *Reliability of observations.* A causal theory is no more reliable than the observations on which it is based. Many promising causal theories have collapsed when subjected to rigorous testing that neutralized or eliminated bias in the observations.

2. *Representativeness of samples.* Since causal theories usually involve generalizations from cases observed to cases not observed, the evidence for causal theories should meet the requirements for sampling discussed in Chapter 7.

3. *Degree of correlation.* We should be particularly wary of causal theories based on low correlations computed from small

samples. Low correlations in small samples may be accidental, or the two variables may be fluctuating in response to a third variable. It is likely, for example, that a comparison of distance of place of birth from Cambodia and the incidence of RLF would have shown a low positive correlation. Even with an adequate sample a high degree of correlation between two variables proves only that a relationship exists between them — it does not prove that the relationship is causal. The high correlation between the incidence of RLF and the number of days kept in an incubator is not enough by itself to pin the blame on the incubators *per se,* but it is more than enough to suggest that other causal theories should be formed and tested for all factors connected with incubators. In order to exercise your talents for creative thinking, stop at this point and try to think of as many of these factors as you can.

Suppose one of the common factors you have thought of is that babies kept in incubators are given oxygen to help them breathe. Even though it seems unlikely that oxygen, which kept the babies alive, caused RLF, a causal theory to this effect should be formed and tested. Judging from what we now know about RLF, a study of case histories of premature babies kept in incubators would have yielded data like that in the scatter diagram below.

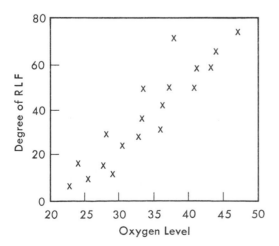

The high degree of correlation in this scatter diagram is sufficient to point an accusing finger at oxygen as a contributory cause of RLF. By itself, however, it is not enough to convict oxygen as the villain. It is still possible that higher levels of oxygen were administered to the babies having more trouble breathing and that whatever caused the trouble in breathing also caused the RLF.

4. *Adequacy of controls.* The closer we can come to establishing controls that eliminate all except one difference, the more likely it is that the factor that differs is a causal factor. In a controlled experiment in which the only variable was the oxygen factor, a high degree of correlation would have proved beyond reasonable doubt that oxygen is a contributory cause of RLF in premature babies. With human beings it is usually impossible to control all factors. Even if we could completely control physical conditions, subjective factors would vary.

Since subjective factors affect observers as well as observed, medical researchers frequently use "double-blind" experimental procedures. The technique is so called because both subjects and observers are "blind" in the sense that they do not know which subjects are in the experimental and which in the control group.

A classic example of the "double-blind" procedure was the experiment conducted in 1952 by the National Foundation for Infantile Paralysis to determine whether gamma globulin was of any value in preventing, or reducing the severity or damage of poliomyelitis. Houston, Texas, was selected for the experiment because a polio epidemic was in progress there. Since parents could not be compelled to have their children injected with the serum, the Foundation had to depend on volunteers. To reduce the possibility that the volunteers would constitute a loaded sample, the Foundation set out to test the serum with 35,000 children. The large sample reduced the probability that the volunteers constituted a loaded sample, and made it more likely that chance would equalize such possibly relevant factors as social and health conditions, which could not be controlled. To eliminate any possible psychological factors, both in children and parents, and in the doctors who would appraise the results, each child was injected with an individually numbered syringe. Half the syringes contained gamma globulin, and half contained a harmless and presumably ineffective gelatin. The syringe numbers were locked in the safe of the company which made the serum, so that no interested person could know which child was injected with which substance until the results were appraised and recorded.

In situations in which it is impossible to control all possibly relevant factors, a large and representative sample should be used, on the theory that the "laws" of probability will tend to compensate for the lack of adequate controls.

5. *Time factors.* You need not stick a pin into your finger many times to prove that sticking a pin into your finger causes pain, because the relationship between cause and effect is immediately obvious. The greater the time lapse between the occurrence of the alleged cause and the appearance of the phenomenon, the greater is the number of factors that might be causes. Proving that water you drank in Cuba caused your typhoid fever would be a different matter, because the symptoms might not appear for a month after you left. During this time you doubtless drank many beverages from many sources, and many of them must be suspect until tested. In general, then, the greater the lapse of time between cause and effect, the stronger the evidence must be.

6. *Thoroughness of the investigation.* The weakness in evidence from agreement is the difficulty of demonstrating that the instances in which the phenomenon under investigation has occurred have *only one* factor in common. Similarly, the weakness in evidence from difference is the difficulty of demonstrating that the instances in which the phenomenon did and did not occur are

different in *only one* respect. The weakness in evidence from concomitant variations is the difficulty of demonstrating that there are no other concomitant variations that would explain the phenomenon in question. Only by a thorough investigation can we eliminate reasonable doubt that there may be another common factor.

To conclude the story of RLF, enough evidence had accumulated by 1954 to satisfy all of the above criteria and demonstrate beyond reasonable doubt that premature birth and oxygen administered in excess of a certain level are causal factors. A large number of cases had been observed in hospitals all over the country. It was demonstrated in one large hospital that when oxygen was reduced below a certain level there was no lasting damage from RLF. Furthermore, some sixty other causal theories had been formed, tested, and discarded, thus reducing the likelihood that some other undiscovered common factor was the cause.

In retrospect it seems that the cause of RLF should have been discovered long before 1954. There was evidence from the beginning that oxygen was a causal factor since the appearance of the disease coincided with the introduction of the use of oxygen in the care of premature babies. Furthermore, several researchers called attention to oxygen as a common factor, though they did not suspect it of being a causal factor. Dr. Theodore H. Ingalls explains the difficulty by quoting Conan Doyle:

> The principal difficulty in the case, remarked Holmes in his didactic fashion, lay in the fact of there being too much evidence. What was vital was overlaid and hidden by what was irrelevant.[4]

It should be pointed out also that the people working on the problem did not have the benefit of hindsight. In terms of creative thinking, however, the procedures of think-

[4] For a history of RLF, see "The Strange Case of the Blind Babies," *The Scientific American*, Vol. 193, No. 20 (December, 1955), pp. 40–44.

ing used were not impeccable. Apparently some investigators settled on a single causal theory instead of forming several. Consequently they tended to become attached to a single theory. Furthermore, a guideline stated in Chapter 11 was not followed until late in the investigation: *causal theories should be formed and tested for all possibly relevant factors.*

Suggested Supplementary Reading

HAROLD A. LARRABEE, *Reliable Knowledge,* rev. ed. (Boston: Houghton Mifflin Company, 1964), Chapter 9.

BERTON ROUECHÉ, *Eleven Blue Men* (New York: Berkley Publishing Corporation, 1956). Stories of medical detection.

EXERCISE 12

For the full value of this exercise, complete each item before reading beyond it.

1–16. *These items continue the problem begun in Exercise 11.*

1. Consider the following causal theory in the light of all evidence accumulated in Exercise 11: Drinking quemolia is a sufficient cause of your asthma. With respect to which criteria is the evidence weak?

degree of correlation; thorough of investiga-tion

2. For which common factors have causal theories not yet been formed and tested?

trip by boat; environment of Bungolia

3. Rate the reliability of the causal theory above. *highly probable*

4. What type of evidence does the table in Exercise 11, Item 8, provide?

difference

5. Consider this causal theory: Something in the air you breathed on the boat trip to and from Bungolia is a contributory cause of your asthma. What type of evidence do you have for this theory?

agreement

6. With respect to what criteria is this evidence weak?

degree of correlation, thouroughness; controls

7. Rate the reliability of this theory. *improbable*

8. Devise a procedure for testing this theory more thoroughly.

observe foliage, etc., take a different route

9. On the twelfth Sunday the chief is away on a hunting trip and you limit your evening meal to American canned goods. That night you have a mild attack. What is the effect of this evidence on the causal theory stated in Item 5 above?

makes it more probable

10. You remember reading in a medical book that air-borne fungi and pollens are among the allergens that cause asthma. What type of evidence does this provide for the causal theory stated in Item 5 above?

converging causal theory

11. From all evidence in hand, rate the reliability of this causal theory: Something in the air in Ambogulia is a contributory cause of your asthma.

im probable

12. On the thirteenth Sunday night you have a violent attack. As you struggle to breathe you try to recall the possibly relevant differences between this and other weekends. You recall that on the boat trip back to Ambogulia you picked some exotic yellow flowers. If you conclude that the yellow flowers caused your asthma, what fallacy have you committed?

post hoc

13. If you warn your friends that picking these flowers will give them asthma, what additional fallacy have you committed? *hasty generalization*

superstition

14. You recall two other unusual factors: you spent Saturday night drinking American beer with friends, and you drank about seven ounces of quemolia on Sunday evening. Write the causal theory that best fits all of your evidence in hand.

all are contributary factors

15. Rate the reliability of this theory.

probable

16. What action should you take?

elimination

17. As the Wysacki track coach, you wish to test a new vitamin compound alleged to increase endurance. You decide to measure the endurance of your athletes in September by having them ride a machine that measures their output of energy, administer the vitamin compound during the season, and measure endurance again at the end of the season. Describe three of the controls you should use in your experiment.

1.) administer to some a fake compound
2.) try to control diet + training of all
3.) measure frequently (time lapse)

18. Suppose you first measure the energy your athletes are capable of exerting. Then you feed half of them the compound for a week, meantime trying to give all athletes the same diet and training. At the end of the week you again measure the energy they are capable of exerting. Which type of evidence are you using?

difference

13 Evaluation and Decision

1. *Deductive Decisions*

2. *Inductive Decisions*

3. *Proposals for Action*

4. *Predicting Consequences*

5. *Evaluating Consequences*

6. *Acting on Unreliable Conclusions*

Thus far we have concentrated on the first four phases of the decision-making cycle. Let us now turn our attention to Phase 5, Evaluation and Decision.

1. Deductive Decisions

Sometimes our only problem in Phase 5 is to decide whether to accept as fact any of the tentative conclusions formed in Phase 3 and tested for reliability in Phase 4. Sometimes this decision can be made by a simple deductive inference from this premise: *Tentative conclusions should never be accepted as fact until tested by the appropriate procedures and judged to be true beyond reasonable doubt.* This premise applies to *all* tentative conclusions, whether hypotheses, generalizations, causal theories, or deductive inferences. Most of us have violated this rule many times, with the result that our frames of reference include many false premises accepted as true when they are only untested tentative conclusions.

In most situations we must decide not only whether to believe our tentative conclusions but also what to do about them. Sometimes this latter decision also can be made by a relatively simple deductive inference. For example, in the trial of John Gilbert Graham,

the jury reached its verdict by deductive inference from premises provided by the law.[1]

2. Inductive Decisions

When we have no rule, policy, or law we can use as a premise for deductive decisions, Phase 5 requires the use of inductive techniques. Consider the problem the pediatrician in charge of a large hospital nursery might have faced in 1950. To help premature babies survive, he had been following the accepted practice of putting them into incubators and feeding oxygen into the air they breathed. He had been administering oxygen in proportion to prematurity, on the theory that the more premature the baby the greater the amount of oxygen required to sustain life. Fifty per cent of his babies had been afflicted with some degree of RLF, while hardly any RLF had occurred in a hospital nearby. Anxious to eliminate or at least reduce the toll in his hospital, he set out to discover how the treatment of premature babies in the two hospitals differed. He followed the procedures of effective thinking by forming and testing a number of causal theories, one of which was that the adminis-

[1] See p. 61.

125

tration of oxygen, or something connected with it, is a contributory cause of RLF. His testing of this theory justified accepting it as fact.

Note that so far our pediatrician has used the five-phase cycle only to interpret his problem situation. He now has a reliable causal theory, but he must still decide what to do about his premature babies. He could, as many of us do all too often, act on impulse and discontinue the use of oxygen altogether. But if he did, he would be violating a cardinal rule of effective thinking, as we shall see.

3. Proposals for Action

When we must decide what to do about a situation, and neither precedent nor policy gives us satisfactory premises, *the five-phase cycle should be used twice, once to interpret the situation and once to find the best course of action.* In using the cycle to find the best course of action, the phases need not be followed in rigid sequence, but each should be completed.

In this use of the cycle the tentative conclusions formed are *proposals for action.* Two proposals for action that our pediatrician might form are obvious.

   A. Continue using oxygen as before.
   B. Discontinue the use of oxygen altogether.

4. Predicting Consequences

Hypotheses, generalizations, and causal theories are tested for truth, but proposals for action are tested for consequences. In other words, *we test proposals for action by predicting their consequences.*

Our old friend the hypothetical proposition is perfectly suited to the purpose. The procedure consists of forming a hypothetical proposition by making the proposed action the antecedent and adding a consequent that states the *consequences, i.e.,* the advantages and disadvantages that will or may ensue.

Proposal for Action	*Advantages*	*Disadvantages*
A. Continue using oxygen as before	⊃ fewer will die	but 50 per cent *may* contract RLF.
B. Stop using oxygen	⊃ none *may* contract RLF	but more will die.

Three guidelines for adding consequents should be observed.

1. *When there is doubt that the predicted consequence will follow from the action, the consequent should be appropriately qualified.* Note that the consequents for Proposals A and B are qualified by *may.* Since our pediatrician believes that oxygen, or something connected with it, is only a contributory cause of RLF, he cannot be certain that 50 per cent of his babies will continue to contract RLF if he continues using oxygen as before, or that none will contract it if he stops using oxygen.

2. *Long-term as well as short-term consequences should be predicted.* Consider the mathematics professor who is debating whether to give a freshman a passing grade that he does not deserve. Obviously the short-term consequences would be pleasing to the student. But the long-term consequences may be quite different. A failing grade would probably force the student to repeat the course; a passing grade might permit him to take a more advanced course for which he is not prepared. Another possible long-term consequence of a passing grade is that the student might continue in a curriculum for which he is unsuited instead of finding a better one.

3. *Equal attention should be given to desirable and undesirable consequences.*

5. Evaluating Consequences

When the cycle is being used to find the best course of action, one objective of Phase 5 is to evaluate each proposal for action by weighing the predicted advantages against the disadvantages. When there is no reasonable doubt that the predicted consequences will follow, we need only weigh the predicted advantages and disadvantages of each proposal.

When there is some degree of doubt that the predicted consequences will follow, both advantages and disadvantages should be discounted according to our concepts of probability. Suppose a gambler makes this offer: you pay him twenty-five cents for one roll of a pair of dice; he will pay you five dollars if you roll two sixes, and nothing if you roll any other combination. If you accept his offer on the ground that your possible loss is twenty-five cents and your possible net gain is $4.75, you did not learn enough from the two chapters on probability. The advantage of accepting his offer should be discounted by multiplying the advantage (winning $4.75) by the probability that this result will happen ($\frac{1}{36}$). Thus the theoretical advantage is worth only about thirteen cents. Similarly the disadvantage (losing twenty-five cents) should be discounted by the probability that this will happen ($\frac{35}{36}$). Thus the theoretical disadvantage is the loss of twenty-four cents.

While in most situations the probabilities cannot be calculated so precisely, the principle applies nonetheless. Our pediatrician could base his probabilities on statistics compiled from his own hospital records. He already knows that 50 per cent of his premature babies contract RLF when given oxygen. Now suppose a study of his hospital records shows that before 1939, when the practice of administering oxygen to premature babies began, 40 per cent of the premature babies died, whereas when given oxygen only 20 per cent died. On the basis of his evidence in hand, the advantages of using oxygen as before include saving the lives of two hundred out of each thousand premature babies, and the disadvantages include causing RLF in four hundred babies (not counting the 20 per cent expected to die). The advantages of discontinuing the oxygen altogether would include preventing RLF in three hundred babies in each thousand (not counting the 40 per cent expected to die), while the disadvantages would include the death of an additional two hundred babies in each thousand. No pediatrician would evaluate either Proposal A or B as satisfactory.

When no proposal for action is evaluated as satisfactory, additional proposals should be formed. Usually the process of forming proposals and predicting their consequences will suggest new ones or revisions in those already formed. To exercise your creative thinking, stop reading for a moment and try to form a third proposal for action that would be better than either A or B.

At least one pediatrician found a better proposal for action. Dr. Thaddeus S. Szewczyk gradually reduced the oxygen level in the incubators of his premature babies, taking care to provide enough oxygen to sustain life. He reported in 1951 that he had observed no lasting damage from RLF after reducing oxygen levels below a certain percentage. Nor did he find permanent damage of any kind that could be ascribed to the reduction of oxygen.

6. Acting on Unreliable Conclusions

Ideally we should take no action until we are reasonably certain that we have accurately interpreted the situation. Often, however, the threat of decision by indecision forces us to take action before we can be sure what the situation is. In other words, we must act before we can be sure that the hypotheses, generalizations, and causal theories we have formed to interpret the situation are true.

Consider the case of Mary Smythe, who is typical of many students in this era of pressure to get into and graduate from college. Mary was the valedictorian of her graduating class in a small high school. She entered

Wysacki University with high hopes of making the dean's list. But at mid-term she received a warning from the dean's office that if her grades did not improve she would be put on probation at the end of the semester. Since this is a new situation for Mary, her first step in dealing with it should be to use the five-phase cycle to interpret her situation. In Phase 1 she should define her problem as *to discover the causes* of her unsatisfactory performance at Wysacki. In Phase 2 she should gather information relevant to her problem as defined in Phase 1. Let us suppose that the information she gathers includes the following propositions.

1. There are many high school valedictorians at Wysacki.
2. The premedical curriculum she is taking is especially difficult because of the explosion of knowledge in such subjects as chemistry and biology.
3. She is studying only twenty hours a week, which is well below average for Wysacki students.
4. Her College Board scores are below the average for Wysacki students.

These propositions contain sufficient information to enable Mary to move to Phase 3 and form hypotheses. The hypotheses she forms should include the two listed below.

A. Her aptitude for medicine is insufficient.
B. Though her aptitude is sufficient, she is not studying enough and her background and study skills are not adequate.

Since Hypotheses A and B are rivals, their combined probabilities cannot exceed one. Let us suppose that after testing them, Mary rates Hypothesis A to be probable and Hypothesis B to be improbable.

Having formed and tested hypotheses about the cause of her trouble, Mary should now use the five-phase cycle to decide what action to take. In Phase 2 of this use of the cycle she should gather information relevant to actions she might take. Essential information would include Wysacki's rules governing suspension, probation, and graduation. To complete this phase she should consult a counselor, who is likely to have information she could not secure herself. In Phase 3 the objective should be to form proposals for action. The more she forms the more likely she is to include a satisfactory one. Much human folly can be traced to a failure in creative thinking at this point. There is usually more than one way to solve a problem, and the first solution that comes to mind is not always the best.

If Mary had found a hypothesis about the cause of her poor grades that she could rate as true beyond reasonable doubt, she would need to form and evaluate proposals for action only in terms of this hypothesis. But she has two rival hypotheses about her grades, either of which could be true.

When we have two or more rival hypotheses, generalizations, or causal theories about the problem situation, proposals for action should be formed for each rival. Thus Mary should form proposals for action for both of her hypotheses.

Stated below are two of the many proposals for action she might form for Hypothesis A (Her aptitude for medicine is insufficient).

1. Change to a less rigorous curriculum next semester.
2. Marry a boy she met last week and withdraw from Wysacki.

She should also form proposals such as the two listed below for Hypothesis B (Though her aptitude is sufficient, she is not studying enough and her background and study skills are inadequate).

3. Drop out and work on her background and study skills.
4. Transfer to a less difficult college.

Mary could, of course, test one of the four proposals pragmatically by putting it into action and then evaluating the results. But pragmatic testing of proposals for action can be expensive in both treasure and suffering. She is far less likely to rue her decision if she carefully predicts and evaluates the consequences of each proposal.

Since Mary has two rival hypotheses about the cause of her problem, she must predict and evaluate the consequences for each. Shown below are some of the consequences she might predict for Proposal 2 that take into account both of her hypotheses.

Proposal for Action	*Consequences if A is True*
Marry a boy she met last week and withdraw from Wysacki $\supset$	avoid flunking out.
	risk unhappy marriage.
	risk possibly severe limitations on career.
	Consequences if B is true
	unnecessary loss of educational opportunity.
	risk unhappy marriage.

When we use this procedure we can often think of proposed actions whose probable consequences will be satisfactory for all tentative conclusions about the situation. For example, Mary Smythe might consider studying forty hours a week for the rest of the semester and employing a tutor to help her improve her study habits. This action would have advantages whichever hypothesis is true. If Hypothesis A is true, additional study should improve her grades, and better study habits will be valuable in any curriculum. If Hypothesis B is true, this action may solve her problem. Furthermore, this action should yield additional evidence about her two hypotheses. If her grades in chemistry and biology improve, she will have a converging fact for Hypothesis B. If they do not improve, she will have a converging fact for Hypothesis A, and she can then seriously consider changing to a less rigorous curriculum.

Note that Mary should be as objective as possible both in interpreting her situation and in predicting consequences of proposals for action. Her feelings about medicine or low grades are completely irrelevant, and she should not let them influence either her interpretation of her situation or her predictions of consequences. If, because her self-concept is threatened by poor grades or the prospect of failure in medicine, she deceives herself about her academic situation or the consequences of her actions, she may persist in a direction that will prove disastrous. But note also that her feelings are quite relevant in *evaluating* the predicted consequences of her actions — in fact, her feelings are an essential part of the evidence. If she deceives herself into believing that medicine is not important to her and shifts to a different curriculum, she may be making a disastrous decision.

Deciding whether to act on a proposal usually involves some kind of value judgment. If Mary Smythe places a high value on a career in medicine, the proposal that she study forty hours a week is probably a good one. If she places a high value on earning a college degree and if the kind of degree is relatively unimportant to her, then changing to a less rigorous curriculum could be her best action.

Many decisions involve *competing values*, *i.e.*, values that interfere with each other because our time, energy, and money are limited. The varsity football player who plans to study medicine may have a problem with competing values because football and his premedical studies compete for his time and energy, especially during the football season. If he is to be reasonably successful in both, he must budget his time and energy according to the relative demands of both activities. Decisions may also involve *conflicting values*, *i.e.*, values that are rivals in the sense that two hypotheses are rivals: if one is right the other is wrong. A cadet at the United States Air Force Academy might have a problem in conflicting values if he believes that it is wrong to inform on a fellow cadet under any circumstances and also believes in the Academy honor code: "We will not lie, steal, or cheat, nor tolerate among us anyone who does."

Procedures for resolving conflicts in values are discussed in Chapters 14 and 35. If you are tempted to conclude that the Academy code is too stringent, ask yourself whether you would wish your life to depend on an officer who does not adhere to it.

EXERCISE 13

1–10. *You are the commander of the Coast Guard station at Norfolk, Virginia. At 3:15 P.M. on February 7, you receive a telephone call from the president of Marine Tanker Lines saying that the* Marine Sulphur Queen *is overdue and unreported.*

1. Define your problem.

Where the ship is

Your routine questions elicit the following information from the president.

1. The *Queen* left Beaumont, Texas, at 8:00 A.M., February 2, with a cargo of molten sulphur.
2. The *Queen* carried a crew of thirty-nine.
3. The *Queen* was due to dock at Norfolk, Virginia, at noon, February 7.
4. The *Queen* carried a marine telephone and two high-frequency radio transmitters, all operated by separate sets of batteries.
5. The last radio message received from the *Queen* was a personal marine telephone call made by a crew member at 8:25 P.M. on February 3. The ship's position given at this time was 230 miles southeast of New Orleans.
6. Under normal procedure the *Queen* would have sent radio messages to Norfolk forty-eight hours and twenty-four hours before her estimated time of arrival at Norfolk. No such messages were received.
7. The *Queen* did not respond to radio calls sent by marine telephone stations in New Orleans, Miami, Jacksonville, Charleston, and Norfolk on February 7.

On the basis of the evidence now in hand, you form the following two hypotheses.

A. The *Queen's* delay is due to minor difficulties that can be corrected without assistance from the Coast Guard.
B. The *Queen* has had a disaster at sea.

2. Are these two hypotheses rivals?   *yes*

3. Rate the reliability of Hypothesis A.   *improbable*

4. Suppose you rate Hypothesis B as improbable. The regulations governing your performance in office state: "It is the duty of the commander of a Coast Guard station to take appropriate action when a boat or ship of any size is reported overdue, no matter how unlikely it is that the boat or ship is in trouble." You define your next problem to be to decide what action to take. Describe the reasoning used in deciding to redefine your problem. *deductive*

he is repeating cycle, having found out cause of problem

5. This proposal for action occurs to you: Order all available cutters and planes to launch an immediate search of the area from New Orleans to Norfolk. Predict a consequence of this action if Hypothesis A is true.

Give aid — unnecessary waste, danger locate ship

6. Revise, in accordance with the guidelines in this chapter, the following predicted consequence of this action: The crew of the *Queen* will be saved.

the crew of the Queen may be saved

7. You form a second proposal for action: Alert all Coast Guard stations between New Orleans and Norfolk. Predict the consequences if Hypothesis A is true.

ship may be located — unnecessary waste of time + money

8. Predict the consequences of this action if Hypothesis B is true.

survivors may be found - may be too late

9. You form a third proposal for action: Delay launching a search for a few minutes while you form and test hypotheses as to the probable position of the *Queen*. Predict the consequences of this action if Hypothesis B is true.

delay may result in tragedy - position may help locate ship more quickly

10. Which of the three proposals for action should you execute? *5, 7 or 9*

11–16. *You are a coed at Wysacki, where a hundred students major in zymology. You have a blind date with a zymology major and find him dull. You form a tentative generalization that most zymology majors are dull.*

11. Rate the reliability of your tentative generalization. *improbable*

12. Another zymology major, whom you do not know, writes you a note asking you to be his date at the Zymology Zigfest. You consider this proposal for action: Ignore the note. Predict the consequences of this action if your generalization is true.

save yourself a boring evening

13. Predict the consequences of this action if your generalization is false.

you will miss having a good time

14. You then consider a second proposal for action: Accept the date. Predict the consequences of this action if your generalization is true.

you will have a boring time

15. Predict the consequences of this action if your generalization is false.

you will have a good time

16. Write a third proposal for action that is likely to be satisfactory whether your generalization is true or false.

arrange a meeting beforehand

14 Value Judgments

1. *Nature of Value Judgments*
2. *Value Systems*
3. *Exposing Value Premises*

As noted at the end of the preceding chapter, when you choose one proposed action in preference to another, you are usually making a value judgment. Whenever you make a decision to see one movie instead of another, or watch television instead of play tennis, or read one book instead of another, or take one course instead of another, or choose one curriculum instead of another, a value judgment is involved, whether you realize it or not.

1. Nature of Value Judgments

A *value judgment* is a conclusion about the worth of an object, experience, idea, or action in terms of human needs. Value judgments are usually derived by deductive inference from *value premises*. Value judgments and value premises are alike in that both deal with the worth of objects, experiences, ideas, or actions in terms of human needs. The only distinction is that a value judgment is always the conclusion of an argument, whereas a value premise is a part of the evidence from which the conclusion is drawn. What may be a value judgment in one argument may be a value premise in another.

For illustration, let us return to the case of Mary Smythe. Suppose Mary weighs all the evidence she can get and draws the following conclusion:

A premedical curriculum requires more hours of laboratory work than most other curricula.

This conclusion is not a value judgment, for it neither states nor implies that laboratory work is good or bad in terms of human needs. Now suppose Mary uses this conclusion as the minor premise of another syllogism.

Minor Premise: A premedical curriculum requires more hours of laboratory work than most other curricula.

Conclusion: A premedical curriculum is bad for me.

This conclusion is a value judgment, for it asserts that a premedical curriculum is bad for her.

Note that the argument is incomplete, for it contains no evidence that a curriculum requiring more than the average amount of laboratory work is necessarily bad. Actually, the argument above is a syllogism with a missing major premise. The major premise necessary to make the conclusion valid is shown in the complete syllogism below.

Major Premise: A curriculum requires more than average laboratory work $\supset$ it is bad for me.

Minor Premise: A premedical curriculum requires more hours of laboratory work than most curricula.

∴ A premedical curriculum is bad for me.

Note also that this conclusion is a value judgment, whereas the major premise is a value premise.

The principal doubt about the reliability of the above conclusion concerns the reliability of the major premise itself. Let us suppose that Mary has derived this major premise by deductive reasoning from another major premise, as shown in the syllogism below.

Major Premise: A curriculum $\supset$ it is bad for interferes with me.
my social life.

Minor Premise: A curriculum that requires more than average laboratory work interferes with my social life.

Conclusion: ∴ A curriculum that requires more than average laboratory work is bad for me.

Obviously the conclusion of the syllogism above is a value judgment, whereas this same statement is a value premise in the first syllogism. This is the only difference between them.

2. Value Systems

The value premises we use in making decisions constitute a kind of "system" that gives our lives meaning, purpose, and direction. Without a value system life would have neither meaning nor direction, and thinking would have no purpose. We could only describe the world; we could not discriminate between what is desirable and what is not, for man reacts to reality not only in terms of how he perceives it but also in terms of how he values it. Two different people in the clubhouse of a golf course may perceive a steady rain in much the same way and yet react quite differently because of different value systems. The confirmed golfer may react negatively because he places a high value on playing golf. The greenskeeper, on the other hand, may be pleased by the rain because he places a high value on healthy grass.

Value judgments do much to shape the frame of reference. One seeks the kinds of experience he values and avoids the kinds he does not value. Thus value judgments are a factor in selecting the content of the frame of reference. Persons who do not value truth and learning are not likely to develop adequate and accurate frames of reference.

There is a reciprocal relationship between one's value system and self-concept. Value systems help to shape one's self-concept. Most of us, at least to some extent, conform to the culture in which we live by absorbing some of the value judgments of that culture. For example, one who grows up in a culture that values contributing to the welfare of others is likely to picture himself as a person who does so. Similarly, the self-concept helps to shape value judgments. A person who sees himself as contributing to the welfare of his fellow man is likely to set a higher value on occupations which so contribute than on occupations which merely produce material wealth. Value judgments are frequently evaluations of experience which help to maintain and protect the self-concept.

Certain value premises promote effective thinking. Following the New Testament value premise, "The truth shall make you free," may help one become a more effective thinker by providing motivation for the necessary effort. Certain value judgments held by scientists have contributed to the progress of modern science. It is said that Thomas Edison strove to overcome such obstacles as lack of support by fellow scientists, financial difficulties, and repeated failure of experiments with the electric light bulb because he believed that brighter light would benefit humanity.

On the other hand, value premises can lead to self-deception. The value judgments we have absorbed from our culture frequently conflict with our immediate desires. Suppose you want to be an artist, but your parents want you to be an engineer and will put you through college only if you study engineering. Your parents are thwarting you, and you would not be human if you were not tempted to retaliate by thwarting them. Suppose further that your value premises include the Fifth Commandment, "Honor thy father and thy mother. . . ." Your all-too-human desires are now in conflict with a value premise. If you are tolerant enough of your own feelings to recognize them honestly, you are likely to realize that retaliation is not worth the damage to your self-concept, and you are likely to decide against it.

But you can satisfy the desire to retaliate and protect your self-concept too — temporarily. You can retaliate by flunking out of college and can protect your self-concept by deceiving yourself about your motives. You can make yourself believe you really meant to succeed in college but failed through circumstances beyond your control. Thus you can have your cake and eat it — for a while. But the price is high, for when you deceive yourself you distort your frame of reference and thereby blur your view of reality.

The system of value premises one uses in making decisions largely determines what kind of person he is and will become. When the premises in a system are "good" (we examine the criteria for "goodness" in a later chapter) and reasonably consistent with each other, the system gives life meaning, purpose, direction, and richness. But when the judgments in a system are "bad" or in conflict with each other, it is all but impossible to make sound decisions, and life seems without purpose or direction.

If your life seems to lack meaning or purpose, or if you feel unhappy much of the time, you should test the causal theory that your value system is at fault. Unless you are very unusual, some of the premises in your system are unsuitable or even false. Some of these "bad" premises may have been derived by faulty reasoning from your own experience. As college counselors know, many students, especially women, develop false ideas about their abilities in mathematics. Consider the student who for some reason gets a bad start in mathematics and finds her early experience with it frustrating and unpleasant. Since we tend to place negative values on unpleasant experiences, she is likely to place a negative value on mathematics and avoid studying it. Thus she fails to develop her abilities in mathematics, and her experiences with it become more and more frustrating and unpleasant, so that when she becomes a housewife she is unable even to balance her checkbook. Other "bad" premises may have been acquired during childhood from other children, who can hardly be considered good judges of values. Some premises may be "good" in themselves but "bad" for you because they conflict with other premises in your system.

Today's college student is confronted with perhaps the most disturbing array of conflicting value premises of all time. The several roots of American culture have made it the most richly varied in the world and perhaps the most inconsistent. The rapid social change of our era is adding new values that conflict sharply with older and more traditional ones. For almost every value premise you can think of, there is a contradictory one. Consider the conflict between our "Sunday" and "weekday" values. On the Lord's Day we do service to the Golden Rule: "Do unto others as you would have them do unto you." Six days a week we believe that "business is business." If you have never sensed the inconsistency between these precepts, stop and think next time you hear the second one. They are patently at odds, and the real purpose of the second is to set aside the first.

Other inconsistent values relate to conformity. We are exhorted not to be sheep, unthinkingly following others and doing as they do. *The Organization Man* is by now as much a term of contempt as it is the title of a book. But the very path of conformity which we are urged to avoid leads to another cluster of values we are told to pursue: "The day is past when you can get ahead on your own. Teamwork is what counts. Learn to fit in — cooperate, be a good team man in working with others." Nonconformity reaps penalties as well as praise in our society; conformity earns both contempt and rewards.

The fact that we often speak of "doing lip-service" to our ideals is an acknowledgment that we often proclaim one value but practice a contradictory one. It is hardly surprising that many psychologists now believe that inability to find a satisfactory system of values contributes to the high incidence of emotional disturbance among college students.

Society cannot arbitrate among the conflicting values it has taught us. The task of deciding what values are worth building into one's system falls to the individual himself. This is nowhere more evident than in the maturing adolescent. The extent of his maturity is characterized — can even be measured — by the degree to which he makes himself responsible for his own standards. Whether he finally embraces or rejects the teachings of his parents, church, school, or society at large, growing up goes hand in hand with deciding which standards should be followed. No man can be a free individual unless he himself chooses the value premises he uses in guiding his life.

Paradoxical though it may seem, the very procedures of thinking that have brought such progress in science are responsible, at least in part, for confusion and conflicts in value systems. Because new techniques of counting and measuring have been important in science, we tend to feel that *only* things that can be counted or measured are worth thinking about. From this notion has grown perhaps the great fallacy of our age: since value judgments cannot be readily counted or measured they cannot be evaluated or tested.

It is true that value premises cannot be weighed and measured with the precision of the laboratory. But to assume from this that they cannot be evaluated at all is a *non sequitur*. One of the main theses of this book is that certain procedures of thinking can be as valuable in developing a satisfactory system of values as the methods of science have been in dealing with the physical world. Applying these procedures to your own system of value premises can be the most important thinking you will ever do.

You should avoid changing important value premises or adopting new ones without careful testing. On college campuses value premises spring up like mushrooms. Some are harmless or even good, but some are poisonous. Furthermore, your own value premises function as a system. A given value premise may be compatible in one person's system and disruptive in another's. An essential part of testing a value premise is predicting its consequences in terms of your system as a whole.

3. Exposing Value Premises

The first step in evaluating your own value premises is to discover what they are. This is not easy. Most of the value judgments we make are implicit rather than explicit. For example, a student who finds a valuable fountain pen in a classroom and turns it in to his teacher may decide to do so by explicit reasoning. But more than likely his guiding value judgment would be implicit; that is, he would shorten his reasoning process by reaching his conclusion without being consciously aware of the underlying value premise. As a matter of fact, many of our actions are habitual: in certain circumstances we act in habitual ways without giving the matter any thought at all. Yet value premises underlie most habitual behavior.

If all our value premises were sound and consistent with each other, implicit or habitual value judgments would present no problems. Indeed, shortening the reasoning process by skipping the value premise would save valuable time for careful reasoning about other matters. Unfortunately, few of us have value systems that are sound and consistent. For example, many students habitually avoid rigorous and demanding courses, yet it is doubtful that most of these same students would accept the underlying value premise if they examined it carefully.

The hypothetical syllogism is a useful tool for exposing value premises so that they may be examined and evaluated. Suppose you decide that it is a waste of time to study a certain chapter because studying it will not affect your grade. A value judgment underlies this decision, but it is implicit. To reveal it clearly, let us first state your reasoning as the minor premise and the conclusion of a syllogism.

Minor Premise: Learning this chapter will not affect my grade.

Conclusion: Learning this chapter is a waste of time.

If you were reasoning deductively, as you probably were, either you were reasoning invalidly or you were reasoning from a major premise not stated. Assuming that you were reasoning validly, let us find the unstated premise so that we may examine it.

You remember from Chapter 2 that the conclusion of a hypothetical syllogism is valid only if the minor premise affirms the antecedent or denies the consequent of the hypothetical premise. It is usually easier to supply a major premise whose antecedent is affirmed. Below is the antecedent of an incomplete hypothetical proposition affirmed by the minor premise above.

Learning something will not affect my grade ⊃

Now let us complete this hypothetical proposition by supplying a consequent. You can avoid a *non sequitur* simply by using as the consequent the same words that are used to state the conclusion. The completed syllogism is shown below.

~~Learning something~~ will not affect my grade ⊃ it is a waste of time.

Learning this chapter will not affect my grade.

∴ Learning this chapter is a waste of time.

The value premise behind your reasoning is now clearly exposed. You may protest that you apply this premise only to important tests and examinations. But it so happens that many students habitually study only what they think will affect their grades. Many students enter college with the value premise that the purpose of study is to improve their minds. However, for one reason or another, they fall behind in their assignments. Faced with the need to prepare for an important test or examination they decide to study only what will affect the final grade. At the time, this decision seems a sensible concession to a practical necessity. Unfortunately, minor decisions like this, repeated often enough, can lead to a major decision — the unconscious adoption of the value premise that completes the syllogism above.

Many of us become trapped in this pitfall, with the result that we often think we are following a certain value premise when in fact we are following a very different one. The procedure for testing hypotheses discussed in Chapter 6 helps us see whether we are actually following the premises we think we are. To do this, first form the hypothesis that you are following a certain premise, and use this hypothesis as the antecedent of a hypothetical proposition.

I am following the value premise that learning to think is more important than high grades ⊃

Next add one or more consequents that follow from this antecedent.

⊃   except for periods immediately before tests I would emphasize thinking problems through instead of memorizing them.

Then observe your behavior to see whether the consequent is true. If you observe that you consistently memorize instead of trying to understand or think problems through, then the consequent is not true. And if the consequent of this particular syllogism is not true, neither is the hypothesis that you are following the value premise in question.

Once you have discovered your value premises, you can begin to evaluate and modify them as needed to develop a system of values suitable for the kind of person you would like to be. We describe procedures for evaluating and modifying value premises in Chapter 35.

Suggested Supplementary Reading

Evelyn Shirk, *The Ethical Dimension: An Approach to the Philosophy of Values and Valuing* (New York: Appleton-Century-Crofts, 1965).

EXERCISE 14

1–7. *Consider the following statements made by Joe Smythe, a first-semester fresh-man.*

1. I'd like to play billiards with you this afternoon but I can't do that and study chemistry too.
2. Chemistry assignments are longer in college than in high school.
3. It would be better for me to study chemistry this afternoon.
4. The probability that a coin will fall heads up purely by chance is ½.
5. It is impossible to study chemistry without gaining significant intellectual development.
6. There is no intellectual development to be gained from playing billiards.
7. If you must choose between social life and intellectual development, it is better to choose intellectual development.

1. Which of these propositions is a statement of fact? _____4___or___2__

2. Which of these propositions is an observation, free from any value judgment?

_____2_____

3. Which of these statements are observations with implicit value judgments?

_____5, 6_____

4. Which of these propositions is most clearly a value premise? _____7_____

5. A valid syllogism, the conclusion of which is a decision involving a value judgment, can be constructed from four of these propositions. Which is the major premise?

_____7_____

6. Which two propositions can be combined into the minor premise? _____5 and 6___

7. Which proposition is the conclusion? _____3_____

8–12. *Consider these additional statements by Joe Smythe.*

8. When I was in the sixth grade I got a chemistry set for Christmas. Ever since, I've gotten a kick out of what happens when various chemicals are combined.
9. In the seventh grade my teacher punished me by making me memorize poetry. Poetry is for the birds.
10. My parents want me to study business administration so that I can take over my father's business when he retires.
11. My favorite indoor sport is billiards.
12. I think a college student ought to try to please his parents. After all, they make a sacrifice to keep him in college.

8. What has been the probable effect on Joe's frame of reference of the value judgment implicit in Proposition 8?

he is good at chemistry

9. What has been the probable effect on Joe's frame of reference of the value judgment in Proposition 9?

he would not be suited for a career in English

10. Do any of the propositions in this group involve *conflicting* value judgments (*i.e.*, value judgments that are rivals in the sense that two hypotheses are: if one is right, the other is wrong)?

8, 10

11. Which of the propositions in this group involve *competing* value judgments (*i.e.*, value judgments that can interfere with each other because of limitations of time, money, and the like)?

8, 12 and 11, 12

12. Which of the propositions in this group contains the value judgment most likely to be conducive to effective thinking?

12 or 8

13–14. *The following items consist of incomplete syllogisms in which the minor premise describes a situation and the conclusion states a decision Joe Smythe made about the situation. In each item (1) supply the value premise necessary to make the syllogism valid, and (2) in the line below state your opinion of the value premise.*

13. *a course is not interesting ⊃ it is not worthwhile*

I do not find my English course interesting.
∴ it is not worthwhile.

14. *joining a frat. requires conformity to rules ⊃ I will not join*

Joining a fraternity requires conformity to rules.
∴ I will not join a fraternity.

15 Creative Thinking

The importance of creative thinking in the decision-making cycle has been mentioned repeatedly. Without it, man's condition would be little better than that of the ape. For every idea that has led to the improvement of man's lot or to the advancement of civilization has been the product of creative thinking. Even the old ideas we use daily in dealing with routine problems were originally the products of creative thinking.

Failure to think creatively causes failures in all walks of life. We live in a world of constant change, and yesterday's ideas will not always work in tomorrow's situations. Consider, for example, the problems of a football coach. Styles of offense and defense are constantly evolving. Offensive and defensive formations that proved highly successful last year fail to work this year because the team's personnel has changed, or because rival coaches have created new offensive and defensive styles, or because the rules of the game have changed. Head coaches who can think creatively devise new stratagems. Those who cannot soon become former head coaches.

Because of the importance of creative thinking, it is now appropriate to take a closer look to see what it is and how it may be cultivated.

1. The Creative Breakthrough

Usually when we encounter a problem we first try to deal with it by familiar methods, for it is easier to follow a well-traveled path than to blaze a new trail. In using the five-phase cycle, the first tentative conclusions we form in Phase 3 are usually familiar ones. If these solve the problem satisfactorily, there is no point in seeking new solutions. Most of us have too many problems to waste creative thinking on those for which we already have satisfactory solutions. We should try to think creatively when none of our usual conclusions or proposals for action are satisfactory. Consider the problem of screwworm flies. In the late fifties the damage done by these pests to the cattle industry alone was estimated as high as $25,000,000 each year. Screwworm flies lay hundreds of eggs in open wounds of animals. Within hours the eggs become larvae, which burrow deep into the wound and feed on blood and tissue. Unless the infested wounds are treated, the pests can kill an animal within ten days.

In 1938, two young entomologists in the Department of Agriculture, Edward F. Knipling and Raymond C. Bushland, were assigned the problem of developing a chemical treatment for screwworm wounds. The definition of the problem assigned to Knipling and Bushland was quite conventional. It did not take Knipling and Bushland long to solve the problem as defined, for they could do so by following paths familiar to well-trained entomologists. They soon developed a chemical treatment that, if applied to the wounds in time, would save the animals' lives. But Knipling and Bushland were not satisfied with this conventional solution. All too often infected animals were not found in time; treating the wounds was too much like setting up a hospital to treat people injured in automobile accidents instead of trying to eliminate the accidents. They decided that the only satisfactory solution was to get rid of the insects. In making this decision they were redefining their problem.

Knipling and Bushland presumably first tried to adapt conventional methods of killing insects to the problem of exterminating the screwworm fly. But no conventional methods were practical. With chemical insecticides there would always be survivors that would rebuild the population within a short time. A totally new approach was needed, and finding it required a high order of creative thinking. Knipling and Bushland worked hard on the problem for some time, but their efforts seemed fruitless until suddenly a revolutionary hypothesis popped into Knipling's mind — that screwworm flies could be eliminated by sterilizing the males. Even though a method of sterilizing the flies still had to be found, Knipling's hypothesis may be described as a breakthrough, for in forming it he broke through the boundaries of his knowledge.

How and why do such creative break-throughs come about? We do not yet know precisely what the creative process is, and it is doubtful that Knipling himself knows exactly how he formed his revolutionary hypothesis. In general, the creative process seems to consist of searching the frame of reference, selecting certain items from it, and combining them in a new way. Knipling apparently combined the following items of information.

1. The life cycle of the screwworm fly is short, lasting only two or three weeks.
2. Only a small reduction in the rate of reproduction would significantly reduce the population within a short time.
3. Female screwworm flies mate only once.
4. Research on the sterilization of insects had been started about 1916.

Creative breakthroughs seem easy — after they have been made. In fact, when one has made a creative breakthrough he often wonders why he never thought of the idea before. It is easy enough to see the relationship among the four items of information Knipling combined once we think of sterilizing the male flies. Unfortunately, creative breakthroughs are not nearly as easy as they seem to be after they have been made, for two conditions must precede the breakthrough. First, the necessary ideas or information must be available in the frame of reference. It is doubtful that Knipling would ever have formed his revolutionary hypothesis had he not already known that female flies mate only once. Second, the necessary items of information must be put together into a new combination.

The difficulty of putting ideas into new combinations can be illustrated by the theory of probability. Before ideas can be combined into a tentative conclusion, they must first be selected. As a well-trained entomologist, Knipling doubtless knew thousands of items of information potentially relevant to the elimination of insects. To keep our arithmetic in bounds, however, let us assume that

Knipling's frame of reference contained only 1,000 items of information of possible relevance. It so happens that 41,417,124,750 different combinations of four items each can be formed from 1,000 items. It seems unlikely, therefore, that Knipling happened to select these four items purely by chance.

It should be noted that creative breakthroughs vary widely in the degree of creativity involved. The invention of the telephone, for example, involved a high degree of creativity. The invention of the dial system was somewhat less creative, and the invention of push-button telephones was still less so. The degree of creativity involved in a breakthrough is the degree to which the combination of ideas or information involved is new to the person making the breakthrough. What may be routine thinking for one person may be a creative breakthrough for another. Whenever you combine ideas or information into an idea that is new to you, you have made a creative breakthrough, even though the same idea may already have occurred to millions of other people.

Creative breakthroughs are not limited to geniuses like Einstein, inventors like Alexander Graham Bell, or scientists like Sir Isaac Newton. The student who, in writing a term paper, forms a hypothesis that is new to him has made a creative breakthrough even though others before him have formed the same hypothesis. The student who devises for himself a new and more efficient method of study has also made a creative breakthrough. Nor are creative breakthroughs important only to scientists and inventors. In our complex and rapidly changing world, all of us must make creative breakthroughs if we are to achieve our potential as individuals.

The process by which we select certain items from the vast collections in our frames of reference and combine them into creative breakthroughs is still somewhat mysterious. Studies of creative persons in all walks of life indicate, however, that the probability of making creative breakthroughs can be greatly increased by following certain procedures.

2. Preparation

Creative breakthroughs rarely occur to people who have not prepared for them. Making the necessary preparations is the objective of the first three phases of the decision-making cycle. Phase 1 identifies and analyzes the problem that the creative breakthrough is to solve.

Phase 2 supplies information not already in the frame of reference. For example, when Knipling and Bushland first started work on the problem of eliminating the screwworm fly, they did not have the necessary information in their frames of reference. Since they did not know exactly what information they would need, they began an intensive study of the life cycle of the screwworm fly.

A serious attempt to complete Phase 3 seems to be an essential part of the preparation necessary for a creative breakthrough. Usually the first tentative conclusions that occur to us in Phase 3 are the obvious or familiar ones. Forming new or different ones requires additional effort. For this reason it has been repeatedly emphasized that several tentative conclusions should be formed. The more tentative conclusions you form the more likely you are to make a creative breakthrough. In using hypotheses, for example, it is usually easy to form one routine tentative hypothesis. Forming additional hypotheses is usually harder because each additional hypothesis you form tends to lead you farther away from the routine and the familiar. As a rule, in preparing for a breakthrough you should work at forming tentative conclusions until you feel that you cannot possibly think of another one. Usually, when the problem in hand requires a creative breakthrough, none of the tentative conclusions you form at first will be satisfactory.

It is here that creative thinkers are separated from noncreative thinkers. At this point noncreative thinkers usually give up in frustration and settle for some routine solution that is less than satisfactory. The creative thinker, on the other hand, has learned that creative breakthroughs rarely come to mind as the culmination of a smooth step-by-step process such as you would use in calculating the standard deviation from a distribution. He has learned that frustration is usually a necessary part of the process. To the creative thinker frustration is merely a spur to greater effort.

3. Incubation

When the creative breakthrough does not occur after a serious effort to complete Phase 3, an incubation period, *i.e.*, a period of time during which conscious attention is turned away from the problem in hand, is indicated. The experience of creative persons indicates that breakthroughs tend to pop into mind while conscious attention is focused on some other subject. The idea that occurred to James Watt while watching steam coming out of a kettle is a case in point. The explanation seems to be that information is combined into new or unusual combinations by the "unconscious" rather than by the "conscious" mind. We do not yet know exactly what this "unconscious" mind is, but we can be reasonably certain that much of our thinking goes on below the conscious level. You doubtless remember many instances in which you were unable to recall a fact, such as a telephone number, a date, or a name, only to have it pop into consciousness later when you were thinking of something else. Also, you can doubtless recall instances in which the solution of a problem eluded you for a time and then popped into consciousness minutes or days after you had stopped thinking about it. Apparently, when we consciously seek a new or unusual tentative conclusion we tend to stay in familiar chan-

nels. But when we permit the unconscious mind to roam the frame of reference, free from restraint by the conscious mind, it is often able to break out of familiar channels and put information together into new combinations.

While the operation of the unconscious mind is still a mystery, the experiences of many creative people indicate that we can learn to make it an invaluable adjunct to effective thinking. The procedure for using the unconscious mind seems to consist of two steps: (1) preparation, as described above, and (2) an incubation period in which the unconscious mind is allowed to work on the problem free from direction or restraint by the conscious mind. Creative people use many different methods of providing this incubation. They may go fishing, or play golf, or take a nap, or take a walk, or take a leisurely shower, or deliberately turn their attention to something else. Sleep appears to provide one of the more effective incubation periods. Many professional writers follow a set routine. In the morning they write. In the afternoon they prepare for the next morning by deciding what topic to develop next and by reading on the subject. During the evening they go into an incubation period by relaxing in various ways. Many college students discover that they can solve homework problems with less effort and time if they struggle with them just before going to bed. Frequently the solutions will come to them before they have finished breakfast.

Using the unconscious mind to solve problems can save much time, but it will not work at the last minute. Students who wait until the last minute to start working on term papers are likely to find that the ideas will not come. A much more productive procedure is to start work on the term paper as soon as possible so that the unconscious mind can have time to work on the information gathered. How long an incubation period must be is unpredictable. Sometimes the breakthrough occurs after only a few minutes of incubation. Sometimes it requires days, weeks, or even years.

4. Persistence

Merely providing an incubation period is no guarantee that the breakthrough will occur. Sometimes persistent effort is necessary. Knipling and Bushland worked long and hard at their problem before Knipling thought of the hypothesis that screwworm flies could be eliminated by sterilizing the male flies. And this creative breakthrough was only the beginning, for a practical method of sterilizing the flies still had to be found, requiring another creative breakthrough. Knipling and Bushland worked at this problem for a decade before developing a method that seemed promising enough to test. In problems as complex as this one, Phases 1, 2, and 3 may have to be repeated many times.

Major creative breakthroughs are likely to require considerable courage and perseverance in the face of criticism and failure. Any new idea is likely to threaten somebody's self-concept and therefore to meet resistance. When Knipling first discussed his revolutionary hypothesis with other entomologists, some of them laughed outright at the very idea. Knipling persisted in the face of criticism and failure until 1950, when he read an article by Dr. H. J. Muller, a world-famous geneticist, describing experiments in which fruit flies were sterilized by overdoses of X-rays. Even then Knipling had trouble getting sufficient scientific and financial support to complete the project. Bushland, who was committed to another project, could work on the method of sterilization only on weekends.

Knipling's and Bushland's perseverance were to be put on trial yet again. The whole hypothesis was first tested on Sanibel Island, two miles off the coast of Florida. Although the population of screwworm flies on the island was greatly reduced, the procedure did not eliminate them. Hordes of fertile flies migrated from the mainland and rebuilt the population. Knipling and Bushland had to wait two more years before the overall hypothesis was proved in a test made in Curaçao. Several years after this successful test the method was used with spectacular success in Florida and later in the southeastern United States. After eighteen years of intermittent effort Knipling and Bushland had found a solution that satisfied them. Most people would have given up sixteen years earlier because they lacked the courage to pursue an idea in the face of criticism and failure. People who give up as soon as they have formed the conventional tentative conclusions and make no effort to form new ones rarely make even minor breakthroughs. They are either content to stick to, or afraid to venture from, well-trodden paths. They rarely blaze new trails of any kind. Creative people, on the other hand, habitually seek to form new and different tentative conclusions.

Sometimes the breakthrough does not come because the problem has not been correctly defined. The next step, therefore, is to begin again with Phase 1. Sometimes a breakthrough can be precipitated by redefining the problem in such a way as to combine two seemingly separate problems. Suppose a student has two problems: he needs money to stay in college, and he needs to test a hypothesis that he should prepare for a career in hospital management. He can deal with the two problems separately by taking a part-time job off-campus and talking to his counselor about hospital management. But these solutions to the two problems may not be altogether satisfactory. The time spent on the part-time job will reduce the time he has available for testing his hypothesis about hospital management. Furthermore, the wages he earns in the part-time job may be relatively low, and the experience may be of little value. Suppose, however, that he combines the two problems and defines his new problem to be to find a job that will give him the necessary income as well as the experience that will help him test his hypothesis. This new definition is a kind of breakthrough in itself, for it leads directly to a solution — find a part-time job in a hospital.

Sometimes the creative breakthrough does not come because the necessary information is not in a person's frame of reference. If, after redefining the problem, the breakthrough does not come within a reasonable time, it is desirable to repeat Phase 2. Sometimes you fail to collect the necessary information because the tentative conclusions you have formed have misguided your search. Thus it is sometimes necessary to make a broader search for information without reference to tentative conclusions. It is often helpful to examine solutions to other problems, for one of these may contain a clue to your problem. Sometimes a creative breakthrough will not come until you have immersed yourself in the subject. When you have trouble writing a term paper, the trouble may be that you do not know enough. The remedy is immersion in the subject.

Since you do not now know what problems you will have to solve in the future, you should not neglect your general or liberal education. The people who make the important creative breakthroughs tend to be those who are knowledgeable in general areas as well as in a specialty.

5. Mechanical Methods

Sometimes, even though the problem has been clearly and correctly defined and the essential information is available in the frame of reference, the creative breakthrough does not occur because the mind fails to select and combine the necessary items. In these instances a mechanical procedure may be useful. Combining new items of information into new tentative conclusions is analogous to putting together a large jigsaw puzzle

that forms a picture you have not seen. Your procedure, at least until you can see a picture emerging, must be mechanical. You can simply select a piece at random and systematically try the other pieces until you find the one that fits. After a period of frustration in using this procedure a kind of creative breakthrough may occur. For instance, you may suddenly realize that it would be better to start with a corner piece. You therefore look for corner pieces. What you have done, in effect, is to think of a better system.

Systematically combining items is not creative thinking, of course, but it can precipitate creative thinking by forcing the mind to put items into unfamiliar combinations. Suppose you are confronted with this puzzle problem. Three boxes identical in weight and appearance are presented to you. You are given the following information: (1) one box contains two white marbles; (2) one contains two black marbles; (3) one contains a white and a black marble; (4) each box is labeled to show the contents (WW, BB, WB), but the labels have been switched so that every box is incorrectly labeled. You are to receive $2,000 for correctly identifying the contents of all three boxes, but you must pay $1,000 for each marble you inspect, and you must pay a fine of $10,000 if you incorrectly identify the contents of any box. You define your problem to be to make the maximum profit.[1]

Obviously you have to begin by taking a marble from one of the boxes. You could select the box at random, but if you did so you would have violated one of the rules of effective thinking set forth in Chapter 13, for you would have executed a proposal for action without having first tested it. A better procedure would be to list the boxes you might try first, together with the consequences. The box you should try first, of course, is the one that will give you the most

[1] Adapted from a puzzle in *The Scientific American.*

information. The three possibilities and their consequences are tabulated below.

Box Opened First	Consequence (Information Gained)
WW	Marble white $\supset$ this box WW or WB.
	Marble black $\supset$ this box BB or WB.
BB	Marble white $\supset$ this box WW or WB.
	Marble black $\supset$ this box BB or WB.
WB	Marble white $\supset$ this box WW or WB.
	Marble black $\supset$ this box BB or WB.

So far your procedure has been mechanical rather than creative, but it has laid the foundation for creative thinking. For you can readily see from the tabulation above that you will lose money unless you can find a better method. You will have to remove both marbles from the first box and at least one marble from another box before you can be sure of the contents of all boxes. You will find a clue to the solution in the exercise for this chapter, but before you peek, try using all of the techniques described in this chapter.

The example above is unusual in that the number of possible combinations is small. Usually when you try to list the possibilities you will discover that there are too many — that you will never solve the problem unless you find a shortcut. Even so, this discovery moves you closer to the breakthrough, for it gives you a clearer idea of what the problem is.

6. Analogies

Perhaps our most fruitful sources of tentative conclusions are *analogies, i.e., partial resemblances between two or more objects, ideas, or processes*. Analogies provide a link between the known and the unknown. When the problem in hand closely resembles another problem with which we have dealt successfully, we usually encounter little trouble in forming tentative conclusions. We can easily see the analogy between the two

problems, and the analogy suggests the tentative conclusions. Little or no creative thinking is required. The police routinely use analogy in solving crimes. One type of analogy they use involves the M. O., *i.e.*, the criminal's method of operation. If a safe has been cracked by the skillful use of an acetylene torch, they search their records for other instances of safe-cracking in which an acetylene torch has been skillfully used. All criminals in the police records who have been known to crack safes in this manner are automatically suspect until investigated.

When the decision-making cycle stalls because we cannot think of a satisfactory tentative conclusion, searching for analogies may be a useful method of precipitating a breakthrough. The search for analogies should begin by comparing the problem in hand with other problems like it. If this fails, the search should be widened to include situations that bear a less obvious relationship to the problem in hand.

Consider Joe Smythe, who was introduced in Exercise 1. After his first round of tests, Joe recognized a problem — if his grades did not improve, he would be suspended at the end of the term. Joe correctly defined his problem to be to find a way to make better grades. At this point Joe doubtless remembered that when he entered high school he had had a similar problem, which he solved by increasing his study time. Although the two problems are not exactly alike, since high school and college are different in many respects, the analogy is obvious. Accordingly, he decided to increase his study time to forty-five hours a week. Joe's grades on the second round of tests were better, but not good enough. Accordingly, he increased his study time still further until he was studying far into the night, especially on the nights before tests and examinations. This time, however, his grades got worse instead of better. Joe was baffled, because he could think of no experience in high school in which his grades became worse when he increased his effort. This should have been Joe's cue to widen his search for analogous situations to include those not directly connected with grades. Actually, Joe's frame of reference included an analogous experience. While in high school he lost an important tennis match because he had practiced too long and hard the day before. Joe was unable to connect the two experiences, however, until a counselor pointed out the analogy.

Even though a conscious search for analogous situations fails, it may have the effect of getting the unconscious mind to take up the search for more subtle analogies. Also, the conscious effort may alert you to the analogy between some new experience and a problem you have been trying to solve. This may have been what happened when Archimedes discovered the principle of displacement. There seems to be no resemblance between stepping into a tub full of water and determining whether silver has been mixed with gold. Yet this analogy is said to have enabled Archimedes to solve a perplexing problem set for him by Hiero II, King of Syracuse. Hiero had asked him to determine whether silver had been alloyed with gold in a crown. Archimedes was baffled until the overflowing water of his bath suggested the principle of displacement. Since silver and gold are of different densities, equal weights of these metals displace different quantities of water. Thus Archimedes solved the problem, but if he had not been struggling with it, it is doubtful that he would have seen the significance of the water displaced from the tub.

Failure to see a subtle analogy may have been a major factor in the downfall of the Mayan civilization in the fifteenth century.

Although they were able to perfect a calendar as good as the Greek or Egyptian and raise stone cities from the jungle, the Maya used the wheel only in toys for children. It would not have been above Maya technique to install a treadmill that dipped into the giant

cenotes and raised the water to the surface, conveying it then, by means of an aqueduct, to their fields. . . .

There was a mental block against the principle of the wheel in the Americas, where man was the dray animal. None of the practical uses of the wheel, in whatever form, were known. . . . Had the Maya had the latter in that terrible year of 1464, when there was drought followed by a locust swarm . . . they might have survived and weathered the great hurricane that followed. . . .[2]

7. Adversity

Adversity can be a stimulus for creative thinking. Whenever you encounter adversity in any form, you should define your problem to be how to twist the adversity into an advantage. If the Mayans had been creative enough to invent a treadmill to irrigate their fields, this breakthrough could have led to finding other uses of the wheel. Many of man's most important technological developments have resulted from efforts to overcome adversity. Sonar, developed in World War II to detect enemy submarines, is now widely used to find fish and keep small boats off reefs. Another example is radar, now used to protect planes and ships.

Both Cyrano de Bergerac and Jimmy Durante faced the adversity of an enormous nose. Cyrano never overcame it, but Jimmy Durante twisted his adversity into an advantage by using his nose to help him become one of the most successful comedians of his time. Failure in one endeavor can lead to success in another. Many college students have discovered their real potential only after failure. A striking example is the case of a sophomore tackle who was on the verge of academic suspension for unsatisfactory grades in an engineering curriculum. Forced by the threat of failure to reconsider his choice of a career, he discovered that he had a high degree of talent in an unexpected

[2] Victor W. Von Hagen, *World of the Maya* (New York: Mentor, 1960), pp. 67–68.

area — art. Once he changed to a major in art he made high grades. He also succeeded in football: in his senior year he was named to an all-American team. Even when you cannot twist adversity into an actual advantage, as Durante did, you can usually at least reduce the adversity by attacking the problem creatively.

8. Practice

Studies of people who have made important creative breakthroughs indicate that skill in creative thinking can be acquired through practice. Your practice should not be limited to important issues. When you climb a small hill and discover the joys of adventure, you are likely to develop the courage and persistence to climb a larger hill. But if you try the Matterhorn and fail, your spirit of adventure may be crushed.

Practice is more likely to be effective if you form and test causal theories about factors in your life that may have inhibited your creative thinking. Recognizing these factors will make it easier to offset them. You may find some of them in your education, both past and present. The teacher of a large class does not have time to identify creative thinking, much less encourage it. Because he is usually required to cover a large mass of subject matter in a limited time, he is likely to fall into the habit of following standard channels. He may discourage the expression of divergent opinions in class discussion, because diverging opinions would lead him out of standard channels and impede coverage of the required subject matter.

Another inhibiting factor is emphasis on grades. Although some teachers do encourage creative thinking and reward it with higher grades, teachers with large classes often find it impossible to do so. To reward creative thinking the teacher must decide whether the student's diverging answer is an instance of creative thinking or merely an indication of ignorance, and this takes time. Hence students are likely to conclude that the best way to make high grades is to memorize and regurgitate. Students who would like to do their own thinking often feel that they do not have time to learn the assigned material and think about it too.

Thus students who would like to develop their abilities in creative thinking may experience a conflict in values. In the face of this conflict some students give up creative thinking and concentrate on grades; others become disinterested in college and drop out.

This conflict is easily resolved. An excellent way to practice creative thinking is to relate the subject matter of different courses. In this way you can increase your skill in creative thinking by putting subject matter into new combinations, and you can increase your resources for creative thinking by enlarging your frame of reference. You can improve your grades at the same time. When you relate subject matter from different courses you make it much easier to remember. You can do better on examinations by increasing your skill in using information you do have to substitute for information you do not have. Furthermore, your courses will become more interesting and therefore easier to study.

In practicing creative thinking, it is usually helpful to separate Phases 1, 2, and 3 from Phases 4 and 5. Most creative ideas are imperfect in their original forms. If you are too quick to apply the tests of critical thinking, you may destroy a potentially good idea before it has time to develop. Knipling's original hypothesis was incomplete because it did not include a method of sterilizing the male screwworm flies. If he had been too critical of his hypothesis at this point, he might have abandoned it.

On the other hand, constructive criticism of new ideas is essential to their development. A good rule to practice is to give the imagination freedom to range the frame of reference unchecked by critical thinking until a new idea is formed. Then this idea should be subjected to constructive criticism designed to improve or refine the idea rather than to determine whether it is useful. A new idea should not be abandoned until after a serious effort has been made to develop it.

It should never be forgotten that creative and critical thinking are two sides of the same coin: one is of little use without the other. If you cannot create new ideas, you are condemned to following the crowd. But if you act on creative ideas without first subjecting them to careful testing and evaluation, you will make mistakes for which circumstances or the crowd, or both, will punish you. Many child psychologists believe that children are naturally creative but that their creative abilities are stifled during childhood when their creative ideas lead them to make mistakes for which they are punished by their parents, by their peers, or by circumstances. The child's trouble is that he lacks the critical skills and knowledge to balance his natural creativeness. Critical thinking, if properly applied, need not restrict creativity at all, for it enables creative thinking to proceed safely. The motto of the effective thinker is: be bold and adventurous in forming tentative conclusions; be careful and thorough in criticizing them.

In the next two chapters we will return to critical thinking and examine some of the fallacies we must guard against.

Suggested Supplementary Reading

Harold A. Larrabee, *Reliable Knowledge*, rev. ed. (Boston: Houghton Mifflin Company, 1964), pp. 130–142.

EXERCISE 15

Answer each item before reading beyond it.

1. In the problem of the three boxes, what item of relevant information has not been used?

every box is incorrectly labeled

2. Complete the tabulation below, using *all* relevant information given.

Box Opened First	Consequence (*Information Gained*)
WW	Marble white ⊃ this box is _WB_
	Marble black ⊃ this box is _WB or BB_
WB	Marble white ⊃ this box is _WW_
	Marble black ⊃ this box is _BB_
BB	Marble white ⊃ this box is _WW or WB_
	Marble black ⊃ this box is _WB_

3. From which box should you remove the first marble? _____ *WB* _____

4. What is the minimum number of marbles you must examine in order to be sure of the contents of all three boxes?

_____ *one* _____

5. Sue Jordan, aged 23, has been dating Jack Harrington, aged 26, for several years. Jack has treated her more like a good friend than like a prospective wife. Sue is unhappy because he has never even hinted at a proposal. While waiting in a dentist's office one day, she happened to see this sentence in a fishing magazine: "A black bass is more likely to strike a lure if it is jerked away from him when he approaches it." What analogy is there between Sue's problem and fishing for black bass?

Sue is the lure trying to catch Jack, the bass

6–9. *The remaining items conclude the case of the* Marine Sulphur Queen. *In March the Coast Guard conducted a formal inquiry into the disappearance of the* Queen. *Evidence introduced included the following propositions.*

    1. The *Queen* was a World War II tanker converted to carry molten sulphur. She had 15,000 tons aboard when she left Beaumont, Texas, on February 2, 1963.

    2. Cracks in the hull of the *Queen* were patched in February and October, 1962.

3. Despite the fact that the *Queen* carried three separate radios, the last radio contact with her was on February 3, when she was 230 miles southeast of New Orleans.

4. The *Queen*'s normal course would have taken her through a severe storm.

5. Between February 8 and 11, planes flew for five hundred hours searching Atlantic and Gulf waters for the *Queen*. No trace of her was found.

6. Write two specific hypotheses that explain what happened to the *Queen*.

(1) _there was an explosion on board destroying everything_

(2) _the storm knocked out radio system and caused patched hull to leak ⇒ sinking of ship_

6. On February 20, an American shrimp boat reported that Cuban planes fired rockets near it when it passed through the Florida straits.

7. On February 20 and 21, flotsam and life preservers from the *Sulphur Queen* were found in waters off Miami, Florida.

8. The report of the Coast Guard included the following sentence: "The condition of the life preserver indicated that it had been used by a crew member and that the crew member subsequently drowned and slipped out of the preserver or was attacked by a predatory fish."

7. Write a specific hypothesis that takes into account all of the evidence so far introduced and yet leaves the *Queen* still afloat.

Cubans took over the Queen and several crew members went overboard in effort to escape

8. The conclusion reached by the Coast Guard was that the *Queen* sank off the east coast of Florida after an explosion or structural collapse. On the basis of all evidence presented in this text, rate the reliability of this hypothesis.

highly probable

9. Suppose that you are an investigator for an insurance company that has insured the lives of many of the *Queen*'s crew. On March 30, the day before you planned to leave for a vacation in the Bahamas aboard your new boat, you are ordered by your company to investigate the possibility that some of the *Queen*'s crew may still be alive. Write below a plan for investigating this possibility that, if accepted by your company, will turn this seeming adversity into an advantage.

examine waters and nearby islands for survivors

16 Fallacies of Irrelevance

1. *Diversion*
2. *Extension*
3. *Pettifogging*
4. *Argumentum ad Hominem*
5. *Prejudicing the Issue*
6. *Argumentum ad Baculum*

We have emphasized that effective thinking requires a balance between creative and critical thinking: neither is sufficient in itself. If our critical thinking is to be adequate, we must guard against a number of fallacies that can lead us astray in any phase of the decision-making cycle. We have already discussed certain fallacies, such as affirming the consequent, denying the antecedent, *non sequitur*, hasty generalization, and *post hoc*.

A distinction should be made between *fallacies* and *devices of persuasion*. A fallacy is an error in reasoning; a device of persuasion is a kind of argument used to persuade someone to commit a fallacy. Consider, for example, the following premises.

One is a Communist ⊃ he advocates policies officially approved by the Communist Party

Jashowitz advocates withdrawal of American troops from Europe, a policy officially approved by the Communist Party.

If you conclude from these two premises alone that Jashowitz is a Communist, you have committed the fallacy of affirming the consequent. These same two premises can be used as a device of persuasion by a propagandist who knows very well that Jashowitz

is not a Communist. By stating these two premises and leaving you to draw a conclusion, the propagandist does not commit a fallacy — he is trying to persuade others to commit it. Thus the same argument may be a device of persuasion used by the person making the argument, and a fallacy committed by the person who is fooled by the argument.

The presence of a fallacy or a device of persuasion in an argument does not necessarily indicate that the conclusion is false. For example, the conclusion of a syllogism in which the antecedent is denied may still be true. As a matter of fact, an affirmed consequent or a denied antecedent may even raise the probability that the conclusion is true. The point to be remembered is that a fallacious argument or a device of persuasion never demonstrates that the conclusion is reliable.

Let us now turn our attention to a general fallacy, *irrelevance*, and to a group of specific fallacies that involve irrelevance in one way or another. We commit the general fallacy of irrelevance whenever we base a decision on evidence or other factors that do not bear logically on the issue involved. This general fallacy may also be a device of persuasion when evidence known to be irrelevant is deliberately used to influence a decision. A ticket to the opera would hardly be honored for admission to a football game, not on the ground that the ticket is worthless, but that it does not pertain to the event for which it is being presented. In the same way, a fact or argument that would be perfectly valid and usable in one context may be worthless in another. If we decide that Frank should be elected to Phi Beta Kappa partly because he comes from a fine family and has an attractive personality, we are permitting irrelevant items of information to influence a decision. They have no connection with the purposes of Phi Beta Kappa, though they might bear on Frank's chances of making a social fraternity.

Again, if a student decides to study engineering partly because he likes the appearance of the buildings that house the college of engineering, or because his uncle likes engineering, he has permitted his decision to be influenced by irrelevant factors. The real issue is how he himself feels about engineering as a study and as a life work, and on this issue neither the physical character of the college nor his uncle's preferences have any bearing whatever.

To commit this fallacy is, at best, to waste time. American courts have established elaborate safeguards to prevent the introduction of irrelevant evidence. Without these safeguards, court trials would drag on interminably. A more important danger in this fallacy is that the issue may be decided on the wrong evidence, with disastrous consequences.

1. Diversion

Irrelevance may occur in a number of specific forms. One of these is *diversion, i.e.,* a digression from the issue in hand. Consider, for example, the following dialogue.

Chairman: "Is there any further discussion of the motion to pay a dividend of 2 per cent on common stock for the last quarter?"

Cranston: "Mr. Chairman, what are we going to do about the competition from television?"
Chairman: "It may affect our ability to pay dividends in the future, but it had no effect on last quarter's dividends."
Cranston: "But isn't it better to meet the problem before we find ourselves unable to pay a dividend?"

The chairman has stated the issue clearly: whether to pay a dividend of 2 per cent on common stock. Cranston's first question could be relevant if he has in mind that the competition from television is a reason for not paying the dividend. But his second question makes it clear that he has wandered off the issue as defined by the chairman.

Diversions often occur merely because each participant in a discussion is interested in a different aspect of the issue. The following dialogue is a case in point.

Committee Chairman: "This committee has been charged with the responsibility of revising campus parking rules. We now have eight thousand drivers seeking parking places every day, and only four thousand parking places. Obviously we must limit parking to those who need it most."
Allen: "Students who commute from great distances certainly need parking privileges."
Barkley: "I doubt that students who have to commute from great distances should be encouraged to attend college. They lose too much time commuting."
Clayton: "I don't think they lose any more time in commuting than many students do in social life."
Douglas: "Our students fritter away much too much time in social life. I think we should put some kind of limit on extracurricular activities."

Note that in the dialogue above the discussion wanders away from the issue step by step. Allen's statement is relevant, since it bears on the issue of who should have parking privileges. But it apparently stimulates Barkley's interest in a somewhat different issue. Barkley could have made his statement relevant by using it as a reason for denying parking privileges to students who commute from great distances. But apparently Allen's statement has diverted Barkley's attention away from parking. Barkley's statement, in turn, seems to have stimulated Clayton's interest in still another issue. Clayton's statement has no relevance at all to the original issue, although he could have made his statement relevant by using it as an argument against denying parking privileges to students who commute from great distances. Clayton is apparently thinking about social life rather than parking. His statement apparently stimulated Douglas' interest in an entirely different issue, for Douglas' statement is completely irrelevant. The committee has thus fallen into the fallacy of diversion, apparently because each speaker has taken the discussion off on a tangent in which he is interested. When diversions occur in committee meetings it is the responsibility of the chairman to bring the discussion back to the issue.

In a social conversation, no harm is done when the conversation wanders from one subject to another. But when a decision is to be made, any wandering from the subject can be harmful. The amount of time for group discussions of any kind, including committees and legislative bodies, is limited. Diversion can therefore have the effect of a filibuster by preventing a decision from being made. Diversion is often used deliberately for this purpose, in which case it is a device of persuasion.

Diversion is also used deliberately to avoid *any* discussion of an issue. In the following dialogue the student is apparently trying to get the discussion as far away from the issue as possible.

Father: "Young man, the issue I would like to discuss with you is your poor academic performance at the university last term."
Student: "You know, Father, my performance was not the only poor one last term. The football team won only two games. Don't you think we need a new coach?"

In this example, diversion is used as a device of persuasion. The student is trying to persuade his father not to take any action about his poor academic performance. If the father fails to bring the discussion back to the issue, he is the victim of diversion.

A form of diversion frequently used as a device of persuasion in politics and propaganda is the *red herring, i.e.,* a false issue used to draw attention away from the real issues. A person distracted by this kind of diversion may forget the original proposition. A candidate who is asked to make clear his stand on the question of increasing taxes for the improvement of schools may draw a red herring across the trail by remarking that he is opposed to "progressive" education. The original question may then easily become lost in a discussion of progressive education.

A diversion may also be accomplished by the *misuse of humor.* When properly used, humor can promote effective thinking. Since our concentration span is limited, we are better able to follow a serious or complex argument if the speaker or writer permits us to relax for a moment with a bit of humor. Humor may also help to relax tensions when emotions are running too high. If the humor used is related to the issue in hand, it is less likely to divert attention from it.

Humor is misused when it is substituted for evidence or when it diverts attention from the issue. This device of persuasion can completely disrupt effective thinking by choking off further thought. For example, a school board was holding a public hearing on its proposal to consolidate two rural schools. Members of the board were making effective arguments for consolidation by pointing out the advantages to the children of a larger school — until an opponent made this little speech. "All this reminds me of a remark in *Following the Equator:* 'In the first place God made idiots. This was for practice. Then He made school boards.'" The school board was not able again that night to get the audience's attention back to the educational advantages of consolidation. Furthermore, the sarcastic remark had the effect of important evidence, whereas it was not evidence at all.

When we are trying to reach a decision we should guard against diversion by reminding ourselves of the issue at hand and asking ourselves whether the evidence presented is relevant. When others introduce diversionary material, either innocently or deliberately, the best defense is a tactful suggestion that the discussion return to the issue.

2. Extension

Extension is like diversion in that it turns attention away from the subject, but it does so in a special way. If in a discussion or an argument we exaggerate an opponent's position in such a way as to make it easier to attack, we are guilty of *extension*. The more extreme we can represent an opposing position to be, the more successfully we can attack it.

It was once common to hear a person who wished to argue against evolution say, "Evolution teaches that men come from monkeys." When the doctrine is expressed in this form, one may make some telling arguments against it. But when so phrased, the theory of evolution is extended by exaggeration, and proof for or against the extended proposition is not the same as proof for or against the original one.

Again, if a student says frankly to his professor, "I'll admit I haven't put the time on this subject that I should," and the professor answers in annoyance, "How do you expect to get good grades when you admit that you don't study?" the professor's question includes a clear extension of the student's admission. For the student did not admit that he didn't study at all — only that he didn't study as much as he should have. The exten-

sion makes it possible for the professor to rebuke the student more severely than he deserves.

Or if a student, told by his counselor that he will be required to take a certain course, should reply impatiently, "From what you say, a student doesn't have any choice in what he takes at this university," he would be extending the counselor's statement. If the extension were to go unchallenged, the student could easily build on it a forceful set of arguments against an arbitrary and narrow curriculum.

Extension is likely to occur in any discussion in which one of the parties is eager to win or seem to win an argument. It is particularly common in Congressional debates, where both sides wish to impress the voters as having won. When one's primary objective is to win an argument, he tends to interpret his opponent's position in the worst possible light, and extension is an easy method of doing so. Thus in a debate over a new tax bill, one party may propose a slight increase in taxes in the lower income brackets. The opposing party may then attempt, deliberately or otherwise, to argue against the proposal as though it were designed to take the bread from the mouths of wage earners. It is much easier to argue effectively against the proposal when it is interpreted in this exaggerated and derogatory way.

Although both diversion and extension draw the discussion away from the issue, they are quite different. Diversion draws it to a different issue, while extension leads to an extreme or exaggerated version of the original issue. To put it another way, extension might be described as leading one's opponent out on a limb where the wood is thinner and where the limb may be cut more easily. Diversion might be described as getting an opponent off on another limb. Suppose you are contending that a student should be allowed six class cuts instead of three. Your opponent argues that, if students were never required to go to class, they would get into the habit of cutting classes and their education would suffer badly. If you then retort that unlimited cuts would not necessarily cause students to get into the habit of cutting class, you have fallen into the trap of extension. You have let yourself be lured out where the limb is thin by arguing for unlimited cuts instead of your initial proposal of only six cuts. On the other hand, suppose that your opponent argues that men cut class more frequently than women. Whatever your opponent's intentions were, he has introduced a different issue, and can be charged with diversion.

When you argue against or permit the discussion to continue on the extended version of your position, you in effect accept the extended version and thereby increase the difficulty of making your original point. The defense against extension, therefore, is to restate immediately exactly what your position is.

When we become angry in an argument, we tend to become reckless, and we more readily take up the gauntlet in favor of the extended issue instead of the original one. For that reason, some users of extension deliberately irritate or anger their opponents before extending the issue. Therefore the defense against extension also requires a cool head.

3. Pettifogging

A pettifogger is a person who concentrates his attention on petty issues. Essentially, he tries to make an issue of something trivial. Hence, the fallacy of *pettifogging* includes a variety of petty tricks of argument. These include quibbling, *i.e.*, evading the real issue by arguing over the meaning of a word when there is no reasonable doubt about its meaning, making unreasonably fine distinctions, or wrangling about trivial points in such a way as to obscure the real issue or the important evidence.

Let us look at some illustrations. The social committee of a civic organization announced a date for the organization's annual picnic. In the event of rain, the committee said, the picnic would be held a week later. One of the members, who did not wish to miss the picnic but who found it inconvenient to go at the appointed time, sincerely hoped that rain would cause a postponement. On the day of the picnic, although there was no serious threat of rain, there was a very light scattering of raindrops — not enough to settle the dust. This member then called the chairman of the committee and insisted that the picnic be set for the following week, for, as he said, "It's been raining." His effort to interpret the scattering of raindrops as "rain" in the sense intended by the committee was pettifogging.

A student preparing to demonstrate a proposition in geometry drew some circles on the blackboard. A fellow student argued that the demonstration could not proceed because the circles were not perfectly drawn. His argument was pettifogging, for technical perfection in the drawing of the circles was not essential to the success of the demonstration.

The loser of an election bet walked from his home to Washington, D.C., a distance of over five hundred miles, to satisfy the terms of the bet. But when the winner learned that the loser had been obliged, at one point, to cross a stream by ferry, he grumbled, "He was supposed to walk every foot of the way." This trivial complaint, considered in the light of a five-hundred-mile hike, was pettifogging.

A motorist was told to make a right turn when he came to a red billboard. He missed the turn, partly because he was not watching carefully and partly because the signboard was not the shade of red he had visualized. Later, when he was shown the signboard, which was a dusty maroon, he remonstrated with his original informant, "What do you mean by *red?* I don't call *that* red."

Such arguments may be technically relevant, but they have the effect of irrelevancies because they make no significant contribution to the real issue. The two-word retort, "So what?" is a devastating defense against pettifogging. A more tactful defense is simply to point out that the argument in question is not significant.

4. Argumentum ad Hominem

The fallacy known as *argumentum ad hominem,* or "argument against the man," is generally based on the assumption that anything which discredits a man discredits his argument. Thus, instead of meeting a proposition directly with evidence that it is objectionable, we may attack the person who advances the proposition, supposing that, if we can show something to his personal disadvantage, it must follow that his proposition is also objectionable.

If we are suspicious of the results announced by a research scholar, and give as our reason that these results are not to be relied upon because the scholar was recently a principal figure in a notorious scandal, we are using an *ad hominem* argument. We may decline to accept a man's suggestion because he uses questionable grammar. Or we may object to a plan for civic improvement because we know that the originator of the plan is cruel to his family. The irrelevance of these reasons is not hard to see.

Under some circumstances the reputation of a person may be relevant to the reliability of his statements. In a courtroom, for example, the testimony of a witness may be discredited if it can be established that he is an untruthful or a dishonest person. But we must not assume that the defendant is guilty of the offense with which he is charged just because he is notoriously dishonest. The worst scoundrel in town may not be guilty of the particular crime with which he is charged. Even a man with an unsavory reputation may tell the truth as a witness.

To determine just how much a person's character is relevant to a specific issue requires careful analysis. In court this is the responsibility of the judge and the jury.

It is important to note that a slur on a person's character is not necessarily an instance of *argumentum ad hominem.* To be *ad hominem* the slur must be irrelevant to the issue in hand. In a political campaign, for example, the issue is the candidate's character and qualifications for the office he seeks. An attack on a candidate for the position of road commissioner on the ground that he has been convicted of accepting bribes is relevant to the issue. On the other hand, attacks on his family background or religion are instances of *argumentum ad hominem* unless it is clearly shown that these matters are relevant to his qualifications for road commissioner.

We may best defend ourselves against *argumentum ad hominem* by showing that the attack on the man is irrelevant to the issue. To avoid committing the fallacy ourselves, we should be careful that any criticism we make of the person involved is relevant to the issue.

The name *argumentum ad hominem* is sometimes applied to an appeal made to a particular individual's bias and prejudice. This kind of appeal will be discussed later under the topic *attitude fitting.* In this book we use the term *argumentum ad hominem* to mean only an irrelevant reference to the man himself in an attempt to discredit his argument.

5. Prejudicing the Issue

A device of persuasion frequently used, particularly by those who are careless about the logical soundness of their arguments, is *prejudicing the issue.* Although this device looks much like *argumentum ad hominem,* it is actually quite different.

Suppose that the issue in question is whether ROTC should be compulsory. And suppose Colonel Abernathy has stated that ROTC should be compulsory in order to provide an adequate reserve of trained officers. One might try to discredit Colonel Abernathy's argument by pointing out that Colonel Abernathy has been divorced twice and is not, therefore, a successful family man. This would be a clear case of *argumentum ad hominem,* for Colonel Abernathy's family life is irrelevant to his qualifications to speak on the issue of compulsory ROTC.

Suppose, however, someone argues that anyone who advocates compulsory ROTC is a fascist. This is a clear case of prejudicing the issue. Arguments of this kind have four potential effects, all undesirable from the point of view of effective thinking. In the first place, this kind of argument may have the effect of *ad hominem* with respect to any contrary argument: any argument for compulsory ROTC is labeled in advance as coming from a fascist. Yet little or no evidence is given to justify this label. In the second place, putting the label of fascist on those who argue on the other side of the issue also puts the label of fascist on compulsory ROTC itself, with little or no evidence to justify it. In the third place, arguments of this kind may have the effect of a "red herring." Finally, this kind of argument tends to shut off rational discussion of the issue by intimidating those who might otherwise argue on the other side. The effectiveness of prejudicing the issue in this respect is more psychological than logical. When used skillfully it forces an opponent to remain silent or to take a position contrary to his own self-concept. Consider the following dialogue.

Daughter: "How do you like my new dress?"
Father: "If you wear a dress like that, you are no daughter of mine."

If the daughter now defends the dress, she must incur the accusation that she is not a loyal daughter.

In resisting this device of persuasion it is helpful to keep in mind that a person who uses it may feel too insecure about his position on the issue to consider contrary evidence. Direct and logical counterarguments are unlikely to have any effect on him. Little is likely to be gained by continuing a private discussion. In a public discussion, however, serious harm may be done if the use of prejudicing the issue is permitted to go unchallenged. In such a situation a two-part defense should be used. It should be pointed out, as tactfully as possible but as forcefully as necessary, that the person using the device is guilty of name-calling and trying to intimidate his opponents. Then attention should be recalled to the real issue in question.

6. Argumentum ad Baculum

Logically, when one argues in favor of a proposed action, he should restrict himself to sound reasons based on the whole, relevant truth. Often, however, force or the threat of force is substituted for reason. This substitution is known as *argumentum ad baculum,* or argument of the club. This device is commonly used by parents who, in controlling the behavior of their children, substitute the threat of the paddle for sound reasons. Nations also use *argumentum ad baculum* when they hold impressive military maneuvers near the border of a neighboring country in times of tension or while international agreements are being negotiated. The robber uses it when he points his gun at a victim and threatens, "Your money or your life."

While such arguments are often effective, they are always logically irrelevant and may be dangerous to human and to international relations. We should never lose sight of the fact that, even when submission or use of counter force may be deemed necessary, such solutions do not persuade by use of reason, and create resentment and bitterness.

What one should do when faced with this kind of argument depends on circumstances. Sometimes one may oppose the threat of force effectively with reasonable argument;

at other times it may be necessary to submit or to combat force with force.

We should always remember that the self-concept is a factor in the degree to which we are susceptible to all fallacies and devices of persuasion. We are much more likely to be tricked by fallacious arguments in favor of ideas we wish to believe than by those in opposition to these ideas. If we are to protect our objectivity in critical thinking, therefore, we should cultivate the habit of examining with particular care those arguments that support ideas we wish to believe.

EXERCISE 16

1–8. *These items refer to the lettered statements below. Assume that all observations contained in these statements are true.*

    A. *Abrams:* "I nominate Williams for the 'most valuable player' award."

    B. *Bacon:* "I nominate Young. He is vice-president of the student body."

    C. *Clarendon:* "Gentlemen, the donor of this award specifically stated that the sole criterion for this award is value to the football team."

    D. *Dexter:* "I second the nomination of Young. He set a record this season for unassisted tackles."

    E. *Foster:* "I second the nomination of Williams. After all, he was captain of the team."

    F. *Gaines:* "Foster, I'm amazed that you would think being captain is the only consideration in selecting the most valuable player."

    G. *Foster:* "I didn't say that. What I meant was that being captain is one of several considerations."

    H. *Holman:* "I don't know what you mean by 'several.' Do you mean three, or seven, or seventeen?"

    I. *Ingersol:* "I don't think we should give full weight to the opinions of Gaines and Holman. They are Young's fraternity brothers, and all three played together in high school."

    J. *Holman:* "We shouldn't give any weight to Ingersol's opinion. He failed freshman math twice."

    K. *Gaines:* "Say what you please, but anybody who says that Young was not the most valuable player is an ignoramus as far as football is concerned."

    L. *Jackson:* "This team does not have an ignoramus on it. The team's grade average is higher than that of the student body."

1. Which statement defines the issue?   C

2. Which statement(s) introduce(s) relevant evidence and contain(s) no fallacy?   A, D, E

3. Which statement(s) illustrate(s) general rather than specific types of irrelevance?   B

4. Which statement(s) illustrate(s) *argumentum ad hominem?*   J

5. Which statement illustrates an attack on a speaker that is not *argumentum ad hominem?*   I, K

6. Which statement(s) illustrate(s) extension?   F, K

7. Which statement(s) illustrate(s) the proper defense against extension?   G

8. Which statement(s) illustrate(s) pettifogging? _____ H ____

9–16. *Write in the blank the name of the specific type of irrelevance that is most prominent in each item.*

9. The speaker said, "I beg of you, ladies and gentlemen, to remember that a person opposing this move does not have the welfare of this community at heart."

prejudicing the issue

10. *Boy:* "Where did you go with him last night?"
Girl: "I just love the way your eyes do when you get mad." *diversion*

11. *Speaker:* "In a time of national emergency, every citizen, be he man, woman or child, should contribute to his country's cause."
Heckler: "So you want women and children drafted into the armed services."

extension

12. *Speaker:* "And, in conclusion, let me urge you not to vote for the dredging of Otterway Bay. My opponent has been asking you to do this for some time, but you must not forget that he has long been under treatment for alcoholism."

argumentum ad hominem

13. *Political candidate in a debate:* "Since our position is unquestionably beyond attack, anyone who speaks against our platform is either ill-informed or not loyal to the party."

prejudicing the issue

14. *Joe:* "Pete, you don't join any organizations; you don't go to the games; you don't vote in the student elections; you don't read the school paper. Don't you have an ounce of school spirit?"

Pete: "Now, wait a minute. What do you mean by 'an ounce of school spirit'? Is school spirit something that can be measured out and weighed? What exactly is an ounce of school spirit?"

pettifogging

15. The minister had just finished an effective sermon denouncing certain vices prevalent in the community. One of the chief sinners in the congregation said to his friend, "Don't pay any attention to him. He doesn't practice what he preaches."

argumentum ad hominem

16. *Campaign orator:* "My opponent says, and I quote, 'If we are to pay the costs of improved government services, we must increase the government's revenue.' Surely you do not wish to elect a man who will so increase the tax burden that your homes and businesses will be confiscated and sold for taxes."

extension

17 Neglected Aspect

Let us now turn our attention to another kind of general fallacy, *neglected aspect,* and to a group of specific types of this fallacy. We commit the general fallacy of neglected aspect whenever we fail to consider evidence or factors that are both relevant and significant to the issue in hand. Thus neglected aspect is almost the opposite of irrelevance, which is permitting a decision to be influenced by evidence or factors that should not be considered.

Sometimes failure to consider an important part of the evidence can lead to a totally false conclusion. For example, a person who reads of a number of fatal accidents in airplanes and decides, upon this evidence alone, that travel by plane should be prohibited has neglected significant aspects of the question, namely, the great advantages of air transport and the relatively low rate of accidents per million miles traveled. Even in the most careful investigation there is always the possibility that one may fail to take into account all the relevant factors.

Many an ingenious and plausible argument fails to hold up when the powerful searchlights of *all* relevant considerations are turned on it. If someone should argue that reckless driving benefits society as a whole because it furnishes employment to automobile mechanics, ambulance drivers, doctors and nurses, undertakers, and insurance men, we would logically object that at least one important factor was being overlooked — one that we could not possibly agree to leave out — the value of human life.

Suppose someone who is in the market for a motel discovers one for sale that seems to be a bargain. Records for a period of years show consistently high profits and low maintenance costs. Yet within a year after our hypothetical businessman purchases the motel the profits disappear and the value of the property is greatly reduced because a long-planned multilaned highway has been built two miles away from the motel. Failure to consider this discoverable aspect of the truth has led directly to a very costly mistake.

The fallacy of neglected aspect can occur in all phases of the decision-making cycle. In Phase 1 we can commit the fallacy by defining the problem so narrowly as to exclude an important part of it. In Phase 2 we can fail to gather essential information. In Phase 3 we can fail to take into account essential information in forming tentative conclusions. In Phase 4 we can fail to apply essential tests for validity or reliability.

In Phase 5 we can fail to see the consequences of a proposed action, particularly its long-range consequences. Consider the case of a college halfback. While in college the glory he won on the football field satisfied his need for self-esteem, and he studied just enough to stay eligible for football. When his eligibility for college football ran out, he dropped out of college and entered professional football. His career in professional football was successful for ten years, after which he was released because he had become too slow. At this point he made a painful discovery: the world has little use for thirty-two-year-old former halfbacks. When he tried to find another satisfying career, he found the doors closed because he lacked sufficient education. When he tried to return to college, he was told that his academic record was so bad that he could not possibly graduate.

Fallacies of neglected aspect are not easy to avoid. Gathering and properly considering all significant aspects of an issue require both time and hard work. Furthermore, subjective factors make us vulnerable to these fallacies. None of us has a frame of reference so complete and accurate that he can recognize and properly interpret all aspects of all issues. The "psychological Ohm's law" mentioned in Chapter 1 leads directly to neglected aspect by inducing us to overlook, or to refuse to see, or to refuse to believe significant evidence that threatens the self-concept. A high degree of susceptibility to fallacies of neglected aspect may amount to a refusal to deal with reality.

In our time, probably more than in any other period in the history of western civilization, the well-being of both individuals and society depends on our skill and courage in resisting these fallacies. Our best protection against them is the careful use of the five-phase cycle of decision making. When we must counter arguments that involve neglected aspect, it is usually best to call attention to the neglected aspect and point out its significance.

1. Oversimplification

There are a number of specific forms of neglected aspect. One of these is *oversimplification*, which occurs when we think of or describe a situation as though it involved only a few significant facets, whereas in truth it involves a complex of many significant facets.

An inadequate frame of reference almost inevitably leads to oversimplification. To the man in the street, whose knowledge of foreign affairs is limited to newspaper headlines and radio and television newscasts, solutions to international problems are relatively simple. Because he knows only a few of the significant details, he is likely to think foreign affairs should be conducted according to Theodore Roosevelt's axiom, "Speak softly and carry a big stick." His understanding of international problems is analogous to the view one has of a forest while flying over it at an altitude of 15,000 feet. He can see the forest, but he cannot see the trees. Oversimplification is not limited, however, to the ignorant. The specialist who has vast knowledge of his own field may be relatively ignorant in other areas. Specialists in all areas related to human behavior tend to oversimplify human behavior by attaching too much importance to one particular facet and neglecting many others. For example, the economist tends to attach too much importance to economic motives, the biologist to explain too much of human behavior in terms of heredity, the sociologist to attach too much importance to environment, the psychologist to exaggerate the importance of childhood experiences.

One's self-concept often encourages oversimplification. It is important to the self-concept to see oneself as a person who can cope with his environment. In order to feel that one can cope with his environment, one must also feel that he understands it. But few of us have both the frame of reference and the reasoning skills necessary to understand accurately all of the significant aspects of our complex world. Hence some of our interpretations of our world are necessarily oversimplified.

Another cause of oversimplification is our fondness for the dramatic. Sportswriters, for example, tend to describe athletic contests in terms of the performances of one or two star players. A football game in which the most dramatic play was a pass from the star quarterback to the star end may be described as though these two players won the game by themselves. Baseball games are often described as though they were won by the pitcher. The wise coach or manager tries to offset this oversimplification by stressing the contributions of other members of the team.

Even if we could eliminate the influence of subjective factors, we could still not eliminate oversimplification. Our views of some situations in our complex world are necessarily oversimplified because we do not have time to gather and consider all of the relevant and significant information.

Oversimplification frequently results from efforts to be concise. Radio and newspaper headlines, which must be concise, are likely to be oversimplifications whenever they deal with complex subjects. Introductory textbooks usually contain some oversimplification, too, for it is difficult to present a complete and balanced picture of a subject without confusing the beginning student with a mass of detail.

To protect ourselves from oversimplification we should cultivate the habit of being suspicious of simple explanations of, or solutions to, complex problems. When we must counter arguments containing oversimplification, the best defense is to point out the significant neglected aspects.

2. The Black-or-White Fallacy

Another specific form of neglected aspect, the black-or-white fallacy, stems from the fact that, although some objects or qualities can be divided into discrete categories, most cannot. Instead, they are spread over a continuum from one extreme to the other, just as paint can vary in an infinite number of shades between black and white. In some respects, for instance, all students can be definitely categorized. Every student is an in-state student or an out-of-state student, a freshman or an upperclassman, a full-time student or a part-time student. On the other hand, students range on a continuum of academic ability and performance all the way from very good to very bad, and it is difficult to divide them into separate and distinct categories. In principle, the experienced instructor sees a very significant difference between A students and B students, but in practice he finds that many of them are in a grey zone between the two categories.

We commit the black-or-white fallacy when we suppose that in a given situation there are only two alternatives when in fact there are more than two. We are particularly vulnerable to this error when the two alternatives we have in mind are opposite extremes. For between opposites or extremes there are frequently intermediate positions, neutral shades, or different courses of action. Items that are not white are not necessarily black: they may be any shade of gray. Deeds that are not evil are not necessarily good: they may be neutral in moral significance. Water that is not hot is not necessarily cold: it may be tepid.

The black-or-white fallacy is particularly bad in Phase 5 of decision making, for it may lead us into taking extreme action when more moderate action would be wiser. Suppose a man has a wife and a mother who are very jealous of each other, both of whom want all of his attention. If he believes he must either do all his mother wants or all his wife wants, he is probably committing a black-or-white fallacy. Very likely he should do some of what his mother wants and some of what his wife wants.

Greater than average susceptibility to the black-or-white fallacy may indicate immaturity. A child, in his early experiences with people, is unable to make discriminating judgments. To him, people tend to be either all good or all bad. The fairy tales and television programs designed for his entertainment abound in angelic heroines and hideous villains. Many people fail to outgrow these childhood tendencies. In later years they yearn for the security of childhood and tend to forget the bruises and burned fingers suffered because they failed to understand their environment.

To protect ourselves from the black-or-white fallacy we should cultivate the habit of forming a number of tentative conclusions and proposals for action.

3. The Argument of the Beard

Another specific form of neglected aspect, the *argument of the beard,* also stems from the fact that most objects or qualities range on a continuum from one extreme to the other. In a sense, the argument of the beard may be considered the opposite of the black-or-white fallacy. We are guilty of black-or-white reasoning if we fail to admit the possibility of a middle ground between extremes. We are guilty of the argument of the beard if we use the middle ground, or the fact of continuous and gradual shading between two extremes, to raise doubt about the existence of real differences between such opposites as strong and weak, good and bad, and black and white. The gradual shading between extremes may blind us to significant differences. The fact that we cannot determine the exact point at which white ceases to be white does not prove that there is no difference between white and black.

The very name of the fallacy is derived from a classic example. Think how difficult it would be to decide just how many whiskers it takes to make a beard. Surely one whisker is not sufficient. Possibly even twenty-five are too few. Then let us say that three hundred and fifty whiskers make a beard. Why not three hundred and forty-nine? Three hundred and forty-eight? And so on. We would have trouble determining an exact

minimum. Does this fact mean that there is no difference between having a beard and not having one?

The commission of this fallacy reveals an inability to distinguish or acknowledge small differences even when they are of real significance. Seeing such differences is frequently difficult, especially in a field in which we are not well informed, and students will therefore occasionally charge their instructors with "splitting hairs." Usually, though, the instructor is simply insisting that the student must keep struggling with a subject until he can comprehend the distinctions essential to an understanding of that subject. Learning to see close distinctions is a very important part of becoming educated.

Unhappily, in many practical affairs we must make arbitrary distinctions on the basis of small differences. Suppose the scores of 101 students are evenly distributed between zero and 100, and the instructor draws the line so that the lowest passing score is 60. A student with a score of 59 might contend that one point should not make this much difference. If the instructor agrees, however, that he is not justified in drawing the line between 59 and 60, then where is he to draw the line? How is he to draw any line at all? And if he shirks his responsibility for drawing the line, will he not ultimately be treating the students with zero and 100 as if there were no difference between them? We commit the argument of the beard whenever we dispute the right of authority to draw lines simply because the difference between the items on each side of the line is small.

This is not to say that all statements to the effect that a little difference will not matter contain this fallacy, for there are many situations in which a little more or less actually does not matter. When you are putting sugar in your coffee, it is true that a little more or less won't matter *one time.* But if you are on a reducing diet and you argue that having a half-teaspoon more sugar in every cup won't matter, then you are committing the fallacy. The little difference per cup may accumulate into a large difference in your caloric intake.

The argument of the beard is especially tempting in situations in which we wish to deceive ourselves. It is a heaven-sent gift for the person who is looking for a way of rationalizing his behavior.

This fallacy is especially pernicious in moral or ethical judgments because it is frequently used to justify immoral or unethical behavior. The operator of a bolita game, who sells "numbers" to the poorest people in town, justifies his conduct on the grounds that both his specialty and bingo games, as operated for charity among the members of a lodge, are forms of gambling, and that one is not worse than the other. Such a person can be said to be "shade blind," for he is unable to distinguish between shades of grey. Whether a difference is significant can be determined only by reference to the particular situation.

We may guard against the argument of the beard by reminding ourselves that an accumulation of even small differences may bridge the distance between great extremes. When you find yourself tempted to argue or believe that just a little will not make any difference, ask yourself whether the difference involved could be cumulative.

4. Misuse of the Mean

There is yet a third way of neglecting the aspects of a continuum between extremes. When we believe or argue that a position near the center is sound solely because it is near the center of the continuum, we commit the fallacy *misuse of the mean* (the word "mean" is used here in a general sense; it does not necessarily refer to the statistical mean). We would commit this fallacy if we argued that the ideal speed on the highway is forty miles per hour because it is between the extremes of the poky driver and the speed maniac. There are at least four flaws in such reasoning. First, the ideal position may vary with circumstances: forty miles per hour may

be too fast in congested traffic and too slow on a turnpike. Second, it is not enough merely to show that the position is somewhere between the extremes; we must also show that it is the right position. One may drive faster than the poky driver and still be driving too slowly. Third, a position is not necessarily wrong because it is extreme. The poky driver's speed may be about right in a fog. Many ideas we now cherish were once considered extreme. Finally, the location of the middle position depends on how the extremes are defined. If driving at ten miles per hour is defined as one extreme and eighty miles per hour the other, then the center of the continuum is forty-five. But if the extremes are defined as twenty and sixty, then the center is forty. In short, the fact that a position is near the center is not sufficient evidence to establish that it is sound.

Misuse of the mean may also be a device of persuasion. In political campaigns each party frequently tries to define the extremes in such a way that its own position appears to be near the center. President Franklin D. Roosevelt described his political philosophy as "a little left of center," even though it was radical in comparison with the philosophy of previous administrations. The principal issue in the Republican Convention of 1964 was "extremism." Both the conservative and liberal factions in the party tried to make their own positions appear to be in "midstream," and those of the other faction "extreme."

Misuse of the mean is frequently involved in compromises. Suppose the members of an organization are divided over the qualifications for membership. One faction advocates very high and rigid qualifications while the other faction advocates moderate ones. To assume that a compromise position is the best solution without reference to the actual merits of the case is to commit the fallacy. While compromises may often be necessary and desirable in a democratic society, we should never assume that a position is sound merely because it is a compromise. Parties to a dispute often begin by making unreasonable demands in the hope that the eventual compromise will be nearer to what they want. A good defense against misuse of the mean as a device of persuasion is to point out the merits of another position on the continuum.

The distinction between the black-or-white fallacy, the argument of the beard, and misuse of the mean on the one hand, and oversimplification on the other can be explained in terms of an analogy — like the difference between a straight line and a spider web. The black-or-white fallacy, the argument of the beard, and misuse of the mean involve failure to consider different points on a straight line. Oversimplification, on the other hand, involves failure to consider significant parts of a spider web. The former involves differences in degree; the latter involves omissions of many kinds.

5. Half-Truths

Witnesses in court must swear to tell the truth, the whole truth, and nothing but the truth. The requirement to tell the whole truth is included in the oath because just a part of the truth can be as misleading as a completely false statement. In the following anecdote, the omission of a single fact leads to a totally erroneous conclusion. In a trial following a disastrous wreck at a railroad crossing, a trainman testified that he had signaled by vigorously waving a lantern. He demonstrated dramatically to the jury the manner in which he had waved it. After the trial the railway's attorney commended him for the effectiveness of his testimony. The trainman wiped some perspiration from his brow and said, "Whew, I was awfully afraid that other lawyer would ask me if the lantern was lighted!"

The type of neglected aspect illustrated in this anecdote is the *half-truth*, a statement that, although true as far as it goes, creates a false impression because one or more significant, relevant facts are omitted from the statement.

For purposes of deception, the half-truth is often more effective than a lie. It is therefore a favorite device of confidence men and propagandists. A lie is dangerous to the propagandist because if he is caught in it his audience will lose confidence in him. But a half-truth is hard to expose. In fact, the skillful propagandist can frequently use the half-truth in such a way that it is difficult to prove that he was telling anything but the truth. Indeed, what is said in a half-truth is true — it is simply not the whole truth.

An especially tricky and subtle variety of half-truth is sometimes called *card-stacking*. The evidence given appears to be fair to both sides, but in fact the evidence is carefully selected to make one side of the argument much more convincing than it would be if the whole truth were told. A case in point is a program presented on Moscow television entitled "A City without a Soul," a documentary film on New York City. As reported by the Associated Press, the film showed the buildings of Rockefeller Center and the financial district, even though Soviet cameramen usually avoid photographing buildings in the West. Also shown were "photographs of Harlem, blind beggars, dirty streets, and unemployed men lining up for compensation payments." Much attention was given shops selling "girlie" magazines, but there were no views of food stores. "Even the Easter parade on Fifth Avenue was shown. Not about Easter, though. The announcer merely said that once a year traffic is stopped so that women can show their hats."

Card-stacking is present in almost all advertising. Business firms can hardly be expected to spend their advertising budgets to inform the public of the faults in their products. The distinguishing characteristic of the half-truth is one-sidedness. An argument may involve neglected aspect in its general or specific forms without being one-sided. The half-truth is always one-sided. Usually, though not always, the half-truth is used as a device of persuasion: the situation is deliberately distorted by the selection of evidence.

To avoid being victimized by half-truths, we should cultivate the habit of being suspicious of one-sided arguments.

6. Decision by Indecision

In trying to avoid fallacies of all kinds, we must beware of falling into the pitfall of decision by indecision by permitting time and events to make decisions for us. Decision by indecision may itself involve a kind of neglected aspect. For as long as we hesitate to act on a tentative conclusion because it seems insufficiently reliable, we are acting as though we believe the tentative conclusion to be false.

It should be noted that taking no action in a situation is not necessarily decision by indecision. On some issues there may be a clear-cut position of neutrality; during a general war, for example, a country may decide that its national interest requires that it join neither side. The very act of deciding not to take sides is itself a decision; it is a deliberate choice, not a failure to make a choice. If, however, the nation remains neutral through a lack of resolute policy, and its responsible officials by default allow the turn of international events to make their decisions for them, then these officials are guilty of decision by indecision.

Decision by indecision on the part of Adolf Hitler had a vital effect on the outcome of World War II. In the early fall of 1942, the German Sixth Army occupied a salient extending into Stalingrad, many miles in front of the main German lines. Although the Germans held much of the city, it continued to be defended with almost incredible sacrifice by Russian troops, as well as by women and children fighting with sticks, stones, and bare hands. Early in September, the German

General Staff urged Hitler to withdraw the Sixth Army to the main lines. Hitler refused to do so. Several weeks later German military intelligence warned Hitler that the Russians were preparing a massive offensive designed to encircle and destroy the Sixth Army. At this point it could probably have been withdrawn from the salient. But Hitler did not believe the warning and waited for the situation to clear up.

While evidence of the impending Russian offensive continued to mount, Hitler continued to hesitate. Military evidence indicated that the middle of November was the latest possible date for the Sixth Army to withdraw. Still Hitler hesitated. The Russian offensive began on November 19, and within a few days it succeeded in surrounding the Sixth Army. The Sixth Army still had a chance to fight its way back through the loosely organized Russian forces cutting it off from the main German lines. But Hitler publicly ordered it to advance. It was not until early December that Hitler was finally persuaded to permit the Sixth Army to fight its way out of the trap. In the intervening days, however, the Russians had strengthened their position, and the attempt failed.

Even at this late hour, some of the Sixth Army might have been saved. General Zeitzler suggested an emergency airlift of supplies, together with a massive attempt by forces from the main German lines to cut through the encircling Russian forces. Again Hitler hesitated for weeks. He finally decided in January to make the attempt, but it was too late. Consequently the entire Sixth Army was lost. Of the 330,000 well-equipped and well-trained men, only 5,000 survived as prisoners of war. By not deciding until it was too late, Hitler had in effect decided to sacrifice the Sixth Army. Many military historians believe that the loss of this army marked the turning point of the war, for Germany never again recovered the political and military initiative.

Many people try to avoid decision by indecision by acting on impulse and then seeking evidence to convince themselves that the decision was sound. There is a better way, as we shall see. It is wise to recognize that you cannot always be right. Dr. A. Lawrence Lowell, the late president of Harvard University, was fond of saying, "There is a Harvard man on the wrong side of every question." If your self-concept includes a view of yourself as a person who never makes a mistake, you are extremely vulnerable to decision by indecision: the fear of having to admit to yourself that you have made a mistake will make you hesitate to make a decision.

Hitler's self-concept was apparently an important factor in his decisions by indecision. German propaganda had pictured Hitler as a military genius who could do no wrong. Apparently Hitler began to believe his own propaganda. A year or so before the disaster at Stalingrad, he arbitrarily wrested total direction of the armed forces from his General Staff, stating flatly that "where the German soldier sets his foot, there he stays." When the Sixth Army first entered Stalingrad he announced prematurely that the city had fallen and that this was an irretrievable disaster for the Russians. Hitler might have avoided the disaster at Stalingrad and saved his own pride too, had he been able to be objective in his appraisal of the situation. But the threat to his self-concept was so great that he was totally unable to recognize the truth.

Although the results are not always undesirable, decisions by indecision are always bad from the point of view of effective thinking. To the extent that you let time or events make your decisions you are letting time or events be the master of your fate. Furthermore, decisions made by using the procedures of effective thinking will prove to be sound much more often than those made by indecision. Habitually following three procedural rules is helpful in avoiding decision by indecision.

1. *Put first things first.* There is not enough time in any one day to consider carefully and thoroughly every decision that must be made on that day; some decisions by indecision are inevitable. It is therefore desirable to spend one's thinking time on the more important decisions.

2. *Set a time limit for making the decision.* In many situations you can determine fairly accurately when the deadline is. For example, the college catalog may tell you what the deadline is for deciding whether to change your curriculum. When you know the approximate date, you can apply the five-phase cycle as thoroughly as possible and act before the deadline. General Eisenhower recognized the time factor in his decision concerning Operation Overlord. He determined the last possible moment for a decision. Until this moment arrived he considered his decision as thoroughly as possible. When the moment arrived he made the decision. Hitler, on the other hand, delayed his decision concerning Stalingrad for two months after the date his advisers believed was the deadline.

3. *Carefully weigh the alternatives,* using the procedures described in previous chapters, especially those concerned with evaluating proposals for action. Then act within the deadline. To quote Dr. Lowell again, "The mark of an educated man is the ability to make a reasoned guess on the basis of insufficient information." To which we might add that the mark of a courageous man is the ability to act on the basis of a reasoned guess when not to act would be decision by indecision.

EXERCISE 17

1–6. *These items refer to the following statements made at a committee meeting.*

    A. *Abbot:* "Gentlemen, this committee has been charged with the responsibility of revising the academic rules for continued enrollment at Wysacki."

    B. *Baker:* "Under our present rules a student is put on probation if his grade point average for the preceding term is below 1.7. I don't think there should be any probation. A student is either good enough to stay in or not good enough."

    C. *Clark:* "I don't think we should eliminate probation. After all, there is no significant difference between averages of 1.70 and 1.69."

    D. *Davis:* "If we eliminate probation and suspend all students who fail to maintain a certain average, we would suspend many students whose averages have dropped temporarily because of illness or other factors beyond their control. A probationary period would give them a chance to catch up."

    E. *Elton:* "It seems to me that the whole purpose of the rules is to make students study. If we set high standards the students will meet them. I think we should suspend all students who fail to maintain a 2.0 average."

    F. *Gaffney:* "There is much more involved in getting students to study than mere rules. If we want them to study we must provide challenging courses and teachers, an adequate library, and an intellectual atmosphere."

1. Which statements define issues?   A F B

2. Which statement contains a definition of an issue that illustrates oversimplification?

     E

3. Which statement illustrates the black-or-white fallacy?   B

4. Which statement illustrates the argument of the beard?   C

5 Which statement is a proper defense against the general fallacy of neglected aspect?

     D

6. Which statement is a proper defense against the fallacy of oversimplification?

     F

7–13. *These items refer to the statements below.*

    G. *Elton:* "I still think we should change the rules to require a minimum average of 2.0. They adopted this rule at Farmington College five years ago. Since then the student body average has risen from 2.3 to 2.9, and the percentage of students suspended did not increase."

    H. *Clark:* "True enough. But I happen to know that the enrollment dropped sharply after the first year of the new rule, and the faculty solved the problem by lowering the grading standards."

I. *Abbot:* "We seem to have a difference of opinion. Some of you seem to favor keeping the present requirement of 1.7, and others favor raising it to 2.0. I propose that we raise the requirement to 1.85."

J. *Clark:* "There's nothing magic about 1.85. Why not 1.8 or 1.9?"

K. *Davis:* "Before we take any action on this issue, I think we should ask the Registrar to analyze the effect this proposal would have had on the students last term."

L. *Elton:* "If we do that it will be too late to change the rules until next year."

M. *Davis:* "I move that we retain the present rules for another year. During that time we can make an adequate study of the matter."

7. Which statement contains a half-truth? _____G_____

8. Which statement illustrates a proper defense against a half-truth?

_____H_____

9. Which statement calls attention to the danger of decision by indecision?

_____L_____

10. Which statement illustrates a means of avoiding decision by indecision?

_____M or K_____

11. Which statement illustrates misuse of the mean? _____I_____

12. Which statement illustrates a proper defense against misuse of the mean?

_____J_____

13. Which statement illustrates the method of testing a tentative solution by predicting its consequences?

_____K_____

14–15. *Write in the blank the name of the specific fallacy of neglected aspect that is most prominent in each item.*

14. *Irate parent:* "Don't give me all that stuff about the stiff competition at school. I've told you and I'll tell you again that all you have to do to make good grades is study three hours a night."

oversimplification

15. *Politician:* "Chaos and confusion have developed around this and related issues. We can eliminate the confusion by clarifying the issues and by sound reasoning. The issue, uncomplicated by red herrings and smoke screens, is whether we favor giving the defense department the increase it asks for or giving it nothing at all."

black-or-white

18 Pitfalls in Language

All the procedures of thinking discussed in this text must be carried out largely, if not entirely, through the medium of language. Basically, language is a "systematized combination of sounds which have meaning for all persons in a given cultural community."[1] Written language is a symbolic representation of these sounds.

It is the ability to think symbolically that distinguishes the mental processes of man from those of the higher animals. All the intelligent animals use what Susanne Langer refers to as *signs*, but apparently only man uses *symbols*.

A symbol differs from a sign in that it does not announce the presence of the object, the being, condition, or whatnot, which is its meaning, but merely *brings this thing to mind*. It is not a mere "substitute sign" to which we react as though it were the object itself. The fact is that our reaction to hearing a person's name is quite different from our reaction to the person himself. . . .

The difference between a sign and a symbol is, in brief, that a sign causes us to think or act *in face of* the thing signified, whereas a symbol causes us to think *about* the thing symbolized. Therein lies the great importance of symbolism for human life, its power to make this life so different from any other animal biography that generations of men have found it incredible to suppose that they were of purely zoological origin. A sign is always embedded in reality, in a present that emerges from the actual past and stretches to the future; but a symbol may be divorced from reality altogether. It may refer to what is *not* the case, to a mere idea, a figment, a dream. It serves, therefore, to liberate thought from the immediate stimuli of a physically present world; and that liberation marks the essential difference between human and non-human mentality.[2]

The development of language is man's most important achievement. Without language most of man's other achievements would have been impossible, for it is the symbolic nature of language that enables man to think abstractly. The vocabulary of any language is nothing more nor less than a set of symbols that represent objects, actions, qualities, or ideas. When we use the procedures of effective thinking we manipulate the symbols that stand for objects, actions, qualities, or ideas. For example, when

[1] Thomas Pyles, *Origins and Development of the English Language* (New York: Harcourt, Brace & World, 1964).

[2] Susanne K. Langer, "The Language Line." Reprinted in part in Wise, Morris, and Hodges, *College English* (New York: Harcourt, Brace & World, 1960).

we make a statistical analysis of the grades made by students on a test, we do not manipulate the students or their test papers. Instead we manipulate symbols that represent the performance of the students. When we form and test a hypothesis, we do not manipulate people or places or things or actions. Instead we manipulate symbols that stand for them. Without the symbols of language we could not perform these mental processes.

Although we could not think without it, language is by no means a foolproof medium of thought and communication. Just as there are fallacies in procedures of thinking, such as hasty generalization, *post hoc,* and decision by indecision, so there are pitfalls in language itself. Trying to think without understanding the pitfalls in language would be like trying to navigate a great river without understanding how the constantly changing currents create eddies and shoals.

We should never forget that a word is merely a symbol. It is not the equivalent of what it stands for. Any combination of sounds or letters can be made to stand for anything. It does not matter in the slightest what a given word symbolizes so long as those who use it assign the same meaning to it. Thus the only meaning conveyed by a symbol is the meaning assigned to that symbol by the people who use it.

Since a word has no meaning in and of itself, any meaning attached to it must be a function of the frame of reference. A word *denotes, i.e.,* stands for, what a person thinks it stands for. The word "phlogopite" denotes nothing to most people because it is not in their frames of reference. To many people the word "enervate" looks like "energize" and denotes "to fill with energy," though the dictionary defines it as denoting "to deprive of energy" or "to weaken." Thus when someone says, "I feel enervated today," you must be familiar with his frame of reference to know whether he feels weak or strong. The meaning of a word as defined in a dictionary

is merely a kind of consensus, and some people do not subscribe to the majority opinion.

Words also acquire *connotations, i.e.,* suggested meanings, from the situations in which they are frequently used. The same word may have very different connotations for different people. The word "home" suggests to most people a place of happiness and security, but not to the juvenile delinquent who has been confined in an institution called the "home." The word "book" presumably has neither denotation nor connotation for an illiterate Australian bushman. It may have approximately the same denotation but very different connotations for a professional librarian and a censor of foreign literature in a totalitarian country. It may have approximately the same denotation but very different connotations to a Phi Beta Kappa and a student who has flunked out of college.

Language communicates as well as it does because the frames of reference of the people in a given cultural community contain common elements both as to information and as to the language by which this information is symbolized. By the same token, language fails to communicate accurately to the extent that the frames of reference of the people speaking the language differ. Many a student has thought himself stupid or has blamed his professor for being vague when the real trouble was that the student's vocabulary was neither as large nor as accurate as the professor's. And many a student has been puzzled by his inability to make satisfactory scores on objective tests when the real trouble was that his vocabulary was neither large enough nor precise enough for the task.

The difficulties of accurate communication are compounded by the imperfections and inaccuracies of language itself. First, words in common usage do not have exact meanings. Thus Sally Coed insists at various times that she "loves" her mother, her dog, her sorority, her favorite soft drink, or her faithful boyfriend. Obviously she is referring to a very different feeling in each instance, yet she uses the same word. Probably the greatest variations in meaning are to be found in words that denote emotion, such as "love," "hate," "fear," "anger," and so on, but many other categories of words have inexact meanings.

Second, many ideas are relative. For example, an object can be said to be cold or hot only in relation to some standard. Most residents of southern Florida or southern California would consider a day "cold" on which the temperature drops into the forties, whereas an Eskimo visiting either of these areas would doubtless consider it "hot." Science would never have made the progress it has with so imprecise a system of symbolizing temperature. Gabriel Daniel Fahrenheit is listed in the dictionary because he devised a precise standard for measuring temperature and a system of symbols for expressing various temperatures.

Third, the meanings of words are constantly shifting. As new bodies of knowledge develop, ways of symbolizing the new knowledge must also be developed. Sometimes they are new words and expressions, sometimes they are borrowings from other languages of both the past and present, and sometimes they are simply old words or new combinations of parts of them used with new or additional meanings. The vocabulary of the space age is a case in point. "To scrub" originally meant to clean or wash by rubbing or brushing hard. Now it also means to cancel the scheduled launching of a rocket into space. The word "pad" now symbolizes the hard and massive concrete base from which rockets are launched as well as a cushion.

In short, one only deludes himself when he assumes, consciously or otherwise, that the words he hears or reads always symbolize to him precisely what they symbolized to the person who wrote or spoke them. Modern mathematics, symbolic logic, and computers, if used carelessly, can make us more suscep-

tible to this delusion. For these tools carry symbolism to a second level, in which symbols are used for words that are themselves symbols. Consider the following syllogism.

Its citizens are permitted $\supset$ the nation is a
to vote for their leaders   democracy.

The citizens of the U.S.S.R. are permitted to vote for their leaders.
∴ The U.S.S.R. is a democratic nation.

This syllogism can be expressed in symbols by letting p stand for the antecedent and q for the consequent, as shown below.

$$p \supset q$$
$$p$$
$$\therefore \quad q$$

Once the syllogism is expressed in symbols, testing it for validity is child's play. "P" in the minor premise affirms the antecedent; therefore it necessarily follows that "q" is true — if the premises are true.

Second-level symbols have great advantages. In the first place, they can be used to remove the ambiguities inherent in words. Furthermore, extremely complex chains of syllogisms can be translated into symbols and fed into computers, which can then test them for validity in the flicker of an eyelash. If the original meaning is correctly translated into second-level symbols, validity can be tested with complete accuracy.

Unfortunately, there are dangers in this second-level use of symbols. It is easy to overlook the fallacy of uncertain relations while translating premises into symbols. Once the premises have been translated into symbols, it is impossible to tell from the symbols themselves whether they stand for equivalent ideas. Also, the use of second-level symbols tempts us to forget that valid syllogisms are not necessarily reliable. For illustration, examine the syllogism above in its verbal form. The major premise is highly questionable, at least in an American frame of reference, for the privilege of voting is only one of the characteristics of a democratic nation. Furthermore, the words "to vote for" can be interpreted in two very different ways. In the context of the major premise the words seem to denote "to choose," but in the context of the minor premise they could denote "to vote for but not against." Thus the conclusion is far from reliable.

Inherent in the symbolic nature of language are a number of specific fallacies and devices of persuasion that lead the unwary into error.

1. Lifting out of Context

One of these devices, lifting out of context, stems in part from the fact that words do multiple duty. For example, *Webster's New World Dictionary of the American Language* (College Edition, 1957) lists forty-six different meanings of the word "strike." Thus this word in isolation could mean any one of the nineteen transitive verbs, sixteen intransitive verbs, or eleven nouns listed in the dictionary.

The intended meaning of a word must be determined by the *context, i.e.,* the surrounding words and ideas. Consider, for example, the following sentence: "We should strike now." The context of this sentence eliminates the eleven meanings "strike" can have as a noun. Even so, this sentence could have been spoken by a general urging an attack, a labor leader urging that work be stopped, or someone urging some other kind of aggressive action. We can know the intended meaning only by knowing the context in which the statement was made.

Those who would deceive us lift statements out of their original contexts, thereby changing or distorting the original meaning, as shown in the example below.

Laboratory Report: "Our tests of Drain-Free show that it will positively remove the grease from the trap of a kitchen sink, even though the trap is completely clogged. Unfortunately,

this product also removes the metal in the plumbing."

Advertisement: "Laboratory tests show that Drain-Free will remove the grease from the trap of a kitchen sink, even though it is completely clogged."

Although direct quotation adds verisimilitude, lifting out of context can be accomplished by a paraphrase, as shown in the example below.

Medical Writer: "Doctors are concerned about the increasing number of Americans who are exposing themselves to malnutrition by following reducing diets. It is estimated that some 14,000,000 Americans are starving themselves in order to lose weight."

Politician: "We must support the anti-poverty program. Doctors are concerned because 14,000,000 Americans go to bed hungry."

Lifting out of context may easily occur through carelessness rather than intent to deceive. We should never repeat a quotation without checking the original context, for the distortion of meaning in quotations, like the distortion of truth in gossip, tends to increase as it is passed on from person to person. Whenever we quote another person we should be careful that the meaning we convey is accurate.

To avoid being victimized by this device, we should cultivate the habit of being suspicious of any quotation, direct or indirect, that seems to put the person quoted in an unfavorable position. Such a statement should not be accepted as a reliable representation of what the speaker meant until the original context has been checked.

2. Equivocation

Another pitfall in language that stems from the fact that words do multiple duty is *equivocation, i.e.,* the use of the same word in two different senses.

Equivocation is often the stuff of wit and humor. Wordsworth is said to have remarked, "I believe I could write like Shakespeare if I had a mind to try it." To this his friend Charles Lamb is supposed to have responded, "Yes, nothing is wanting but the mind." The word "mind" was used by Wordsworth in the sense of "inclination," and by Lamb in the sense of "intelligence." In such instances, we are intended to see and laugh at the shift in meaning. We are supposed to recognize the wordplay; we are all in on the trick.

Equivocation is a fallacy when an inference is drawn from a word whose meaning has been deliberately or inadvertently shifted in the course of argument. For no logical progression of thought can occur if the terms are used first in one sense and then in another. The very fact that an inference is drawn indicates that we are expected to take the word in one sense only; we are not supposed to spot the equivocation. For example, most of us will grant the premise that a person ought to do what is right. Let us also grant that a person has the right to eat as much as he wishes. But anyone who concludes, or asks us to conclude, that a person ought therefore to eat as much as he wishes is committing the fallacy of equivocation, for the word "right" does not have the same meaning in the two premises. With words whose meanings are complex, words like "democracy" and "fair play," it is especially easy to fall into equivocation. This fallacy may also involve the figurative use of words. It has been argued that the Taft-Hartley law is a slave labor law and that slave labor is prohibited under the Constitution. The catch here is that the term "slave labor" is first used figuratively and then literally.

A careful definition of terms is the best protection against equivocation.

3. Misuse of Evaluative Words

Misuse of evaluative words is an important and pernicious fallacy, as well as a device of persuasion. The fallacy results from the fact that words evaluate as well as symbolize objects, actions, qualities, and ideas. Some words evaluate directly through their denotations. We refer to most common ideas, objects, and actions by a number of different words that can be arranged on a continuum ranging from derogatory, through neutral, to laudatory. For example, the house in which you live can be called a "shack," a "domicile," or a "mansion." Unfortunately for accurate communication, the precise position of these words on the continuum is a function of the individual's frame of reference: one man's mansion may be another's shack.

Evaluative words are *misused* when they cause a false evaluation of the objects, actions, qualities, or ideas to which they are applied. The misuse of evaluative words occurs in three principal varieties.

1. *Misuse of labels.* Words are commonly used as labels for classes of objects, actions, or ideas. For example, the word "desert" is used to designate a category of land that is dry, barren, and sandy. The use of words as labels for categories is a very useful device both in communication and in thinking — as long as the labels are accurate. But words that function as labels are *misused* when they mislead. Suppose a real estate promoter buys a tract of land in the desert and divides it into parcels fifty feet wide and a hundred feet long. If he advertises these plots for sale as "small desert plots," he has correctly labelled them. If he calls them "Desert Acres," he is using a deceptive label, for an acre contains 43,560 square feet. If he calls them "Green Acres" or "Shady Acres," he should be prosecuted for fraud. Note that the evaluative qualities of words used as labels change with the context. The name "Desert Acres" applied to a sanitarium located in the desert for the treatment of patients requiring dry air does not deceive; the same name applied to homesites of 5,000 square feet located in the desert does deceive.

2. *Prestige jargon.* Just as people acquire reputations from the company they keep, words acquire evaluative meanings from the contexts in which they are frequently used. For example, because of the prestige of science in our culture, words used normally in scientific contexts acquire a prestige of their own. We tend to assume, therefore, that objects, actions, or ideas described in language that appears to be technical or scientific are more important or of higher quality than the same objects, actions, or ideas described in common language. Those who would deceive us into exaggerating the value of something take advantage of this unreliable assumption by using prestige words instead of common ones. In the advertising world, toothpaste is a "dentifrice."

The use of technical words is not necessarily a device of persuasion. Such words are appropriate in scholarly and technical writing, where they promote accurate and economical communication. It is when they are used to impress the hearer, rather than because they are necessary to the thought expressed, that the fallacy is committed. Prestige jargon need not come from the dictionary. The words may be coinages that sound technical or scientific. An automobile might be advertised as having *ultraelectronic* ignition, *hydynamic* transmission, or *gyronamic* steering. Although it may be claimed that such words describe new principles in automobile manufacturing, it appears that their principal function is to sound technical and thus exploit the prestige attached to science and technology.

Prestige jargon is not limited to technical terms. The same effect can be achieved by substituting formal words for common ones. A barber shop can be called a "tonsorial parlor," an undertaker a "mortician," a salesman a "field representative," or a janitor a "custodian." New York City had difficulty in employing enough garbage collectors until they were given the title "sanitation men." Commonplace ideas can be dressed up in formidable language and made to seem more

erudite. "A rolling stone gathers no moss" can be expressed this way: "A nomadic portion of the metamorphosed igneous or sedimentary deposit of the Proterozoic era accumulates no bryophytic vegetation." The use of this formidable language has an additional deceptive element: one who does not understand the language is afraid to challenge the idea expressed for fear of revealing his ignorance.

3. *Name-calling.* The evaluative characteristics of words can be used to put individual persons or groups of persons in an unfavorable light. This principle was pointed up by Bertrand Russell in what he described as the "conjugation" of an "irregular verb."

> I am firm.
> You are obstinate.
> He is a pig-headed fool.

It is all too easy to put people in a bad light by calling them uncomplimentary names, such as "reds," "wops," or "commies." Name-calling can increase the effect of *argumentum ad hominem* when applied to an opponent in an argument.

To avoid being victimized by the misuse of evaluative words we should cultivate the habit of looking behind evaluative language. Pasting the label "caviar" on a can of sardines does not change the contents of the can. An ordinary flashlight is still an ordinary flashlight, even though described in pseudotechnical jargon as an "electronic illuminator." Calling a political opponent a "commie" does not make him one.

A rose by any other name would smell as sweet only if we react to the rose instead of the linguistic symbol. Hence we should cultivate the habit of avoiding the misuse of evaluative language in our own thinking. Whenever we are not certain whether evaluative words are accurate or relevant, we should translate them into neutral ones. If you think of your teacher as a "pedagogue," (in the sense of a dogmatic or pedantic person), you are likely to react to him as though he were dogmatic and pedantic, even though he may be a fine teacher. Furthermore, you may begin to react to his course with the same negative attitude and consequently profit less from the course. On the other hand, if you think of him as your "mentor," you may begin to react to him as though he were wiser than he is. Your attitude toward him may make you too credulous about the content of the course. The antidote is to refer to him by a neutral term, such as instructor, at least until it is clear that he deserves a more evaluative name.

Sometimes the antidote itself requires an antidote. Suppose the word "instructor" is relatively neutral in your frame of reference. Suppose further that you apply this term only to an instructor whom you dislike intensely. Eventually this term may become a derogatory label in your frame of reference. If you then apply it to a fine teacher whom you like, you are misusing an evaluative word in terms of its connotations to you. The remedy for this problem is to acquire a large vocabulary so that you will not exhaust your supply of neutral words.

4. Obfuscation

Words may be used to conceal or to obscure as well as to enlighten. The weakness of a questionable argument may be difficult to detect if the structure of the argument is concealed in a mass of words that convey little or no meaning. For this reason, a person may appear to deal with an issue without actually doing so, simply by using an excessive number of words. It is often easier to avoid taking a stand on an issue in a thousand words than in fifty. *Obfuscation,* then, consists in using meaningless word groups either inadvertently or for the particular purpose of obscuring or avoiding an issue.

Consider the statement of a politician trying to avoid committing himself on the issue of federal aid to education: "I firmly believe that every citizen is entitled to the best possible education. In fact, it is my unalterable conviction that it is the solemn obligation of each generation to endow its youth with the knowledge of the noble achievements of the human species, and to make these endowments equally without regard to race, creed, color, or region. I also hold that the burden of providing these rights and privileges should be equitably allotted among those most capable of assuming the burden." The politician has made it clear in his first sentence that he favors education. Does he favor federal aid to education? One cannot tell. As we might expect, obfuscation is frequently combined with diversion and prestige jargon.

Obfuscation is often effective in argument because the mind refuses to trace the meaning through the maze of words and tends to assume that significant meaning is there because the language is impressive. When a person has been favorably impressed with a speech but is unable to remember what was said, the use of obfuscation may be the explanation. One may guard against obfuscation by reducing wordy passages to their simplest elements and barest meaning.

5. Leading Question

The symbolic nature of words is not the only source of pitfalls in language. The structure of language can also be used to trap the unwary through *leading questions*.

Presumably a question is a request for information. But it is often more than this. In a leading question a person is directed to the answer or led to imply or admit something he may not wish to. For example, the question, "You didn't shoot him until he started to draw his gun, did you?" is doubly loaded. It directs the person questioned to answer "No" — an answer in accord with instinctive self-defense. And if he makes such an answer, by implication he admits the shooting — a fact which may not yet have been established.

There are several types of leading questions. One type directs the answers: "You haven't studied your lesson, have you?" (No) "You worked hard on this problem, didn't you?" (Yes) "You haven't seen the defendant before today, have you?" (No) "You and the witness are close friends, aren't you?" (Yes). Courts of law have strict rules to prevent attorneys from asking this kind of question.

A second type of leading question, in which the person questioned is often trapped by the implication of his answer, is illustrated by the experience of a schoolboy who was suspected of stealing candy from a lunchroom. He was asked not whether he took the candy, but "What did you do with the candy?" Surprised by the question, he gave himself away with, "I ate — I mean I didn't have any candy."

A third type of leading question is sometimes used by advertisers. Its effect is to put the reader or listener on the defensive and to capitalize on the implications of his answer. "Is your car entirely safe? Install Sure-Grip Tires today." "Do you want to be popular, make friends easily, and earn enough money to provide you with the things you have always wanted? Then take our Home Study Course and complete your education in twelve easy lessons." "Would your wife and children have security if you died today? If not, shouldn't you buy more Sure-Pay Insurance?" In each of these, the question prejudices the answer in favor of the product advertised.

A fourth type of leading question calls for a "yes" or "no" answer, either of which has a derogatory implication. "Have you stopped beating your wife?" is the classic example. "Have you stopped cheating on examinations?" is another.

Before answering a leading question, rephrase it to eliminate the trap. The second example above might be answered in this way: "I never have cheated on examinations."

Suggested Supplementary Reading

Wallace L. Anderson and Norman C. Stageberg, *Introductory Readings on Language* (New York: Holt, Rinehart and Winston, Inc., 1962).

EXERCISE 18

1. What does *score* mean in the context of this sentence: "The conductor must have forgotten the score"?

<u>music</u>

2. What does *score* mean in the context of this sentence: "The quarterback must have forgotten the score"?

<u>points</u>

3. Arrange the following words on the continuum below: *car, jalopy, limousine.*

derogatory <u>jalopy</u> neutral <u>car</u> laudatory <u>limousine</u>

4–17. *In the remaining items supply the name of the most conspicuous fallacy or device of persuasion.*

4. Instead of writing, "Between seventy-five and one hundred people heard a speech last evening by Senator Smythe at the Evergreen Gardens near the Southside City Limits," a reporter wrote, "A crowd of suckers came to listen to a political hack last evening in that rickety firetrap that disfigures the south side of town."

<u>misuse of labels</u>

5. *Laboratory report:* "We find that Tanka Tea has 3.246 milligrams of caffeine per pound. Two other brands tested had 3.2467 and 3.248 milligrams respectively. For all practical purposes the difference in caffeine content of these three brands is insignificant."

Advertisement: "Drink Tanka Tea. It will let you sleep. An independent laboratory reports that Tanka contains less caffeine than any other brand tested."

<u>lifting out of context</u>

6. *Industrialist:* "Everyone agrees that cooperation is desirable. Yet we have passed antitrust laws directed at large corporations, despite the fact that these corporations are only examples of cooperation."

<u>equivocation</u>

7. *Excerpt from a piece of literary criticism:* "Despite the insistent, denotative matter-of-factness at the surface of the presentation, the subsurface activity of *Hearth and Sea* is organized connotatively around two poles. By a process of accrual and coagulation, the images tend to build around the opposed concepts of Home and Not-Home. Neither, of course, is truly conceptualistic; each is a kind of poetic intuition, charged with emotional values and woven, like a cable, of many strands . . ."

<u>obfuscation</u>

8. *Wife who suspects her husband of gambling:* "Did you win tonight, dear?"

<u>leading question</u>

9. Feeling that Lincoln's administration was not taking a strong enough stand against slavery, a contemporary newspaper denounced "this albino administration, and its diluted spawn of pink-eyed patriots."

name-calling

10. *Book review in the New York* Bugle: "The only mystery about this mystery is where the mystery is. It is about as subtle as a gangster with a tommy gun and about as electrifying as the shock of a flashlight battery."

Book jacket: "New York *Bugle:* 'This mystery . . . is . . . subtle . . . electrifying . . . ' "

lifting out of context

11. The people who have contributed most to the growth of America have been progressive people. Americans should therefore support the Progressive Party.

equivocation

12. *Salesman for a lock company:* "Can you afford to continue to run the risk of having your office accessible to prowlers?"

leading question

13. *Citizen:* "A man who is always democratic is greatly to be admired. Smythe has always voted the Democratic ticket. Therefore, Smythe is greatly to be admired."

equivocation

14. *Mother who suspects her son of having gone in swimming contrary to her orders:* "Son, did you get your hair wet in the river today?"

leading question

15. *Politician:* "When you ask me if I favor the special bond issue for roads, I reply that I have always been for better roads. They are the arteries of our commerce. They are the pathways to progress. And yet I would not deem it wise to bankrupt ourselves even to pay for better roads. This is a serious question — so serious that I think each person should think it through for himself. That is one of the glories of our American way of life — that each person has a right to determine for himself which way he shall vote."

obfuscation

16. *Advertisement:* "Lowtemp Antifreeze consists of a specially inhibited, concentrated methanol base to which has been added esterol, a new organic solvent that makes the metal in your radiator rust resistant."

prestige jargon

17.   Here the Red Queen began again. "Can you answer useful questions?" she said. "How is bread made?"
      "I know that!" Alice cried eagerly. "You take some flour — "
      "Where do you pick the flower?" the White Queen asked. "In a garden or in the hedges?"
      "Well, it isn't picked at all," Alice explained, "it's ground — "
      "How many acres of ground?" asked the White Queen. "You mustn't leave out so many things."

LEWIS CARROLL, *Through the Looking Glass*

equivocation

19 Classification and Definition

Language is essential to *classification,* the principal means by which man organizes the huge body of information in his frame of reference. Language itself is largely based on classification. For example, all common nouns are the names of classes of objects, actions, qualities, or ideas. The noun "automobile" is the name of a class that includes Chevrolets, Cadillacs, Chryslers, Fords, Ramblers, and so on. If man could not put objects, actions, qualities, and ideas into classes, describe these classes with linguistic symbols, and reason from these classes by means of other linguistic symbols, his frame of reference would be of relatively little use. It would be analogous to a vast library in which the books are shelved in random order, and which has no card catalogue. If you needed a certain piece of information from such a library in order to make a decision, the chances are overwhelming that you would be caught by decision by indecision long before you could locate the information. Similarly, if information in your own frame of reference were not organized to some extent by classification, you would have great difficulty in bringing your past experience to bear on any particular problem.

Classification is also an invaluable tool in using the information you have. Suppose you see a bird in the distance, too far away to identify. If you are sure it is a bird, you know a great deal about it, even though you cannot tell whether it is an eagle, or a buzzard, or a bird you have never seen before. You know that it has all of the characteristics birds have: it has a skeletal structure, feathers, and so forth. The more you know about the common characteristics of birds, the more you know about this one.[1]

You will encounter many situations, both during and after college, in which you will need to make your own classifications. The five-phase cycle, with modifications, applies to making classifications as well as to other forms of reasoning. As with all other uses of the cycle, the phases should not be followed in rigid sequence. The objective of Phase 3 is (1) to find a satisfactory basis for division and (2) to name and define the necessary classes and subclasses. In other words, the tentative conclusions formed are systems of classification, with names and def-

[1] See Olive B. Goin, *World Outside My Door* (New York: Macmillan, 1955).

183

initions for each class and subclass. Objects, actions, ideas, qualities, and value premises can be divided into classes according to many different bases or principles. A grocer might divide his merchandise into classes according to such bases as brand, container, size, shape, or quality. A student might divide literature according to author, type, period, or theme.

The basis for a classification should be selected in accordance with the purposes of the classification. Classifications can themselves be divided into two classes, *utilitarian* and *explanatory,* according to the purposes of the classifier.

1. Utilitarian Classifications

The purpose of a *utilitarian* classification is to facilitate finding, handling, or using the matter classified. Suppose you have accumulated such a mass of class notes, college records, correspondence, and the like that you have trouble finding things. The time has come to set up a filing system based on a classification of your material. Your purpose is utilitarian — to store your papers so that you can find them readily.

In a utilitarian classification the basis for division into classes and subclasses can be purely arbitrary, according to the needs or even the whims of the classifier. If you wish, you can divide your papers into classes according to any number of bases, such as size and subject, so that you can file your class notes in three-ring notebooks and your correspondence in an alphabetical filing case. A grocer may arrange his goods on his shelves according to such classifications as bread, soups, cookies, canned vegetables, fresh vegetables, and meats. Any item that does not fit one of these classes can be put into a miscellaneous class.

Classifications cannot be tested for reliability as can hypotheses or causal theories. A classification is a kind of form imposed on groups of objects, actions, qualities, or ideas. While the form should be closely related to the matter, the form cannot be said to be either true or false. The test of a classification, then, is the degree to which it serves the purpose for which it was constructed. Utilitarian classifications are tested *pragmatically, i.e.,* by actual use. You can test your filing system simply by using it. As you use the system you will doubtless discover flaws, but you can correct them as you go.

When the quantity of material to be classified is large, a preliminary test with a sample is in order. Suppose you have just become the manager of a large office with hundreds of filing cabinets full of records. After studying the files you conclude that the records have outgrown the system, with the result that finding items in the files resembles a scavenger hunt. You therefore devise a new classification. You could, of course, test it by having your clerks re-file all records according to your new system. If it is sound, you may get a raise in salary; if it is not, the office may get a new manager. A better procedure would be to have a clerk try your new system on a sample from your files. You can then correct the flaws before applying the system to the entire files. If you follow this procedure, your office is less likely to get a new manager.

2. Explanatory Classifications

The purpose of an *explanatory* classification is quite different. Consider the problem facing a doctor who wishes to learn as much as possible about allergies, a field in which our knowledge is far from complete. His purpose in classifying available information would be explanatory — to help him understand the causes, symptoms, and treatment of allergies. Explanatory classifications may also serve utilitarian purposes. The classifications used by zoologists, for example, facilitate not only understanding the fauna of the world but also storing specimens and arranging exhibits. Since the basic purpose of an explanatory classification is to facilitate understanding the essential nature of the material classified, an explanatory classification must be much more precise than a utilitarian one.

In constructing explanatory classifications, Phase 2 consists in collecting the matter to be classified. Relevant matter for our allergist would include the relevant generalizations and causal theories, as well as case studies of allergy victims. With complex and heterogeneous matter, such as the causes, symptoms, and treatment of allergies, much trial and error is likely to be required before a satisfactory classification is found. It is therefore advisable to begin with a sample of the matter to be classified.

The objective in Phase 3 is to construct a tentative system of classification by dividing the matter into classes and subclasses. Our allergist might begin by dividing his matter into the following classes.

I. Allergens (substances causing allergic reactions)

II. Symptoms

III. Treatment

The next step (Phase 4) would be to test his tentative system by classifying some of his matter and judging the results by the following five criteria for explanatory classifications.

1. *Significant differences.* Classes should be subdivided into as many levels as necessary to reveal significant differences. If our allergist classified all allergens under one main class, with no subdivisions, the classification would reveal very little about the essential nature of the allergens. He should, therefore, search for significant differences in allergens and subdivide them as necessary to reveal these differences. He might, for

example, subdivide allergens on the basis of how they reach the body, as shown below.

I. Allergens
   A. Substances inhaled
   B. Substances ingested

He might subdivide each of the second-level classes on the basis of differences in the nature of the substance, as shown below for substances inhaled.

I. Allergens
   A. Substances inhaled
      1. Pollens
      2. Fungi

He should continue the process of subdividing classes until he has exhausted the significant differences.

2. *Consistency.* Whenever possible the basis for division into classes should be consistent within each given level. The third-level division below violates this criterion.

I. Allergens
   A. Substances inhaled
      1. Sawdust
      2. Dust
      3. House dust

The class *substances inhaled* has not been divided on one consistent basis. "Dust" is a general category including both sawdust and house dust. "Dust" should be a third-level class, along with "pollens" and "fungi," while "sawdust" and "house dust" should be fourth-level classes under "dust."

I. Allergens
   A. Substances inhaled
      1. Pollens
      2. Fungi
      3. Dust
         a. Sawdust
         b. House dust

3. *Comprehensiveness.* There should be enough classes and subclasses to provide a place for every item in the matter to be clas-

sified. The second-level classes of allergens are insufficient, for they do not yet include a place for substances such as cosmetics that cause allergic reactions through contact with the skin. Usually a fault like this one can be remedied simply by adding another subclass. Sometimes, however, it may be necessary to change the basis of division, even at the first level.

4. *Essential properties.* Classes and subclasses should be divided on the basis of the essential properties of the matter being classified. The color of an automobile is not an essential property; the fact that it has wheels is. Most objects have many different essential properties, and the one chosen as the basis for division should be relevant to the purpose of the classification. Consider the following subclassification.

> B. Substances ingested
>   1. White bread
>   2. Vitamin B-1
>   3. Beer

Since our allergist's purpose is to identify the substances that cause allergic reactions, this subclassification is unsatisfactory because it is not based on relevant essential properties. It gives no information about why these substances are allergens. Yet all three of these substances have a common element that is a relevant and essential property: all three contain yeast. If our allergist used this classification, he might needlessly prohibit a patient from eating bread when the offending substance was something in beer other than yeast. The following classification would be better.

> B. Substances ingested
>   1. Substances containing yeast cells
>   a. Bread
>   b. Vitamin B-1
>   c. Beer

5. *Unity.* When the matter being classified cannot be divided on a single basis, the bases

used should be related. Consider our allergist's first-level classification. Allergens, symptoms, and treatment are actually three separate classifications rather than a single classification on a single basis. To make his classification fully useful, the allergist should unify the three elements as far as possible by showing all known connections among them. Our present knowledge of allergies indicates that specific symptoms are more likely to be caused by certain allergens than by others, and that some symptoms respond better to certain treatments. It may be that some day an allergist, with the aid of a computer and a host of assistants to feed it, will succeed in developing a classification with a single basis. Meanwhile the three bases can be unified to some extent by a classification somewhat like the one below.

Allergen	Symptoms	Effectiveness of Treatment
Fungi	Nasal congestion (probable)	Injections (high)
	Nausea (improbable)	Antihistamines (moderate)
		Avoidance (low)

One might suppose that classification is a purely mechanical process, with little or no creative thinking required. Actually, making a satisfactory explanatory classification is usually the culmination of a number of creative breakthroughs. A truly satisfactory classification may require the forming and testing of numerous hypotheses, generalizations, and causal theories. Finding a satisfactory basis for division is much like forming and testing hypotheses. The relevant generalizations and causal theories, as well as the details of the matter to be classified, are the evidence to be "explained." It may be necessary to form and test many different bases before a truly satisfactory one is found. In short, for a complex matter like allergies, finding a satisfactory basis of division may prove to be the ultimate creative breakthrough.

3. Definition

In making classifications an essential part of Phase 3 is defining the classes. Definitions show the limits of the classes. Thus definitions are to classifications roughly as maps are to geographical territory. Just as the value of a map depends in part on its accuracy, so the usefulness of a classification depends in part upon the precision of the definitions involved. In setting up your own filing system you can, of course, define your classes in any way you choose and even keep your definitions a dark secret. But when you become an office manager and set up a filing system, if you fail to define your classes so that their boundaries are clearly understood by your filing clerks, the punishment will fit the crime. In explanatory classifications fuzzy definitions can conceal the very truth you are seeking to find.

Of the many possible types of definition, the one most suitable for our present purpose is known as *definition by genus and difference*. In this type the word or class being defined (the *definiendum*) is put into a larger class (the *genus*) and then differentiated from all other members of the genus. Thus, as shown in the example below, the definition contains three components: the *definiendum*, the *genus*, and the *differentia*, i.e., the words that distinguish instances of the *definiendum* from other instances of the genus. The words that describe the genus and *differentia* are known as the *definiens*.

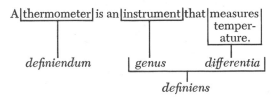

To be entirely satisfactory, definitions by genus and difference must conform to five rules.

1. *The* definiens *and the* definiendum *must be equivalent.* Since the purpose of a definition is to set the limits of the class clearly and accurately, the *definiendum* (the name of the class) should be logically interchangeable with the *definiens* (the limits of the class). Consider the example below.

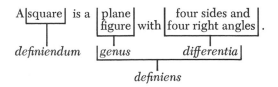

In the above example the *definiens* and *definiendum* are not equivalent. While it is true that all squares are plane figures with four sides and four right angles, it is not true that all plane figures with four sides and four right angles are squares. The fault here is that the *differentia* does not exclude instances of the genus "plane figure" that are not squares, such as rectangles shaped like football fields. This fault is easily remedied by limiting the *differentia* with the word "equal."

A square is a plane figure with four equal sides and four right angles.

In the definition above the *definiens* and *definiendum* are equivalent; the subject and predicate can be interchanged without changing the meaning. All squares are plane figures with four equal sides and four right angles; all plane figures with four equal sides and four right angles are squares.

If *definiens* and *definiendum* are to be equivalent, the genus must be large enough to include all instances of the *definiendum*. The following definition fails in this respect because the genus "glass instrument" excludes thermometers not made of glass.

A thermometer is a glass instrument for measuring temperature.

This fault is easily remedied by removing the word "glass" from the genus.

If *definiens* and *definiendum* are to be equivalent, the genus should be small enough to make differentiation practicable. In the example below the unnecessarily large size of the genus makes it difficult to differentiate "child" from other immature living organisms.

A child is an immature living organism.

The remedy is to substitute a smaller genus.

A child is an immature human being.

Except in closed systems of thought, such as geometry, you will seldom succeed in writing definitions in which the *definiens* and *definiendum* are equivalent. Even so, you should try to come as close as possible. Purely arbitrary distinctions are often necessary to make *definiens* and *definiendum* reasonably equivalent, especially with matters that lie on a continuum, such as hot and cold, or heavy and light. A law requiring higher registration fees for large automobiles than for compact ones would be unenforceable without an arbitrary distinction. A compact car might be defined as any passenger automobile weighing less than 2,500 pounds.

2. *The* definiens *should be suitable for the purpose.* In both utilitarian and explanatory classifications, definitions should make identification of class or subclass unmistakable. In explanatory classifications, differentiation between classes should be made according to essential properties. Compare the following definitions.

Pollen is a yellow substance on plants.
Pollen is the "yellow, powderlike male sex cells on the stamens of a flower."[2]

[2] *Webster's New World Dictionary of the American Language,* College Edition (Cleveland: World, 1966), p. 1132.

The first example would be unsatisfactory in an explanatory classification because it does not describe the essential properties of "pollen." The second definition is better.

3. *The definition should not be circular.* A definition is circular when the *definiens* contains the *definiendum* or words which cannot be understood precisely without knowing the meaning of the *definiendum.* Consider the example below.

A|fallacy| is a |fallacious argument|.
   definiendum   *definiens*

This definition is circular because a key word in the *definiens* is the adjective form of the *definiendum.* Figuratively speaking, this definition moves in a circle, for it begins with "fallacy" and proceeds to "fallacious." If one does not know what "fallacy" means, this definition will not help him. It is little better than saying that a fallacy is a fallacy. Circular definitions are unsatisfactory because they do little to clarify the limits of the class.

4. *The definition should not contain ambiguous, figurative, or obscure language.* Since the purpose of a definition is to describe the limits of a class clearly and precisely, ambiguous or obscure language is obviously out of place. Although figurative language can aid communication by stating or implying a resemblance, it is not likely to describe the limits of a class accurately and can therefore be misleading. Consider this definition: Misuse of evaluative words is a device of persuasion in which words unjustly sneer at or smile upon what they describe. In this context "sneer at" and "smile upon" are used figuratively. Such words might be properly used to amplify the meaning of a definition, but they should not be used in the definition itself because they do not accurately set the limits of the class being defined. Whether the language of a definition is obscure may depend on the frame of reference. Technical language may be quite clear to

one person and completely obscure to another. Prestige jargon should never be used in a definition, for the language of a definition should be selected to communicate accurately rather than to impress.

5. *The* definiens *should not be negative.* Because negative concepts are likely to be vague, they are not suitable for definitions, the purpose of which is to set precise limits. Consider the definition below.

An undergraduate is not a person who has completed the requirements for a college degree.

This definition, which describes an undergraduate in terms of what he is *not*, is logically incomplete until the *definiens* includes every possible item that is not an undergraduate, such as shoes and ships and sealing wax and cabbages and kings.

4. Evaluation and Decision

With classifications, the decision to be made in Phase 5 is whether to adopt the classification as formulated or to continue to refine it. When the mass of items is small, as in your personal filing system, the decision is easy. You can simply start using the classification and refine it as you go. But when the mass is large and the issue important, the procedures described in Chapter 13 should be used.

Certain hazards in classification should be kept in mind. In the first place, classifications are meaningless without their definitions, and definitions must be expressed in language. Definitions are therefore subject to the dangers inherent in the symbolic character of language. In the second place, a classification does not alter the nature of the objects, ideas, actions, or qualities classified. In fact, classifications can be very misleading about the nature of things.

Classification and definition in our day have steadily lost in importance in one direction at the same time that they have gained in another. By the sophisticated, they are no longer regarded as infallible keys to the nature of things. The universe is more complex, more plastic, and more permeated with change than the conceptualizers of earlier periods dared to suspect. . . . The class-member relationship is by no means the only ordering principle which has proved to be useful in dealing with the intricacies of the flux. Many of the characteristics which have long been believed to justify class distinctions have turned out to be superficial, and many of the time-honored demarcations of class boundaries have been shown to be fuzzy matters of shading and degrees.[3]

Finally, classifications tend to deceive us into overlooking the fact that, while all members of a given class have certain characteristics, they may also have very significant differences.

The hazards and difficulties in classification should not make us overlook their great advantages. The explosion of knowledge in our age has made classification more important than ever in organizing and clarifying knowledge. Many objects, actions, ideas, and qualities cannot be divided into discrete classes, but that should not necessarily deter us from using a classification. Anyone who refuses to use the standard classification of animals because there is a border zone between vertebrates and invertebrates may be committing the black-or-white fallacy by reasoning that the classification is bad because it is not perfect. The existence of a border zone may be due to the nature of the matter classified rather than to a flaw in the classification itself. A behavioral scientist who refuses to classify people because he cannot find discrete categories may be falling into the argument of the beard by reasoning that, since there are no discrete differences, there are no differences at all.

Students who resent having to learn classifications in their textbooks are overlooking

[3] Larrabee, *op. cit.*, p. 194.

the fact that a workable classification makes learning much easier. Trying to learn the information necessary to pass even an elementary course in zoology without benefit of classification would be roughly comparable to memorizing the Manhattan telephone directory.

Classification and understanding are inseparable. Before you can construct a satisfactory classification of a complex subject, you must acquire a thorough knowledge and understanding of the subject; the process of constructing and testing a classification helps to pull your knowledge together into a coherent whole, and to reveal relationships between the parts.

Suggested Supplementary Reading

Harold A. Larrabee, *Reliable Knowledge*, rev. ed. (Boston: Houghton Mifflin Company, 1964), Chapter 8.

EXERCISE 19

1–6. *These items refer to the following definition:* An automobile is a motor-powered vehicle made to carry passengers.

1. What is the *definiendum?* <u>automobile</u>

2. What is the *genus?* <u>motor-powered vehicle</u>

3. What is the *differentia?* <u>made to carry passengers</u>

4. What is the *definiens?* <u>vehicle made to carry passengers</u>

5. Is a bus with a capacity of forty passengers an "automobile" in terms of this definition? <u>yes</u>

6. Is a cart powered by an electric motor made to carry two players on a golf course an "automobile" in terms of this definition? <u>yes</u>

7–11. *Which rule(s), if any, of classification by genus and difference is violated by the following definitions?*

7. *Post hoc* is an error in thinking in which it is inferred that one event causes another. <u>not equivalent</u>

8. Hasty generalization is a form of reasoning in which a generalization is made about a group on the basis of an inadequate sample of the group. <u>circular</u>

9. Neglected aspect is an error in reasoning in which the middle part of a continuum is ignored. <u>not suitable</u>

10. *Argumentum ad hominem* is a device of persuasion in which one tries to shoot down a conclusion by blasting the person making it. <u>figurative language</u>

11. A fallacy is not sound reasoning. <u>negative</u>

12. Laws in some states set different speed limits for certain classes of vehicles. Using the method of definition by genus and difference, define "trailers" for the purpose of enforcing the above law.

<u>trailer is a vehicle hauled by another vehicle that serves as dwelling place or place of business when parked</u>

13. Criticize the following as an explanatory classification of the fallacies discussed so far in this book.

Fallacies with Latin names	Fallacies with English names
Post hoc	Hasty generalization
Argumentum ad hominem	Irrelevance
	Diversion

not essential properties

14. Consider the following classification.

I. Fallacies in Inference

   A. Deductive

affirming cons.
denied antecedent
uncertain relation.
non-sequitur

   B. Inductive

post-hoc
hasty generalization

II. Fallacies of Neglected Aspect

over simplification
argument of the board
half-truth
decision by indecision
black-or-white

III. Devices of Persuasion

prejudicing the issue
leading question
misused evaluative words

Test the above as an explanatory classification by inserting the following items in the appropriate blanks above.

Affirmed consequent	Decision by indecision
Hasty generalization	Pettifogging
Prejudicing the issue	Non sequitur
Oversimplification	Half-truth
Leading question	Denied antecedent
Argument of the beard	Black-or-white
Uncertain relationships	Misuse of evaluative words
Post hoc	

15. What first-level class should be added?

fallacies of irrelevance

16. Which of the first-level classes are not mutually exclusive?

Devices of persuasions and irrelevance

17. Is the overlapping of the first-level classes due to the nature of the matter or to a flaw in the classification?

nature of the matter

20 Categorical Propositions

As we have noted in several chapters, effective thinking requires precision in using and understanding language. Vaguely or ambiguously stated observations may be as misleading as inaccurate ones. Premises that are misunderstood may lead to error as easily as false premises. Unless we understand precisely what a premise means, we cannot tell whether it is reliable or whether conclusions drawn from it are valid.

The precise use of language requires an accurate understanding not only of the meaning of the words in a proposition but also of the structure of the proposition. Suppose a general issues the following order: "All units will attack at 10:00 A.M. unless the weather is bad." This order can be misinterpreted in two ways. In the first place, the words themselves can be misinterpreted. "Bad" weather may mean one thing to a fighter squadron and something quite different to an infantry platoon. Also, the word "attack" can mean many different things. Any good general issuing such an order would have previously defined precisely what he meant by "bad weather" and "attack."

In the second place, this order can be misinterpreted if the linguistic structure of the proposition in which it is stated is misused or misinterpreted. For example, the general's order can be written in pure hypothetical form.

"*If* the weather is not bad, *then* all units will attack at 10:00 A.M."

This proposition contains two structure words, *if* and *then,* which identify antecedent and consequent, respectively. These structure words also state the relationship between antecedent and consequent; the consequent necessarily follows from the antecedent, but the antecedent does not necessarily follow from the consequent. Nor does anything in the order state what is to happen if the weather is bad; perhaps some units have been separately ordered to attack even so. Now suppose that at 10:00 A.M. the commanding officer of a unit observes another unit beginning an attack. If he does not understand the meaning conveyed by the structure of the proposition, he may conclude that, since one unit is attacking, all are supposed to be attacking, and that the weather must not be bad even though his own observations indicate that it is. He has thus added probably erroneous meaning that is not conveyed by the structure of the proposition.

The structure of certain propositional forms is clear and unequivocal. When they are misunderstood, the fault lies with the person interpreting them rather than with the proposition. These propositional forms can be useful as a kind of second language into which we can translate propositions to see what they really mean. We have already studied the hypothetical propositional form (Chapter 2). Now let us consider the *categorical* form, which has some advantages over the hypothetical form, especially for stating generalizations and classifications.

1. Relationships between Classes

Whereas a hypothetical proposition states a relationship between an antecedent and a consequent, a *categorical* proposition names or describes two classes and states a relationship between them. For example, the proposition "All whales are mammals" names two classes, whales and mammals, and states a relationship between them. Given accurate definitions of the two classes, the relationship between them is clear and unequivocal to anyone who understands this form of proposition. Almost any idea can be stated as a categorical proposition, although some awkward twisting of language may be necessary.

Categorical propositions occur in four different forms. When an idea is correctly stated in one of these, there can be no reasonable doubt about the meaning — assuming that you are thoroughly familiar with this chapter. A complete understanding of these forms will sharpen your understanding of language and your powers of reasoning.

2. A-Form Propositions[1]

An A-form proposition names two classes of objects or ideas and declares that the relationship between them is *total inclusion, i.e.,* that *all of one class is included within the other.* Two familiar classes of people having this relationship are Baptists and Protestants. We can express this relationship in a categorical proposition.

All people in the class of Baptists are included in the class of Protestants.

[1] The four forms of categorical propositions take their names from the first two vowels in each of the Latin words *AffIrmo* and *nEgO.*

As long as we fully understand that we are talking about classes, we can shorten the statement as shown below, with the parts marked.

Quantifier Term 1   connective   Term 2

All   Baptists   (are included in)   Protestants.

Note that in a categorical proposition the *term* names the class, and the *connective* declares the relationship between the classes. The *quantifier* indicates how many of the class named by Term 1 are included in the class named by Term 2. Because the relationship in an A-form proposition is *total* inclusion, the quantifier must be the word *all* or some word meaning *all.*

Since we will be dealing with many such categorical propositions, let us adopt a shorthand system to save writing. Let us use the symbol < to mean *is* or *are included in.* We can now write our proposition thus.

All Baptists < Protestants.

Now let us take a close look at what the relationship of total inclusion means. To do so let us introduce a system of simple diagrams that will show what we mean.

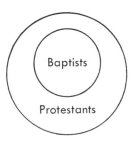

Our diagram is analogous to a map of a county within a state, with the Baptists the county and the Protestants the state.

Note that the symbol for inclusion (<) does not have the same meaning in logic and mathematics. In logic it expresses a relationship between classes; it means only that the first class named is included in the second class. It does not necessarily mean that the first class is smaller than the second. We might say that the weight of a cubic yard of dry earth is *less than* that of the same volume of wet earth; it would be nonsense to say that the class, dry earth, is *included in* the class, wet earth. Note, too, that the circle diagram is only analogous to a map — it is not exactly like a map. If the meaning of the diagram above were exactly like a map, we could assume that there is some territory in the state that is not in the county. We cannot make this assumption logically, however, because of the possibility that the two terms are identical, as would be the case in a perfect definition by genus and difference. An A-form proposition asserts only that all members of the first class are included in the second class; it makes no assertion whatever about how many members of the second class are included in the first.

The four statements below summarize the meaning conveyed by the linguistic structure of an A-form proposition.

1. Anything in the county of Baptists *must be* in the state of Protestants.
2. Anything outside the county of Baptists *may or may not be* in the state of Protestants.
3. Anything in the state of Protestants *may or may not be* in the county of Baptists.
4. Anything outside the state of Protestants *cannot be* in the county of Baptists.

Both in understanding propositions and in dealing with categorical syllogisms we need to know one other important detail. The terms of a categorical proposition may be either *distributed* or *undistributed*. The terminology is somewhat unfortunate, but it has been used by logicians for a long time. The two words have no meaning except in terms of the relationship between the two classes named in the proposition.

A term is distributed when it accounts for all the members of the class in so far as its relationship to the other class is concerned. The term Baptists is distributed because we

have put 100 per cent of the Baptists within the class of Protestants. If Smythe is a Baptist, he has to be a Protestant.

A term is undistributed when it accounts for less than all of a class in so far as its relationship to the other class is concerned. The term Protestants is undistributed because we do not know the relationship between all Protestants and Baptists. Smythe can be a Protestant without being a Baptist.

Now we can add to our shorthand system by using the symbols *d* for distributed and *u* for undistributed. Abbreviating our terms, we may state our proposition in our complete shorthand system thus:

$$\overset{d}{\text{Bap.}} < \overset{u}{\text{Prot.}}$$

Before reading further, test your understanding by writing in shorthand propositions accurately expressing the relationship you believe to exist between the following pairs of classes. (You will find the answers at the end of the chapter.)

1. Virginians — Americans.
2. Citizens — voters.

3. E-Form Propositions

An E-form proposition names two classes and declares that the relationship between them is *total exclusion*, i.e., *that the two classes are entirely separate.* Two familiar classes having this relationship are fraternities and sororities.

We can express the relationship in a categorical proposition this way: The entire class of fraternities is completely excluded from the class of sororities. But this statement is wordy, and if we remember that we are talking about classes, we can shorten it to the form below.

Quantifier	Term 1	connective	Term 2
All	fraternities	are excluded from	sororities.

For our shorthand system let us adopt the symbol $\nless$ to mean *is* or *are excluded from.* We can now write our proposition thus:

All fraternities $\nless$ sororities.

The circle diagram for this relationship appears below.

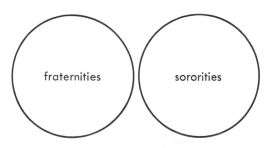

The diagram is exactly analogous to a map of two different states. Anything in one state cannot be in the other. Anything not in one state may or may not be in the other, for it could be in a state not shown.

In an E-form proposition, *both* terms are *distributed,* for we know the relationship of 100 per cent of each class to the other. If Alpha Alpha Alpha is a fraternity, it cannot be a sorority, and vice versa. Stated in shorthand, our proposition becomes:

d   d
Frats. $\nless$ sors.

This proposition could be written in A-form as shown below.

d   u
Fraternities $<$ organizations that are *not* sororities.

Note, however, that the second term of this proposition is stated negatively. Whenever possible, the terms of propositions, like definitions, should be stated positively rather than negatively. Accordingly, wherever possible such words as *no, not, none,* and *never* should be treated as structure words indicating the relationship of exclusion rather than as parts of the terms.

Before reading further, test your understanding by writing in shorthand proposi-

tions expressing accurately the relationship you believe to exist between the following pairs of classes.

3. Professional people — doctors.
4. College graduates — illiterates.

4. I-Form Propositions

An I-form proposition names two classes and states that at least a part of the first class is included within the second class. You run into this relationship when you start calling your friends for a date and find that the first two or three you call already have dates. The classes are *my friends* and *those who have dates.* You do not yet know the complete relationship between the classes: for all you know, the rest of your friends may have dates, or none of them may. All you know is that some of your friends have dates. Expressed wordily, your proposition is: Some of those in the class of my friends are included in the class of those who have dates. Expressed more economically, it is:

Quantifier	Term 1	connective	Term 2
Some of	my friends	(are included in)	those who have dates.

Here is the circle diagram.

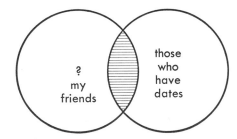

The circles overlap to show that some friends have dates. The analogy to a map no longer holds, for a map drawn this way would indicate that some of your friends are in the territory of those who have dates and some are outside that territory. But all you know is that some of your friends are within the territory of those who have dates — you know nothing about the location of the rest of your friends. To indicate that they may or may not be in the territory of those having dates, a question mark is put in the outside part of the circle for friends. The territory covered by both circles is shaded to show that the part of the class of friends we do know about is within the territory of those having dates. The extent to which the circles overlap is unimportant; we are concerned here only with whether there is overlapping, not with how much.

In an I-form proposition *both* terms are *undistributed,* for we do not know the relationship of all of either class to the other. If I know only that Susan Smythe is a friend of yours, I do not know whether she has a date; if I know only that Alice Jones has a date, I do not know whether she is a friend of yours.

Your proposition is stated in shorthand thus:

u   u
My friends < dates.

It is important to note that a single I-form proposition is not sufficient to state the complete relationship between two overlapping classes, such as mushrooms and edible plants.

u   u
Mushrooms < edible plants.

The I-form proposition above states only that at least some of the members of the mushroom class are included in the edible plant class. If you interpret this proposition to mean that some edible plants are not mushrooms, you are reading into the proposition a meaning that is not conveyed by the proposition's structure.

Before reading further, test your understanding by writing shorthand propositions accurately expressing the relationship you believe to exist between the following pairs of classes.

5. Courses you took last semester — courses flunked. (You have just received your grades; all are B's.)
6. College professors — people who use big words. (You are sitting in your first college class. The professor has just said, "Absences lacking plenary justification by a physician will not be tolerated.")

5. O-Form Propositions

An O-form proposition names two classes and declares that the relationship is *partial exclusion,* that is, at least a part of one class is outside the other.

You encounter this relationship when you try to borrow money from your friends and the first ones you ask will not lend you the money. Your classes are *my friends* and *those who will lend me money.* You do not know the complete relationship between the classes: for all you know, the next friend you try may lend you the money, or it may be that none of them will. All you know is that some of your friends will not lend you money. Expressed wordily, your proposition is: Some of those in the class of my friends are excluded from the class of those who will lend me money. Expressed more economically it is:

Quantifier	*Term 1*	*connective*	*Term 2*
Some of	my friends	are excluded from	those who will lend me money.

Here is the circle diagram.

The circles overlap to show the possibility that some friends *might* lend you the money, and a question mark is put in the overlapping territory to show doubt whether such overlapping exists. The part of the circle for friends outside the other circle is shaded to show that we know some friends are outside the circle of those who will lend you money.

In the O-form proposition the *first term is*

undistributed, because we do not know the complete relationship of the first class to the second. If I know only that your proposition is true and that Smythe is your friend, I do not know whether he will lend you money.

The *second term is distributed.* When part or all of one class is excluded from another, it is excluded from *all* of the other class.

Note the important difference between I- and O-forms. The I-form guarantees that at least some of one class is within the other; the O-form guarantees that at least some of one class is outside the other.

Stated in shorthand, your proposition is:

$$\overset{u}{\text{My friends}} \nless \overset{d}{\text{money lenders.}}$$

The proposition above can, of course, be written in I-form, as shown below.

$$\overset{u}{\text{My friends}} < \overset{u}{\text{those who are }} not \text{ money lenders.}$$

Note, however, that the second term of this proposition is stated negatively. As we have said, the terms of a proposition should be stated positively if possible, and words like *no, not, none,* and *never* should be treated as structure words indicating the relationship of exclusion.

Note that the complete statement of the overlapping relationship between two classes requires both I-form and O-form propositions. Neither will suffice alone.

Now check your understanding of categorical propositions by writing shorthand propositions accurately expressing the relationship you believe to exist between the following pairs of classes.

7. College students — those expected to read books.
8. College students — eighth grade students.
9. Residents of your dormitory — psychology majors. (You have learned that two residents of your dormitory are psychology majors; you know nothing about the others.)
10. Residents of your dormitory — those who have B averages. (You have just learned that at least one resident of your dormitory does not have a B average; you know nothing about the averages of the others.)
11. Residents of your dormitory — those who have B averages. (You now know that ten of the residents of your dormitory have B averages and that the others do not.)

Answers to Self-Check Questions

Page 195: 1. $\overset{d}{\text{Vir.}} < \overset{u}{\text{Am.}}$

2. $\overset{d}{\text{Vot.}} < \overset{u}{\text{cits.}}$

Page 196: 3. $\overset{d}{\text{Docs.}} < \overset{u}{\text{prof. people.}}$

4. $\overset{d}{\text{College grads.}} \nless \overset{d}{\text{illits.}}$

Page 197: 5. $\overset{d}{\text{Courses taken}} \nless \overset{d}{\text{flunked.}}$

6. $\overset{u}{\text{Profs.}} < \overset{u}{\text{users of big words.}}$

Page 198: 7. $\overset{d}{\text{College students}}$
$< \overset{u}{\text{those expected to read books.}}$

8. $\overset{d}{\text{College students}} \nless \overset{d}{\text{eighth graders.}}$

9. $\overset{u}{\text{Residents of your dorm}}$
$< \overset{u}{\text{psych. majors.}}$

10. $\overset{u}{\text{Residents of your dorm}}$
$\nless \overset{d}{\text{those having B averages.}}$

11. $\overset{u}{\text{Residents of your dorm}}$
$< \overset{u}{\text{those having B averages;}}$

$\overset{u}{\text{residents of your dorm}}$
$\nless \overset{d}{\text{those having B averages.}}$

EXERCISE 20

1. *Identify the parts of the proposition by drawing a bracket over the part and writing Q for "quantifier," T1 for "Term 1," T2 for "Term 2," and C for "connective."*
2. *On the line provided, write the proposition in shorthand form.*
3. *Draw a circle diagram for the proposition.*

Item 1 has been worked as an example. Do not change the meaning of the proposition stated; your task is to state the proposition, not your belief, in shorthand and diagrammatic form.

1.
Q   T1   C
⌐All⌐ ⌐Americans⌐ ⌐are included in⌐
T2
⌐believers in democracy.⌐

  d   u
Ams. < bel. in dem.

2.
All metals ⌐are⌐ denser than water.

met. < denser than water

den. than water

3.   Q   T1   C
⌐All⌐ ⌐fascists⌐ ⌐are excluded from⌐
T2
believers in individual freedom.

fascists ≠ bel. in ind. freed

fasc.   *bel. freed.*

4.   Q   T1   C
⌐No⌐ modern automobiles ⌐are⌐
T2
⌐powered by steam engines.⌐

mod. auto ≠ steam eng.

mod. autos   *steam engine*

5.   Q   T1   C
⌐Some⌐ ⌐failures⌐ ⌐are excluded from⌐
T2
⌐failures due to indolence.⌐

failures ≠ failures due to indolence

failure   *fail. ind.*

6.   Q   T1   C
⌐Some⌐ ⌐electricians⌐ ⌐are not⌐ good
T2
insurance risks.

elect. ≠ good insurance risks

elect.   *good risks*

7. Some paintings by Van Gogh are included in masterpieces.

paintings ∠ masterpieces

8. Many so-called communists are merely malcontents.

comm. ∠ malcnts

9. Every case of infection is accompanied by fever.

infection ∠ acc. by fever

10. Re-examinations are never given at Wysacki.

re-ex. ≠ Wysacki

11. Some habits of thinking do not improve decisions.

think. hab ≠ improve decisions

12. All perceptions are subject to error.

percept. ∠ sub. to err.

13. All generalizations are based on samples.

gen. ∠ based on sampes

14. Thinking that is not creative is not effective.

not creative think ≠ eff.

21 Immediate Inference

Let us now sharpen our understanding of categorical propositions by studying the *immediate inferences* that can be drawn from them, *i.e., inferences drawn from a single categorical proposition, without reference to evidence from any other source.* By studying immediate inference we can increase the skill with which we use and interpret language.

1. Conversion

Our concern in this chapter is with the meaning conveyed by the structure of the propositions. Categorical propositions always read from left to right. In other words, the subject term is always included in or excluded from the predicate term. If we read a categorical proposition from right to left, we are making an immediate inference by *conversion, i.e., by interchanging subject and predicate terms.* If you interpret the proposition, "No statesman puts votes ahead of duty," to mean that no one who puts votes ahead of duty is a statesman, you have made an immediate inference by converting the original proposition.

Inference by conversion, like other forms of inference, can be either valid or invalid. The rule is simple: if the conversion is valid, no term in the converted form can be distributed unless it was distributed in the original form.

E- and I-form propositions can be validly converted, as shown in the examples below.

$$\text{Given:} \quad \overset{d}{\text{Mammals}} \nless \overset{d}{\text{insects.}}$$

$$\text{Converted:} \quad \overset{d}{\text{Insects}} \nless \overset{d}{\text{mammals.}}$$

$$\text{Given:} \quad \overset{u}{\text{Students}} < \overset{u}{\text{men.}}$$

$$\text{Converted:} \quad \overset{u}{\text{Men}} < \overset{u}{\text{students.}}$$

Although there may be a difference in emphasis between the given and the converted propositions, there is no difference in the logical meanings. Note that no term that is undistributed in the given proposition is distributed in the converted proposition.

O-form propositions cannot be validly converted. Consider the example below.

$$\text{Given:} \quad \overset{u}{\text{Animals}} \nless \overset{d}{\text{mammals.}}$$

$$\text{Converted:} \quad \overset{u}{\text{Mammals}} \nless \overset{d}{\text{animals.}}$$

In this example we can easily tell from our knowledge of the relationship between the two classes that the converted form is invalid. Knowledge of the subject matter is not necessary, however, for the term "animals" is undistributed in the given proposition and distributed in the converted form.

Thus the converted form makes a claim that is not justified by the evidence.

A-form propositions cannot be validly converted. Consider the propositions below.

$$\text{Given:} \quad \overset{d}{\text{Pennsylvanians}} < \overset{u}{\text{Americans.}}$$

$$\text{Converted:} \quad \overset{d}{\text{Americans}} < \overset{u}{\text{Pennsylvanians.}}$$

Obviously the converted form is invalid, for the given form does not state the relationship of *all* Americans to Pennsylvanians, while the converted form does. Note that "Americans" is undistributed in the original but distributed in the converted form.

2. Obversion

Obversion consists in changing the second term of a proposition from positive to negative, or vice versa, and changing inclusion to exclusion, or vice versa. The two changes offset each other, and the net result is a change in the tone of the proposition, but no change in the meaning.

$$\text{Given:} \quad \overset{d}{\text{Students}} \not< \overset{d}{\text{stupid.}}$$

$$\text{True Obversion:} \quad \overset{d}{\text{Students}} < \overset{u}{\text{non-stupid.}}$$

All true obversions are valid. We can validly obvert A-, E-, I-, and O-form propositions if the changes we make in the given proposition meet the definition above. If the changes fail to meet this definition, we may be guilty of the fallacy of *faulty obversion.*

To avoid such awkward expressions as "non-stupid," we often obvert propositions by changing the second term to an antonym or phrase with an opposite or contrasting meaning. But when we do this we risk inaccuracy, as in the example below.

$$\text{Given:} \quad \overset{d}{\text{The good}} \not< \overset{d}{\text{live to be old.}}$$

$$\text{Faulty Obversion:} \quad \overset{d}{\text{The good}} < \overset{u}{\text{die young.}}$$

This obversion is faulty because there is a change in meaning. The given proposition asserts that the good die before they get old; it does not prohibit them from living to be middle aged. But the faulty obversion asserts that the good die while still young, before reaching middle age. This faulty obversion is invalid because it goes beyond the information in the given proposition. This variety of faulty obversion is not necessarily invalid, however. Suppose the given proposition had read: "The good die young." If we change it to read, "The good do not live to be old," we would have a case of faulty obversion, since dying young is not the equivalent of not living to be old. Although this faulty obversion is not the equivalent of the given proposition, it is valid: if the good die young they cannot live to be old.

In a true obversion the subject term of the given proposition is never changed. In the example below the subject term has been changed, and the obversion is faulty.

$$\text{Given:} \quad \overset{d}{\text{Logicians}} < \overset{u}{\text{wise.}}$$

$$\text{Faulty Obversion:} \quad \overset{d}{\underset{\text{not logicians}}{\text{Those who are}}} \not< \overset{d}{\text{wise.}}$$

This kind of faulty obversion is always invalid because the original information in the given proposition is limited to the class described by the subject term. In the above example the information in the given proposition is limited to logicians; nothing whatever is said about those who are not logicians. In reading poetry it is permissible to draw inferences from what is not said; in logic such inferences are unreliable.

Propagandists and advertisers often exploit people's ignorance or carelessness about drawing inferences from propositions. For example, an advertiser may make this claim: "Every bar of Satin Soap contains lanolin." Assuming that the advertiser is telling the truth, he is not committing a fallacy. But he may be tempting you to commit a fallacy by invalidly converting his statement into, "All bars of soap that contain lanolin are Satin Soap," or by invalidly obverting it into, "No soap that is not Satin Soap contains lanolin."

3. Relationships between Propositions

Another form of immediate inference consists, in effect, in changing the form of a given proposition without changing either its terms or their order. Since our present concern is with the structure of propositions, let us substitute symbols for terms in order to see clearly the function of the structure without being distracted by the denotative and connotative meanings of words. The four forms of categorical propositions can be written in symbols as shown below, with X and Y symbolizing the subject and predicate terms respectively.

$$
\begin{aligned}
&\text{A-form:} && \overset{d}{X\text{'s}} < \overset{u}{Y\text{'s}} \\
&\text{E-form:} && \overset{d}{X\text{'s}} \not< \overset{d}{Y\text{'s}} \\
&\text{I-form:} && \overset{u}{X\text{'s}} < \overset{u}{Y\text{'s}} \\
&\text{O-form:} && \overset{u}{X\text{'s}} \not< \overset{d}{Y\text{'s}}
\end{aligned}
$$

Now *assume that the A-form is true.* What inferences can we draw about the other three forms? We can validly infer that the I-form is true. If *all* Pennsylvanians are Americans, certainly *some* are. We can also validly infer that the E- and O-forms are *false.* If all Pennsylvanians are Americans, no Pennsylvanians can possibly be excluded from the class of Americans.

Now *assume that the E-form is true.* The E-form is the only one of the four forms that states the complete relationship between the two classes — total exclusion. We can validly infer that the A- and I-forms are *false.* We can validly infer that the O-form is *true;* if *all* X's are excluded from the Y class, certainly *some* X's are excluded.

Now *assume that the I-form is true.* We can validly infer that the E-form is *false:*

The I-form asserts that there is at least one X that is a Y; thus the E-form cannot possibly be true. No valid inference can be made about the A- and O-forms. The only meaning conveyed by the structure of the I-form is that somewhere there is at least one X that is a Y. The whole truth could be that all X's are Y's, or that some X's are Y's and some are not; we cannot tell which is true.

Now *assume that the O-form is true.* We can validly infer that the A-form is *false,* since it declares that every X is a Y. We cannot tell, however, whether the I- and E-forms are true or false. All we know from the O-form is that somewhere there is at least one X that is not a Y. The whole truth could be that no X's are Y's, or that some X's are Y's and some are not. We cannot tell from the structure of the proposition which is true. Thus any inference about the I- or E-form is invalid.

In ordinary conversation I- or O-form propositions are frequently used to express both partial inclusion and partial exclusion. For example, your instructor may say to his class, "Some of you passed," when he means that some of you passed and some of you did not. You may, therefore, be justified in concluding from the instructor's statement and its context that some of you did not pass. You should keep in mind, however, that the instructor's proposition itself stated only that some passed. In this chapter we are concerned only with what propositions state, not with what they suggest.

4. Inferences from False Propositions

If we could find a propagandist who is never right, he would be a more reliable source of information than if he were usually but not always right; if we could depend on him always to be wrong, we could draw valid and reliable inferences from what he says. The principles of valid inference apply to propositions known to be false as well as to those known to be true. However, a slightly different approach is recommended. Suppose our dependably erroneous propagandist declares, in A-form, "All Democrats are yeggs." Knowing only that he is wrong, we can infer at least part of the truth about Democrats. For *if a proposition is known to be false, we can validly conclude that its contradictory form is true.* Two propositions are *contradictory* when one of them must be false and the other must be true. The contradictory form of any categorical proposition can be derived by two simple steps, neither of which can be omitted: (1). changing the relationship between terms, and (2) changing the distribution of both terms. Consider the two propositions below.

$$
\left.
\begin{array}{c}
\overset{d}{\text{Democrats}} \overset{u}{<} \text{yeggs.} \\
\overset{u}{\text{Democrats}} \overset{d}{\not<} \text{yeggs.}
\end{array}
\right\} \text{Contradictories}
$$

If it is false that all Democrats are yeggs, then there must be at least one Democrat somewhere who is not a yegg. On the other hand, if it is false that some Democrats are not yeggs, then it is necessarily true that all Democrats are yeggs. We must change the distribution of the subject term in order to derive the contradictory proposition. Also when we change the relationship we must automatically change the distribution of the predicate term, for the predicate term is always undistributed following inclusion and distributed following exclusion. To put the matter another way, the contradictory form of a proposition states the minimum evidence necessary to prove that the given proposition is false. To prove that the slander on the Democratic Party is false, we need produce only one Democrat who is not a yegg.

A- and O-forms and E- and I-forms are contradictories. If the A-form is true, the O-form must be false, and vice versa. Similarly, if the E-form is true, the I-form is false, and vice versa.

Contradictory propositions must not be confused with *contrary* propositions. Contradictory and contrary propositions are alike in that both cannot be true; they are different in that, whereas one of a pair of contradictory propositions must be true, *both* of a pair of *contrary propositions* can be false. Consider the two propositions below.

$$
\text{A-form: } \overset{d}{\text{Democrats}} \overset{u}{<} \text{yeggs.}
$$
$$
\text{E-form: } \overset{d}{\text{Democrats}} \overset{d}{\not<} \text{yeggs.}
$$

Obviously one of these propositions must be false. By definition, however, they fail to qualify as contradictories, for *both* of them could be false. We could prove that both are false merely by producing one Democrat who is a yegg (thus demolishing the E-form), and one Democrat who is not a yegg (thus demolishing the A-form). Thus A- and E-form propositions are *contraries*: both cannot be true, but both may be false. Note that to assume merely from the structure of the propositions that one of a pair of contrary propositions is necessarily true is to commit the black-or-white fallacy.

We can easily determine the validity of inferences drawn from any proposition known to be false simply by changing the proposition to its contradictory and testing the inferences by using the contradictory form as the truth. For example, suppose that our dependably erroneous propagandist declares that no Republicans are sane. His declaration is shown in shorthand below.

$$
\overset{d}{\text{Republicans}} \overset{d}{\not<} \text{sane.}
$$

We can derive the truth from this falsehood by changing the relationship and the distribution of both terms. The resulting proposition is necessarily true because it is the contradictory of a false proposition.

$$
\overset{u}{\text{Republicans}} \overset{u}{<} \text{sane.}
$$

We can test other immediate inferences by using the above proposition as the truth. Since it is an I-form, the corresponding E-form will be false. The A- and O- forms will be invalid, and their truth will be in doubt.

EXERCISE 21

1–4. *Assume that the italicized proposition in each group is true. Evaluate each of the other propositions in the group, using the letter T if it can be validly inferred to be true, F if it can be validly inferred to be false, and D (doubtful) if its truth or falsity cannot be validly inferred from the italicized proposition.*

1. *All students like to sleep late.* A-form

   (a) No students like to sleep late. E   F – relationship

   (b) Some students like to sleep late. I   T – relationship

   (c) Some students do not like to sleep late. O   F – relationship

   (d) All who like to sleep late are students. A   D – converted

   (e) None who like to sleep late are students. E   F – conversion of (a)

2. *Some professors like to tell jokes.* I-form

   (a) All professors like to tell jokes. A   D – relationship

   (b) Some who like to tell jokes are professors. I   T – converted

   (c) Some professors do not like to tell jokes. O   D – relationship

   (d) Some students like to tell jokes. I   D

   (e) No professors like to tell jokes. E   F – relationship

3. *Some doctors are not surgeons.* O-form

   (a) All doctors are surgeons. A   F – relationship

   (b) No doctors are surgeons. E   D – relationship

   (c) Some doctors are surgeons. I   D – relationship

   (d) Some surgeons are not doctors. O   D – conversion

   (e) Some medical students are not surgeons. O   D

4. *No old men are drafted.* E-form

   (a) All old men are drafted. A   F – relationship

   (b) Some old men are drafted. I   F – relationship

   (c) Some old men are not drafted. O   T – relationship

   (d) None who are drafted are old men. E   T – conversion

   (e) All who are drafted are young men. A   D

5–8. *In the next four groups, assume that the italicized proposition is false.*

5. *Some dictators do not restrict liberty.* o-form
   (a) All dictators restrict liberty. A   T   F - relationship
   (b) Some dictators restrict liberty. I   T   D - relationship
   (c) Some dictators do not restrict liberty. O   F   I
   (d) No dictators restrict liberty. E   F   O - relationship
   (e) Some who restrict liberty are not dictators. O   D   O - conversion

6. *Some men are indispensable.* I - form
   (a) No men are indispensable. E   T   F - relationship
   (b) Some men are not indispensable. O   T   D   "
   (c) None who are indispensable are men. E   T   F
   (d) All men are indispensable. A   F   D - relationship
   (e) No women are indispensable. E   D

7. *All tugbeets are dragdites.* A-form
   (a) Some tugbeets are dragdites. I   D   I - relationship
   (b) Some tugbeets are not dragdites. O   T   F   "
   (c) No tugbeets are dragdites. E   D   F   "
   (d) All dragdites are tugbeets. A   D   D - conversion
   (e) Some dragdites are not tugbeets. O   D   D

8. *No nabberocks are pearlgates.* E - form
   (a) No pearlgates are nabberocks. E   F   I - conversion
   (b) No nabberocks are pearlgates. E   F   I
   (c) Some nabberocks are not pearlgates. O   D   I - relationship
   (d) Some nabberocks are pearlgates. I   T   F   "
   (e) All nabberocks are pearlgates. A   D   F   "

9–10. *Write in logical shorthand (1) the obverse of the following propositions (2) the converse of any propositions that can be validly converted.*

9. Some students are inattentive at lectures. I
   (1) students ₴ attentive O   (2) inattentive < students

10. Some students are not mature. O
    (1) students < immature I   (2) immature < students

206

22 Categorical Syllogisms

Having studied the meanings of categorical propositions, let us now examine their uses in decision making. As we noted in Chapter 2, when the decision-making cycle follows a deductive pattern, Phase 4 (testing tentative conclusions) includes testing inferences for validity. We usually make deductive decisions so quickly that we must be able to test simple deductive inferences for validity almost instantly and automatically if we are to avoid fallacious conclusions. The ability to do this requires a thorough understanding of certain syllogistic forms. We have already studied the hypothetical form. We now turn to the categorical.

As we study the categorical syllogism, let us keep in mind two objectives. One is direct: to learn the rules of validity so well that we never, or almost never, misapply classifications, generalizations, causal theories, and value premises. The other objective is indirect but no less important: to sharpen our skill in using and interpreting language. The focus in this chapter will be on validity, but let us not forget for an instant that a valid conclusion is no more reliable than the premises on which it is based.

1. Structure

A categorical syllogism consists of two categorical propositions used as premises and a conclusion in categorical form drawn from the premises by inference. Both the premises and the conclusion have two terms, each of which names a class of objects, ideas, or qualities. A connective describes the relationship between the two classes; this relationship must be inclusion or exclusion. The quantifier tells how much of the first class named is related to the second class. Note that the minor premise names a new class or subclass not mentioned in the major premise and declares that this class is included in or excluded from one of the classes named in the major premise.

An example of a categorical syllogism with all its parts labeled is shown on the following page.[1]

A syllogism is valid only when its premises close all possible loopholes, so that the relationship between classes claimed by the conclusion must exist if the premises are true. Vast experience with students has shown that when they like a conclusion they tend to rate the syllogism valid; and when they dislike a conclusion, to rate the syllogism invalid. You will do well to learn a better system.

All possible loopholes in a categorical syllogism are closed only when it meets four

---

[1] Technically, the major premise is the one which contains the predicate term of the conclusion ("subject to error"), while the minor premise contains the subject term of the conclusion ("books").

	Quantifier	Term 1	Connective	Term 2
Major Premise:	All	things created by men	are included in	things subject to error.

	Quantifier	Term 3	Connective	Term 1
Minor Premise:	All	books	are included in	things created by men.

	Quantifier	Term 3	Connective	Term 2
Conclusion:	All	books	are included in	things subject to error.

rules of validity. If the syllogism violates a single rule, it is invalid and its conclusion, though possibly true, is not reliable. The remainder of this chapter describes a procedure for applying these four rules. Unless your instructor suggests a different procedure, you should follow it precisely until you can do it automatically. Otherwise you will become confused or omit steps. When you have had sufficient practice you can eliminate or consolidate some of the steps. Eventually you should be able to check a simple syllogism in a few seconds, but in the beginning the long way around is best.

The first step in this recommended procedure is to write the syllogism in logical shorthand, observing the rules stated in Chapter 20. The syllogism above would be written this way.

$$\overset{d}{\text{Things created by men}} < \overset{u}{\text{subject to error.}}$$

$$\overset{d}{\text{Books}} < \overset{u}{\text{created by men.}}$$

$$\therefore \overset{d}{\text{Books}} < \overset{u}{\text{subject to error.}}$$

When correctly written in shorthand, it is relatively easy to determine whether a syllogism meets the four rules of validity.

2. The Four-Terms Fallacy

The next step in our procedure is to determine whether the syllogism meets the first of these four rules. If the syllogism is valid it must follow the rule in the next column.

> A valid syllogism must have exactly three terms, each used exactly twice to refer to the same class.

If the syllogism violates the rule in any way — by having four terms, by using one term only once or more than twice, or by using the same term to refer to different classes (equivocation) — it is invalid. This error is called the *four-terms fallacy*.

You can see the reason for this rule by studying the valid syllogism above. Note that the minor premise introduces a third term ("books") and relates it to one of the terms in the major premise ("created by men"). Note further that the conclusion relates this same third term to the other term in the major premise ("subject to error"). If a syllogism fails to do exactly this, it contains a loophole and is invalid. In order to do this, it must contain exactly three terms, each used exactly twice. There is no other way. The four-terms fallacy corresponds in some respects to the fallacy of uncertain relationships between premises in hypothetical syllogisms.

Now suppose your instructor tells you that you are good for nothing, because all who flunked this course are indolent and you made the lowest grade in the class. If you are unwilling to accept this allegation, you must attack either the premises or the validity of the argument. Let us test it for validity first. The instructor's premises are written in shorthand on the next page.

$$\overset{d}{\text{Those who flunked this course}} < \overset{u}{\text{indolent.}}$$

$$\overset{d}{\text{You}} < \overset{u}{\text{made the lowest grade in the class.}}[2]$$

You can see the four-terms fallacy in this argument without bothering to write the conclusion. The minor premise introduces a new term ("you"), but it does not clearly relate this term to either term in the major premise. Even if you did make the lowest grade in the class, it is not necessarily true that you flunked the course. Perhaps everybody passed.

When you call attention to his fallacy, suppose your instructor changes his syllogism to the version below.

$$\overset{d}{\text{Those who flunked this course}} < \overset{u}{\text{indolent.}}$$

$$\overset{d}{\text{You}} < \overset{u}{\text{flunked this course.}}$$

$$\therefore \overset{d}{\text{You}} < \overset{u}{\text{good for nothing.}}$$

The minor premise does its work perfectly by relating "you" to those who flunked the course, but the conclusion violates the rule. For this syllogism to be valid, the conclusion must relate "you" to the "indolent." Instead, it relates you to the "good for nothing," which is quite a different class. Although in categorical analysis we call this a four-terms fallacy, you will recognize this particular example as a *non sequitur*. The instructor's syllogism would have been valid if he had merely accused you of being indolent.

In writing syllogisms in shorthand you must be very careful to identify and state the classes accurately. Otherwise you may accept a fallacious syllogism like the one below.

Smoke is a nuisance.

Bill and Jack smoke.

Therefore, Bill and Jack are nuisances.

The four-terms fallacy becomes obvious

when the premises are correctly written in shorthand, for "smoke" and "smokers" are not the same class.

$$\overset{d}{\text{Smoke}} < \overset{u}{\text{nuisances.}}$$

$$\overset{d}{\text{Bill and Jack}} < \overset{u}{\text{smokers.}}$$

3. The Fallacy of Faulty Exclusion

Suppose your boy friend gives you an argument you do not like. Since it is often easier to destroy an argument by showing it to be invalid than by disproving a premise, you test it for validity. When you write his argument in logical shorthand, it looks like this.

$$\overset{d}{\text{Ladies}} \not< \overset{d}{\text{break dates unnecessarily.}}$$

$$\overset{d}{\text{You}} \not< \overset{d}{\text{ladies.}}$$

$$\therefore \overset{d}{\text{You}} < \overset{u}{\text{break dates unnecessarily.}}$$

You can quickly see that his argument meets the four-terms rule, so the next step is to check it for the second rule of validity, stated in the box below.

> A valid syllogism must have no exclusions, or exactly two, one of which must be in the conclusion.

You would be justified, though tactless, in suggesting to your boy friend that he be more logical, for his syllogism contains the fallacy of faulty exclusion by having exclusions in both premises.

The reasons for the rule on exclusion are easy enough to see. Two exclusions in the premises prove nothing because the third term is not linked to anything. In the example above, "you" are linked in no way to the class "those who break dates unnecessarily." Now suppose that your boy friend changes his argument to this.

---

[2] "You" is distributed because it refers to a single individual.

$$\overset{d}{\text{Ladies}} \overset{d}{\nless} \text{break dates unnecessarily.}$$

$$\overset{d}{\text{You}} \overset{u}{<} \text{ladies.}$$

$$\therefore \overset{d}{\text{You}} \overset{u}{<} \text{break dates unnecessarily.}$$

Although your boy friend is now being more tactful, you can still chide him about his faulty logic. This syllogism also breaks the rule on exclusions. His premises actually prove the opposite of his conclusion. Thus if there is one exclusion in either premise, the conclusion must also contain an exclusion. Otherwise, the syllogism contains the fallacy of faulty exclusion.

4. The Fallacy of Undistributed Middle

Suppose you park overtime, and the traffic officer makes the unpalatable accusation in the syllogism below.

$$\overset{d}{\text{Criminals}} \overset{u}{<} \text{lawbreakers.}$$

$$\overset{d}{\text{You}} \overset{u}{<} \text{lawbreakers.}$$

$$\therefore \overset{d}{\text{You}} \overset{u}{<} \text{criminals.}$$

This syllogism clearly passes the first two tests for validity. The next step, therefore, is to test it for the third rule, stated in the box below.

> In a valid syllogism the middle term must be distributed at least once.

The middle term is easily identified. *It never appears in the conclusion; it must appear in both premises.* It must be distributed at least once because it is the middle link in the chain of argument. Look at the valid syllogism on page 208. "Things created by men" is the middle term because it is the only term that appears in both premises. In the major premise, all "things created by

men" are included in the class "things subject to error." In the minor premise, "books" are included in "things created by men." Thus the middle term links "books" and "things subject to error" as surely as a town is linked to a state because it is in a certain county in the state. Note that the middle term is distributed in the major premise.

Now look at the impolite policeman's syllogism. The middle term is "lawbreakers." But this link has a gap in it. Even if you knew nothing whatever about the two classes in the major premise, you know from the structure of the proposition that the second class, "lawbreakers," is possibly, even probably, larger than the first class, "criminals." Proving that you are a lawbreaker does not prove that you are a criminal, for the same reason that living in a certain state does not prove that you live in a certain county. Now note that the middle term is *undistributed* in *both* premises. Thus the syllogism violates the rule and is invalid.

Now suppose you tactlessly point out to your policeman that his logic is unworthy of his profession, and suppose he changes his syllogism a bit, as shown below.

$$\overset{d}{\text{Lawbreakers}} \overset{u}{<} \text{criminals.}$$

$$\overset{d}{\text{You}} \overset{u}{<} \text{lawbreakers.}$$

$$\therefore \overset{d}{\text{You}} \overset{u}{<} \text{criminals.}$$

The fallacy of undistributed middle has been eliminated. But before you let your self-concept be damaged by this syllogism, compare its major premise with the one in the policeman's original argument. Both major premises are classifications. The first is generally accepted; the second is not.

These two syllogisms illustrate a problem you will frequently encounter: the evidence in hand, depending upon how you write the premises, gives you either an invalid syllogism with reliable premises or a valid syllogism with unreliable premises. In these situations you cannot afford to throw away the evidence in syllogisms with undistributed middle terms, for these syllogisms are like hypothetical syllogisms with affirmed consequents. The conclusions are not proved, but the probability that they are true is increased.

When either or both of the premises are expressed in statistical terms, the probability that the conclusion is true can sometimes be estimated with a fair degree of accuracy. Consider the following example.

Twenty-three per hundred thousand Americans will be killed in motor-vehicle accidents next year.[3]
You are an American.
Therefore, you will be killed in a motor-vehicle accident next year.

The middle term, "Americans," is undistributed in both premises (in the major premise because the quantity referred to is less than all; in the minor premise because it follows inclusion). Thus the conclusion is invalid. But the probability that it is true on this evidence alone, assuming that the premises are true, is easily computed: it is the probability that any given American will be killed in a vehicular accident this year, or $23/100,000$. Although this probability is low, it is still high enough to justify a decision to drive carefully.

5. The Fallacy of Illicit Distribution

It is not enough to check only the arguments you dislike. You should be particularly careful in checking arguments you like to offset your natural tendency to accept them. Consider the syllogism below.

$$\overset{d}{\text{Stupid people}} < \overset{u}{\text{swallow propaganda.}}$$
$$\overset{d}{\text{Logic students}} \nless \overset{d}{\text{stupid.}}$$
$$\therefore \overset{d}{\text{Logic students}} \nless \overset{d}{\text{swallow propaganda.}}$$

[3] Based on data in the *World Almanac.*

It meets the test of all three rules studied so far. But there is one more rule.

> In a valid syllogism, every term distributed in the conclusion must be distributed in the premise in which it appears.

Note that this rule applies only to distributed terms in the conclusion. The first term, "logic students," is distributed in the conclusion; it meets the rule because it is also distributed in the minor premise. The second term, "those who swallow propaganda," is also distributed in the conclusion, but it is undistributed in the major premise. Thus the rule has been violated, and we have the fallacy of *illicit distribution.*

The reason for the rule is easy to understand. The essence of validity is that the conclusion must never go beyond the evidence actually stated in the premises. The conclusion above claims that 100 per cent of those who swallow propaganda are accounted for with respect to logic students. Yet the major premise accounts for only *some* of those who swallow propaganda, because this latter class follows inclusion. It is possible, even probable, that there are people who swallow propaganda who are not stupid, and some of these people could, alas, be logic students. The fact that you do not live in a particular county is not enough to prove that you do not live in the state.

Consider another example.

$$\overset{d}{\text{Students}} < \overset{u}{\text{alert.}}$$
$$\overset{u}{\text{Women}} < \overset{u}{\text{students.}}$$
$$\therefore \overset{d}{\text{Women}} < \overset{u}{\text{alert.}}$$

Note that the term "women" is distributed in the conclusion, but not in the minor premise. The minor premise puts *some* women in the class of students, and these women are certainly in the class of the alert. But the conclusion claims that *all* women are in the class of the alert. Had it modestly claimed only that some women are alert, it would have been valid.

Consider another example, using the same major premise.

$$\overset{d}{\text{Students}} < \overset{u}{\text{alert.}}$$

$$\overset{d}{\text{Coeds}} < \overset{u}{\text{students.}}$$

$$\therefore \overset{u}{\text{Coeds}} < \overset{u}{\text{alert}}$$

If you think this is invalid, go back and reread the rule. Given these premises, the conclusion could validly claim that all coeds are alert. But there is no law of validity that prohibits claiming too little. Claiming too little may be wasteful of evidence, but it never invalidates an argument. The laws of validity prohibit claiming too much.

Assuming that the premises are true, syllogisms with illicit distribution are not always worthless as evidence. Consider the following example.

$$\overset{d}{\text{Reference books}} < \overset{u}{\text{on reserve.}}$$

$$\overset{d}{\text{The book I want}} \not< \overset{d}{\text{reference books.}}$$

$$\therefore \overset{d}{\text{The book I want}} \not< \overset{d}{\text{on reserve.}}$$

The second term in the conclusion is illicitly distributed; the conclusion is therefore invalid. Even so, the two premises do increase the probability that the book is not on reserve.

The time you invest in acquiring a thorough knowledge of syllogisms will pay rich dividends when you are required to analyze complicated arguments, as you will see in Chapters 25 and 26.

EXERCISE 22

In the space provided, rewrite each syllogism in categorical shorthand. Then analyze it by the recommended procedure and write in the blank the number of the appropriate statement from the key list.

KEY LIST

1. The syllogism contains the fallacy of four terms.
2. The syllogism contains the fallacy of faulty exclusion.
3. The syllogism contains the fallacy of undistributed middle.
4. The syllogism contains the fallacy of illicit distribution.
5. The syllogism meets all rules and is valid.

1. No good students neglect their studies.

He neglects his studies.

Therefore, he is not a good student.

good students ≯ neglect studies
he ≮ neglects studies
∴ he ≯ good student
5 - valid

2. All violent persons must be restrained.
John often does not know when to stop.

Therefore, John must be violent.

violent persons ≮ restrained
John ≮ know when to stop
∴ John ≮ violent
2 - invalid

3. All surgeons have steady nerves.

John is not a surgeon.
Therefore, John does not have steady nerves.

surgeons ≮ steady nerves
John ≯ surgeon
∴ John ≯ steady nerves
4 - invalid

4. Some Southern Democrats favor states' rights.
Senator Smythe is a Southern Democrat.
Therefore, Senator Smythe favors states' rights.

Southern Dem. ≮ favor st. rights.
Sen. Smythe ≮ South. Dem
∴ Sen Smythe ≮ favors st. rights.
3 - invalid

5. All good tests are difficult.

    All tests on deductive reasoning are difficult.

    Therefore, all tests on deductive reasoning are good.

[handwritten: good tests < difficult / tests on ded. reas. < diff. / ∴ tests on ded. reas. < good / 3 — invalid]

6. All industrialists are capitalists.

    Most industrialists are not politicians.

    Therefore, politicians are capitalists.

[handwritten: industrialists < capitalists / industrialists ≠ politicians / ∴ politicians < capitalists / 2 — invalid]

7. All radicals are communists.

    All progressives advocate changes.

    Therefore, all progressives are communists.

[handwritten: radicals < communists / progressives < advocates of change / ∴ progressives < communists / 1 — invalid]

8. All difficult courses are worthwhile.

    All courses in ichthyology are difficult.

    Therefore, all courses in ichthyology are worthwhile.

[handwritten: difficult courses < worthwhile / ichthyology courses < difficult / ∴ ichthyology courses < worthwhile / 5 — valid]

9. Most good blockers are star players.

    All our backfield men are good blockers.

    Therefore, some of our backfield men are star players.

[handwritten: good blockers < star players / backfield men < good blockers / ∴ backfield men < star players / 3 — invalid]

23 Alternative and Disjunctive Syllogisms

To complete our study of syllogisms we must consider two more types, the alternative and the disjunctive. Although more limited in their applications than the categorical or the hypothetical syllogism, they serve a necessary purpose. You have doubtless used them hundreds of times without realizing it, and some costly errors can probably be charged to their misuse. As you study these syllogisms you should keep two objectives in mind: first, to learn them so well that you will never, or almost never, again make an error in using them; second, to sharpen your skills in using and interpreting language.

1. Structure of the Alternative Syllogism

Suppose you are a doctor. You can think of only two diseases which would account for your patient's symptoms, malaria and rheumatic fever. This knowledge can be the major premise of an alternative syllogism.

	Alternative 1		Alternative 2
Either	the patient has malaria	or	he has rheu-matic fever.

The words *either* and *or* are the connectives showing the relationship between the two parts of the premise. They indicate that there are only two possibilities in the situation. The two possibilities are called *alternatives,* from which the syllogism gets its name.

The minor premise may do two things: (1) it may declare that one of the alternatives is true, or (2) it may eliminate one alternative by declaring it false.

2. Affirming an Alternative

Suppose you run a test and find that the patient does have malaria. You now have a minor premise that affirms the first alternative, *i.e.*, declares that the condition described by the first alternative is true.

	Alternative 1		Alternative 2
Major Premise: Either	the patient has malaria	or	he has rheu-matic fever.

Minor Premise: He has malaria.

Given these premises, it is invalid to conclude that the patient does not have rheumatic fever. Your original information does not prohibit the patient from having both; it merely asserts that the explanation of his symptoms is limited to the two diseases. As a matter of fact, the patient could have both. Affirming an alternative is an invalid form. Note that in the example above the second alternative is affirmed by the minor premise. It does not matter which alternative is affirmed — the principle is the same.

Consider another example.

	Alternative 1		*Alternative 2*
Major Premise: Either	the tank is empty	or	the ignition is faulty.

Minor Premise: The ignition is faulty.

You might be tempted to conclude that the tank is not empty. Your conclusion would be probable, but it would be invalid because the major premise declares only that one of the two alternatives must be true. It says nothing whatever about the probabilities that both could be true. Any estimate of the probability that your conclusion is true must be based on evidence not in the premises.

The words "either . . . or" limit the possibilities to two; *they do not prohibit both possibilities from being true at the same time.*[1]

3. Denying an Alternative

The other possibility for the minor premise is to deny one of the alternatives by declaring that the condition or situation it describes is not true.

	Alternative 1		*Alternative 2*
Major Premise: Either	the tank is empty	or	the ignition is faulty.

Minor Premise: The tank is not empty.

Conclusion: The ignition is faulty.

[1] Sentences containing "either . . . or" are not necessarily alternative propositions. When the waitress says, "You *may* have ice cream or cake for dessert," she does not mean that you must have one or the other. The word "may" indicates that the choice is permissive rather than mandatory.

Certainly if the possibilities stated by the major premise are limited to two, one of which is demonstrated to be false, then the other must be true. The inference is valid.

Denying an alternative is a *valid* form. As in the hypothetical syllogism, a valid form permits only one valid conclusion. Before you rate an alternative syllogism valid, you must check the conclusion to see that it is the proper one. To be valid, the conclusion must declare that the other alternative (the one not eliminated by the minor premise) is true. The principle is the same, regardless of which alternative is denied. Any other conclusion is a *non sequitur*.

Alternative syllogisms are particularly prone to weaknesses in the major premise. In the example above, the major premise is actually a statement of two hypotheses. When you reason this way, you are really concluding that there can be only two possible explanations, because you can think of only two. Unfortunately, the fact that you can think of only two hypotheses does not make your premise reliable.

Many an alternative premise is actually a black-or-white fallacy. The following example is a case in point; although the conclusion is valid, it has little or no reliability.

Either she is perfect or she is a horrible person.
She is not perfect: her nose is crooked.
Therefore, she is a horrible person.

Although our focus in this chapter is on validity, we should never forget that a valid conclusion is no more reliable than the premises on which it is based.

4. Structure of the Disjunctive Syllogism

The disjunctive form of syllogism is the complement of the alternative form. The major premise of a disjunctive syllogism names two possibilities and declares that the two cannot exist together. These two possibilities are called *disjuncts* because they are completely separate. If one is true, the other cannot be. You can see this in the disjunctive premise below.

<u>*Disjunct 1*   *Disjunct 2*</u>

The patient cannot both be well and have a fever.

The words *cannot* and *both* assert that these two disjuncts cannot occur together. There are only two possibilities for the minor premise: (1) it may declare that one of the disjuncts is true, or (2) one is false.

5. Affirming a Disjunct

The minor premise may affirm one of the disjuncts by declaring that it is true in the particular case involved.

                Disjunct 1
Major Premise: The patient cannot be well

           Disjunct 2
     and have a fever.
Minor Premise: The patient is well.
Conclusion: The patient cannot have a fever.

The conclusion is *valid;* since the patient cannot be well and have a fever at the same time, and since he is declared to be well, he cannot have a fever. Should a clinical thermometer show his temperature to be 105°, then there is something wrong with the premises or with the thermometer, for the argument is valid. The argument will always be valid when the minor premise affirms one disjunct and the conclusion denies the other.

The principle is the same regardless of which disjunct is affirmed. Given the major premise above, should the minor premise declare that the patient has a fever, we can validly conclude that the other disjunct is not true: the patient is not well. Any other conclusion would be a *non sequitur.*

6. Denying a Disjunct

The minor premise may also deny one of the disjuncts by declaring that the condition or situation it describes is not true in the particular situation involved.

                        Disjunct 1
Major Premise: The patient cannot be well

               Disjunct 2
   and have a fever.
Minor Premise: The patient is not well.

No valid conclusion can be derived from these two premises. The major premise did not guarantee that the patient had to be either well or feverish. The patient may be ill with or without a fever.

Denying a disjunct is an *invalid* form. The major premise prohibits both disjuncts from being true at the same time; it does not guarantee that either one of them is true. There may be, and often are, many other possibilities. It does not matter which disjunct is denied. Any conclusion drawn will be invalid.

7. Combined Alternative and Disjunctive Syllogisms

Suppose your adviser tells you, "You must take Math A or Math 100, but you cannot take both." He has not only limited you to two alternatives but also prohibited you from doing both. Thus you have a major premise that combines the essential elements of both alternative and disjunctive propositions.

           Alternative-Disjunct 1
Major Premise: Either   take Math A

       Alternative-Disjunct 2
   or take Math 100, but not both.

Note that the structure words of both alternatives ("either . . . or") and disjuncts ("not both") appear in this premise. Any minor premise that clearly affirms or denies either alternative-disjunct will yield a valid conclusion. Not just any conclusion will be valid, of course. If the minor premise affirms one alternative-disjunct, the conclusion must deny the other; if the minor premise denies one alternative-disjunct, the conclusion must affirm the other. Otherwise the conclusion is a *non sequitur.*

In testing a syllogism for validity, do not consider it an alternative-disjunctive form unless the structure words (or their equivalents) of both alternative and disjunctive propositions are present. Should the major premise declare, "Either you continue your education or you join the armed forces," consider it an alternative form. Your frame of reference may tell you that you cannot do both, but this information is not in the premises. Besides, there may be ways you do not know about for continuing your education while in the armed forces. Should your professor declare, "You cannot stay in my class and refuse to prepare your assignments," you are not entitled to consider his declaration a combination form. He has nowhere said that you have to do either.[2]

In reasoning from your own premises, cultivate the habit of saying and thinking what you mean. If you believe that the situation

[2] Sometimes our frames of reference tell us that two alternatives cannot both be true. Consider this alternative proposition: "He is either in the library or in the lab." You would be justified in assuming that he cannot be in both places. But note that your assumption comes from your frame of reference rather than from the form of the proposition.

presents only two choices, both of which cannot be true together, put in the "either . . . or" and the "not both." Putting in the words may save you from a serious error by making you realize that you are reasoning from a false assumption.

8. Uncertain Relationship between Premises

In alternative and disjunctive syllogisms, as in hypothetical ones, the minor premise must clearly affirm or deny one of the possibilities of the major premise. Otherwise, the syllogism is invalid, no matter what the form.

Suppose your professor gives you this major premise in combination form: "Either you turn in an acceptable term paper by Tuesday and pass the final, or you fail the course, but not both." Should I learn only that you turned in a term paper and passed the final, I am not entitled to conclude that you passed the course, for my information does not clearly affirm all conditions set forth by the first alternative-disjunct. I do not know that the term paper was acceptable or that it was turned in by Tuesday. On the other hand, if I know that you did not pass the final, I can conclude that you failed the course, because I have sufficient information to deny that first alternative-disjunct.

Alternative and disjunctive syllogisms are valid only under the conditions summarized below.

▶ THE MAJOR PREMISE SAYS:	AND THE MINOR PREMISE:	AND THE CONCLUSION DECLARES:
either . . . or, or words to that effect	clearly denies one alternative	the other alternative true
not this . . . and this, or *not both,* or words to that effect	clearly affirms one disjunct	the other disjunct false
either . . . or, but not both, or words to that effect	clearly affirms one alternative-disjunct	the other false
	clearly denies one alternative-disjunct	the other true

EXERCISE 23

1–8. *In these items:*

　　1. Write in the blank the number of each statement from the key list below that applies to the item.

　　2. Following this number, write V if the conclusion is valid or I if it is invalid.

KEY LIST

　　1. An alternative is affirmed.
　　2. An alternative is denied.
　　3. A disjunct is affirmed.
　　4. A disjunct is denied.
　　5. An alternative-disjunct is affirmed.
　　6. An alternative-disjunct is denied.
　　7. The relationship between premises is uncertain.
　　8. The form is valid but the conclusion is a non sequitur.

1. Either he is seriously injured or his wind is knocked out.
His wind is certainly knocked out.
•Therefore, he is not seriously injured.　　___1___　　___I___

2. You cannot break training and still play on our teams.
You broke training.
Therefore, you cannot play on our teams.　　___3___　　___V___

3. He cannot know the facts and be prejudiced too.
He is not prejudiced.
Therefore, he must know the facts.　　___4___　　___I___

4. Either the radiator is clogged or it has sprung a leak. 6
But it is not leaking.　　　　　　　　　　　　or　　V
Therefore, it must be clogged.　　___2___　　___V___

5. Either he lacks the ability or he is not studying.
We know that he is studying hard.
Therefore, he must lack the ability.　　___2___　　___V___

6. He cannot fail to satisfy his needs and still be happy.
He is not happy.
Therefore, he is failing to satisfy his needs.　　___4___　　___I___

7. Either his fever must break soon or he will die.
His fever is definitely breaking right now.
Therefore, he will recover completely.　　___7___　　___I___

8. Either John is broke or he would have sent me a corsage.
I did not receive a corsage.　　　　　　　7 2　　V
Therefore, he is broke.　　_____　　___I___

9–16. *If the premises in the following items yield a valid conclusion, write it in the blank. If not, write the name of the fallacy.*

9. One cannot be registered in both the Lower Division and the College of Business Administration. Smythe is not registered in the Lower Division.

invalid - denies one disjunct

10. This snake is either a deadly coral snake or a harmless milk snake. It does not have the coloration sometimes found on the milk snake.

invalid - uncertain relationship

11. He is either a Rotarian or a Kiwanian, but not both. He is not a Rotarian.

He is a Kiwanian

12. Either he is an elusive runner or he has unusual speed. He is certainly an elusive runner.

invalid - affirming alternative

13. Either Calgonia will receive American aid or the Communists will attempt to gain control of the government. Calgonia will not receive American aid.

∴ Communists will attempt to gain control

14. Either the rain must stop before noon or the game will have to be postponed. The Weather Bureau has predicted showers for the afternoon.

invalid - uncertain relationship

15. It cannot be that he was innocent of evil intentions and still aware of the consequences of his act. This evidence proves that he could not have been aware of the consequences of his act.

invalid - denying a disjunct

16. This man's behavior is such that we can be sure that he is either guilty of a crime or shielding someone who is guilty. The evidence makes it clear that he is not guilty of a crime.

∴ he is shielding someone who is guilty

24 Interpreting Propositions

1. Categorical Forms

2. Hypothetical Forms

The propositional forms we have studied up to this point have been limited to those in which the normal English sentence and the logical proposition closely resemble each other. But many sentence forms in common use require special treatment when we put them into logical form. Before we begin our consideration of them, it should be helpful to understand that in Old English, some nine hundred years ago, word relationships within sentences depended upon the same kind of inflectional word endings as in Latin, rather than on a consistent pattern of word order.

Many of these inflectional word endings have disappeared. In modern English, meaning depends to a considerable extent on word order. In the modern English sentence the normal word order is simply subject-predicate. When we deviate from it, we sometimes fail to convey the meaning we intend.

1. Categorical Forms

There are five types of sentences that require special treatment when we transform them from ordinary English into categorical propositions.

One type may be easily identified by the presence of any one of the following structure words or their equivalents: *only, none but, none except,* and *alone.* In ordinary English these expressions enable us to achieve emphasis and variety in sentence structure by stating the predicate first and the subject second, thus reversing the normal

sequence. But, as we know, logical structure is based on normal English word order, with the first or "subject" term corresponding to the grammatical subject and the second or "predicate" term to the grammatical predicate. Hence, when we translate into logical propositions sentences in which "only," "none but," "none except," or "alone" indicate a reversal of subject-predicate order, our rule must be to *use the A-form and reverse the original order of the sentence elements.*

All the following sentences have the same meaning.

Only students may attend the game.
None but students may attend the game.
None except students may attend the game.
Students alone may attend the game.

In logic, each of these propositions should be stated in the A-form, with the subject and predicate terms in the normal order, as shown below.

$$\overset{d}{\text{Who may attend the game}} < \overset{u}{\text{students.}}$$

The second type of sentence is similar to those considered above in that the predicate is stated first. It differs from the first type in that it has an easily identifiable structure instead of easily identifiable key expressions: a modifying word or words, stated first, constitutes the predicate, followed by the verb and subject. When we translate them into categorical form, our procedure is the same as for the first type of proposition: *use the A-form and reverse the original order of the sentence elements.* The following sentences illustrate this type.

Ill lay John Smith.
Happy is the boy who dates a pretty girl.
Blessed are the meek.
Foolish are they who reason from false premises.

Again, in logic, each of these propositions should be stated in the A-form, with the subject and predicate terms in the order shown below.

d u
John Smith < those who lay ill.

d u
Boys who date pretty girls < the happy.

d u
The meek < the blessed.

d u
Those who reason < the foolish.
from false premises

The third type of troublesome sentence involves only the subject of the sentence and, accordingly, only the first term of its logical propositional form. The subjects and predicates of such sentences are in normal word order, and the sentences may be easily identified by the expressions *all but, all except,* and *unless,* or words that have the same meaning. In ordinary English these expressions have a negative meaning which always attaches itself to the subject of the sentence. When we transform the sentence into a logical proposition, therefore, we must be careful to make the first term (the subject term) negative and avoid the error of attaching the negative meaning to the connective, which expresses the relationship between the subject and predicate terms. The following sentences illustrate this third type.

All but John came to the party.
Everyone in the class except Marie preferred to postpone the test.
Unless excused, everyone must attend class.

When expressing them as logical propositions, we need only *retain the A-form* (since subject and predicate are in the normal order) *and make their first terms negative.*

d u
Those who are not John < those who came to the party.

d u
Those in the class < those who preferred
who are not Marie to postpone the test.

d u
Those who are not excused < those who must attend class.

Sentences with "unless" sometimes cause needless confusion because the "unless" can be in almost any position in the sentence. The example above, for instance, could also be stated, "Everyone must attend class unless excused." We need only remember that the word or words immediately following "unless" form the first term of the logical proposition and must be negated.

The precise meaning conveyed by the expressions "all but," "all except," and "unless" is often a subject of controversy. Very likely when we state that "All but John came to the party" we mean that John was the only one of those expected at the party who did not come. But logic is a discipline designed to clarify meaning, and all that is guaranteed by the logical propositional form of this sentence is that all persons other than John came to the party; strictly speaking, no information whatever about John himself is conveyed. In the second example cited above, it is possible that Marie was the only member absent at the time the class's opinion was determined, and to assume that she preferred *not* to postpone the test would be unwarranted. The proposition conveys no information about Marie or her preference; it merely states the preference of all members of the class other than Marie. We should understand that, however reasonable the belief may seem to us that something about John or Marie or the excused is conveyed in these three propositions, the structure of the proposition actually conveys no such information. In important matters, we should assume that the logical meaning is all that is conveyed.

Finally, note that "all but" and "all except" must never be confused with "none but" and "none except" — their meanings within sentence contexts are vastly different, as we have seen.

A fourth type of troublesome sentence involves the O-form (partial exclusion). Every expression of partial exclusion in ordinary English must be made by means of one of the following structures (or an easily identifiable variant); they are cited in the order of their frequency in everyday usage.

> Some X's are not Y's.
> Not all X's are Y's.
> All X's are not Y's.
> It is false that all X's are Y's.

In logical form, all of these sentence structures express partial exclusion.

$$\overset{u}{X's} \not< \overset{d}{Y's}$$

At first glance, we may be tempted to assume that "Not all Wysacki coeds are beautiful" and "All Wysacki coeds are not beautiful" are E-form propositions, expressing total exclusion. But suppose two male Wysacki freshmen arriving on the Wysacki campus for the very first time form these statements from their own experience. If they visit the lounge of one of the coed dormitories, placing themselves in strategically located chairs near the front door traffic area, they can confirm what they have heard about the beauty of Wysacki coeds. Let us assume that the first three coeds who enter are indeed beautiful, but our two freshmen wish to avoid hasty generalization and decide to observe further. After another coed enters, one freshman may say sadly, "Well, not all Wysacki coeds are beautiful." The other may reply with equal regret, "You're right. All Wysacki coeds are not beautiful." Obviously, having decided that the last one does not

meet their criteria for beauty, the two freshmen are conveying to one another that at least one Wysacki coed is excluded from the beautiful. The truth is that whatever confusion arises is a result of the written forms, for in our speech, stress and pitch patterns will usually make the meaning clear. If, in speech, one stresses the *all* as in "*All* Wysacki coeds are not beautiful," probably no one would miss the partial exclusion, the only meaning logically conveyed.

Similarly, if we insert the same subject and predicate in the last O-form example cited above ("It is false that all Wysacki coeds are beautiful"), the meaning conveyed must be that at least one Wysacki coed is *not* beautiful. Hence, in logical propositional form,

$$\overset{u}{\text{Wysacki coeds}} \not< \overset{d}{\text{the beautiful.}}$$

The last of our five kinds of troublesome sentences in categorical form are those that contain the expressions *few* and *a few*. When we state that "Few men are truly brave," we seem to be expressing partial inclusion (I-form), but what we mean — and also what we are conveying — is that "Most men are not truly brave," or partial exclusion (O-form). By the same reasoning, what we mean and convey by "Few men are not truly brave" is that "Most men are truly brave," or partial inclusion (I-form). Our rule, therefore, is that when we transform sentences containing "few" into logical propositions, we must *use the partial quantifier (some) and change the relationship between the terms (the connective).* The propositions below illustrate the rule.

Ordinary English	*Logical Propositional Form*
Few children smoke.	$\overset{u}{\text{Children}} \not< \overset{d}{\text{those who}}$ smoke.
Few men do not drive automobiles.	$\overset{u}{\text{Men}} < \overset{u}{\text{those who drive}}$ automobiles.

The expression "a few" differs in meaning from "few," for it simply indicates the quantifier *some*. Hence when we transform any sentence containing "a few," into a logical proposition, our rule is *to use the partial quantifier (some) and to keep the original relationship between the terms (the connective)*, as shown in the following examples.

Ordinary English	Logical Propositional Form
A few women are brave.	Women $\overset{u}{<}$ the $\overset{u}{\text{brave.}}$
A few women are not patient.	Women $\overset{u}{\not<}$ the $\overset{d}{\text{patient.}}$

2. Hypothetical Forms

Three types of troublesome propositions occur in hypothetical form, two of which contain the expressions *if and only if* and *only if*. Occasionally we encounter a hypothetical proposition like the one below.

Major Premise: If and only if it rains, our crops will be saved.

Minor Premise: It is not going to rain.

Given these premises, we can validly conclude that our crops will not be saved, even though the antecedent is denied. The presence of the words "if and only if" in the major premise indicates a reciprocal relationship between antecedent and consequent. Fully expressed, the premise means: If it rains our crops will be saved, and if it does not rain our crops will not be saved.

When you see the words "if and only if" or a similar phrase, such as "given these and only these conditions," all four hypothetical forms are valid. If the antecedent is the only condition under which the consequent can occur, and if the antecedent does not occur,

then the consequent cannot occur either, and vice versa. If the consequent occurs, the antecedent must occur, and vice versa. But when testing a syllogism for validity you must not add information to that given in the premises; for the syllogism to be valid in all four forms the words "if and only if" or their equivalents must be included in the premise.

"Only if" does not mean the same thing as "if and only if." "Only if you study will you pass" means simply that studying is one condition necessary for you to pass. Thus we cannot assume from this major premise that studying is *sufficient* in and of itself to enable you to pass, for there may be other necessary conditions. We can be certain only that (1) if you do not study, you will not pass, or (2) if you are to pass you must study. Accordingly, restating the major premise in either of these two forms yields a conventional hypothetical proposition. Our rule is to *restate propositions containing "only if . . ." either by negating both antecedent and consequent or by making the original antecedent the consequent and the original consequent the antecedent.*

The third and last of the hypothetical forms brings us back to the familiar *unless*, which has the same kind of negative meaning in hypothetical form it has in categorical form. In the hypothetical form the negative meaning of "unless" attaches itself to the antecedent of the proposition.

> Unless I hurry, I will be late.
> I will not hurry.
> Therefore, I will be late.

The syllogism is valid, and the major premise, in the hypothetical form, should be stated as follows.

> If I do not hurry, then I will be late.

EXERCISE 24A

1–14. *Write the following sentences in the logical shorthand for categorical propositions.*

1. A few men are cowards.

men < cowards _____ I

2. All except English majors may take this course.

those not English majors < those taking this A course

3. Only the brave deserve the fair.

those who deserve the fair < brave A

4. Long is the road to Paradise.

road to Paradise < long A

5. All models have gyrosteer unless manufactured this year.

those not manufactured this year < gyrosteer A

6. Not all teams have winning streaks.

teams ≮ have winning streaks O

7. None except Elizabeth's friends are welcome here.

those welcomed here < Elizabeth's friends A

8. Few men earn more than the President.

men ≮ earn more than President O

9. All that glitters is not gold.

those that glitters ≮ gold O

10. All but the first group of passengers were quarantined.

those not in 1st group of passengers < quarantined A

11. None but the lonely heart can know my sadness.

those what know my sadness < the lonely heart A

12. It is completely untrue that all women gossip.

women ✗ gossip O

13. Commanders alone are entitled to make such decisions.

those entitled to make such decisions < commanders A

14. Happy are the sounds of children playing.

sounds of children playing < happy A

15–18. *Write the following sentences in the logical shorthand for hypothetical propositions.*

15. The mission will be scrubbed unless all components function perfectly.

if all components function do not perfectly, then mission will be scrubbed

16. Only if you meet all requirements will you receive your degree.

you do not meet all req. ⊃ you will not receive degree

17. If you are the only one present, the meeting will be cancelled.

if you are only 1 present, then meeting will be cancelled

18. Given these conditions, you can expect an explosion.

given these condition ⊃ you can expect explosion

19–20. *Analyze the following hypothetical syllogisms. Write V in the blank if valid, or the name of the fallacy if invalid.*

19. A student receives a diploma if and only if he meets all requirements for graduation. Baker has his diploma. Therefore, he met all requirements for graduation.

_____V_____

20. A student can graduate from Wysacki only if he passes the proficiency test in swimming. Clark graduated from Wysacki. Therefore, he must have passed the proficiency test in swimming.

_____V_____

EXERCISE 24B

Translate these syllogisms into logical shorthand and analyze them for validity.
State the fallacy involved in every invalid case.

1. Diligent are they who work harder than their friends.

John does not work harder than his friends.

Therefore, John is not diligent.

Fallacy

those who work
harder than friends < diligent

John ≠ work harder

∴ John ≠ diligent

illicit distribution

2. Few teachers are free from financial worry.

All physicians are not teachers.
Therefore, all physicians are free from financial worry.

Fallacy

teachers ≠ free fin. worry

physicians ≠ teachers

∴ physicians < free fin worry

faulty exclusion

3. Only men may bowl today.

Jim is a man.

Therefore, he may bowl today.

Fallacy

those bowl today < men

Jim < man

∴ Jim < bowl today

undistributed middle

4. Not all sixteen-year-olds are sweet.

Sue is sixteen.

Therefore, Sue is not sweet.

Fallacy

16-yr-olds ≠ sweet

Sue < 16

∴ Sue ≠ sweet

undistributed middle

5. All but those who have seen a counselor must make an appointment today.

John is among those who have not seen a counselor.

Therefore, he must make an appointment today.

Fallacy

those who have
not seen counselor < appointment

John < not seen counselor

∴ John < make an app.

valid

6. None except freshmen may use the pool today.

Mary may use the pool today.

Therefore, Mary is not a freshman.

Fallacy

those who may use pool today < freshmen

Mary < may use pool

∴ Mary ≁ freshmen

faulty exclusion, illicit dis.

7. A few lazy students do not prepare for class.

Bill prepares for class.

Therefore, Bill is not a lazy student.

Fallacy

lazy students ≁ prepare

Bill < prepares

∴ Bill ≁ lazy student

illicit distribution

8. All Wysacki men are not A students.

John is an A student.
Therefore, John is not a Wysacki man.

Fallacy

Wysacki men ≁ A students

John < A student

∴ John ≁ Wysacki man

illicit distribution

9. One should study at least two hours for each credit hour, unless he is exceptionally brilliant.

I am exceptionally brilliant.
Therefore, I should not study at least two hours for each credit hour.

if he is not ex. bri, ∴ then he should study 2 hrs.

Invalid denies ant

Fallacy

those who are not brilliant < study 2 hr. /credit

I ≁ except. brilliant

∴ I ≁ study 2hr /credit

illicit distribution

10. The plane can make the flight if and only if we have sufficient fuel.

We do not have sufficient fuel.
Therefore, the plane cannot make the flight.

Fallacy

IFF we have sufficient fuel ⊃ plane can make flight

we do not have fuel

∴ plane can't make flight

valid

25 Involved Arguments

Nearly all of the syllogisms we have studied so far have been arranged in neat packages, with premises and conclusions clearly identified. Our purpose has been to learn how our tools work before applying them to the more involved arguments we encounter daily in articles, editorials, speeches, and dormitory "bull sessions." These arguments are seldom stated simply, or with premises and conclusion neatly arranged in order. Often the basic structure of the argument is concealed in several paragraphs or pages, and the careless thinker is tempted to accept the conclusion offered rather than take the trouble to pick out and analyze the argument. Those who would deceive us do not advertise the fallacies in their arguments. Learning to analyze simple syllogisms without going farther and learning to analyze long or involved arguments would be a waste of good tools.

1. Finding the Parts

The first step in analyzing an involved argument is to pick out the structure of the argument. It is usually best to look first for the conclusion. If you mistake the major premise for the minor premise, it is still possible to analyze the argument correctly, but if you mistake the conclusion for a premise, you may analyze *an* argument correctly, but not the one you started with. It is hardly fair to the other fellow to use his evidence as the conclusion of his argument.

The conclusion is the statement of what the speaker or writer is claiming to prove. It is not necessarily the last statement in the argument. People who believe they have a sound argument and wish to present it fairly often state the conclusion first so that the hearer or reader can check the evidence as it is presented. Sometimes the conclusion appears near the middle of the argument, with introductory material at the beginning and with evidence stated after, or both before and after, the conclusion.

Sometimes the conclusion is easily identified because it is introduced by such words or phrases as "therefore," "consequently," "then," "for this reason," "it follows that," and the like.

Sometimes, as in the example below, no such introductory words appear.

> Spectator sports cannot be considered educational, because only activities that increase knowledge or intellectual skill can be considered educational, and spectator sports do neither.

But the conclusion can still be easily identified, for the word "because" indicates that what follows is evidence. The conclusion must, therefore, be the first statement, "Spectator sports cannot be considered educational." Other words or phrases used to introduce evidence, or premises, are: "for," "since," "inasmuch as," "the facts are," "granted that," and "it is known that."

Sometimes, as in the example below, no introductory words appear to identify either premises or conclusion.

No regulation that interferes with learning can be good for Wysacki. The proposed regulation cannot be a good one. It would discourage students from studying except immediately before tests and final examinations.

Even so, the structure of the argument can be identified. The first sentence cannot be the conclusion, for it states a general principle, while the two following sentences discuss a specific regulation. The speaker would hardly attempt to prove a general principle by means of two statements about a specific regulation. The first sentence must, therefore, be a premise. The last sentence does not follow as a conclusion, but the middle sentence follows nicely; it completes, in fact, a valid argument.

Suppose you hear this argument from a foreign short-wave station beamed to South America. The sentences have been numbered for convenience.

(1) The news today proves again that Americans are grasping imperialists. (2) Today the American Development and Investment Associates bought two thousand acres of land in Colombia for a coffee plantation. (3) Imperialistic peoples always make investments in foreign countries. (4) In that way they can fatten themselves by sucking the blood of other peoples. (5) The purchase of land in Colombia by an American corporation is only one of thousands of American investments in foreign countries. (6) Few Americans have no foreign investments. (7) This is ample proof that all Americans are imperialists.

Though this particular argument is fictitious, it is not unlike the propaganda disseminated in South America. To a Latin American wishing to think the worst of North Americans, it doubtless sounds convincing. But, in addition to a number of misused evaluative words, it contains a basic fallacy.

Let us begin to find the fallacy by locating the conclusion. In this argument the propagandist put his conclusion in the first sentence and repeated it in the last sentence, doubtless for emphasis.

The next step in analyzing an involved argument is to locate the major premise. When the major premise is in hypothetical, alternative, disjunctive, or alternative-disjunctive form, it is usually easily recognizable by the structure words "if . . . then," "either . . . or," "not both." In the categorical form, the structure words may be the same for both major and minor premises. Even so the *major premise* can be identified because it *contains the predicate term of the conclusion.* In the example above, the conclusion is "All Americans are imperialists." The predicate term of this conclusion is "imperialists." We can, therefore, expect the major premise to speak of "imperialists." Sentence 3 makes a statement about "imperialistic peoples." The rules of validity do not require that the terms be worded identically. In this context "imperialists" and "imperialistic peoples" refer to the same class. Thus Sentence 3 qualifies as the major premise. We have now identified the conclusion and the major premise, as shown below.

Major Premise: Imperialistic peoples always make investments in foreign countries.

Minor Premise:

Conclusion: All Americans are imperialists.

The minor premise is now easily identified. If this argument is valid, the minor premise must include the terms that have been used only once: "Americans," and "those who make investments in foreign countries." Sentence 6 (Few Americans have no foreign investments) contains these two terms.

WORDS AND PHRASES THAT INDICATE CONCLUSIONS

▶ Therefore   Thus
Consequently   Hence
So   It follows that
For this reason
It must be
Then

WORDS AND PHRASES THAT INDICATE PREMISES

▶ Because   The facts are
For   It is known that
Since   Granted that
Inasmuch as

2. Putting Arguments into Syllogistic Form

Once the parts have been identified, the next step is to write the argument in logical form. Although many premises can be written in any of the four basic propositional types, it is usually best to write a premise in the logical form which it most closely resembles. The more you change the wording of a statement the greater is the risk of changing its meaning.

In the argument above the major premise deals with classes: "imperialistic peoples" and "those who make investments in foreign countries." The categorical syllogism is therefore the most suitable form for analyzing this argument, shown below in shorthand.

$$\overset{d}{\text{Imperialistic peoples}} < \overset{u}{\text{make investments in foreign countries.}}$$

$$\overset{u}{\text{Americans}} < \overset{u}{\text{make investments in foreign countries.}}$$

$$\therefore \overset{d}{\text{Americans}} < \overset{u}{\text{imperialistic peoples.}}$$

Note that the premises and conclusion have been interpreted in accordance with the rules set forth in Chapter 24. The two fallacies in the argument are now clearly exposed: undistributed middle and illicit distribution. This argument, like many others, loses its effect once its skeleton is exposed.

To avoid introducing fallacies that are not in the original argument, *both premises and conclusions should always be interpreted in the context of the whole argument.* There is no rule of logic or rhetoric requiring that a term be stated in exactly the same words in the two places it appears in a syllogism. In fact, terms are frequently stated in different words for the sake of variety in expression. Thus it is often necessary to "edit" premises and conclusions in order to avoid introducing fallacies that were not there originally. For example, consider the following syllogism.

All except aliens are eligible.
None of these applicants is an alien.
Therefore, all of these applicants are eligible.

If the minor premise above is considered in isolation, our rules would require that it be written in E-form, as shown below.

$$\overset{d}{\text{These applicants}} \nless \overset{d}{\text{aliens.}}$$

When the minor premise is so written, the syllogism seems to contain two fallacies: four-terms (those who are not aliens, those who are eligible, these applicants, and aliens) and faulty exclusion. Properly interpreted, however, the conclusion is valid.

To avoid introducing fallacies it is usually best to begin by writing the major premise in logical form. Consider the major premise from the above argument, properly written in categorical shorthand.

$$\overset{d}{\text{Those who are not aliens}} < \overset{u}{\text{eligible.}}$$

Note that, in accordance with the rules for interpreting propositions, the word *not* is interpreted to be a part of the class rather than the sign of exclusion. The major premise as so written identifies two of the classes. The minor premise and conclusion should then be interpreted in the context of these two classes. Now consider the minor premise: None of these applicants is an alien. The third term, introduced by this premise, is "these applicants." The issue with respect to the four-terms fallacy is whether the minor premise clearly relates "these applicants" to one of the classes in the major premise. If we consider the minor premise in the context of the two classes stated in the major premise, clearly these applicants are included in the class of those who are *not* aliens. The complete argument is thus revealed to be valid when properly "edited."

$$\overset{\text{d}}{\text{Those who are not aliens}} < \overset{\text{u}}{\text{eligible.}}$$

$$\overset{\text{d}}{\text{These applicants}} < \overset{\text{u}}{\text{those who are not aliens.}}$$

$$\therefore \overset{\text{d}}{\text{These applicants}} < \overset{\text{u}}{\text{eligible.}}$$

When "editing" arguments to conform to the context, we must never change the meaning or add meaning that was unstated. The meaning of the minor premise above has not been changed at all, for it is actually a valid obversion of the original premise.

Now let us try another involved argument. Suppose you hear this argument from your commencement speaker.

(1) First let me congratulate the members of the graduating class. (2) If you really deserve high congratulations on the excellence of your education, you must be better educated than 99 per cent of the people of the world's population. (3) As nearly as I can estimate, less than 2 per cent of the world's people are college graduates. (4) Graduates of Wysacki are certainly in the upper half of college graduates in excellence of education. (5) It follows, then, that the graduates of this great institution are better educated than at least 99 per cent of the people in the world. (6)

Therefore, the members of this graduating class deserve high congratulations.

You should not accept the speaker's conclusion merely because it is pleasant. The speaker's data would be hard to check, but we can easily test his argument for validity. Let us try the hypothetical form this time. Sentence 6 is the conclusion: clues are "therefore" and the fact that it states what the speaker has been building up to. Sentence 2 is the major premise: it is a hypothetical proposition, and it links those who deserve high congratulations to those who are better educated than 99 per cent of the world's population. Sentence 5 looks like the conclusion because of the words "It follows, then." But it is actually the minor premise, for it relates the graduates to those who are in the top 1 per cent. It is in the form of a conclusion because it has been derived from data in sentences 3 and 4. Sentence 1 is introductory material. The basic argument is shown below in hypothetical shorthand.

Deserve high congratulations $\supset$ better educated than 99 per cent of the world's population.

Wysacki graduates are better educated than at least 99 per cent of the people in the world.

$\therefore$ Wysacki graduates deserve high congratulations.

It is now clear that the argument is fallacious, for the consequent is affirmed. Note that the words "at least" appear in the minor premise but not in the consequent of the major premise. This is not a case of uncertain relationship, however, for the minor premise contains more than enough information to affirm the consequent. The fallacy of uncertain relationship occurs when the minor premise does not contain enough information.

You will frequently encounter arguments containing categorical propositions with missing quantifiers, such as the one below.

Students do not study as much as they should.

In this proposition there is no quantifier to indicate whether the term "students" is distributed. The decision as to whether such terms are distributed should be based on the context and the situation. When the context clearly indicates that a proposition is a definition or a classification, terms with missing quantifiers should be considered to be distributed because classifications and definitions refer to a whole class. The term "mammals" in the syllogism below is a case in point.

Mammals have mammary glands.
This animal does not have mammary glands.
Therefore it is not a mammal.

When you are basing a decision on a premise with a missing quantifier it is usually advisable to be conservative and consider the term to be undistributed. Otherwise you may base a decision on what amounts to a hasty generalization. In your own speech and writing you should always supply a quantifier to avoid the risk of being misunderstood.

3. Missing Parts

We often omit basic components of an argument because the meaning is obvious from the context. Sometimes those who would deceive us leave out a basic part because the argument is more convincing without it.

The missing part may be the conclusion.

My opponent in this race believes in government ownership of basic industry, and the Communists believe in government ownership of basic industry. Now, my friends, you may draw your own conclusion about my opponent.

If the speaker had stated the conclusion he suggested, we could devastate his argu-

ment by pointing out the undistributed middle. But since he has not stated it, we can blame only ourselves if we credulously jump to the conclusion he is suggesting. The trick often works, perhaps because we are so flattered by being trusted to draw the conclusion that we forget all about logic. The careful thinker cultivates the habit of resisting suggested conclusions until he has tested them for validity.

The missing part may be a premise. Even without help from outsiders we can and do deceive ourselves with missing premises. There is an assumption behind nearly every decision we make, even though we often fail to recognize it. When we reason from an assumption without realizing it, the assumption is in effect a missing premise. Whether or not the argument is his own, the careful thinker wants to know what the premises are. Otherwise, he cannot judge the argument for reliability. When a premise is missing, he dredges it up for examination.

Suppose you hear the following argument.

(1) It is obvious that all Demopublicans are dissenters. (2) They condemn the administration's foreign policy. (3) They proclaim that domestic programs are archaic. (4) They predict that the administration's tax policy will lead to economic disaster. (5) Clearly, therefore, all Demopublicans promote progress.

You may never know what this speaker was actually assuming, but you can find out the minimum he had to assume to make his argument valid. You can do this by trial and error, but a better way is to analyze the syllogism backwards. The first step is to write the known parts in the appropriate syllogistic form, beginning with the conclusion. Since the conclusion (Sentence 5) states a relationship between two classes, the appropriate syllogistic form is the categorical.[1]

---

[1] The procedure for finding missing hypothetical premises is described in Chapter 14.

The minor premise must contain the subject term of the conclusion, "Demopublicans," or its equivalent. Sentences 2, 3, and 4 contain the pronoun "they," the antecedent of which is "Demopublicans," but note that all three support the claim in Sentence 1, which is the real minor premise.

The major premise must contain the predicate term of the conclusion, "[those who] promote progress." The only sentence containing this term is the conclusion; therefore, the major premise is missing. The minor premise and the conclusion appear below in shorthand.

Major Premise:

Minor Premise: Demopublicans $\overset{d}{<}$ dissenters.$\overset{u}{}$

Conclusion: Demopublicans $\overset{d}{<}$ [those who]$\overset{u}{}$ promote progress.

The major premise needed to make the argument valid can now be easily supplied by using the rules of validity for categorical syllogisms. One of the terms in the major premise must be the middle term, which is "dissenters" (since this term does not appear in the conclusion). The other term must be "[those who] promote progress," since this term appears only once.

The relationship between terms in both minor premise and conclusion is inclusion. Therefore, the relationship in the major premise must also be inclusion; otherwise the argument would violate the faulty exclusion rule.

The middle term, "dissenters," must be distributed at least once. Since the relationship in the major premise is inclusion, only the subject term can be distributed. Thus "dissenters" must be the subject term.

By elimination, the predicate term in the major premise must be "[those who] promote progress." Because it follows inclusion, it must be undistributed. This same term is undistributed in the conclusion, and may therefore be undistributed in the major premise. The major premise needed to make the argument valid is now clearly revealed.

$$\overset{d}{\text{Dissenters}} \overset{u}{<} \text{promote progress.}$$

You will note that this major premise is a sweeping generalization. You could prove it false merely by finding a single dissenter who does not promote progress. The argument was more convincing without the major premise.

Since you are trying to find the minimum assumption needed to make the argument valid, never make a term distributed unless necessary. Sometimes either term may be put in the subject position. If both missing terms are undistributed, or if both are distributed, it will not matter which is put first, since both forms are validly convertible. But if one of the two terms must be distributed, and you cannot tell which to make the subject, choose the form that claims the least.

Sometimes you will find an argument with a missing premise that cannot be made valid with any premise you can supply. An example is an argument with a term distributed in the conclusion but undistributed in the stated premise. Disregard all such arguments.

When decisions you have made prove to be "bad," try to remember your reasoning and test it by this system. It may be that you were reasoning from an unstated premise that you would not accept as fact.

EXERCISE 25

1–6. *Write the following arguments in categorical shorthand. Then use the key list below to indicate your analysis of the argument.*

KEY LIST

1. Four-terms
2. Faulty exclusion
3. Undistributed middle

4. Illicit distribution
5. Valid

1. Most good political speakers would not use this story. Since Blythe used it, he must not be a good political speaker.

good pol. speakers ≠ use story
Blythe < used story
∴ Blythe ≠ good pol. speakers

_____4_____

2. No temperamental people ever learn to accept criticism gracefully. But Smythe is not the least bit temperamental, so we can conclude that he knows how to accept criticism gracefully.

temp. people ≠ learn to accept criticism
Smythe ≠ temp. people
∴ Smythe < learn to accept criticism

_____2_____

3. It is evident that some devices of persuasion are not reliable, for some devices of persuasion are invalid arguments, and no invalid arguments are reliable.

꓂ devices of persuasion < invalid arguments
invalid arguments ≠ reliable
∴ devices of persuasion ≠ reliable

_____5_____

4. Since some European nations have not signed the Atlantic Pact, these nations must belong to the Comintern, for no nation which signed the Atlantic Pact belongs to the Comintern.

nations signing At. Pact ≠ Comintern
European nations ≠ nations signing A.P.
∴ European nations < Comintern

_____2_____

5. According to the laws of physics, water must be lighter than air, for water contains hydrogen, and certainly hydrogen is lighter than air.

hydrogen < lighter than air
hydrogen < water
∴ water < lighter than air

_____4_____

6. This plant must be certified, because all certified plants have been inspected, and this plant has a tag showing that it has been inspected.

certified < have been inspected
plant < has been inspected
∴ plant < certified

_____3_____

7–12. *Write the following arguments in hypothetical shorthand. Then use the key list below to indicate the relationship between premises. Also write V in the blank if the conclusion is valid or I if it is invalid.*

KEY LIST

1. The antecedent is affirmed.
2. The antecedent is denied.
3. The consequent is affirmed.
4. The consequent is denied.
5. The relationship between premises is uncertain.

7. Smythe must not have gone to college, because he is ignorant. If he had gone to college, he would not be illiterate.

he went to college ⊃ he would not be illiterate
Smythe is ignorant   5   I
∴ Smythe did not go to college

8. This specimen must be an insect. If this specimen were an insect, it would have only three pairs of legs. You can see that it does.

This specimen were an insect ⊃ it would have 3 prs. legs
This specimen has 3 prs. of legs   3   I
∴ this specimen is an insect

9. Smythe would certainly have called for a pass in the left flat had he noticed that the Wysacki right end was rushing in on every play. Since he called for a slant off tackle, he must not have noticed how the Wysacki end was playing.

he noticed Wy. rght. end rushing in on every play ⊃ Smythe
      would have called a pass in left flat
Smythe called for slant off tackle   5   I
∴ Smythe did not notice how Wy. end was playing

10. If he had liked your qualifications, he would have sent you a personnel data sheet to fill in. You can be sure that he likes your qualifications, because he has sent you one of these sheets.

he liked qualifications ⊃ he would have sent personnel data
      sheet
he sent personnel data sheet   3   I
∴ he liked qualifications

11. The primary motivation of the "beatniks" must be to get revenge on society. They would not revolt against society if they were successful members of it. Their behavior leaves no possible doubt that they are in revolt against society.

beatniks were successful members of society ⊃ wouldn't revolt
      against it
they are in revolt against society   5   I
∴ their motivation is revenge on society

12. Last week Smythe went to one movie, one dance, and two basketball games. He also spent some time working on his hi-fi set. He must not have studied as much as he should have, for if he had, he would have put in at least fifty hours in classes and study.

Smythe studied necessary amt. ⊃ he put in 50 hrs.
Smythe spent time on pleasure   5   I
∴ Smythe did not study necessary
      amount

26 Complex Syllogistic Forms

1. *Dilemmas*
2. *Chain Arguments*
3. *Syllogisms within Syllogisms*
4. *Deductive-Inductive Arguments*

We have now studied four basic types of syllogisms: hypothetical, categorical, alternative, and disjunctive. The major premise of each type states some kind of relationship between two terms. In the hypothetical syllogism, this relationship is conditional: the major premise states that the consequent is true on condition that the antecedent is true. The categorical type deals with classes: one class is totally or partially included in or excluded from another class. In the alternative syllogism the major premise states two possibilities and declares that at least one of them must be true. In the disjunctive type, the major premise states two possibilities and declares that at least one of them cannot be true. There are other possible relationships, but if you have thoroughly mastered the basic four, you should be able to manage the others without serious difficulty.

The four basic types of propositions can be put together in an almost infinite number of combinations. We cannot even begin to study all of the possible combinations. Fortunately, it is not necessary to do so. A careful study of two basic types will enable us to deal with most of the complex deductive arguments we encounter. The techniques of analysis we have studied so far must be modified to make them applicable to some of these combinations.

1. Dilemmas

Deductive arguments can be composed of a mixture of propositional types. One such mixture is the *dilemma*. Dilemmas may occur in several varieties. In common speech, however, the word is usually used to refer to a situation in which there are only two choices, both of which are unpleasant. This variety of dilemma is composed of a mixture of hypothetical and alternative propositions. The major premise is a pair of hypothetical propositions; the minor premise and the conclusion are alternative propositions. Consider the student who has wasted his time during the semester and finds himself at the end of the term with insufficient time to prepare adequately for all his examinations. If he distributes his time about equally among his courses, he will make low grades in all of them. If, on the other hand, he devotes enough time to some of his courses to make good grades in them, he will fail other courses. The consequences of both choices are undesirable. Our student now has the major premise of a dilemma.

If I study all courses about equally, I will make low grades in all of them; if I study some enough to make good grades, I will fail others.

He does not yet have a complete dilemma,

for the major premise does not force him to take either choice. But if he reasons that he must do one or the other, he now has this minor premise:

> I must either study all courses about equally, or study some enough to make high grades.

This minor premise affirms the antecedents of both hypotheticals and forces this unpalatable conclusion:

> I must either make low grades in all courses or fail some of them.

Our student can be said to be caught on the "horns" of a dilemma, for if he chooses either antecedent he is "stuck" by its consequent. Since this variety of dilemma is valid, the only possible attack is on the reliability of the premises.

One way to attack the premises of a dilemma is to "break a horn," *i.e.*, to choose one of the antecedents without incurring the consequent attached to it. Consider the following dilemma in which a Congressman might find himself.

Major Premise:
> *Alternative 1*   *Horn 1*
> If | I vote for this farm bill, | I shall lose labor votes. |
>
> *Alternative 2*   *Horn 2*
> If | I vote against this bill, | I shall lose farm votes. |

Minor Premise: But I must either vote for or vote against this bill.

Conclusion: Therefore, I must lose labor votes or farm votes.

Should the Congressman choose the first alternative by voting for the farm bill and still keep the labor votes by convincing his constituents that his position is sound, he would break the first horn. Note that in so doing he would demonstrate that the first hypothetical of the major premise is false. He might break the second horn by voting against the bill without losing the votes of farmers by convincing them that the passage of the bill was not in their best interests.

The Congressman might avoid the unpleasant consequences described in the dilemma above in another way. According to the minor premise he is restricted to two choices, voting for and voting against the bill. He might, however, be conveniently ill or out of town on the day of the vote, or he might pair his vote with another Congressman, thereby choosing neither alternative and avoiding both consequences. Should he do so he would be *escaping between the horns,* which may be defined as finding a possibility not included in the minor premise. In so doing, of course, he is demonstrating this premise to be false, for it stipulated that the two choices mentioned were the only possible ones.

The dilemma form should be scrupulously avoided in decision making because there is a serious psychological hazard inherent in it. Suppose you find yourself in a situation like one that occurred in a hotel in Atlanta, where a fire originating in the basement swept flames and deadly gases through most of the structure, which was supposed to be fireproof. You are trapped in a room on the thirteenth floor. If you try to escape through the halls of the building, you know that you will be burned to death unless the gases kill you first. If you try to escape by jumping from the window, you know that you will be smashed on the pavement below. You now have the major premise of your dilemma. If you add a minor premise that limits your choices to jumping or going into the hall, you tend to fix your attention on the terrible consequences of your two choices instead of on finding a better solution. As you think about the horns of your dilemma, your fears are likely to rise higher and higher and make you less and less able to think constructively. Many people in this particular fire apparently did just that and lost their lives by jumping, by feeble attempts to reach the stairways, or by decision by indecision, hesitating in their rooms until overcome by the deadly gases. Cooler heads in this same episode escaped between the horns of the dilemma. They neither jumped nor went out through the halls. Instead, they stopped the cracks around their doors with newspapers or cloth to keep out the gases, opened their windows for fresh air, and quietly waited to be rescued by the firemen.

A situation in which you find yourself thinking that you must choose between two evils should become an automatic stimulus for repeating the five-phase cycle, with special emphasis on forming other proposals for action. Even if you can find no third alternative, you can usually find some way of mitigating the undesirable consequences of at least one of the choices.

2. Chain Arguments

Syllogisms can be combined to form a chain of reasoning with any number of links. Consider the argument below.

> All insects are invertebrate animals.
> All mosquitoes are insects.
> All anopheles are mosquitoes.
> Therefore all anopheles are invertebrate
>   animals.

The procedures for analyzing syllogisms we have studied thus far are applicable only to arguments with two premises. They will not apply directly to the argument above because it has three premises. The problem of analyzing arguments with more than two premises is analogous to computing complex probabilities. We found that we could work complex problems in probability with simple procedures merely by dividing the problems into installments and then working each installment separately. Similarly, the procedures we have studied for analyzing syllogisms can be applied to arguments with

more than two premises simply by analyzing these arguments in installments.

For the first installment, let us analyze the first two premises in the argument above. They yield a valid conclusion, as shown in shorthand below.

$$\overset{d}{\text{Insects}} < \overset{u}{\text{invertebrate animals.}}$$

$$\overset{d}{\text{Mosquitoes}} < \overset{u}{\text{insects.}}$$

$$\therefore \overset{d}{\text{Mosquitoes}} < \overset{u}{\text{invertebrate animals.}}$$

Now let us use the valid conclusion above as the major premise of a second installment, using the original third premise as the minor premise. We get the following.

$$\overset{d}{\text{Mosquitoes}} < \overset{u}{\text{invertebrate animals.}}$$

$$\overset{d}{\text{Anopheles}} < \overset{u}{\text{mosquitoes.}}$$

$$\therefore \overset{d}{\text{Anopheles}} < \overset{u}{\text{invertebrate animals.}}$$

Thus all the evidence necessary to make the conclusion valid is explicitly stated in the premises.

In the example above the premises are arranged in a descending order of magnitude. In the example below the premises are arranged in an ascending order.

> All residents of Precinct 5 are residents of the city.
> All residents of the city are residents of the county.
> All residents of the county are residents of the state.
> All residents of the state are residents of the U.S.A.
> Therefore, all residents of Precinct 5 are residents of the U.S.A.

This argument is more easily analyzed backwards, using the last premise as the major premise of the first installment, as shown on the next page in shorthand.

d   u
Residents of the state < residents of the U.S.A.

d   u
Residents of the county < residents of the state.

d   u
∴ Residents of the county < residents of the
U.S.A.

The conclusion above then becomes the major premise of the second installment, as shown below.

d   ·   u
Residents of the county < residents of the U.S.A.

d   u
Residents of the city < residents of the county.

d   u
∴ Residents of the city < residents of the
U.S.A.

In turn, the conclusion above becomes the major premise of the third installment, which shows that the conclusion is valid.

Chains of hypothetical premises can be analyzed in installments too, using the rules of the hypothetical syllogism. Consider the example below.

 If the defendant is guilty, then he had the murder weapon in his possession.
 If he had the murder weapon in his possession, he must have stolen it.
 If he stole the murder weapon, he must have been in Chicago on December 11.
 He was seen in South Bend on December 11.
 Therefore the defendant cannot be guilty.

This example is invalid because the fourth premise (He was seen in South Bend on December 11) is in uncertain relationship with the third premise.

Chain arguments should be handled with care. They are no stronger than the weakest link, and the conclusion is valid only if every link is valid. Furthermore, the conclusion is reliable only if every premise is reliable. Consider the following chain argument.

(1) Perhaps the most spectacular issue of the Democratic Convention of 1952 was whether to permit the Virginia delegation to participate in the convention after it refused to subscribe to the loyalty pledge prescribed by the new rule adopted by the convention. (2) Near the end of the voting it appeared that Virginia would not be seated, but the Illinois delegation reversed its vote and the tide was turned in favor of Virginia. (3) When Illinois first voted on the issue, the chairman of the delegation was out of the hall eating a sandwich — the convention had then been in session for nearly eight consecutive hours. (4) If he had not returned when he did, Illinois would not have changed her vote. (5) If Illinois had not changed her vote, Virginia would not have been seated. (6) If Virginia had not been seated, several Southern states would have bolted the Democratic Party. (7) If they had bolted, the Republican Party would have become a real factor in Southern politics. (8) Therefore, if the chairman of the Illinois delegation had not returned when he did, the Republican Party would have become a real factor in Southern politics.

The chain argument begins with Sentence 4 and ends with Sentence 8, which is the conclusion. Note that the conclusion merely condenses the argument to a single proposition composed of the antecedent in Sentence 4 and the consequent in Sentence 7. The conclusion is valid, for the consequent of each proposition in the chain affirms the antecedent of the succeeding proposition. But this conclusion is far from reliable. The conclusion of a chain argument is unreliable unless *all* propositions in the chain are reliable. In this example no link is reliable, for each is a hypothesis contrary to fact (see Chapter 33).

We learned in our study of probability that the greater the number of events that must occur, the lower is the probability. Similarly, the greater the number of premises in a chain argument, the lower is the probability that all links are valid and that all premises are reliable.

3. Syllogisms within Syllogisms

Some arguments contain syllogisms within syllogisms. Consider the following argument.

(1) This tax cannot serve the best interests of the country as a whole and at the same time discourage the development of heavy industry. ~~(2) All military experts of any reputation as-~~ sert that heavy industry is essential to national defense. (3) Had this tax not discouraged the development of heavy industry, our capacity for making steel would have increased by at least 5 per cent during the past year. (4) Instead, it has dropped by 2 per cent. (5) This tax cannot be in the best interests of the country as a whole.

The conclusion of this argument is Sentence 5 (This tax cannot be in the best interests of the country). The major premise is Sentence 1 (This tax cannot serve the best interests of the country and at the same time discourage the development of heavy industry). Sentence 2 presents evidence in support of the major premise, and is not a part of the skeleton of the argument. The minor premise in this argument is not stated. However, Sentences 3 and 4 constitute the premises of a valid syllogism within the main syllogism.

This tax had not discouraged the development of heavy industry	⊃	our capacity for making steel would have increased by at least 5 per cent during the past year.

Our capacity has dropped by 2 per cent.

The minor premise clearly denies the consequent and yields this valid, though unstated, conclusion: This tax discouraged the development of heavy industry. This unstated conclusion is the minor premise of the main argument, as in a chain syllogism. Thus the argument contains enough information to yield a valid conclusion: This tax cannot be in the best interests of the country.

4. Deductive-Inductive Arguments

Deductive and inductive reasoning are frequently combined. Consider the argument below, which might be made by a prosecutor in summing up his evidence in a murder trial.

~~(1) If the defendant fired the fatal shot with~~ malice aforethought, then he is guilty of murder in the first degree. (2) Reliable witnesses have testified that the defendant owned the murder weapon, that his fingerprints were on it when it was found at the scene of the crime, and that he was seen leaving the scene of the crime shortly after the fatal shot was fired. (3) Reliable witnesses have also testified that the defendant had a powerful motive and that he had several times threatened to kill the deceased. (4) There can be no reasonable doubt that the defendant fired the fatal shot and did so with malice aforethought. (5) The defendant is therefore guilty of murder in the first degree.

Sentence 1 states the law under which the defendant is being tried. It serves as the major premise, Sentence 4 is the minor premise, and Sentence 5 is the conclusion. Note, however, that Sentence 4 actually states a hypothesis, which is supported by Sentences 2 and 3. If the hypothesis is true, the defendant is clearly guilty. The issue, then, is whether the hypothesis is sufficiently reliable to be rated true beyond reasonable doubt. This is the decision the jury must make.

There is nothing logically wrong with combining deductive and inductive reasoning. In fact, many of our decisions involve a combination of both. It is important to know the difference, however, because the methods of testing are quite different. Deductive inferences are always tested for validity, using the rules appropriate to the particular logical form involved. Inductive inferences are tested for reliability by methods appropriate to the particular type of inference. In earlier chapters we studied methods of testing the principal types of inductive inferences: hypotheses, generalizations, and causal theories.

In testing deductive inferences we should never forget that conclusions, even though valid, are no more reliable than the premises on which they are based. Up to a point, premises can be tested for reliability by deductive inference from other premises. Ultimately, however, this process reaches a premise that must be tested by inductive methods or not tested at all.

Since absolute certainty obtains only in closed systems of thought, the person who seeks to base decisions only on certainty will find himself beset by many difficulties. He will too often be caught by decision by indecision. He will be prone to rate premises more reliable than they are. When he makes a bad decision, as inevitably he will, he will feel unjustified guilt for his mistake. His ability to solve problems by creative thinking will be narrowly circumscribed, for he will tend to reject promising hypotheses, causal theories, and proposals for action. If uncertainty bothers you, consider how unpleasant a world of certainty would be.

EXERCISE 26A

1–3. *These items refer to the following situation:*

Smythe's father wanted him to be a doctor. He told Smythe, "If you go into engineering, I won't give you a dime to finance an education." Mary, his fiancée, did not want to be a doctor's wife. She threatened, "If you go into medicine I won't marry you."

1. Smythe's situation can be stated as the major premise of a dilemma. Write it below.

*if he goes into engineering, his father won't finance him;
if he goes into medicine, his fiancée won't marry him*

2. Write below the minor premise necessary to make his situation a dilemma.

he must either go into engineering or medicine

3. Write below the conclusion of his dilemma.

he must either finance himself or not marry Mary

4–8. *Select from the key list below the statement which describes the method used to solve the problem.*

KEY LIST

1. *Breaking the first horn*
2. *Breaking the second horn*
3. *Escaping between the horns*
4. *Accepting the consequences of an alternative.*

4. Smythe went into medicine but persuaded Mary to marry him anyway.

_____2_____

5. Smythe went into business and married Mary. _____3_____

6. Smythe went into engineering and persuaded his father to pay part of his educational expenses.

_____1_____

7. Smythe went into medicine and remained a bachelor. _____4_____

8. Smythe went into a new field of research known as engineering medicine, married Mary, and kept his father's support.

_____3_____

9–16. *Analyze the following chain arguments. If the conclusion is valid, write V in the space provided; otherwise, write the name of the fallacy involved.*

9. If Smythe values learning, he is studying tonight.
   If he is studying tonight, he is in the library.
   He does value learning.
   Therefore, he is in the library now. *non sequitur* _____✓_____

10. Nothing that hurts other people is moral.
    Nothing that improves the mind hurts other people.
    Studying effective thinking improves the mind.
    Therefore, studying effective thinking is moral. *I - faulty exclusion*

11. All who deserve to pass study faithfully.
    All who study faithfully study thirty hours per week. *deserve to pass ∠ study 30 hrs*
    All Beta Beta Betas study thirty hours per week.
    Therefore, all Beta Beta Betas deserve to pass. *I - undistributed middle*

12. This policy will not improve education.
    All policies that improve education improve society. *policy ≠ improve society*
    All policies that improve society are good.
    Therefore, this policy is not good. *I - illicit distribution*

13. If it rains during the game, we cannot pass effectively.
    If we cannot pass effectively, our offensive team cannot score.
    If we cannot score one touchdown, we will lose.
    If we lose, we will be very unhappy.
    It is certain to rain during the game.
    Therefore, we will be very unhappy. _____✓_____

14. All medicines are exempt from the sales tax. *drugs prescribed ∠ exempt from tax*
    All drugs prescribed by doctors are medicines.
    Some products containing alcohol are prescribed by doctors.
    Therefore, all products containing alcohol are exempt from the sales tax.

    I - illicit distribution

15. None who choose the wrong career are happy in it.
    All who chose a career for which they are not qualified have chosen the wrong career.
    All who are weak in mathematics and chose engineering as a career have chosen a career for which they are not qualified.
    Therefore, none who are weak in mathematics and who chose engineering as a career will be happy in it. _____✓_____

16. If you do not study this term, your grades will be poor.
    If your grades are poor, you will be put on probation.
    If you are put on probation, you will lose your scholarship.
    If you lose your scholarship, you will have to drop out.
    If you drop out, you will be unable to finish your education.
    Therefore, if you do not study this term, you will be unable to finish your education. ✓ *uncertain*

EXERCISE 26B

1–5. *Strip the following arguments down to essentials and rewrite them in hypothetical, alternative, or disjunctive form, as indicated by the structure words in the argument. Then analyze them by the rules for the form of syllogism you have used. Use the key list to indicate your evaluation of the argument. Write the number of your choice in the blank.*

KEY LIST

1. *Denied antecedent*
2. *Affirmed consequent*
3. *Affirmed alternative*
4. *Denied disjunct*
5. *Uncertain relations*
6. *Non sequitur*
7. *Valid*

1. Wysacki students cannot leave town every weekend and still do justice to their studies. Smythe must do justice to his studies, for he never leaves town.

Wysacki students cannot both leave town + study
Smythe never leaves town
∴ Smythe does justice to his studies.   I – 4

2. Her silence can be accounted for in only two ways. Either she is sick or very busy, or she has lost interest in you. I can assure you that she has been exceedingly busy studying for exams ever since Christmas. You can stop worrying that she has lost interest in you.

Either she is sick or busy or not interested
She is busy
∴ she has not lost interest   3

3. This man should not be hired. If he were a graduate of Wysacki, he would be well trained, but he never attended Wysacki, so he cannot be well trained. If he is not well trained, he should not be hired.

graduate of W → he'd be well-trained
he never attended W
∴ he cannot be well-trained   I – 1

syllogism within a syllogism

4. When Smythe found a burglar in his home, he leaped out of an upstairs window and ran for help. Had he had any common sense, he would have called for help instead of performing such a dangerous feat. Consequently, we can see that Smythe is not a person of common sense.

he had common sense → he'd called for help instead
he performed dangerous feat
∴ he has no common sense   V – 7

5. If the following premises are true, you are guilty of either the black-or-white fallacy or misuse of the mean. If you believe that you must either conform completely to the values of your group or reject them completely, you are committing the black-or-white fallacy. If you believe that you must conform to roughly half of these values and reject the remainder, you are committing the fallacy of misusing the mean. You must either reject them all or reject roughly half of them. One of these premises is not true. Therefore you are not guilty of either fallacy.

I – 1

6–13. *Analyze the following arguments, from which the conclusion has been omitted. If the premises yield a valid conclusion, write it in the space provided. If they do not yield a valid conclusion, write the name of the fallacy.*

6. Only if the present administration in Chilihuahua *~~succeeds~~ does not* succeeds in balancing the budget can it claim in the next election to be the party of economy. It is now certain that the administration will succeed in balancing the budget.

  ∴ – denies antecedent

7. Unless a student is willing to put his mind to analyzing involved arguments, he cannot hope to improve his thinking ability significantly. These problems you are trying hard to solve are involved.

  ∴ uncertain relationship or antecedent denied

8. In selecting a modern automobile, one may choose a car with the speed, comfort, and roadability desirable on the highway, or one with the agility and short turning radius needed in city traffic. No one car provides both. The Urbancar has unusual agility and a very short turning radius.

  ∴ Urbancar does not have speed, comfort and roadability desirable on the highway

9. John Stuart Mill argued that if a belief is not grounded on conviction, it is likely to give way to the slightest of arguments. Many of our beliefs, on which we base our most important judgments, are not based on conviction at all, but are carelessly and unconsciously adopted.

  ∴ they are likely to give way to the slightest of arguments

10. During presidential campaigns many people listen only to those speeches which are favorable to the side for which they intend to vote. If one takes one side of an issue without examining the evidence for the other side, he has no adequate ground for taking either side.

  ∴ he has no adequate ground for taking either side

11. If a press association releases a news report without checking it, it runs the risk of being inaccurate; if it takes the time to check the report, it runs the risk of having a competitor release the report. Obviously, however, the press association must either release the report without checking it or delay it for the time necessary to check it.

  ∴ it either runs risk of being inaccurate or having a competitor release the report

12. Scouts reported that whenever State's star passer intended to carry the ball on a sweep around left end, he unconsciously put his hand on his left knee. At a critical point in the game, with State on Wysacki's eleven, the Wysacki captain noted that the passer was resting his hand on his left knee.

  ∴ – affirms consequent

13. Those who are ignorant of the facts in a case should never criticize a judicial decision. Most reporters, however, are not ignorant of the facts.

  ∴ – illicit distribution

27 Need-Directed Thinking

If man were a thinking machine that ground out accurate answers solely on the basis of the data fed into it, we could end our study of effective thinking at this point. But man is not a mere thinking machine. He is a biological organism who lives in a society of his kind and acquires a personal point of view and personal characteristics of thinking, with the result that the decisions he makes are strongly influenced by subjective factors within himself as well as by the information available to him. Any study of procedures of thinking that does not embrace a study of these subjective factors is certainly incomplete and possibly even dangerous. For man can and does misuse the very procedures of thinking we have been studying to conceal the truth from himself, just as he misuses automobiles when he turns them into lethal weapons.

When we face personal problems, especially where strong feelings are involved, we often forget efficient procedures of thinking. We eagerly follow false hypotheses. We become prone to most of the major fallacies, especially *post hoc*, hasty generalization, and neglected aspect. We seem to remember logical form only after we have hit upon an answer we like. Then, because we like to think that we are rational beings, we try to make our thinking seem logical by putting it into logical form. But the logical form is only a façade. In short, instead of searching for reliable evidence from which to draw reliable conclusions, we search for plausible premises that will make the conclusions to which we have already leaped seem valid.

In fact, man seems to have much greater skill in using his logic to justify the conclusion he wants to reach than in using it to find the right answer in the first place. He is highly sensitive to evidence that supports the answers he wants, and adept at using this evidence to construct arguments convincing to himself. He is equally good at ignoring evidence contrary to the conclusion he likes, and at discounting the evidence he cannot ignore. He is quick to make the hasty generalizations he wants to make, and just as quick to apply all the logical tests to generalizations he does not like. Indeed, he is so skillful in these gymnastics that he has often been accused by psychologists of first deciding what he wants and then using his mental activity solely for the purpose of making it seem logical.

1. Why We Think

This accusation is not as unjust as it might appear. Two well-supported hypotheses about human behavior indicate that man seeks the truth only when impelled to.

The first is that life is a dynamic, ongoing

process which must be kept in approximate equilibrium by constant adaptation to changes both within the organism and in its environment. Whenever the physiological processes are disturbed, or when any of the elements necessary for life are missing or inadequately supplied, the organism experiences a need to have its equilibrium restored. The need manifests itself in inner tensions and stresses which drive the organism to try to satisfy the need. Only when the need has been satisfied and equilibrium approached do the tensions diminish.

Unlike a factory, which can close down for the weekend, man must continue to work to maintain his equilibrium. His supply of water, air, and food are constantly being depleted and must be replenished. He can take in at one time only enough water to keep him comfortable for a few hours, and he must eat several times a day to avoid hunger. Man, like the whirlwind, is a process; when the process stops, he ceases to be. He must continually adapt to constant changes in both his physical and his social environment. All of this is profoundly important to the nature of his thinking — indeed, to the very fact that he thinks at all. For the intricate process of human life is only partly automatic. Man must think to keep it going.

This brings us to our second hypothesis, that the primary and probably the sole purpose of thinking is to satisfy needs. Even daydreaming occurs in response to some unsatisfied need. When you find yourself daydreaming in class instead of listening to the professor, you may be responding to a need to solve some problem not connected with your studies, or to a need to get away from class because you are failing, or to any number of other needs you may not be conscious of at the time.

For convenience in discussion we can divide the needs to which we must respond into two categories, physiological and psychological. We should not forget, however, that these needs are closely interrelated.

2. Physiological Needs

The primary category of needs, in point of origin, stems from our nature as biological animals and has to do with the maintenance of physiological equilibrium. This category includes: (1) the maintenance of body chemistry by providing a constant supply of air, water, and suitable food, by eliminating waste materials, and by keeping body temperature within a narrow range; (2) response to sex drives; (3) the avoidance of pain; (4) protection from external danger; (5) activity and rest, in proper balance.

The need for activity is particularly interesting to the student of logic. Since the mind is part of the total organism, mental activity is included in this need. Out of this need arises a drive to search for knowledge and experience which may be totally irrelevant to the satisfaction of any other need. Indeed, the drive may become so strong that it makes the child miss his dessert in order to continue his exploration of the mysteries of the road scraper parked in front of his house, or makes the engineering student lose needed sleep while he attempts to solve a problem which has nothing to do with his assignment. Because learning satisfies this drive, it can be one of our most pleasing activities. For the same reason, thinking too can be fun, provided the problem in hand is not too serious. This drive to search for knowledge and experience is invaluable in improving thinking, for our thinking can be no better than our information. Information acquired today through this drive may be the clue to solving tomorrow's problem. It is a drive which should be carefully nurtured.

Physical needs influence thinking in obvious ways. You will find it increasingly difficult to keep your mind on what the professor is saying when the classroom gets too warm, when you become thirsty, or when lunch time approaches. The idea of eating raw fish would normally be repulsive, but if you were ever stranded long enough on a life raft without food you would come to regard raw fish with the same enthusiasm you normally have for T-bone steak. After spending a day in strenuous activity you will yearn for rest, but after enough rest you will yearn for activity. You will be less likely to accept a job requiring hard mental work immediately after a grueling examination period than after a vacation. These needs also influence our thinking in other more subtle but none the less important ways, as we shall see.

3. Psychological Needs

Psychological needs center on the development and maintenance of a satisfactory self-concept (a review of Chapter 1, Topic 4, is in order at this point).

Through interacting with and learning to get along in his universe, the child develops a concept of himself and of his relationship to other people and to the physical world. Presumably the newborn infant has only a vague, impersonal awareness of himself. As far as observers can tell, he is unaware of any distinction between himself and his environment. It is doubtful, for example, that he recognizes his toes as belonging to himself. Only gradually, with the growth in complexity of his nervous system and the accumulation of experience with objects outside himself, such as cribs, toys, blankets, and parents, does he become aware of the boundaries between his body and the world outside. Somewhere in the process, possibly from the beginning, he begins to like and dislike. He exhibits a strong tendency to like those experiences which help to maintain his equilibrium and promote his growth, such as being fed and learning to wiggle his toes, and to dislike those experiences which threaten his equilibrium, such as being cold or hungry. In other words, his first value judgments are determined largely by organic needs. Gradually objects he perceives become associated with his likes and dislikes. The pleasant sensation of being fed becomes associ-

ated with his mother's entrance into his room, and he stops crying when she appears. As his understanding of language increases, he begins to make evaluations of himself. These are based primarily on his observations of how other people react to him. When he cuddles in his mother's lap, he is called a "good, sweet boy." When he satisfies his hunger by raiding the cookie jar, he is "naughty." From these experiences he develops a picture of himself which he himself can view. For the rest of his life psychological needs will not only motivate most of his thinking but will also affect most of his decisions.

The development and maintenance of a satisfactory self-concept is a dynamic process that seems to involve a number of interrelated needs.

1. Affection. First to appear is the need of the child to feel secure in the affection of his parents, especially his mother, for he depends on them for the satisfaction of most of his other needs. It is primarily from his mother's reaction to him that he forms his initial conception of his own worth. Apparently one can adequately sense his own value only through the high value placed on him by another's affection. The need for the deep affection of at least one other person continues throughout life.

2. Approval. The need for the approval of others first manifests itself in the need of the child to feel secure in the approval of his parents. It is probably originally derived in the same way as the need for affection. To the child, affection and approval are probably much the same thing. When his parents indicate that they approve of his behavior he feels worthy of their affection. When they indicate otherwise, he feels unworthy. In time the need for approval spreads from parents to playmates and schoolmates, and eventually to friends, neighbors, and associates. The need continues to influence behavior and thinking in a marked way all through life.

Since individuals tend to disapprove of behavior too different from their own, satisfaction of this need requires reasonable conformity to the ideas and standards of behavior of one's group. For this reason you will find it more difficult to accept ideas at variance with those of your social group than those that conform. Thus your ideas will tend to be radical or conservative depending on whether you look upon yourself as a member of a radical or a conservative group. On the other hand, you may gain approval by being different in some matters if your group values originality.

Individuals who fail to satisfy this need tend to seek attention, and while attention may indicate disapproval as well as approval, it is better than nothing. For this reason a child who cannot get the attention of his parents any other way may misbehave until he is punished. For though the punishment indicates disapproval, it is a form of attention. Similarly, adults will sometimes seek the spotlight even though they have to make fools of themselves to do so.

3. *Acceptance.* Indispensable to feeling that one has the approval of others is acceptance in one's family, school, vocational, and social groups. One needs to feel that he is a full-fledged member of each group. Many a child has trouble satisfying this need when he is rejected by or kept on the fringe of his school group. The problem is especially common with children who are frequently moved from one school to another. Before they can win acceptance in one school group they must start over in a new group. As a result they come to feel that they must be inferior in some important way. Many a college freshman who made a fine academic record in high school does less well in his studies in college because he is too busy getting himself accepted by the college groups that are important to him.

4. *Autonomy.* Even though one needs to feel that he is accepted by his group, he must also feel that he is an autonomous individual who is not exactly like any one else

and who is, at least to some degree, the master of his own situation. You can observe this need in the little boy who persists in learning to skate in spite of falls and failures. The student who is failing in his studies is likely to be unhappy because he is not satisfying this need for autonomy. He is not just failing his courses; he is also failing to demonstrate mastery over his own situation. The remedy lies either in improving his efficiency as a student or in changing his situation to one in which he can succeed.

The ability to think effectively helps to satisfy this need in two important ways. It improves one's chances of success in any endeavor. And it helps build the feeling that one is in control of one's own destiny, not the helpless pawn of chance.

The four needs discussed above arise primarily within the individual, and presumably manifest themselves in some form and to some degree in any culture. Still other needs, though closely related to these, seem to be determined largely by the kind of society and culture he lives in. A person growing up among the Manus natives of New Guinea, who live in huts built on stilts in shallow lagoons and who wrest their living mainly from the sea, can hardly earn the respect of his fellows and hence of himself, unless he becomes skillful in the arts of swimming, canoeing, and fishing. In the environment. of an American college, on the other hand, one can do quite well without any of these accomplishments. In this environment it is such matters as the social graces, skill in organized athletics, and academic talent that are important. The next five needs, discussed below, seem to be essential to most people living in western culture.

5. *Achievement.* Closely related to autonomy is the need for achievement, such as the production of useful articles or the acquisition of knowledge or skills. Whereas autonomy seems to be a universal need in any culture, the kind of achievement that satisfies

one's need seems largely determined by the particular culture. A knowledge of classical literature is valued in western civilization, whereas in Manus culture it would not be esteemed. Achievement of the kind approved in one's culture enhances the self-concept because it helps to earn approval and to demonstrate autonomy. Looking back over your life you are likely to find that the things you now value most are not the parties you attended but your achievements, such as holding a good job, making good grades, or winning athletic victories.

6. *Prestige*. Achievement is not enough without recognition. We need not only to feel that we are persons of worth but to be recognized as such. In other words, we need prestige — basically a form of social recognition and honor. Coming within one semester of graduation from college is a genuine achievement, for it means getting nearly all of the intrinsic value of a college education. But it is much more satisfying to graduate and gain the prestige of a college degree. The amount of prestige attached to an achievement is, of course, largely determined by the culture. Your college degree would carry little prestige among the Manus people.

The need for prestige affects our thinking in many ways. We tend to select activities that bring prestige and to avoid those that do not. Thus college students tend to go into white-collar occupations instead of trades, even though some of these students would be more successful in the trades. Many students who do not have the necessary preparation and intellectual abilities undergo great hardships to earn a college degree because of its prestige value, when they would be more successful in the long run spending the same effort on getting ahead in a job. We tend to select our recreational activities on the same basis. Members of middle- and upper-class social groups will continue to prefer golf to pitching horseshoes as long as golf carries the higher prestige. When or if

our culture matures to the point that it awards more prestige to reading books than to watching color television, we will read more books.

7. *Conformity to conscience*. Conscience may be defined as the value premises that distinguish right from wrong. It is impossible to maintain a satisfactory self-concept without following these premises reasonably well, for they are so strongly reinforced, both by religion and by society, that a person feels guilty and unworthy when he violates them. Society must have some way of holding the individual in line, for if everyone followed his impulses unchecked the result could only be anarchy. Society has several methods of doing so. It can punish you for violating its laws by fining you or by putting you in jail. Or it can withhold approval and prestige or subject you to ridicule or criticism for violating its customs. But perhaps most effective is the punishment you inflict on yourself when you do something you consider wrong, for this punishment hits hardest where it hurts most: it damages the self-concept.

Your conscience serves as the moral judge of your behavior. There are many ways of satisfying your personal needs which are not approved by your culture and which you consider wrong. You might, for example, gain the prestige of high grades by cheating on your examinations. Or you might satisfy your craving for a new automobile by stealing one. But if you have absorbed the moral tenets of western culture, you consider these methods wrong. You may avoid punishment from your fellows, but you cannot escape the punishment of guilt feelings. If you are to maintain a satisfactory self-concept you must live in reasonable conformity to the moral principles you have accepted and which make up your conscience.

Conscience exercises a strong influence over thinking as well as over behavior. Western culture prohibits evil thoughts as well as evil deeds. Thus you will find yourself reluctant to reach conclusions which are in conflict with western standards of morality.

8. *Contributions to others.* It is not enough merely to avoid the violation of one's moral code. It is also necessary to feel that one is making an important contribution to the welfare of others. Helping others is, of course, a means of satisfying the need for approval, achievement, and prestige, but it is more than that. One of the best ways of enhancing your self-concept is to feel that others are dependent on you for their happiness and welfare. Perhaps this is one of the reasons married people have a longer life expectancy than single ones: they feel that their mates or children are dependent on them for care, or affection, or the necessities of life.

It is not only more blessed to give than to receive, but it is also more enhancing to the self-concept. Thus we need to give approval as well as receive it, to improve the world as well as to profit from it, to respect and protect the rights of others as well as to receive protection. By these means we strengthen our security in feeling that we are valuable and worthy members of our society.

9. *Enhancing the self-concept.* The self-concept, like the process of adaptation, is dynamic rather than static. To be satisfactory, it must be continually enhanced. We set up an ideal self-concept and try to make the real one match it. Then, as the real approaches the ideal, we tend to raise the ideal. Thus a self-concept that is satisfactory today will not be so tomorrow unless it has been enhanced. This need for enhancement is doubtless part of the force which drives us ceaselessly to achieve something better — better jobs, better housing, better clothes, better social relationships. The standards by which we measured our prestige yesterday are too low today — we raise them and then strive to meet the higher standards.

But raising one's standards is not enough; we must also expand the area of the self-concept. If the self-concept is limited strictly to the interests of one's own organism, the opportunities for enhancement are similarly limited. The individual who so limits his interests tends to become more and more ingrown. Like the small town cut off from contact with the outside world, such a person shrinks and shrivels instead of growing. He is called *selfish,* and his fellows react to him accordingly by withdrawing approval and affection. On the other hand, the individual who expands his interests to include those of others is like the town at a busy crossroads, which grows and expands through contact with the outside. Such a person is outward-looking. He is described by and reacted to by his fellows as *unselfish,* and his self-concept gains from their approval.

Expanding the area of the self-concept is accomplished through identification, *i.e.,* through looking at oneself as though he were in the place of the other person and sharing his feelings. At a movie, when you suffer with the hero and exult in his triumphs, you identify yourself with him. The baby, in his early stages of development, makes no very clear distinction between himself and others. He identifies himself with those about him, particularly with his mother. Perhaps through the mechanism of the conditioned response, since she is present when his needs are satisfied, he associates his mother with the pleasure which accompanies the satisfaction of his needs. In this way the mother becomes the most important single fact of a typical child's existence. Even when he later develops a concept of himself as separate from others, his sense of identification with his mother remains strong. Through this identification with his mother he comes to share her feelings. When he senses that she is happy, he tends to feel happy; when he senses that she is sad, he tends to feel the same way. Gradually, through this process of identification, he includes other persons, things, and ideas in his self-concept. Thus, to some extent at least, the college freshman includes in his self-concept his friends, his fraternity, his team. Even though he is not a member of the football team he develops loyalty toward it, rejoicing when it wins and groaning when it loses. Hence, to a degree, he himself is winning or losing. It is partly from identification that man's nature as a social being arises. In this way he becomes sensitive to the feelings of others and considerate of their interests.

Through identification with institutions, causes, other people, and the like, we immeasurably increase our opportunities for self-enhancement. It might seem that we would also increase the risk of injury. But this does not seem to happen. The person with an expanded self-concept is better able to stand disappointment or injury to something he loves. It is the person with the shriveled self-concept who runs the risk — perhaps because he has so little he can ill afford to lose any of it.

4. Balanced Satisfaction of Needs

All needs must be satisfied in a reasonably balanced way. In times of emergency, when one's very existence is threatened, physiological needs may assume paramount importance. For example, the paramount need of the drowning man is for air — he has no time to concern himself with matters of prestige or self-enhancement. But this does not mean that physical needs are generally more important. In the mature individual the psychological needs assume equal if not greater importance in shaping behavior and thinking. You can doubtless recall many instances in your own life where you put other needs ahead of physical ones. The point is that all needs must be satisfied — in general the one not being satisfied becomes the sore point, receives the most attention, and does the most to shape our thinking.

We can to some extent compensate by strength in one area for weakness in another. For example, one can compensate to some extent for inadequate housing with affection

or approval. But no amount of these satisfactions will completely remove the unpleasantness of poor housing. And no amount of prestige will eliminate the tensions arising from a feeling that one is not contributing to the welfare of others. Nor will any amount of achievement suffice to eliminate the tensions induced by a lack of affection from others. It is the balanced satisfaction of all needs that brings happiness.

The balanced satisfaction of all needs in a complex society such as ours requires high-grade thinking, especially for young people. The satisfaction of one need often conflicts with the satisfaction of another. The freshman who must spend nearly all his time studying in order to satisfy his need for achievement in his courses is likely to experience inner tensions because he is failing to satisfy his need for acceptance in his new social group.

Furthermore, it is difficult to avoid the fallacy of neglected aspect in thinking about problems of need satisfaction. Few of us understand ourselves so well that we always know the cause of our inner tensions. Often in response to tension we strive all the harder to satisfy certain needs at the expense of others. For example, in our highly competitive culture many of us strive so hard for success that we neglect families and friends. When the unsatisfied need for affection manifests itself in tension, we fail to realize the true cause and relieve the tension temporarily by striving even harder for success. Many of us fail to realize the true cause of the tension until it is too late.

Inner tension may also be caused by interpreting a situation as a threat to future satisfaction of needs. People who oppose change or resist new ideas may be responding to such a threat. A successful football coach may oppose a change in the rules of the game because he fears that such a change will threaten his success in the future. A psychologist may resist a new hypothesis about human behavior because it threatens other hypotheses that are important to his feeling of achievement. Thus our psychological Ohm's law may operate in part as a response to a threat to future need satisfaction.

If you find yourself uneasy or unhappy without knowing why, an unsatisfied need or a threat to future need satisfaction may be the cause. The procedures of effective thinking are useful both in identifying the need or the threat, and in finding a way to satisfy the need or to deal with the threat.

Needs and value systems are inextricably linked. Our value systems are the guidelines we use in judging the relative importance of needs, as well as the means by which we satisfy them. If your value system is inadequate, or if premises in the system are in conflict, you are unlikely to achieve balanced satisfaction of needs. We shall consider difficulties in the balanced satisfaction of needs, together with suggestions for dealing with them, in the chapters to come.

EXERCISE 27

1–12. *Indicate whether the following statements agree with the hypotheses presented in this book by writing in the blank T if true or F if false.*

1. Sufficient skill in logical techniques will eliminate subjective factors in thinking. _____F_____

2. Even when the problem we are thinking about seems unrelated to personal problems, our definition of the problem is likely to be shaped by our needs. _____T_____

3. Psychological needs probably exercise less influence on thinking than physiological needs. _____F_____

4. There is little interaction between physiological and psychological needs. _____F_____

5. One's need for affection is usually satisfied permanently if his parents give him adequate love and care. _____F_____

6. The need for approval affects thinking by tending to make one accept ideas held by others whose approval he wishes to have. _____T_____

7. In order to satisfy his need for autonomy, a person must succeed in all his ventures. _____F_____

8. Any kind of success will satisfy the need for achievement as long as the success is hard to attain. _____F_____

9. The amount of prestige involved in a given achievement is determined by the culture. _____T_____

10. In western culture, at least, making a contribution to the welfare of others is necessary for a satisfactory self-concept. _____T_____

11. Making $50,000 a year speculating in real estate would for most persons be more effective in satisfying psychological needs than making $15,000 a year as a rural physician. _____F_____

12. Identification with others helps to expand the area of the self-concept. _____T_____

13–21. *All attempts to interpret the motives of other people must be regarded as speculative reasoning and should therefore be made with caution. However, as an exercise, use the key list below to identify your best guess as to which need is manifesting itself in the following instances.*

EXERCISE 27

KEY LIST

1. *Affection*	4. *Autonomy*	7. *Conformity to conscience*
2. *Approval*	5. *Achievement*	8. *Contributions to others*
3. *Acceptance*	6. *Prestige*	9. *Enhancement of self-concept*

13. Appleton, a freshman, made a brilliant record in high school, but is now failing most of his courses. He was not invited to join a fraternity in the fall rushing period. He tells his counselor that he spends most of his time working for a campus political party. _____3_____

14. Baker is a Phi Beta Kappa, co-captain of the varsity football team, and president of a campus service organization. He is highly respected as an able and conscientious person but has no intimate friends. To the surprise of everyone, he eloped with a high school girl of low social status and inferior intellect. _____1_____

15. Carter had the choice of acting behind the scenes and being the most powerful student on the campus, or being elected to a high office in which he would be a figurehead. He chose the latter. _____6_____

16. Dakin chose to work his way through Wysacki rather than live with his parents and attend a college near home. _____4_____

17. Easterton was working hard to win a national contest for the best original essay on political science, the rules of which prohibited the use of any quotations. While searching for material, he found a brilliant article in an obscure foreign journal. He appropriated the best passages from the article by simply leaving off the quotation marks. _____5 - 9_____

18. Franks, in the same situation, decided that it would be better to present some of the ideas in the article in his own words, giving credit to the author in a footnote. _____7_____

19. Grangerford writes a sports column for the campus newspaper. The student body was up in arms over an incident occurring in the homecoming game in which players of the rival school had repeatedly piled on the star quarterback. Grangerford thought it would be better to forget the matter, but in his column he advocated breaking off athletic relations with the rival school. _____2_____

20. Hannay declined to run for president of the student body, even though he would almost certainly have won, because he wanted to devote his time to his premedical studies. _____5_____

21. After Hannay declined to run, Ireland also declined, because he was too busy conducting the campus drive for funds for research on the causes of a vicious disease. _____8_____

28 The Personal Point of View

Of all newborn creatures, the human infant has the most complex set of needs to be met and is the least able to meet them without the ministrations of others. He must learn how to get along in a vastly complicated material and social universe. His early drives are unlearned and have to do entirely with the maintenance of his physiological equilibrium. His behavior is likewise unlearned and relatively simple. About all he can do when he is hungry or uncomfortable is to squirm and squall until someone comes to relieve the stress.

But with his first breath in his new universe he begins to interact with his physical and social environment, and to learn new, more varied, and more complex methods of satisfying needs. His first efforts seem to be pure trial and error. For example, when a finger is pressed constantly against a newborn infant's chin, he throws arms and legs about in jerky fashion, occasionally striking the annoying finger by chance. When he hits upon a solution, he tends to repeat the action on future occasions.

1. The Organization of Experience

Presumably the child begins to develop his frame of reference at the same time he begins to use language. Before experience can become a part of the frame of reference, it must be translated into some form of mental symbol. When the child gets too close to the hot stove and burns himself, he might learn to avoid getting too close to that and similiar stoves merely through the operation of the conditioned response, and without the operation of any conscious thought process. But before he can think about such matters, and hence make full use of his experience in avoiding hot objects in general, he must translate his experience into symbols, usually verbal, such as "Stove hot; stove hurt." If you do not believe that you must use symbols in order to think, try making a simple little decision, such as whether to take a drink of water, without allowing any form of symbol to enter your mind.

Experience can be used in thinking as soon as it has been translated into symbols, but it is more useful when organized into what the logician calls propositions. Experience in getting along with a particular person is useless in getting along with other persons until it has been formed into some kind of generalization. For example, you would probably have considerable trouble in doing your work to the satisfaction of your college professors unless you had already made certain generalizations based on your experience with high school teachers, such as "Teachers like to have assignments turned in on time." Even when generalizations prove inexact, they are usually more useful in thinking than no generalizations at all. It is only through his ability to organize his knowledge of the physical world into generalizations that man has been able to unlock the secrets of the universe and put them to use.

No amount of experience with stomach pains brought on by eating green apples will suffice to make the child stop eating green apples until he has organized the experience, usually with the help of his parents, into the causal theory that eating green apples causes stomach pains. The usefulness of this theory in thinking is increased when it is generalized to cover the eating of all unripe fruit.

As soon as his language is adequate for the task, the child begins to develop his self-concept in verbal terms. From the way others treat him, and from what they say to and about him, he forms propositions about what he is like as a person.

At about the same time he begins to develop his value system. Since his primary motivation is to satisfy his needs, he makes positive value judgments about those experiences that seem to satisfy his needs and negative ones about those that interfere with need satisfaction or intensify unsatisfied needs. In time he organizes specific value judgments into value premises, which he then uses in guiding his conduct.

2. The Influence of Culture

Some of the propositions included in the self-concept, the value system, and the frame of reference are derived by induction directly from experience. For example, after several bruises and abrasions from running, skating, or riding his bicycle too fast, the youngster may generalize that excessive speed is dangerous. The dislike of many students for mathematics may be based on a value judgment derived from experience. In his early contacts with the subject a student may be frustrated because he cannot solve the problems. This frustration, together with the embarrassment of low grades and of inability to recite correctly in class, causes him to evaluate his personal experience with mathematics as unsatisfying and to form the value judgment that mathematics is unsatisfying and to be avoided.

Most propositions, however, are acquired directly or indirectly from his culture — that complex body of knowledge, beliefs, customs, laws, morals, and arts which man acquires as a member of society. We can only speculate on the amount of knowledge you could acquire if you had to get it all by trial and error and induction, as you would have to do if you did not live in a culture. If you lived alone and had to start from nothing, presumably you would not acquire a language. Abstract thinking would thus be beyond your capacity. You might have to live a million years before accidentally noticing the effect of fire on meat. You might have to live even longer before discovering so simple a mechanical aid as the wheel. If you lived ten million years, you might conceivably acquire as many propositions about the world as an average American child has at the age of three. For it has been largely through the interchange of ideas and experience, as provided in a culture, that man has risen so far above the level of other animals.

If society is to maintain itself so that it can provide the individual with the tremendous advantages of living in a culture, it must to some extent regulate his behavior. By prohibiting the individual from assaulting his neighbor, society gives him freedom to walk the streets without carrying a weapon. By forcing persons into specialized roles, it provides the individual with the necessities of life at smaller cost in time and effort, thus freeing some of his time and energy for the development of his individual capacities. By setting up schools and libraries, together with rules and regulations for their use, it makes available to the individual the experience accumulated by billions of people in thousands of years. It is through its culture that society controls the behavior of the individual. The manners, morals, customs, and beliefs of the culture in which the individual lives become the propositions by which he runs his life.

Some of these propositions are taken over directly. The individual hears them from other people, or reads them, or observes other people following them, and simply adopts them as his own, without examining them critically or seeking evidence to support them. This is not to say that such propositions are right or wrong. The point is that they are adopted from the culture without actual evidence.

Other propositions are adopted from the culture through *introjection*, the process by which a person reacts to incidents and to other persons as though they were within himself. Early in the development of the child, when he is making his first value judgments about himself, he encounters one of the most frustrating facts of human life — the satisfaction of organic needs frequently conflicts with the maintenance of a satisfactory self-concept. When, in response to hunger, the child steals cookies from the neighbor's kitchen, he finds the action pleasant because it satisfies an organic need. But when his mother scolds him by calling him "naughty" or "bad," he may infer that he is not loved or lovable when he steals cookies. Now he has two conflicting evaluations of his action, one from his own senses and one from his mother. Because of strong identification with his mother, he may introject his mother's evaluation of his action, just as though he himself had found the action bad by his own experience, *i.e.*, he takes over from his mother a cultural prohibition, despite the contrary evidence of his own senses and despite the fact that he understands nothing of property rights.

The culture is not only the mold which shapes the individual, but also a part of the environment to which he must adjust. For the manners, customs, and morals of the culture stand between the individual and the satisfaction of his needs. If he satisfies his need for food by throwing a brick through the bakery window and helping himself, he risks being put in jail. Even worse, assuming that he has absorbed the culture's moral prohibition against stealing, he is punished for his act by his conscience. The culture is also the only source of satisfaction of such needs as approval and prestige. By attaching approval or prestige to certain activities and discredit or shame to others, a community can prod the individual into approved behavior. It can, for example, induce a busy businessman to give to the management of a charity drive time and energy worth hundreds of dollars. It can force a man to wear uncomfortable clothing on a hot day. And it can control his thinking to a considerable degree, for it is uncomfortable to think thoughts not approved by one's culture. Every person finds his own desires in conflict with his culture on many occasions. Yet, to be happy he must live in reasonable harmony with his culture. Such conflicts can be satisfactorily resolved, but high-grade thinking is necessary.

The culture also helps to account for differences in thinking, for no two of us are exposed to exactly the same cultural influences. Cultural patterns differ, sometimes sharply, between families, neighborhoods, social groups, communities, regions, and nations.[1] You can find, for example, definite differences in the prevailing value judgments between two social fraternities on the same campus. If you wish to develop certain characteristics in yourself, it is advisable to mingle with a social group that values those characteristics.

All in all, the culture has a hand in virtually everything you think, in your taste in food and books, your ambitions, your moral

[1] For a study of cultural differences, see Ruth Benedict, *Patterns of Culture* (Boston: Houghton Mifflin, 1943).

code, your political opinions, and your beliefs about health, wealth, and happiness. It is hard for any individual to realize the full extent of cultural influences, for he has always been subject to them. Like the fish that has never been out of water, he does not know what it is like to exist in a different element. One of the best ways to realize how much culture has influenced you is to become acquainted with one that is different from your own. You can do this by reading anthropological studies of primitive cultures.[2]

3. The Individual Character of Thinking

As powerful as the culture is in shaping the development of the individual, it cannot eliminate individual differences. For each of us develops his own unique personal point of view, the dominant components of which are self-concept, value system, and frame of reference. These three components function as a triad that has a profound effect on the decisions we make.

Figuratively speaking, this triad functions as the selector of experience. We are physically incapable of observing more than a fraction of what goes on about us at any given time. At a football game we can watch the ball, or the scoreboard, or the officials, or the star halfback, or the plane flying overhead, but we cannot pay attention to all of them at the same instant. At any one time, one aspect of the scene is the foreground and the rest of it is the background.

The selection of the foreground is made primarily on the basis of needs. That is why different individuals observe different aspects of the same scene. At the football game, the scout concentrates on the tactics of the team; the spectator who has bet on the outcome concentrates on the progress of the ball; the fashion editor concentrates on what the spectators are wearing; and the coed watches for something in the game that she can call by its technical name and so impress her escort.

Incidents in the background of the scene may, of course, impinge upon the attention if the stimulus is strong enough. The scout may be distracted by a fight between spectators. But in general what is in the background makes little impression; it does not as a rule become part of the individual's experience.

Each proposition that becomes a part of the triad tends to set the pattern for the selection of other propositions. For example, the child who is rewarded by his parents for being agreeable is likely to incorporate into his self-concept the proposition that he is an agreeable person. This proposition leads to the adoption of the value premise that it is good to be agreeable. From then on he will tend to resist ideas that are incompatible with this value premise. The child who resents parental interference is likely to resent authority in any form. The child who is punished severely by parents or by experience for being venturesome may adopt the proposition that it is better to be safe than sorry, and may come more and more to resemble Caspar Milquetoast as he grows older. The child who is successful in asserting himself may adopt the proposition that nothing is gained unless something is ventured, and so may grow into an aggressive business executive.

Thus, by directing the selection of experience, the triad directs its own development, with the result that each person develops his own unique self-concept, value system, and frame of reference.

Because of its uniqueness, the triad makes the thinking of each person assume particular characteristics different from those of any other person. Figuratively speaking, the triad plays many roles in the thinking process. One role is to serve as the agency through which needs are recognized, interpreted, and translated into thought and action. It serves, so to speak, as Chairman of the Committee on Need Satisfaction. And

[2] Such as Margaret Mead, *Growing up in New Guinea* (New York: The New American Library of World Literature, 1953).

like a good committee chairman, it tries to keep the thinking relevant to the issue at hand. The relevant issue at any given moment is the most pressing need of that moment. We do not concern ourselves with needs of the past unless they are manifesting themselves in the present. When you are trying to solve a problem in chemistry, the only logically relevant factors are those having to do with the problem. But while you are thinking about the problem you may recall a slur the instructor made about your ability to work simple equations. Defending your self-concept against this slur may become the most pressing need of the moment, and you may find yourself forgetting about chemistry and daydreaming instead about avenging the slur. Thus your reaction to the situation within and without determines what you think about.

The triad also functions as the interpreter of outside phenomena. We noted in Chapter 4 that all perception is limited and shaped by the frame of reference. Thus we can observe only what the frame of reference permits us to observe. The triad also exerts a strong influence on the inferences we draw from our observations.

Suppose you know these facts: Smythe has not returned from a fishing trip in the Gulf of Mexico. It is now Tuesday morning and Smythe was due back late Monday afternoon. He left the dock alone Monday morning in a sturdy skiff, powered by an outboard motor. He carried a spare motor. No storms have occurred in that area. Smythe was an expert swimmer and boatman. He was emotionally depressed, having recently learned that the severe pain in his abdomen was caused by an incurable cancer. He was heavily in debt. He carried an insurance policy of ten thousand dollars.

A number of plausible hypotheses might be formed to explain the information in hand. Smythe has met with an accident; he is lost; he is still out fishing, not caring any longer about his business; he has committed suicide. In general, you will tend to pick the hypothesis most favorable to your personal point of view. The owner of a helicopter, eager to demonstrate its usefulness in rescue work, would probably choose the hypothesis that Smythe is lost. Since Smythe's insurance policy is invalid in case of suicide, the insurance agent might choose the suicide hypothesis. Smythe's friends would probably choose any hypothesis but that one. If you had recently urged Smythe not to go fishing in the Gulf alone, you might choose the hypothesis that he is lost or has had an accident.

The triad also influences the significance you attach to the facts. The insurance agent might pick as most significant the facts that no storm has occurred, that Smythe is an expert boatman and swimmer, and that he carried a spare motor, and interpret these facts as ruling out any hypothesis except suicide. Smythe's friends, on the other hand, might attach little importance to these facts, reasoning that anyone could have an accident or get lost. The owner of the helicopter might reason that these facts are significant in supporting the hypothesis that Smythe is still alive and in need of rescue. When you were urged in Chapter 5 to form the habit of setting up rival hypotheses and testing the supporting facts by certain criteria, the purpose was to help you overcome the bias of your personal point of view.

Perhaps the most important of all the roles in thinking played by the triad is that of evaluator of experience. It is the Bureau of Standards by which experience is judged to be desirable and hence to be repeated, or undesirable and hence to be avoided. The value system provides the standards used. Is reading a mystery story a waste of time or a desirable relaxation? Is the current fad in popular music really music or mere noise? Your opinion depends on your value judgments. Many value judgments are self-centered: they evaluate experience in terms of the individual's own interests rather than the interests of mankind in general. When you circulate a scandalous story about a political opponent it is "practical politics," but when such a story is circulated about you, it is likely to be "dirty politics." When four tacklers gang up on the ball carrier and slam him to earth, whether the play was "good football" or "unnecessary roughness" may depend on which team you favor.

Thus to a considerable degree we create the world in which we live. We react to reality not as it is but as it appears to us through our personal points of view. We can no more see reality independently of this personal point of view than we can listen to a broadcast of a football game independently of the radio announcer. If he is skillful and accurate, we get a reasonably accurate picture of the game. Similarly, if we have an adequate supply of accurate propositions, we get a reasonably accurate and workable view of life. But if the propositions in the personal point of view are inadequate or inaccurate, poor thinking is inevitable.

4. Thinking and Health

Nothing we have said so far should be interpreted to mean that the mind and body are independent. On the contrary, man functions as a total organism, and what affects the organism affects thinking. Most of us know that the quality of our thinking is affected by illness, fatigue, and physical discomfort. The close interrelationship between body and mind is shown by the effect of certain substances in the blood stream bathing the brain. Some drugs, such as opium and LSD, produce hallucinations. We have all observed the effects of alcohol on otherwise well-behaved people. Certain endocrine products in the blood stream affect what one remembers or imagines by raising or lowering the thresholds of perception. This relationship is so close that many of us have learned the wisdom of maintaining good bodily health and, where practical, of postponing important decisions while tired, sleepy, ill, or under the influence of drugs.

We are also beginning to learn that this interrelationship works the other way too — that thinking has a far-reaching effect on bodily operations, that certain kinds of thinking promote the health and well-being of the whole organism, and that other kinds may prolong or intensify illness and even cause or contribute to the cause of such ailments as insomnia, stomach ulcers, hysterical paralysis, and high blood pressure.

The American public is becoming steadily more aware of the problem of mental health, and with good reason. More than a million patients are treated each year in mental hospitals, and nearly half the hospital beds in America today are occupied by mental patients. It has been estimated that as many as three-fourths of the patients visiting their physicians today are suffering from ailments that are psychosomatic rather than purely physical.

A vast amount of research aimed at determining the exact causes of these illnesses is now under way, and the evidence is still far from complete. Some mental illness is undoubtedly caused by disease or damage to brain tissue. Some of it may prove to be due to biochemical disturbances in the organism. Meanwhile it seems probable that much mental illness is traceable to failure to cope successfully with life, which in turn is traceable to poor decisions about one's objectives and about how to achieve them. This is not to suggest that, if you have made a number of bad decisions, you are in danger of mental illness. The human personality is basically tough and can endure a great deal of punishment without permanent damage. No one thinks so well that he can avoid bad decisions entirely. It does suggest, however, that you should try to increase your skill in decision making, for health, as well as happiness, is a by-product of skillful decision making.

EXERCISE 28

1–24. *The items in this and the following exercises are intended to raise issues as well as to test knowledge of facts. Indicate whether the following statements agree with the hypotheses presented in this book by writing in the blank T if true and F if false.*

1. We tend to use logical techniques for the purpose of attacking evidence contrary to what we want to believe. _____ F T

2. Psychologists have accused man of first deciding what he wants and then thinking for the purpose of making it seem logical. _____ T

3. Finding the truth is necessary for any kind of need satisfaction. _____ F T

4. Conditions within the human organism have little effect on thinking. _____ F

5. So far as we now know, thinking has little effect on bodily operations. _____ F

6. Much mental illness seems to be due to chronic bad thinking. _____ T

7. The major components of the personal point of view are self-concept, frame of reference, and the concept of culture. _____ F

8. Experience must be translated into some form of symbol before it can be consciously used in thinking. _____ T

9. Experience is more useful when generalized in the form of a proposition. _____ T

10. One's personal point of view is involved in all his interpretations of the world outside him. _____ T

11. It is impossible to perceive reality except in terms of one's personal point of view. _____ T

12. Value judgments determine to a large extent which experiences we seek and which we avoid. _____ T

13. The propositions which make up the personal point of view are always consistent with each other. _____ ? F

14. Once a proposition has been adopted into the personal point of view, it is never changed or abandoned. _____ F

15. The issue you think about at any given moment is likely to be the most pressing need of that moment. _____ T

16. What you observe in any given scene is determined more by your physical equipment than by your personal point of view. _____ F

17. Consciously or unconsciously we select to a considerable extent the evidence we use in forming propositions. _____ T _____

18. The hypotheses you set up to explain any given situation are determined largely by your personal point of view. _____ T _____

19. Most of the propositions making up the personal point of view are derived by induction from experience. _____ F _____ T

20. Most of one's knowledge is acquired by trial and error. _____ F _____

21. Culture and need satisfaction are often in conflict. _____ T _____

22. An introjected value judgment may be in conflict with the evidence of one's senses. _____ T _____

23. Culture helps to promote adaptation and at the same time is the source of many problems of adaptation. _____ T _____

24. Cultural differences can be noted between groups on the same college campus. _____ T _____

25–29. *Suppose that both students and faculty of Wysacki are voting on the issue of whether ROTC should be compulsory for physically fit college freshmen. Given below is brief information about the personal points of view of a number of fictitious persons. Using this information, make a reasoned guess how each would vote on the issue.*

25. Colonel Andrew Anderson is Professor of Military Science at Wysacki. He was required to take ROTC when he was a freshman. _____ for it _____

26. Barry Basque is a freshman at Wysacki. He is a member of the campus Ban-the-Bomb Society. He is a brilliant student and is carrying the maximum academic load permitted. His father was a conscientious objector in World War II.

_____ against _____

27. Candy Calhoun, a sophomore at Wysacki, is a candidate for Queen of the Military Ball. _____ for it _____

28. Debbie Davis is a senior at Wysacki. She is also a candidate for Queen of the Military Ball. Debbie plans to join the Peace Corps after graduation. Her father is the author of two books: *Disarmament, the Only Hope,* and *The Rigidity of the Military Mind.*

_____ against _____

29. Earle Edwards, a music major, plays the trombone in the ROTC band. His value premises include the following: another major war would probably destroy civilization; communism is immoral. _____ for it _____

29 How We Distort the Evidence

It is unfortunate that man cannot be thoroughly trained in the techniques of effective thinking before birth. For as soon as the child matures enough to think at all, he begins to make errors in reasoning about matters of great importance to him. Because of these errors, some of the propositions he adopts into his personal point of view are faulty. He hastily generalizes about other people from the single instance of himself. He readily assumes that his way of life is the only one, and that other people live and think as he does. Particularly troublesome are the faulty propositions he adopts about himself. He may make a hasty generalization about his abilities on the basis of a single failure. Or he may acquire false value premises through *post hoc* reasoning. When his mother, hard pressed and harried by household matters, punishes him severely for a trivial act, it is only natural for him to reason that, since his act came first, it was the sole cause of his mother's irritation. From such trivial incidents as this a child may begin to form a false concept of himself as unworthy and unloved.

1. Self-Defense

As the child matures he slowly improves his techniques of reasoning, but he tends to retain many of the erroneous propositions he has already adopted.

In some respects we behave toward ourselves like dictators. Doubtless most dictators like to see their countries flourish and thereby shed glory on themselves. But their primary motivation is to protect their persons, power, and prestige. When the welfare of the country and the prestige or power of the dictator are in conflict, it is usually the country which suffers. The citizenry soon learn that they are free to criticize the dictator only once. And the palace guard soon learns that it is unhealthy to bring the dictator evidence that indicates an error on his part — dictators do not like to acknowledge errors. Thus evidence is kept from the dictator, and he falls into further error. Truth does not flourish in a dictatorship.

All of us behave somewhat like dictators in that we protect ourselves from the truth when it is threatening to the self-concept. We would like to know reality as long as it is a credit to us, for knowing the truth is in itself a source of self-satisfaction. But above all we must protect our good opinion of ourselves, for this is our most cherished possession. When knowing the truth conflicts with protecting our good opinion of ourselves, truth is often the loser.

If we shielded ourselves from the truth only when it threatened our good opinion of ourselves, presumably we would constantly glow with self-satisfaction. But the findings of behavioral science directly contradict the consequent of the above proposition. Clinical records are filled with cases of individuals who damage their lives by refusing to give up harmful and false beliefs about themselves. In fact, we are far more likely to have too low rather than too high an opinion of ourselves.

The explanation of this paradox appears to be that we defend our personal points of view as wholes. We must defend our value systems and frames of reference as well as our self-concepts. To acknowledge that any significant proposition in the triad is false is to weaken confidence in the entire triad: if the triad is false in one respect, it may be false in others. One who has no confidence in his frame of reference is as badly off as a mariner who has no confidence in his compass. No matter how warped the personal point of view is, it is a source of security so long as we are unaware of its inaccuracy, for no matter how distorted it may be, it is the only lens we have through which to view reality. For that reason we are often no more tolerant of criticism of our propositions than

the dictator is of criticism of his regime. Like dictators, who are notoriously cool to the suggestions of others, we are reluctant to accept suggestions that conflict with propositions in the triad. If you do not believe this, try to convince your professor that he would be more successful in teaching if he would change some of his methods. Thus we often conceal the truth from ourselves, much as the palace guard conceals bad news from the dictator.

The degree to which we distort reality varies widely with the individual and the situation. In general, the more important a proposition is in the personal point of view, the more zealously it is defended. The propositions making up the personal point of view interlock like the stones in an arch. When a major proposition is threatened, the whole structure is threatened, just as the arch falls if the keystone crumbles. The girl who has adopted the major premise that her mother does not love her tends to resist or ignore evidence to the contrary. Even though she would like to be loved by her mother, to abandon her major premise would threaten her whole personal point of view. A major proposition about one's abilities, even though unfavorable, will usually be defended vigorously, whereas a minor proposition about how to play chess may be abandoned readily. Your boss, for example, may readily accept your suggestion about how to improve his golf and yet be offended at your suggestion about how to run his business.

The child who has dismantled the family alarm clock may interpret his father's comment that he cannot put it back together as meaning that he lacks mechanical ability. This he may generalize and introject as "I have no mechanical ability." Later, when he succeeds in repairing the chain on his bicycle he interprets the incident in the light of his previous generalization and fails to recognize it as evidence that he does have mechanical ability. Later still, when he goes to college, he may reject the evidence of vocational tests that he has high ability in engineering and choose a less suitable vocation.

In general, the less sure a person is of himself, the more defensive he is likely to be. For example, the instructor who is confident of himself will usually not hesitate to acknowledge a mistake he has made in class, for he does not feel that his position is threatened. But the instructor who is unsure of himself may argue vigorously over some minor point. He feels he cannot afford to lose. The person who is sure of himself in one area, however, may be unsure in another. When your roommate begins to argue violently over a seemingly unimportant point, the chances are that in some way you have threatened his personal point of view.

2. Mechanisms of Self-Defense

A perfect thinker, finding evidence contrary to a proposition he has accepted, would carefully evaluate the evidence and make the necessary modifications in the proposition. He would have no distortions to defend. When he encountered a threatening situation he would deal with it directly and realistically. Or, if his realistic perception of the situation told him that he could do nothing constructive about it, he would accept the situation and adapt to it. For example, the college student who found his need for achievement unsatisfied because of poor grades would set to work to improve his grades by more effort and improved study habits. If he found that his grades could not be improved, he would accept the fact and seek achievement in some other area.

But none of us attains perfection. None of us has thought so soundly that he has no faulty propositions to defend. For most of us there is a great deal of evidence in our environments that would be threatening if clearly perceived and accurately interpreted. Instead of dealing directly with this evidence, we resort to various mechanisms of self-defense by which we ignore, or distort, or misinterpret the evidence so as to avoid or minimize the threat. We often combine several of these mechanisms. You probably use them sometimes without even realizing that the situation is threatening. Even when consciously aware of the threat in a situation, you may be unaware at the time that you are using defense mechanisms. Let us examine some of the more important of these mechanisms. You will doubtless observe them more readily in others than in yourself.

3. Sophistical Defense

When you find an idea threatening, you can defend yourself against it with a device named after the Sophists, who acquired a reputation for teaching dishonest tricks of argument to young Athenians. This device uses the procedures of effective thinking in reverse, not to establish the truth but to attack it. If the threatening idea is a hypothesis, you can counter with another hypothesis which accounts for the evidence in a more satisfying way. If it is a generalization, you can convince yourself that it is based on a loaded sample. If it is a theory of causation, you can point to the strong possibility of *post hoc*. If someone criticizes you, you can use an array of logical tricks. You can attack the critic with *argumentum ad hominem*: "He is prejudiced and uninformed." You can prejudice the issue: "Those who criticize me are liars." And so on. The trouble with sophistical defense is that it keeps you from dealing with the real issue, thus necessitating more maneuvers. When you find yourself vigorously attacking an idea, it is well to try to discover the real reason you dislike it.

4. Avoidance

If a situation is threatening, you can consciously and deliberately avoid it by *remov-*

ing yourself from the situation. For example, if you are unprepared for your next class, you can cut it. By so doing you make it harder to deal with your instructor, but you escape the threat — temporarily. If there is something threatening in a situation, you can look the other way. Suppose you are the chairman of the student honor system. The knowledge that wholesale cheating was going on would be a threat to your self-concept as an effective official. If you suspected that wholesale cheating was occurring in a course you were taking, you could look the other way by keeping your eyes glued to your own paper. By so doing you could minimize the threat: it is less threatening to suspect than to know. But you would not have solved the real problem, and sooner or later conscience would catch up with you.

If you have an unpleasant duty to perform, you can avoid it by *forgetting* it. If you are ashamed of something you have done, you can forget it as you would a telephone number you no longer need. What you do not remember does not bother you — at the moment. Forgetting, of course, is not necessarily self-defensive. You may forget the matter simply because it is of no importance to you, like the telephone number. But if the things you forget tend to be unpleasant ones, you are probably avoiding them.

If an idea is sufficiently threatening, you can keep it entirely out of consciousness by *perceptual defense.* You may shift the spotlight away from the threat and keep it so deep in the background that it is not perceived at all. Suppose you have strong feelings of loyalty to your football team and strongly negative feelings about poor sportsmanship. When you see the fist of one of your players start toward the face of an opponent, you may shift your attention elsewhere before you can perceive or symbolize the act of slugging. Thus many of the neglected aspects in our observations are self-defensive maneuvers. The remedy, in part, is to practice and take pride in being an accurate and objective observer. Some avoidance is beneficial, if there is nothing you can do about the matter, there is no point in remembering it. There is no use in remembering that you broke your roommate's watch after you have had it repaired and learned your lesson about how to handle watches. But it is different when you forget a situation you could improve or a thing you ought to do, such as going to the dentist. Some problems have a way of getting worse the longer they are avoided.

5. Distraction Devices

Avoiding an unpleasant situation is easier if you employ a distraction device to keep your attention elsewhere. It is easier to ignore a toothache if your attention is absorbed by a movie. Do you dread studying for that biology test? You can distract your attention from it by playing a few rounds of bridge after supper. Are you hurt because he did not ask you for a date? You can divert your attention by absorbing yourself in biology. If the pain is too great for this, you can try a stronger distraction. The variety of distraction devices is endless. Radio, television, sports, and even work can be so used.

Up to a point distraction devices are beneficial. But when you find yourself seeking diversion excessively without knowing why, self-deception is probably involved, and it would be well to search for the real reason. Some distraction devices, like alcohol and narcotics, usually make the matter harder to deal with.

6. Rationalizing

Are you ashamed of the motive behind something you wish to do? For example, do you want to drop a course because you do not like to study? If you drop it for that reason you will suffer loss of self-esteem — it is painful to acknowledge that you are lazy. So you can drop the course and ease the pain with psychological aspirin, one form of which is *rationalizing, i.e.,* substituting acceptable reasons for the real reasons for an action. You can easily find acceptable reasons for dropping the course. "The course is dull, the instructor a bore, the class too crowded. And I will make better grades on my other courses if I reduce my load." Rationalizing comes in several popular brands.

One is known as *sour grapes.* You cannot reach the grapes? "They were sour anyway." You failed to make Phi Beta Kappa? "I wouldn't want to be a bookworm." She wouldn't give you a date? "I can spend my time better studying."

Another popular brand of rationalizing is called the *sweet lemon.* Is that car you bought a lemon? "But it is a sweet lemon. Even if it does break down every other day, it has many virtues. It is comfortable, the tires are good, and it has more prestige than cheaper models."

Still another is *excuse making.* Did you fail the course because you did not study enough? "It wasn't all my fault. I was in the infirmary three days early in the semester. I lost my book. And I had a headache the day of the final."

A similar one is *blaming others.* "It wasn't my fault I failed. The instructor didn't teach me anything, and besides he had it in for me." One trouble with this one is that your social standing is not improved when your remarks get back to the person blamed.

A worse form of rationalizing is *criticizing others.* You can raise your own relative position by tearing your competitors down with criticism. Or you can use it to rationalize jealousy. Suppose you are jealous of your roommate because he has a new convertible and you have to walk. Jealousy is not an acceptable reason for disliking him, so you find better reasons: he is lazy, he wastes his father's money, he's a parasite on society, and selfish as well. The aspirin works whether he has these faults or not — as long as you can convince yourself that he has

them. Criticism of others is not necessarily self-defensive; you may have other motives or adequate evidence for your criticism. But when you use it as psychological aspirin you deceive yourself about your own motives, make false appraisals of others, and alienate those who hear about it. When you find yourself critical of others, it is well to seek your real motive.

Rationalizing is bad for thinking on three counts. (1) Like morphine, it tends to be habit-forming. It is easier to make excuses than to face the issue squarely. (2) Like aspirin, it eases the pain without removing the cause. The student who excuses himself for failing a course instead of correcting the cause is likely to fail other courses. (3) By obscuring motives, it tends to make behavior irrational. The individual who rationalizes excessively tends to act on impulse without applying Phase 5, and to depend on psychological aspirin to ease the pain of his mistakes.

Reducing one's dependence on psychological aspirin is a complex matter. A general practice which helps to eliminate all forms of self-deception is to cultivate a concept of yourself as an individual who is willing and able to face reality frankly and objectively. You can help yourself strengthen this self-concept by being alert for your minor rationalizations and by taking pride in catching yourself in them. It is unlikely, however, that you will be able to catch yourself in many of your major rationalizations; you will be too anxious to avoid the pain of the issue you are evading. Dealing with major rationalizations requires a general reduction of the need for self-defense, a matter discussed in a later chapter.

7. Repression

When a threatening idea is too serious to be dealt with by the devices already mentioned, you can repress it, that is, you can block it from entering consciousness.

In effect, you lock the evidence in the closet, as you would the family skeleton, because you cannot face it. Consider the student who is having an argument with his father over what vocation he will follow. His father wants him to study accounting, but the student has no interest in the subject. Partly for this reason and partly because he wants to prove to his father that he should not study accounting, he fails the course. Failing a course is bad enough, but failing it for such a base motive offends the conscience. It is not fair to his father, whom he loves, to fail a course deliberately, especially when his father is sending him to college at considerable sacrifice. The student refuses to admit to himself that the real reason for failing the course was to prove his father wrong — that is too shameful. But he must have some reason, for it is also threatening to self-esteem to realize that one has done something important without a reason. So the student combines repression and rationalizing, and invents some acceptable reasons — such as the course was too hard and he had too heavy a load — and sincerely believes them to be the real reasons.

There is much popular misconception about repression. It should not be confused with *suppression*. Repression is unconscious; suppression is conscious and deliberate. When you say to yourself, "I'll not think about that," you are suppressing the idea. Repression is not the equivalent of self-control. When you consciously acknowledge that you would like to punch your roommate in the nose but resist the impulse because you believe the action unwise, you are suppressing the impulse. The parent does not necessarily repress the child by punishing him for drawing pictures on the wallpaper. Parental control of the child leads to repression only when the parent makes the child feel unworthy or guilty for wanting to do things and thus unable to face his own feel-

ings or wishes without damage to self-esteem.

Repression is perhaps the most pernicious of all self-defensive maneuvers. In the first place, it tends to spread. Even though repressed, the threatening idea is still there — in the closet. To keep it out of consciousness, you must avoid contact with ideas which might force it into consciousness through association. You may, for example, be unable to remember names associated with the repressed idea. To keep the skeleton securely locked in the closet, you must also lock up things closely connected with it. This requires further self-deception and distortion of reality, which enlarge areas of self-defensiveness. When you find yourself using any self-defensive device without quite knowing what you are defending against, repression may be at the bottom of it.

In the second place, repression reduces the control of thinking over behavior. You cannot use in thinking the evidence you have hidden from yourself. The result is behavior which one can neither understand nor approve. Skeletons locked in the closet by repression seem not to lie quietly — the inner tension is still there. And tension that is not allowed expression seems to increase in pressure like steam in a boiler. When you repress the idea causing the tension you block or inhibit the normal expression or release of the pressure. So it builds up and breaks out somewhere else.

One of the strongest moral commandments in our culture is to love and honor our parents. It is introjected in childhood from parents and others. But even the best of parents block many of our desires. Parents can be particularly frustrating to college students when they try to retain control at a time when young people normally strive to become independent. It is as normal as breathing to dislike whatever frustrates us, but our introjected value system prohibits disliking parents. Instead of recognizing frankly that it is natural to have mixed feelings about one's parents and that one can love and honor them and still retain some hostility, many of us repress the hostility instead of controlling its expression.

It is also as natural as breathing to want to attack a cause of frustration. If we never experienced any such desire, we would be spineless masses of protoplasm, hopelessly unable to defend ourselves or to progress in the face of resistance. But we cannot openly and directly attack our parents. So the aggressive feelings build up pressure until they break out somewhere else. We can express the tension, without knowing why, by expressing hostility to someone who reminds us of the parent. Or the hostility can break out in some other way. If your parents are ambitious for you, you can attack them indirectly by failing your college courses without having the faintest suspicion of the real reason for your poor work. College counselors can testify to the frequency with which repressed hostility to parents seems to be at the bottom of poor college work.

Finally, repression is hard to deal with. Since it is unconscious, you cannot catch yourself at it. For that reason many people refuse to believe that there is any such thing. It is hard to correct unsatisfactory behavior without knowing the cause, and repression keeps the cause hidden. The essential step, therefore, is to induce yourself to admit the repressed idea to consciousness. Before the total effect can be removed, the skeleton must be taken out of the closet and decently buried.

8. Verbal Distortion

Accurate use of words is of great importance, for you react to the words rather than to what they describe. When your roommate removes your book from your desk you can symbolize his act in many ways: "He removed it," "He took it," "He absent-mindedly took it," "He stupidly took it," "He took it for meanness," "He borrowed it," or "He stole it." If you choose "He stole it" the word "steal," with all of its implications, is what you react to. If he merely borrowed the book, when you say "He stole it," you have distorted reality by the way you have symbolized it.

It is highly desirable, therefore, to strive for accuracy in the use of language. Accuracy of statement is particularly important in value judgments and generalizations. "All professors are dull" and "All professors are more interested in their subjects than I am" are two very different propositions. It is also helpful to cultivate the habit of avoiding the misuse of evaluative words especially in describing one's personal experience. "I was stupid" is more damaging than "I made a mistake." Describing an experience in neutral words may enable you to face at least part of the experience, whereas if it is stated in strongly emotional words, the whole experience may be repressed.

9. Projection

When you possess a trait too shameful to face, you can not only repress it but project it as well. That is, you can repress the recognition of it in yourself and transfer it to other people, as the movie projector transfers to the screen the image on the film. If you treat your parents shamefully and cannot face the fact, you can ease the pain by finding that other students treat their parents shamefully: they are ingrates, they deceive their parents, they spend tuition money on strong drink. The truth of your accusations does not matter — when you project you need little evidence.

Projection is a strong and dangerous form of psychological aspirin. In the first place, it breeds intolerance. People who recognize their own faults are usually tolerant of those same faults in others; but people who are projecting their faults are notoriously intolerant of those faults in others. In the second place, projection leads to aggression. When you repress a fault you cannot attack it in yourself, but you can release the tension by attacking others. Such behavior is typical of the fanatic who viciously attacks a certain sin wherever he finds it — and he finds it everywhere.

Projection is hard to deal with because it springs from unconscious motives. Perhaps the best practice is to think twice before criticizing others. You should also think twice before concluding that others are projecting. Not all people who criticize others or attack what they consider evil are projecting. They may have other and more acceptable reasons. Clues that indicate the probability, but not the certainty, of projection are: intolerance, unreasonableness, hatred, and extremely aggressive attack.

10. Evaluating Defense Mechanisms

Some use of defense mechanisms is inevitable. None of us can live so well that there are no painful elements in our lives. Mental suffering can be much harder to bear than physical suffering. Without defense mechanisms all of us would have difficulty maintaining a satisfactory self-concept. But, like powerful drugs, the less they are used, the better. No hard and fast rules for their use can be established, for whether a given device is helpful or harmful depends on a highly complex relationship between the individual and the situation. However, the two following criteria will prove useful.

1. *A defense mechanism can be considered helpful or harmful according to whether it promotes or interferes with long-run adaptation.* Consider the student who finds himself unprepared for approaching examinations. As he surveys the work yet to be done and the time left to do it in, he may become so disturbed that he is unable to concentrate. He may use a distraction device such as the

movies, thus escaping the situation and forgetting his problem temporarily. If he comes back to his studies the next day refreshed and able to concentrate, presumably the device helped him solve his problem. But if he finds it so pleasant to escape that he spends most of his time at the movies, presumably the distraction device is making the solution of his problem more difficult, if not impossible.

2. *The more self-deception involved in a defense mechanism, the more likely it is to be harmful.* Consider the student who convinces himself that being unprepared for approaching examinations is not his fault. By so doing he may succeed in easing the pain for the moment. But the problem is still there: the examinations must still be faced, and the penalties for failure are still the same. By deceiving himself about the causes of his failure, he has made it more difficult to remove those causes in the future. Or consider the student who uses rationalizing and perceptual defense to keep himself from realizing that he is not suited for the career toward which he aims. The longer he avoids the realization, the more time and effort he will waste pursuing the wrong course. Or consider the student who uses sophistical defense whenever he encounters evidence contrary to what he believes. He has in effect built a barrier against new learning. The more we blind ourselves to the realities of life, the more difficult it becomes to deal with them. While some self-deception is inevitable, it can be carried to the point where one becomes unable to deal with reality at all.

Any improvement you can make in your ability to think soundly will reduce your reliance on defense mechanisms. The more personal problems you solve, the fewer you will have left to hide from. The more accurate your frame of reference, the less you will need to distort or ignore reality in order to protect false propositions.

EXERCISE 29

1–15. *Indicate whether the following statements agree with the hypotheses presented in this book by writing in the blank T for true or F for false.*

1. Errors in induction, such as hasty generalization or *post hoc*, may distort one's frame of reference.   T

2. Most individuals would rather know reality than protect the personal point of view.   F

3. The individual is usually reluctant to recognize an error in his frame of reference.   T

4. Even though inaccurate, the frame of reference gives the individual a sense of security.   T

5. The individual is more likely to distort, misinterpret, or ignore evidence than see it as conflicting with his frame of reference.   T

6. People often hold to false and uncomplimentary beliefs about themselves rather than revise their frames of reference.   T

7. As a rule, we distort evidence to protect only those beliefs that are favorable to ourselves.   T

8. One's beliefs tend to interlock, so that evidence which threatens one threatens others.   T

9. The maladjusted individual whose personal point of view is distorted probably has too high an opinion of himself.   F   T

10. Evidence contrary to what one believes is likely to stimulate sound thinking.   F

11. The less sure of himself a person is, the less likely he is to distort evidence.   F   T

12. All people use mechanisms of self-defense to some extent.   T

13. Forgetting almost always indicates self-defense.   F

14. When, because of fear of being caught, a student resists the temptation to cheat on an examination, he has indulged in repression.   T   F

15. The correlation between the damage done by the use of defense mechanisms and the amount of self-deception involved is high-positive.   T

16–26. *Write in the blank the name of the defense mechanism probably used in each of the following instances.*

16. Axton, one of the candidates dropped from the football squad after the second week of practice, said: "I've changed my mind about football. It takes a lot of time that I can spend better."

rationalization
sour grapes

17. Bascot, who was also dropped from the squad, went home every week end when a football game was played on campus.

avoidance

18. Caseman, likewise dropped, explained: "I didn't have a fair chance. I've always played fullback, and the coaches made me try out at guard."

rationalization
blaming others

19. Dolton also had an explanation: "I had a run of bad luck. Every time the coaches looked at me I was playing against the first string. Also, I hurt my leg and couldn't go at full speed. I played single wing in high school and didn't have time to get used to the split T."

rationalization
excuse-making

20. After Egmont was dropped from the squad, he spent a lot of time watching practice and chatting with other spectators. Typical of his remarks were: "Crayton is not as good a quarterback as he thinks he is." "Coach is getting ready to play last year's style of football."

rationalization
criticizing

21. Dora Fayme has long been a Democrat. When a number of newspapers began to criticize the Democratic administration, she retorted: "Republicans control most of the newspapers. They put Democratic mistakes on the front page and leave out Republican mistakes."

avoidance
sophistical

22. Beatrice Ghait comes from a family which has voted Republican for two generations. When a news magazine began criticizing Republican policies, she stopped reading the politics section of that magazine.

avoidance

23 Cora Hepplewaite's fiancé was killed in an accident. Cora is now carrying the maximum academic load and participating in dramatics and sorority activities.

distraction
device

24. When Dora Ingerton's boy friend married his high school sweetheart, Dora fumed, "The fickle fool threw me aside like an old shoe."

verbal distortion

25. Evelyn Jelker was once engaged to three boys at the same time. When her roommate refused a second date with a student she had recently met, Evelyn accused her of being fickle.

projection

26. When Fran Kepple was a child, she knocked over a candle, starting a fire which killed her grandmother. When her sorority president asked her to light the candles at a formal dinner, Fran burst into tears. Even Fran was puzzled by her behavior.

repression

30 Emotions and Thinking

Have you ever, under the stress of excitement, made a decision so foolish that you wondered later how you made it? Have you ever become so panic-stricken while making a speech or taking an examination that you could not remember material you knew well? Have you ever become angry in an argument and made rash statements that your opponent turned against you? Have you ever been so excited or angry that you could not sleep at night, only to discover later that the situation was not nearly so serious as you had thought? If you have done any of these things — and you have probably done all of them — you have been in the grip of emotion.

Emotions are the product of the close linkage between mind and body. Emotions may be thought of as consisting of two interacting phases: (1) intensified feelings about a situation, and (2) a pattern of changes within the body for meeting the situation. Perhaps we can clarify this definition with an analogy. Suppose that in wartime a merchant vessel is cruising in waters not usually frequented by the enemy. The weather is clear and the sea calm. The situation is normal. Then the lookout sights an enemy submarine astern. The feelings of the officers on the bridge can now be said to be intensified, for

presumably they interpret the situation as a state of emergency. They issue certain orders to the crew. In response, the engineer opens the throttle to the maximum, the firemen increase the flow of fuel, the navigator plots a course for the nearest point of safety, and so on. These actions within the ship follow a pattern, designed to meet the emergency by flight.

Or suppose the ship encounters a severe storm. The feelings of the officers are again intensified, and certain orders are issued, but the pattern is different. In this situation, speed is not called for: the engineer closes the throttle to middle or low speed, and the firemen decrease the amount of fuel consumed. Meantime the crew is busy closing bulkheads and battening down hatches. Your own emotions operate in much the same way: when you encounter a threatening situation you experience intensified feelings, and your body, like the crew of the ship, prepares to meet the situation.

1. Physiological Changes in Emotions

The pattern of physiological changes and the degree to which they occur vary according to the intensity of feelings and the type of situation. When the feelings involved are mild, the physiological changes are correspondingly slight. In mild fear, for example, the changes include increases in pulse rate, blood pressure, and rate of breathing. In effect, the body has opened up the throttle a notch or two: the individual is "keyed up"; he has the energy to work longer and more intensely, and is thus better able to meet the situation that causes the fear.

When feelings are strong, however, the accompanying physiological changes are extensive. In strong anger or fear, the changes have the effect of preparing the body for a fight. Suppose that on a camping trip you are surrounded by a raging forest fire. Presumably you would interpret the situation as a critical threat to your life, calling for a supreme effort. You would experience strong fear; hence, automatically and instantly, your body would begin to put into effect a pattern of extensive changes.

Under strong fear the adrenal glands begin to release adrenalin into the bloodstream, stimulating the heart to greater activity and thereby increasing circulation. The circulatory system begins to redistribute the blood supply, taking it away from stomach and intestines, where it is not needed at the moment, and sending it to the big muscles of arms and legs, where it will be needed. The liver begins to pump glycogen into the bloodstream, providing a quick source of extra energy. Rate of breathing increases, and the spleen begins to dispatch large numbers of additional red corpuscles into the bloodstream, thus enabling the lungs to extract more oxygen from the air. Meanwhile, the pupils of the eyes dilate a little, admitting more light. The hair bristles. Blood-clotting hormones appear in the blood, providing some protection against bleeding to death in the event of a wound. The body is on a full emergency footing — the throttle is wide open. You are prepared either to run or to fight. But you are not prepared to think, for the redistribution of the blood supply tends to decrease the supply to the higher

brain centers and to leave them undernourished, so that they cease to function effectively.

In grief or despair, the pattern may be quite different. Suppose you have your life's savings invested in a small manufacturing plant. You have failed to renew your insurance, and the plant is destroyed by fire. At the moment you can see no way to start again. Presumably you would experience feelings of despair. The resulting physiological changes would probably have the effect of lowering energy rather than mobilizing it. They would include a reduction in pulse rate, blood pressure, breathing, appetite, and muscular strength. The general numbness of body and mind that results makes the blow easier to bear, and since you see nothing you can do at the moment anyway, no surge of energy is called for.

Thus the pattern of physiological changes varies according to the individual's feelings about the situation. You can often observe the phenomenon operating in athletic teams. When the football team suddenly finds itself a touchdown behind in an important game, the players may react with fear or anger, summon reserves of energy, and quickly drive for two touchdowns. But if, in their drive for the tying touchdown, a fumble or intercepted pass puts the opponent two touchdowns ahead, the players may react with despair and suddenly become tired.

2. Feelings

The feeling phase of an emotional reaction is essentially the individual's interpretation of the total situation, including conscious awareness of conditions within the body. Suppose you are walking on a dark street late at night and hear someone approaching rapidly behind you. Your first hypothesis might be that a thug intends to assault and rob you. You are unarmed, you do not know how to deal with thugs as the heroes in the movies do, and you are carrying a large amount of money. You evaluate the situation as threatening. Instantly your body puts into effect the pattern of response for fear. You cannot feel all these changes taking place: you cannot, for example, feel your adrenal glands secreting adrenalin or your liver pumping glycogen into your bloodstream. But you can feel the effect of the changes: for example, the removal of blood from your abdomen may feel like "butterflies" in your stomach. And you can certainly feel the surge of energy. Thus, your feelings include not only your interpretation of the situation but some awareness of your physiological state as well.

3. Effect of Emotions on Thinking

Emotions are an indispensable part of our adaptive machinery. Without them we would be like an engine without a throttle: we would be condemned to go through life at a constant pace, unable to adapt ourselves to changing conditions. Without emotions, we would presumably lack the drive for more than a bare existence. A man incapable of anger would be at the mercy of others. A man incapable of fear could not summon reserves of energy with which to meet emergencies. The energy provided by emotions has been responsible for man's finest achievements.

In some ways mild emotions promote sound thinking. The physiological changes have a tonic effect on the mind, increasing mental alertness and endurance. You can therefore study longer, harder, and more effectively when you are a bit afraid that you will not make the grades you want. You can usually make a better speech if you are a little worried, for then you put forth more effort. Under the influence of mild emotions you can probably write better poetry or better term papers, and you are more likely to take the trouble to put facts together into hypotheses.

On the other hand, even the mildest of emotions hamper sound thinking in any situation where objectivity is required, for they intensify self-defensive behavior. Whenever you feel threatened you react to defend yourself. You become more alert, not to the truth but to methods of defense, and you use vigorously whatever weapons seem necessary. Thus, if you have just failed a course, you had better not decide whether to major in that subject until your emotions have subsided, for you may make one of two errors. You may use self-deceptive mechanisms to minimize the threat and hide from yourself evidence that you should not major in the subject. Or you may rationalize your failure to study adequately by convincing yourself that the subject is dull and unimportant.

Strong emotions, especially fear and rage, are about as useful in thinking as lighted matches in a dynamite factory, for they interfere with effective thinking in at least five ways.

First, strong emotion *interferes with learning*. The student who is too fearful of academic failure finds himself frantically reading words but retaining little meaning. He is on an emergency footing, has plenty of energy, and can study for many hours without seeming to tire. But he is unable to learn.

Second, strong emotion tends to *inhibit recall*. The student who is too fearful that he will fail an examination is unable to recall much of what he actually knows.

Third, strong emotion *narrows perception*. When you are afraid, you tend to perceive only those elements in the situation that stimulate your fear. The soldier who is afraid tends to perceive the enemy everywhere, and he tends not to perceive the allied soldiers at his side or the strong bulwarks protecting him. When you are angry you tend to perceive only the elements in the situation that feed your anger. The student who is angry at his roommate tends to perceive all of the roommate's bad behavior and none of his good behavior.

Associated with the narrowing of perception is the inhibition of creative thinking, especially the formation of rival hypotheses. Critical thinking is also inhibited. You become prone to most of the fallacies of thinking, especially hasty generalization and neglected aspect. For example, when you feel threatened by another person you are likely to exaggerate a particular flaw in his character and then generalize about his whole character. Then you are tempted to extend this generalization to his brothers and even to his associates.

Fourth, whenever we interpret a situation as critical, we tend to become so concerned with the threat that we are *unable to concentrate on the problem.* We are like a person trying to work a difficult problem in calculus while suffering from a severe stomach ache. Many students are unable to concentrate while preparing for examinations because their thoughts continually drift toward the painful consequences of failure. One who suffers from stage fright is unable to concentrate on his speech because he is too busy worrying about what people will think about him; he stutters and stammers and forgets the words he planned to say. Thus, fear helps to bring about the very things we fear.

Finally, emotions tend to *reduce the control of behavior by thought.* Under strong emotional tension, we feel an urge to do something immediately, even if it is wrong, rather than wait until we can consider the situation in the light of accumulated experience. We tend to act first and think later — and later we are likely to have a lot of thinking to do to get out of the mess caused by our impulsive behavior.

One hypothesis developed to explain such behavior is that our responses in the face of threat are determined by the *old brain,* a relatively small area of tissue located near the end of the spinal column. Overlying this is a larger area, the *new brain,* which supposedly developed later in the evolution of the race. The old brain, operating below the conscious level, is the source of impulsive behavior. When we encounter a threatening situation, the natural impulse, originating in the old brain, is to do violence to the threatening object, or to flee from it. Thus, a yearning to do physical violence to the teacher who failed you in a course presumably originates in the old brain. But in a civilized society there are severe penalties for yielding to certain impulses. It is the function of the new brain to restrain these impulses and to substitute another kind of reaction that will be more suitable in the long run. When you restrain your impulse to do physical or verbal violence to the teacher because you realize it would not pay, the decision was made by the new brain. But the control of the new brain over the impulses originating in the old brain is only partial. Soldiers sometimes flee in battle despite their training; students sometimes attack their teachers despite the known consequences; we sometimes make verbal attacks on those we would be afraid to attack physically, even though we know that the verbal attacks are unwise in the long run. Under the influence of emotion, our thinking is likely to be primitive in quality at the very time when the highest grade of effective thinking is needed.

Living as we do in a highly complex society, the emergency situations we face — and we must face them in abundance — usually threaten self-esteem rather than physical safety. Instead of roaring lions we face examinations, the uncertainties of military service, the difficulties of achieving satisfactory social position. It makes no difference to the body whether the threat is an examination or a roaring lion; as long as the situation is interpreted as a serious threat, the body puts into effect its inherited pattern of adjustment — it prepares for physical rather than mental action. But examinations require thinking — not bristling hair, dilated pupils, or high blood pressure. And the net effect of these physiological changes is to make effective thinking much more difficult, if not impossible. Thus we are frequently unable to think clearly at the very time when we most need to do so.

4. Anxiety

One of the most troublesome forms of emotion is anxiety, *i.e.*, the anticipation that needs will not be satisfied in the future. Anxiety is like fear in that the accompanying physiological changes prepare for action. It differs from fear in two respects. Fear is a reaction to one's interpretation of the present situation, whereas anxiety is a reaction to one's interpretation of the future. Furthermore, fear tends to subside when the stimulus has been removed, whereas anxiety is a persisting state of tension.

Within limits, anxiety, like fear, promotes adaptation. When we find ourselves in a difficult situation, we experience anxiety that we will encounter it again. Anxiety is an unpleasant state, and we will go to great lengths to get rid of it. Hence we are driven to learn how to avoid difficulties in the future, and to take measures for dealing with anticipated emergencies before they occur. Thus the student who is anxious enough about his final examinations may study throughout the semester to prepare for the anticipated emergency.

Like other forms of emotion, however, anxiety is harmful when excessive. If you worry about events in the future that usually fail to come about or prove less serious than you anticipated, or if you worry in general about the future without knowing why or without sufficient reason, your anxiety is probably excessive and is doing you more harm than good.

While a "healthy" anxiety promotes adaptation by driving us to make reasonable preparations for the future, an intense degree of anxiety actually interferes with adaptation. The overanxious person is so concerned with relieving the pain of anxiety that he tends to deal with the anxiety itself rather than with its cause. Like the individual who habitually takes aspirin to ease physical pain instead of consulting a doctor, the overanxious person resorts to psychological aspirin instead of constructive action. The student who is reasonably anxious about his examinations may study conscientiously all semester. But the student who is overanxious finds his anxiety so unbearable that he seeks escape through numerous distraction devices. As the examination period approaches and his anxiety mounts, he increases the dosage of psychological aspirin. By now the emotional tension is so acute that he is unable to study even when he tries. He reads his assignments frantically, but he remembers little. And the more he reads the more he realizes how much he does not know. In the end he may seek escape by withdrawing from college or by going to the infirmary with a psychosomatic illness. Excessive anxiety is at the bottom of many psychosomatic illnesses, for it keeps its victim in a chronic state of emotional tension.

5. Emotions and Health

There is another difficulty with emotions. Only seconds are required to put the physiological changes into effect, but hours, days, or weeks may be required to restore the body economy to normal. Usually we do not return to normal until the disturbing situation has been successfully dealt with and the excess energy has been expended. Since most situations we face do not require the expenditure of great amounts of energy, we continue in a state of tension, like the steam locomotive that arrives at its destination with more steam pressure than it needs: we are all steamed up with no place to go. But, unlike the locomotive, we have no handy valve that can be opened to release the extra pressure. The unrelieved tension tends to keep the pressure up, or it may even increase it. The effects are as damaging to the body as is constant overfiring of a furnace. When severe emotional tensions are prolonged or intense enough, they reach the disruptive stage, resulting in serious impairment of both physical and mental functions.

Psychosomatic medicine has traced a number of physical as well as mental ailments to the emotional relationship between body and mind. Emotional disturbance is suspected of causing or contributing to such ailments as heart trouble, asthma and allergies, skin eruptions, stomach ulcers, high blood pressure, migraine headaches, backaches, diabetes, and disorders of the colon. The body-mind relationship works the other way, too. Disturbances of the endocrine glands, such as toxic goiter, seem to heighten emotional tension.

Thus emotions are a mixed blessing. They have been responsible for many of man's finest achievements but they have also been responsible for some of his greatest follies, including wars.

6. Controlling Emotions

Learning to control your emotions is essential to achieving your maximum potential, just as learning to use the accelerator is essential to becoming a good driver. There will never be a better time to learn than now, for the older you are the more difficult it is to acquire emotional control. Furthermore, in this age of intense competitive pressure on college students, you will have ample opportunity to practice.

Control does not mean elimination of emotions. There are times when you should run or fight. If you were not afraid or angry in some situations, your frame of reference would be giving you a false picture. Emotional control means becoming emotional in the right amount, in the right way, at the right time. The following procedures will help you achieve emotional control.

1. *Recognizing the symptoms.* Perhaps the first step in controlling emotions is to recognize the symptoms of excessive emotions. The optimum tension level varies with the person and with the situation. When the situation calls for vigorous or prolonged physical action the optimum level is relatively high. The optimum tension level for studying and decision making is relatively low. While there is considerable variation among individuals, the following symptoms usually indicate a tension level that is excessive for studying or decision making: insomnia, sweaty palms, lack of concentration, a feeling that you must constantly hurry.

2. *Expending energy.* When your tension level is high you may find yourself unable to think rationally about a situation because your higher brain centers are being starved by the redistribution of your blood supply. Until you can use up some of the excess energy generated, your tension level may stay too high for effective thinking. In such a situation the remedy is to burn up some of the energy with relaxing forms of exercise. For example, if you find yourself so keyed up that you cannot study, a game of tennis, or a swim, or a long walk may reduce your tension level sufficiently to enable you to study.

3. *Avoiding tension-producing stimuli.* When you find your emotional level too high, a distraction device may prove helpful. For example, if you are fearful of examinations, it may be helpful to avoid other students who are fearful of examinations, for they may easily communicate their fear to you and thereby reinforce yours. When your tension level is too high, it is unwise to engage unnecessarily in highly competitive activities. For example, a basketball player who is already too keyed up for a game should avoid playing poker for high stakes.

4. *Taking constructive action.* Constructive action in response to a threatening situation will usually reduce your tension level. You will often find yourself in situations in which you cannot possibly do every-

thing you should do on time. The constructive procedure is to do the most important things first. In this way you can use the energy generated by your emotions to deal with the threatening situation. Consider the student who is unprepared for an examination he must take within a day or two. If at this late hour he tries to learn all the minutiae the examination might cover, every topic he tries to learn becomes a tension-producing stimulus and his tension level rises higher and higher. A more constructive approach to the problem would be to study the main topics first.

5. *Using neutral language.* We have already noted that we react to situations in terms of the words we use to describe them. Evaluative words have in themselves the power to arouse the same emotions as the situations they describe. Poets and dramatists, as well as advertisers and propagandists, use evaluative words to stir our emotions.

Words often acquire the power to stir emotions quite apart from their standard evaluative meaning. Suppose you have a teacher whom you dislike intensely. And suppose this teacher often addresses you as "friend" and then scolds or insults you. Through this experience the word "friend" could acquire the power to stir your anger even in quite different contexts. When a real friend addresses you as "friend," you might find yourself irritated even though you know what your friend means. Thus the same word may have quite different emotional meanings for different people. To avoid reacting emotionally to a situation, you should cultivate the habit of thinking about the situation in terms of words that have neutral meanings for you.

6. *Reinterpreting the situation.* While all these procedures can help to bring your emotions within desirable levels, they do not actually control the emotions themselves. They do not keep you from becoming angry or afraid. And you cannot control these feelings by resolving not to have them. You can

no more keep yourself from becoming emotional when you feel threatened than you can keep your knee from jerking when the doctor taps the right spot, for both reactions are involuntary. Nor, as we have noted, can you restore your body to normal merely by an act of will. Your adrenal glands will continue to pump adrenalin into your blood as long as you feel threatened.

The secret of real emotional control lies in your interpretation of the threatening situation. For you react to the situation not as it is but as you interpret it. Thus the emotional reactions of different individuals may be quite different in what appears to be the same situation. Suddenly encountering a rattlesnake in the woods may cause a strong fear reaction in a city dweller and hardly any reaction at all in a professional snake handler. One student may interpret an approaching examination as a grave threat and experience an acute fear reaction, while another student may interpret the same examination as an opportunity to display his achievement and experience only feelings of pleasure. We may react as strongly to an insult as to a blow in the face. Or, we may interpret a threat to self-concept, value system, or frame of reference as seriously as real danger to life. When you interpret a situation as an emergency, the glands go to work automatically. Their job is not to reason why, but to open the valves. As Montaigne said, "A man is hurt not so much by what happens, as by his opinion of what happens."

When you find your emotional reaction inappropriate or excessive, a reinterpretation of the situation is called for. Since our interpretations of situations are actually hypotheses, the procedure for reinterpreting most situations has already been described in Chapters 5 and 6. When you are reinterpreting a situation for the purpose of reducing emotional tension, a special attempt should be made to form nonthreatening hypotheses.

Suppose you find yourself in this situation.

When you entered college, your parents brought you to the campus, selected your room and your roommates, told you what courses to study, paid your fees for the semester, gave you twenty-five dollars for pocket money, and instructed you to write for more when needed. Your grades for the first semester were low. Now, at the beginning of the second semester, your parents hand you a check for your expenses for the semester, tell you that you will receive no more, let you get back to the campus by yourself, show no interest in what courses you will take or where you room, and make no comment about your low grades.

You might, as many students would, conclude that your parents are angry because you made low grades. But these facts could be explained by three other hypotheses: (1) your parents are too occupied with other matters to give you their usual attention; (2) they are disappointed with your grades and believe you will do better if left on your own; (3) your parents now have enough confidence in you to let you manage your own life. The habit of setting up rival hypotheses is a good one to cultivate, especially in interpreting personal matters. You will often discover that you have interpreted a situation inaccurately, and that your fear or anger was not justified.

7. *Avoiding rash decisions.* Excessive emotions tend not only to make us exaggerate the threat in a situation but also to make rash decisions. When you find that your emotional level is high, it is advisable to postpone making important decisions until your emotions have subsided or until you must act to avoid decision by indecision. When you must make a decision before your emotions have subsided, you should carefully follow the procedures for forming and testing proposals for action discussed in Chapter 13. Since the actions you may take under the influence of emotions are likely to be extreme, you should try to find proposals for action that will not be disastrous if your interpretation of the situation proves wrong. You should also keep in mind the fact that emotions tend to make you forget the long-term value premises experience has taught you. For example, when someone has hurt you, your anger may make you value striking back. Later, when your anger has subsided, you may realize that you have followed the wrong value premise.

If the measures just described fail to keep your emotions within desirable levels, the trouble may be due to false propositions in your personal point of view that cause you to interpret your situation as more threatening than it really is. In subsequent chapters we shall discuss methods of identifying and correcting these false propositions.

EXERCISE 30

1–27. *Indicate whether the following statements agree with the hypotheses presented in this book by writing in the blank T if true or F if false.*

1. It might be appropriately said that in emotional states the body impedes effective thinking.   T

2. The physiological changes occurring with emotions usually follow the same pattern and reach about the same degree.   F

3. The physiological changes occurring with strong anger include an increase in blood supply to the higher brain centers.   F

4. The feeling phase of emotions includes some awareness of bodily conditions.   T

5. How one feels about a situation may depend more on his interpretation of it than on the situation itself.   T

6. Threats to self-esteem bring about the same kind of physiological reaction as physical threats.   T

7. Emotions have no beneficial effects on thinking.   F

8. Even the mildest emotions can interfere with objectivity.   T

9. Fear and rage interfere with sound thinking by fixing attention on the threat rather than the remedy.   T

10. Strong emotions tend to transfer the control of behavior to primitive brain centers.   T

11. Under the influence of strong emotion, one is more likely to invent rival hypotheses.   F

12. Emotions tend to make one more susceptible to the fallacy of oversimplification.   T

13. The impulse to take aggressive action against a frustrating object probably originates in the old brain.   T

14. In our society we probably face more threats to self-esteem than to physical safety.   T

15. We are frequently unable to think clearly at the very time we most need to be able to do so.   T

16. It usually takes longer to stir up emotions than for the body economy to return to normal.   F

17. Strong emotions broaden the field of perception.   F

18. A strong resolution not to have emotions is an effective means of controlling them. *F*

19. The secret of effective control over emotion lies in your interpretation of the situation. *T*

20. Emotions that are excessive for the circumstances may indicate errors in one's frame of reference. *T*

21. The best indication of adequate emotional control is the absence of emotions. *F*

22. Excessive emotion often indicates failure to set up rival hypotheses. *T*

23. A recommended method of controlling emotions is to make a more favorable interpretation of the threatening situation. *T*

24. Anxiety is a fear reaction to past events. *F*

25. The emotional tensions of anxiety usually disappear as soon as the threatening situation has passed. *F*

26. The probable cause of excessive anxiety is faulty propositions in one's personal point of view. *T*

27. Anxiety tends to make one exaggerate the significance of favorable evidence. *F*

28–30. *Write your answers to the following questions in the space provided.*

28. You and your neighbor have a common lawn and no fence between your houses. Because you have been ill, you have neglected to mow your side of the lawn, and the grass has grown quite high. Finally your neighbor mows both your side and his. If you conclude that he has tired of seeing your ugly lawn and has meddled in your business, what defense mechanism have you possibly used?

Sophistical defense
rash decision (narrow perception)

29. Write another hypothesis to explain your neighbor's behavior.

doing it out of kindness because
you were sick

30. Your parents have always pushed you to make high grades. No matter how hard you studied, your grades never seemed good enough to satisfy them. Now you are trying to decide whether to go into business or study medicine. To get into medical school you must pass a medical aptitude test. List the emotional influences on your thinking which you should guard against in making your decision.

anxiety tension,

31 Hidden Propositions

1. *Expert Help*
2. *Self-Help*
3. *Insecurity*
4. *Inferiority Feelings*
5. *Guilt Feelings*

In Chapter 28 we developed the hypothesis that the decisions we make are largely a function of the personal point of view. In Chapter 29 we developed two more hypotheses: that errors creep into the personal point of view and that we tend to distort the evidence available to us in order to make it conform to these errors. In Chapter 30 we added the hypothesis that these errors can cause excessive and inappropriate emotion. None of us reaches college age without having adopted at least a few false propositions. Even if all our propositions were true at the time we adopted them, some would now be false, for the world is constantly changing.

Unless we make some effort to correct these errors a vicious cycle may result. Distortions in the personal point of view often lead to bad decisions, which in turn may lead to emotional disturbances. These disturbances may then lead to intensified self-defensive thinking, which may lead to more distortion in the personal point of view, and so on. If one permits this vicious cycle to continue, he may find himself unable to cope with the real world. No matter how valid his reasoning may be, his efforts to cope with the world are doomed to failure because his evidence is false. He is like a mariner trying to guide himself to a port that does not exist by a compass that does not work. It is now appropriate to examine more closely the manner in which these errors cause bad decisions and to suggest procedures by which the offending errors can be identified and corrected.

In trying to identify these errors it is helpful to remember that many of the propositions that influence decisions are submerged like icebergs. The submerged propositions may include value premises, propositions making up the self-concept, and propositions in the frame of reference used in interpreting the situation. Some of these propositions do not reach the conscious level merely because we do not take the time to recall them. Self-defense may keep others below the conscious level.

1. Expert Help

When your decisions seem to be consistently bad and when you find yourself feeling instead of thinking about your personal problems, expert help in identifying the offending propositions can be very useful. You probably have a professional counselor on your own campus, in the office of the dean, in the department of psychology, or at the infirmary. His services are probably free, and the sooner you see him the better.

Many people refuse to take their personal problems to an expert because of false shame. They will brag about the length of the surgeon's incision, but they would rather be caught robbing a bank than be seen entering the office of an expert on psychological problems. Fortunately, that attitude is changing rapidly. The notion that any stigma is attached to professional consultation about personal problems is becoming as outmoded as the belief that illness can be cured with charms. Many modern students think no more of seeking expert help with personal problems than they would of going to a doctor for treatment of an infection. They realize that modern living can be exceedingly complex, and that they are too close to their own problems and too involved emotionally to see them objectively.

The difficulty in solving your own problems is in seeing all the relevant evidence. While methods differ according to the school of thought to which the counselor belongs, most professional counselors have one practime in common — they help you solve your problem; they do not solve it for you. They do not give you a lecture about your false beliefs; instead, they help you put all the relevant propositions on the table, where you can examine them.

While it is not our purpose to advocate any particular view about counseling, one school of thought is especially worth examining because it advocates an objectivity and tolerance that you can apply yourself in bringing submerged feelings to the surface. As Carl Rogers describes this school of thought, the counselor operates from the basic premise that you are capable of making your own decisions. He treats you as an equal. He makes no attempt to reform you; he accepts you as you are, without blame or praise. He lets you tell him what you will. He has only one purpose: to give you complete and sympathetic understanding, to think about you and your problems as you do. He tries to put himself into your frame of reference, to see you as you see yourself.

He does this by acting as a sensitive and accurate sounding board for what you say. When you make a statement, he rephrases it for you in accurate, matter-of-fact language without a trace of criticism, and in a friendly tone of voice. When you hear him state your value judgments, hypotheses, and other propositions, you can more easily see the inaccuracies in them.

Advocates of this method of counseling believe the secret of its effectiveness lies in the atmosphere of the interview. You probably have friends or teachers to whom you feel you can talk freely on some subjects because they will understand you, but you hesitate to discuss other subjects because you fear they will not understand, or will have a personal reason for wanting you to think in some particular way. But the counselor tries to understand you in *all* respects, to accept you just as you are, and to exclude his own interests. When you discover this, you become less self-defensive. You gradually strip away, layer by layer, your areas of self-deception, so that you can admit the relevant evidence to consciousness and correct the errors in it.

2. Self-Help

You would be wise to take important problems to a counselor. But you can borrow a leaf from the counselor's book and combine it with the procedures of effective thinking to help yourself.

It is worse than useless to persuade yourself that you have no feelings about your problem and can view it objectively. Furthermore, if you refuse to consider your feelings in making a decision, you can make grievous errors. Suppose you are trying to decide whether to take a new job. You like the job you have, and you have an emotional attachment to the community in which you live. The new job will take you to a different kind of community far away and will involve work you do not like, but it offers a better salary and better prospects for advancement. If you ignore your feelings about job and community, you may spend the rest of your life regretting your decision. Your feelings are relevant evidence.

The leaf to borrow from the counselor's book is to look at your feelings objectively, as he tries to. Suppose your problem is getting along with your roommate. He gives you too much advice, which you resent. But you like him, and you feel that it is wrong to resent his advice. You are having feelings about your feelings. These feelings about your feelings of resentment make it as hard to discuss the matter frankly with yourself as with another person who you think would disapprove of your resentment. But if you can accept these feelings as the counselor does, without being critical of them, you are well on the road to solving the problem. Using the procedures of effective thinking will help provide the necessary atmosphere. They will not be friendly and sympathetic like the counselor, but neither will they bite.

3. Insecurity

If, because of your previous behavior and academic record, you were being permitted to stay in college on strict probationary terms, you would have good reason for feeling uncertain about your position in college. Many people, however, suffer from feelings of uncertainty out of proportion to the situation or with no basis in fact. There are students, for example, who feel uncertain of themselves academically even though they are meeting the standards of Phi Beta Kappa. These students are suffering from insecurity, which we may define as an unduly pessimistic personal point of view. Because of this pessimism the insecure person is predisposed to be more sensitive to potential threats and to interpret situations as more threatening than they are. Thus he is an easy prey to anxiety. He is unduly fearful that he will lose his job and be unable to sustain himself, or that he will lose the affection or approval of those whose affec-

tion or approval is important to him, or that he will lose his health, and so forth. The insecurity may be limited to one area of need, or it may spread to all.

Insecurity can be a major problem. Since he is uncertain of himself and of others, the insecure person is more prone to self-defensive thinking and behavior than the secure person. He tends to be unwilling to adopt a course of action unless it has a very high probability of success. He is intolerant of criticism. He takes defeat more seriously than he should. He is likely to be troubled by anxiety, guilt feelings, and feelings of inferiority. When his fears are aroused they may reach high intensity with little cause. His fear reactions may take either of the basic forms: anger and aggression toward the threat, or flight from it. Thus, when you make a mild objection to some idea he has proposed, he may snap at you in angry rebuttal, or he may break off the conversation and leave the room. The insecure person may reject an exciting but uncertain vocation, in which he might have been a brilliant success, for a dull but secure one, in which he will never be happy. If he feels insecure about his college work, he may study into the late hours of the night but fail to accomplish much because he has worked himself into an emotional lather. Or he may give up and stop studying altogether. Chronic emotional tension hampers thinking in all areas.

Should you find yourself suffering from insecurity — and *suffering* is the appropriate word — the first step is to find the false propositions in your personal point of view. Insecurity may originate in some severe emotional shock. It may be intensified, if not caused, by the discovery that the premises by which you have guided your life no longer work. Students from small communities or rural areas often feel insecure in the strange new world of a large college.

The most probable cause, however, is the way you were reared as a child. If your parents, especially your mother, made you feel unloved, or were harsh or cruel, or made you feel that your work was never good enough, or disciplined you by withholding affection, or made you feel that they would withdraw their affection if you did not live up to their standards, or were inconsistent in their treatment of you so that you were unable to learn how to please them, or were themselves insecure or in conflict, especially if they used you as a pawn in their intramural warfare, you would be unusual if you did not adopt pessimistic generalizations about getting and keeping the affection of those most important to you. If when you were a child your parents were hard pressed to pay the rent, you may feel economically insecure no matter how much money you have in the bank. Many students feel insecure in their studies, especially in tests and examinations, because in the past they have found it very difficult, if not impossible, to meet the standards set for them by parents or teachers.

Finding the cause is itself an aid in overcoming insecurity. When you find the cause you will be able to see that it is a hasty generalization, based on instances that are too few and no longer representative of your life as a whole.

The rest of the remedy is to correct the generalization. Complete correction will be difficult, but any progress you can make will increase your happiness. A number of procedures should prove helpful. The first is to make a realistic appraisal of what you can expect from the world. You can hardly feel secure if you set your standards of security too high. You are hardly justified in expecting everyone to love you exclusively, or in believing that you can succeed in all you attempt, or that you can keep everything in your present situation exactly as it is.

Your appraisal of what to expect from the world will be more accurate if you deepen and broaden your understanding of other people. When you understand them, their behavior will seem less inconsistent and capricious; being better able to predict their behavior, you will be more able to deal with them successfully. By learning what to expect of other people, you will be less likely to make impossible demands of them and to experience frustration when these demands are not met.

Another procedure for overcoming insecurity is consciously and consistently to cultivate the habit of setting up rival and less threatening hypotheses for situations which seem to intensify your feelings of insecurity. For example, if the she of your dreams frowns when you ask her for a date, do not jump immediately to the conclusion that she does not like you. Set up at least three rival hypotheses which are less pessimistic, such as (1) she experienced a sudden pain, (2) she has a conflict between having a date with you and doing some much-needed studying, (3) she is now regretting that she has made another date.

4. Inferiority Feelings

When you make a failing grade in French, you are justified in feeling incompetent as a student of French. Knowing that there are some things you cannot do very well is a necessary part of honest self-appraisal. But the correlation between actual incompetence and feelings of incompetence is quite low. Some of our ablest people feel incompetent to cope with life. They are suffering from inferiority feelings, which amount to a chronically unsatisfactory self-concept.

The effects of inferiority feelings on thinking and behavior are manifold. The person so afflicted is likely to be unduly afraid of failure. Hence he approaches examinations and other tests of ability with foreboding. He uses the mechanisms of self-deception, especially the several varieties of rationalizing, to protect his battered self-concept. And, as we have noted, he may even use these mechanisms to preserve his view of himself as incompetent. He seems to lack ambition, whereas the truth is that his ambitions are excessive. He makes no effort because he is afraid of failure. As long as he does not try, he has an alibi — he could have done it if he had tried. He is sensitive to criticism; his self-concept is so battered that he can stand no further damage to it. Because of jealousy, he is prone to dislike those who seem superior. He may make excessive and foolish attempts to demonstrate his own superiority and thus may appear to think too highly of himself, whereas in reality he thinks too little of himself. He may, like James Thurber's Walter Mitty, withdraw from reality and live in a world of dreams in which he is the all-conquering hero. Or he may seek to establish his superiority by excessive aggression against others. The Napoleons and Hitlers of the world suffer from feelings of inferiority.

Since inferiority is essentially a faulty generalization about oneself, the first step in dealing with it, as with insecurity, is to search out the cause so that you can correct the generalization. Childhood is a good place to look. If your parents punished you in such a way as to make you feel unworthy of their love, or pushed you to achieve goals which were beyond your capacity, or compared you unfavorably with your brothers or sisters, you are likely to suffer the pangs of inferiority feelings. If your parents overprotected you by giving you everything you needed without effort on your part, solving all your problems, and shielding you from trouble, you may be suffering from inferiority feelings now because you failed to gain the experience in running your own life that you now need in your new environment. When you have found the apparent cause of your feelings of inferiority, you can begin the process of improving your self-concept. But do not expect to finish the job in a day.

Your next step is to make a careful appraisal of your own assets and liabilities. The person suffering from inferiority tends to discount evidence of success and dwell on evidence of failure, especially recent evidence. Thus the student who has a good academic average may suffer out of all pro-

portion because of one poor grade, ignoring the fact that his average is still good. The problem, therefore, is to make a new generalization about yourself which takes into account *all* the evidence.

Another necessary step is to revise your goals to make them consistent with your abilities. The person suffering from inferiority feelings tends to set his goals impossibly high, on the theory that only by great achievement can he disprove his inferiority. He thereby condemns himself to certain failure and a new scar on his already battered self-concept. A counselor can help you with this step. By giving you a battery of tests, and making a thorough study of your record, he can give you a more objective appraisal of your abilities than you can give yourself. Striving to achieve a goal for which you lack the ability is an almost certain way of intensifying inferiority feelings. A more modest goal is much to be preferred.

The tonic the person suffering from inferiority most needs is a good dose of success. Instead of working hard for success, however, he is likely to sit and dream of the day, always in the future, when he will dazzle the world with brilliant achievement. But the day never arrives, for brilliant achievements are usually built of countless little achievements made over a long period of time. No matter how hard you try you are unlikely to change from a wallflower to a social daisy in one easy step, but if you work at it steadily, taking small steps one at a time, the probability is high that you will succeed. You are most unlikely to succeed in learning the new language of biology in a brief period of superhuman effort just before the examination; your chances of success are much better if you work at it every day during the semester. The tonic you need, therefore, is to set for yourself small, modest goals for each day and to achieve them. By so doing you will gradually build up a balance of success. You will also be reducing your emotional tension by using your energy in constructive effort.

5. Guilt Feelings

If by careless driving you caused injury or death to others, you presumably would suffer guilt feelings, for you would have violated a section of your moral code. The unpleasant guilt feelings are a form of punishment inflicted by your conscience.

As long as the punishment fits the crime, guilt feelings are indispensable to society. No amount of laws and policemen would suffice to hold society together were it not for the fact that individuals suffer from guilt feelings when they violate their codes, and anticipate more guilt feelings when they are tempted to violate them again. Within limits, guilt feelings also aid adaptation. The person who had no moral code or guilt feelings would have a high probability of spending most of his life in jail. But the punishment does not always fit the crime. As innumerable clergymen and counselors have observed, those who suffer most from guilt feelings are frequently the least guilty. The correlation between guilt feelings and real guilt is low, if not actually negative.

When guilt feelings are excessive, as they often are, they tend to prevent rather than promote adaptation. Feelings of guilt are extremely painful, for they imply a belief that one is unworthy of love and respect. The afflicted person will go to great lengths to rid himself of the pain. In extreme cases he may spend a lifetime trying to atone for a relatively minor offense. Or he may seek to reduce the guilt by self-punishment, such as denying himself certain pleasures and comforts. Or, as some psychologists believe, he may unconsciously court accidents as a means of self-punishment. Or he may seek to excuse himself from blame by the use of mechanisms of self-deception. If he cannot rid himself of the pain in any other way, he may repress the knowledge of guilt. But then he has only driven the trouble underground; he continues to feel guilty, but he does not know why. A person afflicted with excessive guilt feelings tends to do nothing constructive about the situation, partly because he is too occupied with the pain to think about constructive action, and partly because he is afraid to do anything for fear he will make another mistake and have added reason for guilt. Thus he builds up a state of emotional tension without taking action that would utilize the accumulated energy and help solve the problem. When combined with feelings of inferiority, as is frequent, guilt feelings constitute a very difficult problem.

When you make a mistake for which you feel guilty, it is important to face the issue squarely and deal with it as soon as possible. Otherwise, you will suffer unnecessarily, and you may take some unwise action or resort to self-deception. If your mistake has injured someone, you can relieve your feeling of guilt by making appropriate reparation. If the circumstances do not permit direct reparation to the person injured, you can relieve the pain by doing a good turn for someone else. Or you can use the mistake as a lesson to help you avoid future mistakes. Once you have faced the issue squarely and taken appropriate action, you can afford to forget the whole thing.

If you suffer from excessive guilt feelings, the trouble may be that one or more major premises in your value system are impossible to live up to. Procedures for examining and refining your value system are discussed in Chapter 35.

Suggested Supplementary Reading

Carl R. Rogers, *On Becoming a Person* (Boston: Houghton Mifflin Company, 1961).

EXERCISE 31A

Indicate whether the following statements agree with the hypotheses presented in this book by writing in the blank T if true or F if false.

1. Few college students do not base decisions on false propositions. _____

2. If one makes no effort to identify and correct his false beliefs, a vicious cycle may result. _____

3. We are aware of most of the evidence on which we base decisions. _____

4. Expert help is usually useless in identifying and correcting false beliefs. _____

5. One of the functions of a professional counselor is to help you see all of the relevant evidence. _____

6. Logical techniques are of relatively little use in solving personal problems. _____

7. A person who can reason objectively and skillfully about problems outside himself is usually able to do so about his personal problems. _____

8. The chief difficulty in solving personal problems is getting yourself to see all the relevant evidence. _____

9. Most professional counselors give you full instructions on how to solve your personal problems. _____

10. Most professional counselors operate on the theory that you are incapable of solving your own problems. _____

11. In trying to solve personal problems it is desirable to recognize frankly your own feelings and accept them as relevant evidence. _____

12. Insecurity is usually the result of a realistic appraisal of one's total situation. _____

13. The characteristics of an insecure person usually include: excessive self-defensive thinking, intolerance of criticism, and a readiness to undertake any course of action which has some chance of success. _____

14. A common cause of insecurity is conflict between parents. _____

15. A recommended remedy for insecurity is the revision of basic propositions in the personal point of view. _____

16. In dealing with insecurity it is useless to try to set up rival hypotheses that are less threatening, for this is likely to involve further self-deception. _____

17. The correlation between real inferiority and feelings of inferiority is usually low. _____

18. The ambitions of a person suffering from feelings of inferiority are usually too modest. _____

19. Feelings of inferiority may lead either to aggressive behavior or to withdrawal from a threatening situation. _____

20. The causes of inferiority feelings are usually found in childhood experience. _____

21. If you are suffering from inferiority feelings you should avoid any realistic appraisal of your abilities, lest you find real reason for feeling inferior. _____

22. Persons who suffer from inferiority feelings tend to discount evidence of their own success and exaggerate evidence of their own failures. _____

23. A necessary step in dealing with feelings of inferiority is to revise your goals to make them consistent with your abilities. _____

24. The correlation between the intensity of guilt feelings and the real degree of guilt is high. _____

25. A faulty value judgment may cause excessive guilt feelings. _____

EXERCISE 31B

Answer each question before reading beyond it. Use all the evidence presented up to and in the question, but do not use evidence presented in later questions.

You teach freshman English at Wysacki University. You have noticed that the themes turned in by Jack Cratchit are unusually poor. Not knowing that Cratchit was out for football, you are surprised when he starts at quarterback in the first freshman game of the season. Cratchit receives the kickoff. Trying to dodge a tackler, he runs toward his own goal, and is tackled on the ten-yard line. On the first play from scrimmage he fumbles and is downed on the five. Then he throws a wild pass which is almost intercepted. On the next play he calls for a quarterback sneak, which gains three yards. At that point the coach takes Cratchit out of the game.

1. Rate the hypothesis that Cratchit's intelligence is low. _____

The following Monday afternoon you drop by the practice field and find Cratchit working out at tackle. When you comment to the coach, he replies, "I can't understand it. He's the smartest quarterback prospect we've had in a long time." The next morning you look up Cratchit's entrance record. He barely graduated from high school, but his scores on intelligence tests place him only slightly below the genius class.

2. Rate the hypothesis that Cratchit's intelligence is low. _____

3. Write a rival hypothesis to explain Cratchit's poor performance, in high school, in English, and in football.

_____

The following week your class is making speeches. When you call on Cratchit, he mumbles that he is unprepared. You invite him to come to your office for a conference. When he explains that he simply does not know anything to make a speech about, you shift the conversation to football. In response to a question, he gives you a brilliant exposition of the respective advantages of the "T" and the "Split T" systems of football. After some urging he agrees to make a speech about football at the next class. He cuts the next class. The following day you go to the second freshman game. Cratchit plays brilliantly at tackle.

4. List the antecedents common to all instances of poor performance by Cratchit.

_____

5. Rate the hypothesis that Cratchit's poor performances are due to laziness. _____

6. Write a rival hypothesis to explain why Cratchit did well at tackle but not at quarterback or in school work.

_____

When Cratchit cuts class again on Monday you send for him. He explains that he cut class because he could not make a speech.

7. What defense mechanism has he used? _____

When you ask Cratchit why he played so much better at tackle than at quarterback, he replies, "It was the wool jersey I was wearing. Wool makes me itch and gives me the willies. They gave me a nylon jersey when I played tackle."

8. What fallacy has he apparently committed? _____

You explain to Cratchit that he has fine prospects as a student and that you would like to help him improve. He replies, "It's no use, Prof. I just don't like to study."

9. Write the faulty generalization Cratchit seems to believe about himself.

_____

You ask Cratchit about his ambitions. He replies, "I'd like to be a surgeon, but I'd have to go to medical school. I guess I'll play pro ball until I'm too old, and then open a restaurant." You say, "You really like football that much?" His reply is, "I'm not crazy about it. I'd rather be a surgeon. But playing football is the only thing I can do well, so I guess I'll stick to it."

10. Write a hypothesis to explain why Cratchit does not want to go to medical school.

_____

You tell Cratchit that you will excuse him from making speeches if he will take a medical aptitude test. He agrees, "O.K., Prof., but you know I'll flunk it." The test shows Cratchit to be at the ninety-eighth percentile among college freshmen. When you explain the significance of the test to Cratchit, he replies, "The test was too easy. It doesn't prove anything. I wish it did."

11. What conflicting ideas does Cratchit have?

_____

You tell Cratchit that with his ability he should have made a good record in high school. He replies, "Yeah, all my teachers told me that, but they didn't understand. When I was five the doctors thought I had rheumatic fever, and they kept me in bed for a year. I must not have had it, because the docs say my heart is O.K. Anyway, the year was half over when I started to school. I started behind and I never caught up. I guess that's part of the trouble. But I'm not as smart as they think, either. My parents were always disappointed in my grades."

12. Write a rival for Cratchit's hypothesis about his behavior.

_____

32 Psychological Pitfalls

We have noted the damage such fallacies as *post hoc* and hasty generalization can do by causing us to adopt false propositions into the personal point of view, with the result that we defend these false propositions instead of seeking to correct them. We have also examined a number of devices of self-defense by which we distort evidence to make it correspond to our own distorted views of the world. We turn now to another cluster of pitfalls in thinking which also lead to serious errors. The pitfalls in this cluster involve a psychological element in addition to faulty procedures in thinking.

1. Mind-Sets

A pitfall that has cost the human race dearly is the mind-set, a tendency of the human mind to view a situation in a certain way despite contrary evidence. In its simplest form a mind-set is a perceptual error. Suppose that as you approach a busy traffic intersection you notice that the traffic light for your lane is green. While entering the intersection you focus your attention on other cars and you fail to notice that the

light has changed even though you have been looking in the general direction of the light. If you have an accident or get a traffic ticket, a mind-set is the villain. Mind-sets account in part for our tendency to perceive what we expect to perceive. When you are looking for a diamond you lost in the grass, you mistake shiny dewdrops for the diamond because it is what you expect to see.

Mind-sets extend well beyond the perceptual level. The damage a mind-set can do is dramatically illustrated by the sinking of the *Titanic* on her maiden voyage in 1912, with the loss of 1,513 lives. Designed to be the safest ship afloat, the *Titanic* was equipped with a double bottom and sixteen watertight compartments. A mind-set that she was unsinkable seems to have been largely responsible for the disaster.

She carried lifeboats sufficient for only one third of her capacity, and no assignment of passengers was made to these boats; nor were any drills held. The *Titanic* was unsinkable.

Three days out of Queenstown, she received her first wireless warning of icebergs in the steamer lanes. A few hours later she received another message about icebergs, but the wireless operator was too busy with his accounts to bother recording the message. The *Titanic* was unsinkable.

That afternoon another warning was received. This time the operator sent it to the Captain, who glanced at it casually and handed it without comment to the managing director of the White Star Line. By 9:30 that night at least five warnings of icebergs had been received, and the *Titanic* was nearing their reported location. But no precautions were taken other than to warn the lookouts to be alert. The owners wanted a speed record; the *Titanic* steamed ahead into the darkness at twenty-two knots. The *Titanic* was unsinkable.

She had yet another chance. At 11:30 P.M. the wireless crackled with a message from the *Californian*: "Say, old man, we are stuck here, surrounded by ice." But the mind-set held, and the *Titanic*'s operator replied, "Shut up, shut up, keep out. I am talking to Cape Race; you are jamming my signals." The *Titanic* steamed ahead at twenty-two knots; she was unsinkable.

Ten minutes later the lookout spotted a giant iceberg dead ahead. Officers on the bridge did what they could to avoid the crash, but it was too late. The collision ripped a hundred-yard gash in the ship's double bottom. Although the watertight doors were closed immediately, the bulkheads not already damaged gave way, one by one. The great ship was doomed.

The loading of the lifeboats went slowly and badly, in part because the passengers would not believe that so safe a ship could sink. The boats left the ship with nearly five hundred passengers less than capacity. At best there would have been room for no more than a thousand. Even so the casualties might have been few. Distress calls were sent out within minutes after the collision, and the ship did not sink until more than two hours later. A number of ships raced to the scene, in spite of the ice. But they were too far away to save the fifteen hundred who did not get into the lifeboats. Meantime, the *Californian* was lying within sight of the *Titanic*, possibly no more than five miles away. Her radio operator did not hear the *Titanic*'s wireless calls; he had gone to bed shortly after being told to "shut up." Some of her crew did see the *Titanic*'s lights and rocket signals but did nothing more than try to communicate with the unknown ship by blinker. Testimony in the investigation of the disaster showed that the sea was calm and the night clear, and that the *Californian* might easily have pushed through the ice field to rescue most if not all of the passengers. Perhaps her officers, too, had a mind-set.

Another classic example of mind-set is the error the political poll takers made in the 1948 presidential elections. As early as July some of them were so sure Dewey would win over Truman that they stopped gathering evidence. Yet evidence was already available to show a change in trend, had they been willing to look for it.

The antidote for mind-set is to cultivate the habit of stopping occasionally to reconsider the course you are pursuing. The recommended technique is to set up rival hypotheses about other courses you might follow, giving more attention to contrary than confirmatory evidence, in order to offset your natural tendency to persist in the old course. For example, you should take stock at least once a semester to see whether you are following the academic program best for you. Many a student has graduated before realizing that he has pursued the wrong curriculum, though evidence available to him as early as his freshman year may have pointed toward a change in his program of study. This antidote can be overdone, of course, for if you become too anxious to avoid mind-sets you will fall into decision by indecision. The trick is to steer a middle course between the Scylla of "he who hesitates is lost" and the Charybdis of "look before you leap."

2. Thought-Habits

First cousin to mind-set is thought-habit, a tendency to persist in a particular method of attack on a problem. Thought-habits are not necessarily undesirable. On the contrary, making thought-habits of the procedures of effective thinking described in this text should keep you from many a pitfall. A thought-habit becomes a handicap when it does not work. For example, despite repeated failure in college, many students persist in using the study habits they acquired in high school. Many who depended on cramming in high school continue the practice in college. When they fail, instead of trying a new method, they merely cram harder. Unfortunately a method that has been successful in one set of circumstances may not work as well in others.

The antidote is to use failure as a signal for fresh thinking. When you fail in any endeavor, examine the methods you used. Then set up some rival hypotheses, and check them by adding and testing consequents. The more times you have failed in an endeavor, the more imperative it is to try new methods. Many problems are solved by trial and error anyway, and the more new methods you try the more likely you are to find a good one. It is desirable from time to time to test even successful methods by setting up rival hypotheses. You may find still better ones.

3. Attitudes

Our attitudes can be major pitfalls in thinking. An attitude is a persisting state of readiness to react favorably or unfavorably, affirmatively or negatively, toward a stimulus, according to one's system of values. Many a capable student wastes his time in college because he has acquired an unfavorable attitude toward study. Even before he knows what an assignment is, his attitude has prepared him to react to it unfavorably, as being a useless, unpleasant task which will interfere with more desirable activities. The professor must present very convincing evidence to persuade him that the assignment is worth doing. On the other hand, the student who has acquired a favorable attitude toward study is prepared in advance to react to the assignment as an opportunity for self-improvement. The stronger his attitude, the more evidence will be required to persuade him that the assignment is not worth doing.

When attitudes are put into words they are value judgments. Often, however, they are not put into words; in fact, we are often unaware of our attitudes and their influence on our thinking. We would condemn many of our attitudes if we expressed them as value judgments and critically examined them. One such attitude is hostility to authority. This attitude usually begins with resentment toward a parent or some other figure in authority and may then be generalized to cover all forms of authority. Persons afflicted with this attitude act as though they believe that all authorities are always wrong. Hence they tend to reject ideas they associate with authority. They have, in effect, closed their minds to certain ideas. The antidote for this attitude is not reverence for authority, since authorities are not always right. A better antidote is to analyze and evaluate ideas in terms of their own merit rather than in terms of their sources.

Attitudes are usually backed by some degree of emotion. Consequently, when an idea encounters a strong attitude, we react to the idea emotionally. If the attitude is favorable, we react to the idea as to a long-lost brother; if the attitude is negative, we put the idea through a Spanish inquisition and usually burn it at the stake.

This is not to say that all attitudes are

hazards to thinking. Like other persisting tendencies of mind, they are indispensable. They help us plot our way through unknown waters. We would have no time for anything else if we had to decide how to react to every stimulus. If all our attitudes were sound, all would be well. The trouble is that they are often in conflict with our basic goals.

The antidote for faulty attitudes is to use any unsatisfactory condition in your life as a signal to examine your attitudes and values.

4. Stereotypes

Mind-sets, thought-habits, and attitudes all have a profound influence on our relations with other people. In our highly mobile society we must deal with many people about whom we know nothing. A thought-habit all of us resort to in some degree is classifying people according to personality types and dealing with them as instances of the type instead of as individuals. Up to a point, this thought-habit helps in getting along with people, for it enables us to generalize past experience with people and use it in dealing with strangers. How helpful this thought-habit is depends on how accurately we type people and how readily we recognize that they are individuals.

But dealing with people by personality types may be a serious pitfall when the types become *stereotypes,* that is, over-simplified, relatively fixed, and identical conceptions of all persons in a category. We form many kinds of stereotypes: according to races and nationalities, such as Nordics and Russians; occupations, such as professors and salesmen; physical types, such as red-heads and fat people; regional types, such as Southerners and Northerners; and so on.

Stereotypes usually involve a cluster of personality traits that are assumed to go together. The conventional stereotype of college professors includes impracticality and

unworldliness as well as absent-mindedness. Another stereotype, fostered by cartoons and comic strips, pictures backwoods mountaineers as ignorant, extremely provincial, naïve, superstitious, poverty-stricken, untidy, lazy, none too honest, and fond of moonshine. Some stereotypes are derived from our personal experience with people; others are derived from the culture through newspapers, movies, radio, television, and other media of communication.

Even if stereotypes were accurate, which they usually are not, their use would be hazardous. We tend to put persons into stereotypes on the basis of some superficial clue, such as dress or mannerisms. Once we have "typed" a person, the stereotype becomes a mind-set. We continue to treat him in terms of and expect him to behave in accordance with the traits of the stereotype, despite contrary evidence. We expect all Frenchmen to be polite, and all Irishmen to be witty. Such mind-sets as these keep us from knowing persons as individuals. Thus some professors tend to deal with students (and students with professors) as though they were all carbon copies, despite wide differences among members of the class.

Another difficulty with stereotypes is that they often involve strong attitudes which reinforce our readiness to act toward an individual according to the stereotype he has been put into, whether he deserves it or not. When the attitudes are strong, we label the classes with emotional words, such as "Chink," "Wop," and "rube." Thus stereotypes are the basis of social prejudice.

The antidote for stereotyping is the same as for other faulty generalizations. We should remember that differences among individuals classified in a stereotype are frequently greater than the differences between stereotypes. You should be constantly alert to see that your classifications do not become fixed and that you revise them as new evidence becomes available. And you should stop dealing with a person in terms of a classification as soon as you have enough knowledge to treat him as an individual.

5. Displacement

Another pitfall in thinking is the result of frustration. One type of response to frustration is a desire to destroy the object that blocks us from reaching our goals. But this is frequently impossible or unwise — the frustrating object may be too big or powerful. But the tension demands release, and the next best thing is to take it out on some less dangerous object. This reaction is known as *displacement,* the transferring of aggression from the object that stimulated it to one less capable of retaliation. The boy whose father has punished him dares not express his resentment by kicking his father in the shins; instead, he kicks the innocent cat. The student who is angry at his teacher for not excusing a class cut may fly into a rage with his roommate over some trivial incident; the roommate, in turn, may work off his resentment by snapping at the cashier in the cafeteria.

Displacement may also take a form that is the opposite of *argumentum ad hominem.* If the person who has frustrated you is too big or powerful to attack directly, you can attack his ideas. You can see displacement in operation in almost any session of Congress. It is against Congressional etiquette for political enemies to come to blows on the floor, though they sometimes do. But no rule prohibits voting against a measure because it is favored by one's opponent, and justifying the action by plausible argument.

Displacement often has the effect of cutting off your nose to spite your face. You can indirectly attack the instructor you do not like by refusing to study or to take any interest in his course. But your course grade goes on *your* record, not his. You can express your resentment against a fraternity brother by refusing to cooperate with him in a fraternity project. But it is *your* popularity that suffers, not his. Or you can oppose a suggestion made by someone you want to attack and find yourself upholding an issue which your own reason tells you is wrong.

A satisfactory antidote for displacement requires three elements. One is to remember that when you are angry or frustrated you are like a little boy with a new gun yearning for a target. The second is to offset this yearning by making a special effort to be tolerant of everyone who crosses your path. The third is to use constructively the energy generated by anger or frustration before it explodes in the wrong place.

6. Identification

Identification is another mental process which, though generally desirable, conceals a pitfall. By identifying with others, we acquire understanding of and sympathy for them and thus expand our self-concepts. The pitfall is our tendency to accept uncritically the ideas of those with whom we have identified. We tend to borrow our ideals, attitudes, and stereotypes from these people without stopping to question whether they are right or wrong, true or false. We behave as though we were playing to a grandstand in which sit the people with whom we have identified. Thus the student tends to pattern his behavior after that of his coach, or professor, or fraternity brother. Through identification we adopt many false or conflicting ideas.

The antidote is to examine critically all ideas before accepting them, and to be particularly careful about adopting the ideas of those you admire. As a citizen in a democracy it is your duty, as well as privilege, to think for yourself. Citizens invite a dictatorship if they fall into the habit of adopting uncritically the ideas of their leaders, no matter how worthy the leaders or their ideas may be.

7. Faulty Communication

A major pitfall in sound thinking is faulty communication with others. Doubtless you have had the experience of discovering that the cause of a bitter argument was not a real difference of opinion but a failure to communicate accurately. Your thinking can be no better than the evidence on which it is based, and much of this evidence comes from communication with others, especially in the important area of human relations. Many a bitter fight has originated from faulty communication.

One barrier to accurate communication is the nature of language itself. As we noted in Chapter 18, words are not the equivalents of the objects they name; they are symbols, and they are used differently by different people. As Humpty Dumpty said, "When *I* use a word, it means just what I choose it to mean." Even when we use words exactly as defined in the dictionary, our emotional reactions to them differ because we have had different experiences with them. Emotional associations with the word "strike" are different for batter and pitcher, and for union member and business executive. The sound thinker must learn not to put too much faith in language as an accurate means of communication. As Thomas Hobbes put it, "For words are wise men's counters — they do but reckon by them; but they are the money of fools."

When you studied syllogisms, you prob- ably noticed another barrier to accurate communication: your own tendency to be inexact in saying what you mean and in interpreting the statements of others.

A third barrier to accurate communication is our tendency to so occupy ourselves with our own thoughts that we do not take the trouble to listen carefully or try to decide what the other person really means by the symbols he uses. We are too busy evaluating what the other person says in terms of how it affects us, or thinking up counter-arguments. Mind-sets play a part, too; we tend to hear the other person say what we expect him to say. Many of us talk much better than we listen, and pay a price for it in misunderstandings and missed information.

The antidote is to cultivate the habit of listening carefully when the matter is important, of trying to put yourself into the other person's frame of reference in order to see the matter exactly as he does. When he makes an important statement, restate it in your own words and ask him if that is what he means. Keep trying until he agrees that you have stated his position accurately. He will be more likely to regard you as a sympathetic and understanding person, and you will make fewer mistakes. You will discover that many seemingly irreconcilable differences of opinion are not differences of opinion at all, but merely differences in wording.

EXERCISE 32

1–18. *Indicate whether the following statements agree with the hypotheses presented in this book by writing in the blank T if true and F if false.*

1. The mind-set is a habitual way of thinking about a certain kind of problem. _____

2. The antidote recommended for mind-sets is to stop occasionally to examine the methods you are using in solving your problems. _____

3. A thought-habit is a tendency to persist in holding to an idea. _____

4. The antidote recommended for faulty thought-habits is to stop occasionally to examine the plan of action you are following. _____

5. The antidotes recommended for both mind-sets and thought-habits involve some risk of decision by indecision. _____

6. Thought-habits are an aid as well as a hazard in efficient thinking. _____

7. One is usually aware of the influence of attitudes on his thinking. _____

8. Attitudes are both an aid and a hazard to efficient thinking. _____

9. Attitudes often reinforce thought-habits and mind-sets. _____

10. Feelings are usually not involved in attitudes. _____

11. The antidote recommended for unsound attitudes is to use any unsatisfactory condition in your life as a signal for examining your attitudes. _____

12. A stereotype is a generalization about human nature used as a guide in dealing with people. _____

13. Classification of people by personality types will not help avoid mistakes in dealing with other people. _____

14. An antidote for stereotyping is to deal with people as individuals as soon as you know enough about them to do so. _____

15. Displacement is the tendency to let one idea replace another without sufficient evidence. _____

16. Nearly all ideas acquired by identification are false. _____

17. The barriers to accurate communication include the nature of language and our tendency to occupy ourselves with our own thoughts.   _____

18. A recommended antidote for faulty communication is to repeat what the other fellow says in his own words and ask if that is what he means.   _____

19–23. *Using the key list below, identify the pitfall probably involved in each of the following instances.*

KEY LIST

1. *Mind-sets*   3. *Attitudes*   6. *Identification*
2. *Thought-habits*   4. *Stereotypes*   7. *Faulty communication*
                 5. *Displacement*

19. Askroth did not enjoy his trip home. His semester report had preceded him, and his father greeted him with a tongue lashing about his poor grades and the announcement that he could not take his car back to college. That night he quarrelled with his girl, and the next day he had a bitter argument with his best friend over a trivial issue.   _____

20. When Askroth got back to the campus he resolved to double his efforts to make good grades. He had been studying only two hours or so the night before a test. He resolved to study a minimum of four hours the night before each test.   _____

21. As Boskom drove through barren country late one night he mused, "What a mess I'd be in if the weak coil on this jalopy conked out now!" A moment later his motor sputtered once and stopped dead. "That's it," thought Boskom. He walked eight miles to the nearest town, but could not get a new coil until morning. When he got back to his car, he found that a wire on the distributor had come loose. He could have fixed the trouble easily the night before.   _____

22. Crayder took a job as credit manager for a large store in a cosmopolitan city. He was told by his predecessor, "Don't trust the Bolkonians; they'll cheat you out of your eye teeth." Crayder followed the advice, turning down all requests for credit from Bolkonians. When he lost his wallet containing a considerable sum of money, it was returned to him intact by a young Bolkonian.   _____

23. Eversole admired his professor of literature, whose favorite novel was *Tom Jones*. Even though Eversole had never read the book, he always included it in his list of great novels of the world. When he did attempt to read it, he never made his way beyond the first volume.   _____

33 False Assumptions

Sometimes we reach false conclusions because we fail to realize that we are reasoning from false assumptions. Let us now examine a cluster of these false assumptions. Phase 4 of the decision-making cycle should always include a check for them.

1. Composition

Suppose an architect combines in a design for a church the best features of Gothic, Renaissance, neo-classic, and modern styles, assuming that his design as a whole will have the excellence of the individual features of each style. In making this assumption he has committed the fallacy of *composition, i.e.,* assuming that an organized whole retains the characteristics of its component parts.

In general, the greater the element of organization involved, the less likely it is that the whole will retain the characteristics of the parts. A team composed of the four best golfers at Wysacki is likely to defeat a team composed of the next best four, because in golf the members of the team perform as individuals. There is little organization as far as actual play is concerned. On the other hand, a touch football squad composed of the best players on the campus, who have been brought together to play just one game, would be less likely to defeat the intramural champions because a touch football team functions as an organized whole rather than as individuals.

Superficially, composition resembles the fallacy of hasty generalization. The difference lies in the nature of the "wholes" involved in each of the fallacies. As we have seen, hasty generalization is reasoning from a *sample* to a *greater number* of instances, whereas composition involves reasoning from *each* to an *organized whole.*

It is the element of organization that is central to the fallacy of composition. People in organized groups do not think or behave as each person does by himself, a fact which may be illustrated by the verdict of a jury or the violence of a mob. Things taken in relation to each other do not have the same properties as when taken singly, as any person knows who is acquainted with the compounding of chemicals. The interaction and interrelationship of parts produce changes that are hard to predict from knowledge of the separate parts.

It is far from true that an organized whole necessarily has the characteristics of its component parts; indeed, sometimes it may have characteristics exactly the opposite of those of the parts. A stone wall, for example, may be graceful and pleasing to the eye although every stone in it is rough and crude. Individual flowers used in a decorative scheme may be especially pretty, but the arrangement may give a total impression of ugliness. Every residence in a community may in itself be most attractive, yet the community as a whole may not be so; the various types of architecture may not harmonize, or the houses may be too closely packed or otherwise badly located in relation to one another.

It is fallacious, then, to assume that the whole necessarily possesses the characteristics of its parts.

2. Division

Exactly the reverse of composition is the fallacy of *division*. Division is the assumption that what is true of an *organized whole* is necessarily true of *each part*. We may have an outstanding team without any individual stars. Our political system is based on a belief in the wisdom of the electorate, but it would be an error of division to assume, therefore, that every voter is wise. If we were to argue that a man is a good lawyer because he belongs to a good law firm, that a person is a democratic person because he is a citizen of a democratic country, or that another is a communist because he is a citizen of a communist country, we would be committing the fallacy of division.

You are likely to be mistaken if you assume that the parts necessarily possess the characteristics of the whole.

3. Argumentum ad Ignorantiam

When we assume that mere failure to prove a proposition proves that its contradictory proposition is true, we commit the fallacy of *argumentum ad ignorantiam, i.e.,* argument from ignorance. We would commit this fallacy if we argued that, since we have no proof that there are human beings on other planets, there must not be any. We would be arguing in effect that something does not exist because we have no knowledge of it or no positive evidence in hand.

The lack of knowledge or evidence is significant only in proportion to the probability that the evidence would have been found if it existed. Suppose you argue that Joe Smythe was not in the library last week on the ground that you did not see him there. The fact that you did not see him there is significant only in proportion to the probability that you would have seen him had he been there. We encountered the problem of *argumentum ad ignorantiam* in testing both hypotheses and causal theories. Your inability to think of a rival hypothesis or causal theory to explain the relevant evidence becomes significant only to the degree that you have eliminated the possibility of other rival hypotheses or causal theories by careful investigation.

In order to give protection to the innocent, our courts assume that everyone is innocent until proven guilty. This assumption does not mean that a person is actually innocent in the absence of convincing evidence of guilt, but that he is legally innocent. Many guilty men have been declared innocent by law simply because there was not enough evidence to establish guilt. It would be possible to base our court procedures on the opposite assumption — that every suspect has to prove his innocence. But then a guiltless defendant might be convicted because he could not prove his innocence.

The best defense against *argumentum ad ignorantiam* is to remember that the absence of evidence for a given proposition supports its contradictory proposition only to the extent that the thoroughness of the investigation has reduced the probability that such evidence exists.

4. Hypothesis Contrary to Fact

Consider this proposition: If Smythe had taken Highway 441 instead of 41, he would not have had an accident. This kind of proposition is a *hypothesis contrary to fact*. It is contrary to fact because the antecedent describes something that did not happen. The statement involves an unjustified assumption, for one can never be certain what would have happened had he taken a different road or made a different decision. The statement is only a hypothesis posing as a statement of fact. It is true, of course, that Smythe would not have had that particular accident had he taken Highway 441; the statement that he would not have had any accident is pure hypothesis.

A hypothesis contrary to fact should be tested for reliability just as any other hypothesis. Consider the example below.

If Smythe had not dropped that pass in the end zone, Wysacki would have won.

If we know also that this play was the last one in the game, that there were no infractions of the rules by the offense on this play, and that Wysacki was no more than five points behind, this hypothesis deserves a rating of true beyond reasonable doubt. If, however, we know that the play occurred late in the second quarter, the reliability of the statement is low: if Wysacki had scored at that point, the situation during the remainder of the game could have been quite different.

Consider the two arguments below, both of which have been used in political campaigns.

If the Democrats had been in power between 1928 and 1932, there would have been no depression in the early 1930's.

If the Republicans had been in power between 1932 and 1944, the United States would not have been involved in World War II.

Both propositions are hypotheses contrary to fact, because the Republicans *were* in power between 1928 and 1932, and the Democrats *were* in power between 1932 and 1944. Both are unreliable because the consequents do not necessarily follow from the antecedents. We can only speculate about what would have happened had the other party been in power. The depression might have been avoided, or it might have been worse. The United States might or might not have been involved in World War II.

The hypothesis contrary to fact is commonly used in rationalizing. "If I had had a better professor, I would have passed." "If I had not been tired, I would not have made that mistake." On the other hand, committing this fallacy can cause unjustified guilt feelings. When you make a decision that has unfortunate consequences it is easy to conclude that if you had not made the decision, your situation would now be good. Many a parent has needlessly blamed himself for something that happened to his child. As we noted in Chapter 1, perfect thinking is impossible. One should not blame himself for a regrettable decision if he followed the procedures of effective thinking reasonably well.

To avoid falling into the pitfall of hypothesis contrary to fact, always qualify the consequent with an appropriate phrase indicating the probability, such as "might have," or "possibly would have," or "probably would have."

5. Begging the Question

If we assume just what we wish to prove, we are committing the fallacy known as begging the question. There are several ways in which a person may commit this fallacy. If we say, "She had an antipathy for football because it was a game she did not like," we beg the question by using an equivalent proposition which simply repeats the first one.

A more subtle way of committing this fallacy is to state in descriptive words or epithets a proposition that should be supported by evidence. For example, when a person complains that "students of agriculture should not be compelled to waste their time studying such subjects as literature, philosophy, and the fine arts," he is begging the question by the use of the phrase "waste their time." He has done nothing to establish that such study is a waste.

A third way of begging the question is to reason in a circle. If we argue that we need more automobiles on the road because we need more money from gasoline taxes so that we can build more roads in order to have more automobiles, we have completed a circle without proving anything. We have in effect argued that we need more automobiles because we need more automobiles. Our reasoning is analogous to that of the three morons, each of whom tied his horse to another's, thinking that he had thereby secured his own horse.

A fourth way to beg the question is to imply that the issue under discussion has been settled by shifting attention to a secondary issue that is relevant only when the primary issue has been settled. Suppose a fraternity brother pleads for the loan of your car during the next weekend and you politely refuse. When Friday comes he asks you what kind of gasoline you want put in your car when he uses it during the weekend. He has begged the question, for the kind of gasoline is a relevant issue only after you have agreed to the loan, which you have not.

The best protection against begging the question is to cultivate the habit of being alert for unsupported assumptions.

6. Cliché Thinking

Proverbs, maxims, aphorisms, and familiar quotations have a special persuasiveness. Because they are pithy and terse, and often in rhyme, they are easily remembered. Many of them have the prestige of age; some are almost as old as language itself. But using them as premises in decision making is flirting with disaster.

In the first place, many clichés are stated in figurative language and have no precise meaning. Suppose you are trying to decide whether to sell a stock for a small profit or hold it in the hope that you can make a larger profit later. If you decide to sell your stock on the ground that "a bird in hand is worth two in the bush," the cliché has led you into the fallacy of four terms or uncertain relationships. The real issue is whether the stock is more likely to go up or down. When you have decided this question you have no need for the cliché. But if you make your decision in terms of the cliché you are probably overlooking the real issue.

In the second place, clichés are usually oversimplifications. It is true in some situations that "haste makes waste," but in other situations "he who hesitates is lost." In some situations it is true that "nothing ventured, nothing gained," but in others it is "better to be safe than sorry." The real issue is whether the particular situation calls for haste or caution. Unfortunately, the clichés are so persuasive that we tend to act on the first one that occurs to us, without considering the real issue.

In the third place, clichés often state as truth what are only unproved generalizations or causal theories. "Like father, like son" is true only sometimes and in some respects. "Early to bed and early to rise" does not necessarily make one "healthy, wealthy, and wise."

Finally, clichés often express value premises that may be good in isolation but are incompatible with other premises in one's value system. "Better to be safe than sorry" seems to be a sound value premise. But if this cliché is interpreted to mean "never take any risk," it would be incompatible with other premises in the system of a person who values achievement in areas in which the probability of success is low. "Hitch your wagon to a star" can be pernicious in the value system of a person who tends to judge himself by excessively high standards.

Cliché thinking should not be confused with the use of trite language. Consider the statement, "If you don't study more, you will fail this course as surely as the sun will rise tomorrow." The words "as surely as the sun will rise tomorrow" are a cliché in the sense that the language is trite. But the statement is not a case of cliché thinking because the cliché is not used as a premise.

The remedy for cliché thinking is to strip the cliché of its persuasive language by translating it into a logical proposition and then examining it for reliability. "Silence is golden" loses some of its persuasiveness when translated into a literal categorical proposition.

$$\overset{d}{\text{Saying nothing}} < \overset{u}{\text{the best thing to do.}}$$

Obviously this proposition is unreliable, for often it is better to speak up. We can make the proposition reliable by changing it to an I-form.

$$\overset{u}{\text{Saying nothing}} < \overset{u}{\text{the best thing to do.}}$$

7. Conflicting Propositions

Another kind of false assumption involves basing a decision on two propositions that are contradictions, or contraries, or in conflict at least to some degree. Failure to see the conflicts in propositions results in inconsistent arguments. Consider the alumnus who contends that Wysacki lost the football game because of bad breaks. He points to a Wysacki fumble late in the game that led to the winning touchdown by the opposition, and argues that fumbles are bad breaks.

When reminded that a fumble by the opposition led to Wysacki's only touchdown, he argues that this fumble was not a bad break because hard tackling by Wysacki caused it. The alumnus is arguing from contradictory propositions: "All fumbles are bad breaks," and "Some fumbles are not bad breaks." The businessman who favors regulation of freight rates but opposes price control on the ground that it involves governmental influence in free enterprise is arguing inconsistently, for presumably regulation of freight rates is also a form of price control and it is certainly a form of governmental influence.

The candidate who promises to reduce taxes, and also to improve the schools, pave the highways, build new parks, provide old-age pensions, and build new hospitals is probably arguing from propositions that conflict at least to some degree. It is unlikely that he can fulfill all of his promises.

Conflicting propositions often appear in social problems. John W. Gardner has called attention to a pair of these: "All men are equal," and "Let the best man win."

> Some Americans have gone considerably beyond this [equality of opportunity] in their equalitarian views, insisting that no man should be regarded as better than another man in any dimension, and that there should be no difference in status whatever.[1]

> •   •   •   •   •

> Many Americans have always assumed that the only sensible way to organize society is to allow each individual to enjoy whatever status, privileges and power he is capable of winning for himself out of the general striving.[2]

To argue that any society can provide absolute equality and absolute opportunity for the best man to win is to commit the fallacy of contradictory assumptions, since

[1] John W. Gardner, *Excellence: Can We Be Equal and Excellent Too?* (New York: Harper, 1961), p. 13.
[2] *Ibid.*, pp. 15–16.

any measure taken to protect the less competent restricts to some degree the opportunity for the best man to win. It is possible, of course, to achieve a balance between the two values, but any argument that absolute equality and absolute opportunity for the best man to win can be achieved at the same time is a case of conflicting propositions.

Procedures for resolving such conflicts within value systems are discussed in Chapter 35.

EXERCISE 33

Using the key list below, identify the most conspicuous fallacy in each of the following arguments.

KEY LIST

1. Composition
2. Division
3. Argumentum ad ignorantiam
4. Hypothesis contrary to fact
5. Begging the question
6. Cliché thinking
7. Conflicting propositions

1. "My roommate tells me that he enjoys reading only good books."
   "How does he know when they are good?"
   "He says that if they're not good he doesn't enjoy them."   _____

2. The wife thought they should not get a new automobile. The husband said they should. They had not yet agreed either way. Yet, as the husband left the house, he asked, "Which shall it be — a Pontiac or an Oldsmobile?"   _____

3. A farmer failed to plant any beans the very season they brought their highest price in fifty years. Berating himself for his lack of foresight, the farmer complained to his wife, "If only I'd put in beans instead of those fool cucumbers, we'd be driving to Florida next winter in our own Cadillac."   _____

4. *Speaker who advocates a society almost completely planned and administered by a central government:* "Let the Government manage your affairs so that you may have more time to enjoy liberty and freedom to do as you wish."   _____

5. "You ought to buy one of these attachments for the carburetor of your car."
   "Why?"
   "Well, you don't want to be penny-wise and pound-foolish, do you?"   _____

6. *Student:* "This argument is fallacious. I know it is fallacious because it is not valid. It is not valid because it contains a fallacy."   _____

7. *Fraternity man, to prospective pledge:* "Our fraternity has taken the highest scholastic rating at the university for the past four years. So you can see that every man in it must be a topnotch scholar."   _____

8. *Student:* "Inasmuch as water extinguishes fire, and oxygen is a component of water, we may be sure that oxygen will also extinguish fire."   _____

9. *Student:* "Since we cannot disprove extrasensory perception, we must conclude that there is something to it."   _____

10. *Wife:* "I need fifty dollars."
    Husband: "Oh, no, you don't! Remember that the love of money is the root of all evil."

    _____

11. *News analyst:* "If the South had won the Civil War, we would have two weak nations today instead of one strong one."

    _____

12. An African medicine man decided to combine into one superior medicine all the herbs he knew which seemed to be beneficial to man, reasoning that if one herb is good, many will be better.

    _____

13. *Professor:* "Since you have not been to the office for a conference and since I have not seen you in the library, you must not be doing the work of this course."

    _____

14. Critics of the Truman administration argued that if the Americans had occupied Berlin before the Russians did, we would not later have had the explosive Berlin situation.

    _____

15. *Julia:* "This is a beautiful work of art."
    Anne: "I don't think it is."
    Julia: "Can you prove that it is not a beautiful work of art?"
    Anne: "Of course not."
    Julia: "Then you must accept my statement that it is a beautiful work of art."

    _____

16. *Speaker:* "Since we have so far been unable to discover any limit to the universe, we must conclude that space is infinite."

    _____

17. One Nazi explained to another in 1938 that Germany had to go to war in order to acquire more living space for her crowded population. Moreover, the German birth-rate had to be increased greatly to furnish future soldiers and to populate the conquered living space.

    _____

18. *Music critic:* "The Cantwell Chorus is the finest in the world because its members are selected from the finest singers available."

    _____

19. *Speaker:* "A mob is no worse than the individuals that make it up, because a mob is just a large group of individuals."

    _____

sarily an expert in others. Whenever the opinion of an authority is presented as an argument, therefore, one ought always to ask himself what competence the person has concerning the point at issue. For competence in one field is no guarantee whatsoever of competence in another.

4. *Testimonials.* The testimonial is a favorite device of advertisers. Distinguished people or just plain citizens of no particular distinction are quoted in advertisements as using, preferring, or recommending the product being advertised. The person is frequently selected to fit specific attitudes. Athletes are selected to endorse razor blades; drunkards are never selected to endorse alcoholic beverages.

This device of persuasion overlaps misuse of authority, for frequently the person giving a testimonial is an authority in some field, or at least a person who has prestige and whose name is well known. But frequently, too, the testimonial is a statement by an "average" citizen. This kind of testimonial is used to suggest that people "just like yourself" have found the particular brand of soap, or insurance, or headache pills to be "best."

3. Repeated Assertion

Both attitude fitting and meaning from association are frequently used in conjunction with *repeated assertion.* Advertisers and propagandists repeat their messages over and over again, on the theory that the public will believe anything it hears often enough. Even though most of us realize that repeating a statement does not make it true, we succumb to this device all too often. Repeated assertion is used in the "technique of the big lie," in which propagandists persuade their victims to believe falsehoods merely by repeating them over and over again. The effectiveness of slogans is due not only to the immediate response that the slogan urges, but also to the delayed re-

sponse that comes from suggestion as repetition fixes the slogan in one's mind. We unconsciously permit repetition to influence our beliefs.

4. Confident Manner

Repeated assertion is often reinforced by a device called *confident manner,* i.e., the use of words, gestures, and intonations that suggest certainty. In radio and television commercials the voices of the announcers ooze confidence, on the theory that the listeners will assume that the announcer must be right because he sounds so certain. The advertising agency knows that on the battlefield, in the public forum, in sports, and in many other circumstances a show of confidence is so persuasive that it frequently carries everything before it.

A candidate for public office uses the confident manner when he says, "I can tell you what's going to happen in November. The fine, honorable people of this district are going to the polls and they are going to send me to the legislature to represent *their* interests — not the interests of the lobbyists — that's what is going to happen." Such a display of confidence often convinces voters who are eager to be on the winning side. People who know often show confidence, but those who show confidence do not always know. Careful observation will demonstrate that people who know the least are frequently those who make the most confident and convincing statements, especially about complex and difficult matters.

5. Argumentum ad Misericordiam

If a person appeals to sympathy or to pity instead of presenting relevant evidence, he is employing the device of persuasion called *argumentum ad misericordiam.* This kind of argument is frequently heard in courtroom trials, when an attorney for the defense ignores the relevant facts and tries to elicit

34 Devices of Persuasion

1. *Attitude Fitting*
2. *Meaning from Association*
3. *Repeated Assertion*
4. *Confident Manner*
5. *Argumentum ad Misericordiam*
6. *Misuse of Analogy*

One of the important functions of critical thinking is to protect us against devices of persuasion. We are subjected to a constant barrage of these devices from propagandists, advertisers, politicians, teachers, preachers, relatives, friends and even ourselves. Sometimes these devices are used with the best of intentions to persuade us to accept the truth or do what we should do. But sometimes they are used to manipulate our thinking for less worthy purposes.

It is difficult to study the history of the persuasive arts without concluding that man has been more interested in manipulating the minds of others than in discovering the truth. Among superstitious people there was usually a witch doctor skillful in the use of eyes of newts, toes of frogs, legs of lizards, and tongues of bats to manipulate the minds of his ignorant fellows and thus maintain his status in his community.

The Greeks had no sooner developed some of the fundamental procedures of rational thinking than the masters of persuasion learned to adapt them to their own uses. By the time of Socrates the Sophists, a once respectable school of philosophers, had become notorious for teaching tricks of argument to wealthy Athenian youths. From

this practice came the word *sophistry,* a clever and persuasive but misleading argument.

When behavioral scientists began to accumulate significant new information about human motivation, the masters of manipulation promptly invented "motivation research," the study of deeper human motivation for the purpose of manipulation. Motivation research has not been as successful as advertisers would like, but it may become more successful as behavioral scientists learn more about human motivation.

Four-color, high-speed printing presses, radio, and television are vastly effective tools for the dissemination of knowledge. But it is interesting to note that it has not been the scholars or educators who have learned to use these tools most effectively — it has been the advertising agencies. Their persuasive skill has become a legend in our time, and "Madison Avenue" now connotes the center of the advertising industry just as "Wall Street" connotes the center of finance.

The arts of persuasion have always been important to politicians. In the 1964 Presidential Campaign most of the devices of persuasion now known were employed. Particularly bad from the point of view of effective thinking was the widespread use of "spot" broadcasts and telecasts, which were too short to permit presentation of evidence to support the claims made, even if the authors had wanted to present evidence. Both candidates employed advertising agencies to create favorable "images" of themselves in the minds of the voters. The possibility that a candidate might be elected President of the United States because he chose the better advertising agency is frightening.

These remarks are not meant to condemn the arts of persuasion or those who use them. Products that are persuasively advertised are frequently of good quality, and politicians gifted in the arts of persuasion may be excellent public servants. Furthermore, it would be unfair to put all the blame on the users of devices of persuasion. There is no particular virtue in being a defeated politician. As long as masses of voters are swayed more by devices of persuasion than by fact and reason, we should not be surprised that politicians rely much more on persuasion than on fact. Nor is there any particular virtue in being a bankrupt advertiser or business man. As long as the public is gullible, we should not be surprised to find little factual content in advertising. Nor should we criticize preachers, teachers, relatives, and friends for trying to present their ideas convincingly. They can hardly be blamed for using a device of persuasion here and there if they think we will not be convinced by the truth alone. The point is that we should choose the best candidate rather than the one who is most effectively presented, the best product rather than the one that is most effectively advertised, and the best idea, rather than the one that is presented most persuasively. To do so we must be able to detect and resist a cluster of devices of persuasion. These devices are all designed to manipulate the personal point of view of the victim. The cluster discussed here is not complete, for the masters of persuasion are constantly inventing new devices or variations and combinations of old ones. If you learn to resist the ones discussed here, however, you can probably detect and resist the others, even though you may not be able to apply specific names to them.

1. Attitude Fitting

A favorite device of the masters of persuasion is *attitude fitting*, which exploits the fact that our attitudes make us readily accept certain ideas and reject others. The device consists of presenting an idea in a manner designed to appeal to the attitudes of those for whom the argument is intended.

The attitudes of individuals vary widely. One man's meat is another's poison. When trying to persuade an individual, the attitude fitter adapts his argument to suit what he believes to be the attitudes of the person he is addressing. Thus a student who wants to persuade his parents to let him join a fraternity may emphasize to his mother the social advantages, while pointing out to his father the contacts he can make that will be valuable to him later on in business.

Attitudes also vary from group to group and from region to region. Candidates for political office tend to color their proposals accordingly. Candidates speaking in a coastal region, for example, may stress the rights of the individual states in such matters as ownership of tideland rights; they may not mention this matter at all when speaking in a region far from the sea, but may advocate instead building interstate highways. In both instances they are attempting to appeal to the prevailing attitudes of the particular group and region.

The methods of presentation used in attitude fitting may involve both statement of idea and selection of supporting arguments. The political candidate who is campaigning on a platform of economy stresses the reduction of the crushing burden of taxation, rather than the reduction of governmental services. Advertising agencies carefully avoid arguments that appeal to unfavorable attitudes.

Attitude fitting often employs the misuse of labels. A textbook entitled *Zymology Made Easy* can be a mass of confusion, but the label can still have a strong appeal to the attitude of a student who finds zymology difficult. Totalitarian political parties seem to have no hesitation in calling themselves by such names as "The People's Party," "The Freedom Party," or "The Liberators." The fact that a label is false does not prevent it from appealing to attitudes.

Skillful attitude fitting is not easy to resist. The former behavioral scientists who now work on Madison Avenue will doubtless make it even more difficult by discovering our hidden attitudes and learning how to exploit them. If we are to protect our right to make our own decisions, we must cultivate the habit of looking behind labels and slogans, and applying our critical skills to arguments that seem pleasing but are not supported by reliable evidence.

2. Meaning from Association

Attitude fitting is frequently used in conjunction with *meaning from association*, a device by which the victim is persuaded to transfer his attitudes about one object or idea to another with which it is associated. An advertiser of an automobile, for example, tries to establish a connection between his automobile and some object of high prestige — say orchids, diamonds, or movie stars — in the hope that the prospective customer will transfer to the automobile the same attitudes and meanings he attaches to the object of high prestige. The association need not be a favorable one. A political propagandist, for example, may try to associate the candidate of the opposing party with some person or idea generally condemned by the voters.

Four kinds of meaning from association are commonly used.

1. *Association by contiguity*. Meaning from association may be produced merely by mentioning in the same breath or in the same sentence the two objects or ideas to be connected. Merely to print on the same page pictures of priceless old books and of a bottle of beer may be sufficient to suggest to many people that the beer is as fine an example of its kind as the books are of the printer's art. Obviously, however, the qualities of the books are not relevant to beer.

2. *Prestige of great names*. Sometimes meaning by association takes advantage of the proper regard we have for great men, institutions, and ideals which have stood the test of time. During national political campaigns the names of George Washington, Abraham Lincoln, and Thomas Jefferson are heard almost as often as the names of the current candidates. These names are injected into speeches in the hope that the public will transfer to the party or candidates some of the esteem in which the great names are held.

3. *Misuse of authority*. To quote a respected authority on an issue in his own field is a legitimate kind of argument, for in many situations we are forced to rely on the opinions of authorities. This kind of argument becomes a device of persuasion, however, when we cite an authority on an issue unrelated to his field of competence. The opinion of a leading industrialist would be relevant evidence on a matter of manufacturing processes, for this is his field of special competence. But his opinions on modern art or bringing up children, however interesting in themselves, would presumably carry no more weight as evidence than those of your next-door neighbor. The misuse of authority gains its effectiveness not only from the suggestion that whatever the authority considers good must be good, but also from the mistaken assumption that a person who is an expert in one field is necessarily...

favorable consideration for his client by playing upon the sympathy of the jury.

Although evaluative words may play an important part in *argumentum ad misericordiam,* they are not essential; a play on sympathy can be achieved without the use of words. The attorney for the defense may, for example, bring into the courtroom the poorly-dressed wife of the defendant, surrounded by pathetic children in rags, and thus say in effect to the jury, "If you send my client to the electric chair, you make a widow of this poor woman and orphans of these innocent children. What have they done to deserve this?"

Argumentum ad misericordiam is by no means confined to the courtroom. The beggar on the street emphasizes his appeal for money by prominently displaying his blind eyes or twisted limbs to the passers-by. A student's mother says to a faculty member, "How can you fail my boy, Professor Flunkmore? You have always been a good friend of the family, and you know the financial difficulties we have in sending him to college."

While sympathy is a noble human emotion, and should motivate many of our actions, we should not allow it to obscure the relevant facts. When we base a decision on sympathy we should at least be aware that we are doing so.

6. Misuse of Analogy

We noted in our study of creative thinking that analogies are invaluable as sources of new ideas. Concrete analogies are also useful in promoting understanding of abstract ideas. You will find a number of analogies so used in this book.

Invaluable to effective thinking as they are, analogies can be *misused.* They are misused when they are offered as proof. Consider this advertisement. "Your television set is a delicate and complicated mechanism. You should select your service-man with the same care you would select your doctor." This advertisement argues, in effect, that since the human body and a television set are alike in that both are delicate and complex, they must also be alike in that both require professional care. The weakness in this argument is that two objects, ideas, or actions, though alike in some respects, can be significantly different in others. The following exaggerated analogy should make this point clear.

The human body and an automobile engine are alike in many respects: both must operate within certain temperature limits, both last longer if cared for, both consume fuel. Since adding tetraethyl lead to the gasoline makes an automobile engine run better, you should put tetraethyl lead in your coffee.

Analogies are frequently misused by advertisers and propagandists because they can combine the persuasiveness of attitude fitting with meaning from association. Consider an advertisement by an association of electric power companies. The upper part of the page shows a picture of an unusual football scene. An official is carrying the ball; another official is blocking for him. The caption, in large letters, asks "What's going on here?" The text below the picture then asks these questions: "Would you let the officials referee and play too? Then why let the government compete with private electric power companies and regulate them too?" The analogy to a football game encourages transferring to the government the American attitude of anger at such unfairness.

To protect ourselves against misusing analogy, we must remember that two things may be alike in many ways and yet be different in others. It is possible to neutralize the effect of analogy by posing a counter-analogy. An opponent of capital punishment may say, "The execution of a human being for a crime is useless. It is like locking the barn door after the horse has been stolen." To this, an advocate of capital punishment may respond, "But we are not locking a barn door. We are destroying a rabid animal before he does further damage." It should be recognized, however, that both the analogy and the counteranalogy are inadequate and misleading as arguments. Neither throws light on the disputed subject. A counteranalogy is not adequate evidence, but it may point up the inadequacy of the original analogy by suggesting other possible comparisons.

34 Devices of Persuasion

1. *Attitude Fitting*
2. *Meaning from Association*
3. *Repeated Assertion*
4. *Confident Manner*
5. *Argumentum ad Misericordiam*
6. *Misuse of Analogy*

One of the important functions of critical thinking is to protect us against devices of persuasion. We are subjected to a constant barrage of these devices from propagandists, advertisers, politicians, teachers, preachers, relatives, friends and even ourselves. Sometimes these devices are used with the best of intentions to persuade us to accept the truth or do what we should do. But sometimes they are used to manipulate our thinking for less worthy purposes.

It is difficult to study the history of the persuasive arts without concluding that man has been more interested in manipulating the minds of others than in discovering the truth. Among superstitious people there was usually a witch doctor skillful in the use of eyes of newts, toes of frogs, legs of lizards, and tongues of bats to manipulate the minds of his ignorant fellows and thus maintain his status in his community.

The Greeks had no sooner developed some of the fundamental procedures of rational thinking than the masters of persuasion learned to adapt them to their own uses. By the time of Socrates the Sophists, a once respectable school of philosophers, had become notorious for teaching tricks of argument to wealthy Athenian youths. From this practice came the word *sophistry,* a clever and persuasive but misleading argument.

When behavioral scientists began to accumulate significant new information about human motivation, the masters of manipulation promptly invented "motivation research," the study of deeper human motivation for the purpose of manipulation. Motivation research has not been as successful as advertisers would like, but it may become more successful as behavioral scientists learn more about human motivation.

Four-color, high-speed printing presses, radio, and television are vastly effective tools for the dissemination of knowledge. But it is interesting to note that it has not been the scholars or educators who have learned to use these tools most effectively — it has been the advertising agencies. Their persuasive skill has become a legend in our time, and "Madison Avenue" now connotes the center of the advertising industry just as "Wall Street" connotes the center of finance.

The arts of persuasion have always been important to politicians. In the 1964 Presidential Campaign most of the devices of persuasion now known were employed. Particularly bad from the point of view of effective thinking was the widespread use of "spot" broadcasts and telecasts, which were too short to permit presentation of evidence to support the claims made, even if the authors had wanted to present evidence. Both candidates employed advertising agencies to create favorable "images" of themselves in the minds of the voters. The possibility that a candidate might be elected President of the United States because he chose the better advertising agency is frightening.

These remarks are not meant to condemn the arts of persuasion or those who use them. Products that are persuasively advertised are frequently of good quality, and politicians gifted in the arts of persuasion may be excellent public servants. Furthermore, it would be unfair to put all the blame on the users of devices of persuasion. There is no particular virtue in being a defeated politician. As long as masses of voters are swayed more by devices of persuasion than by fact and reason, we should not be surprised that politicians rely much more on persuasion than on fact. Nor is there any particular virtue in being a bankrupt advertiser or business man. As long as the public is gullible, we should not be surprised to find little factual content in advertising. Nor should we criticize preachers, teachers, relatives, and friends for trying to present their ideas convincingly. They can hardly be blamed for using a device of persuasion here and there if they think we will not be convinced by the truth alone. The point is that we should choose the best candidate rather than the one who is most effectively presented, the best product rather than the one that is most effectively advertised, and the best idea, rather than the one that is presented most persuasively. To do so we must be able to detect and resist a cluster of devices of persuasion. These devices are all designed to manipulate the personal point of view of the victim. The cluster discussed here is not complete, for the masters of per-

suasion are constantly inventing new devices or variations and combinations of old ones. If you learn to resist the ones discussed here, however, you can probably detect and resist the others, even though you may not be able to apply specific names to them.

1. Attitude Fitting

A favorite device of the masters of persuasion is *attitude fitting*, which exploits the fact that our attitudes make us readily accept certain ideas and reject others. The device consists of presenting an idea in a manner designed to appeal to the attitudes of those for whom the argument is intended.

The attitudes of individuals vary widely. One man's meat is another's poison. When trying to persuade an individual, the attitude fitter adapts his argument to suit what he believes to be the attitudes of the person he is addressing. Thus a student who wants to persuade his parents to let him join a fraternity may emphasize to his mother the social advantages, while pointing out to his father the contacts he can make that will be valuable to him later on in business.

Attitudes also vary from group to group and from region to region. Candidates for political office tend to color their proposals accordingly. Candidates speaking in a coastal region, for example, may stress the rights of the individual states in such matters as ownership of tideland rights; they may not mention this matter at all when speaking in a region far from the sea, but may advocate instead building interstate highways. In both instances they are attempting to appeal to the prevailing attitudes of the particular group and region.

The methods of presentation used in attitude fitting may involve both statement of idea and selection of supporting arguments. The political candidate who is campaigning on a platform of economy stresses the reduction of the crushing burden of taxation, rather than the reduction of governmental services. Advertising agencies carefully avoid arguments that appeal to unfavorable attitudes.

Attitude fitting often employs the misuse of labels. A textbook entitled *Zymology Made Easy* can be a mass of confusion, but the label can still have a strong appeal to the attitude of a student who finds zymology difficult. Totalitarian political parties seem to have no hesitation in calling themselves by such names as "The People's Party," "The Freedom Party," or "The Liberators." The fact that a label is false does not prevent it from appealing to attitudes.

Skillful attitude fitting is not easy to resist. The former behavioral scientists who now work on Madison Avenue will doubtless make it even more difficult by discovering our hidden attitudes and learning how to exploit them. If we are to protect our right to make our own decisions, we must cultivate the habit of looking behind labels and slogans, and applying our critical skills to arguments that seem pleasing but are not supported by reliable evidence.

2. Meaning from Association

Attitude fitting is frequently used in conjunction with *meaning from association,* a device by which the victim is persuaded to transfer his attitudes about one object or idea to another with which it is associated. An advertiser of an automobile, for example, tries to establish a connection between his automobile and some object of high prestige — say orchids, diamonds, or movie stars — in the hope that the prospective customer will transfer to the automobile the same attitudes and meanings he attaches to the object of high prestige. The association need not be a favorable one. A political propagandist, for example, may try to associate the candidate of the opposing party with some person or idea generally condemned by the voters.

Four kinds of meaning from association are commonly used.

1. *Association by contiguity.* Meaning from association may be produced merely by mentioning in the same breath or in the same sentence the two objects or ideas to be connected. Merely to print on the same page pictures of priceless old books and of a bottle of beer may be sufficient to suggest to many people that the beer is as fine an example of its kind as the books are of the printer's art. Obviously, however, the qualities of the books are not relevant to beer.

2. *Prestige of great names.* Sometimes meaning by association takes advantage of the proper regard we have for great men, institutions, and ideals which have stood the test of time. During national political campaigns the names of George Washington, Abraham Lincoln, and Thomas Jefferson are heard almost as often as the names of the current candidates. These names are injected into speeches in the hope that the public will transfer to the party or candidates some of the esteem in which the great names are held.

3. *Misuse of authority.* To quote a respected authority on an issue in his own field is a legitimate kind of argument, for in many situations we are forced to rely on the opinions of authorities. This kind of argument becomes a device of persuasion, however, when we cite an authority on an issue unrelated to his field of competence. The opinion of a leading industrialist would be relevant evidence on a matter of manufacturing processes, for this is his field of special competence. But his opinions on modern art or bringing up children, however interesting in themselves, would presumably carry no more weight as evidence than those of your next-door neighbor. The misuse of authority gains its effectiveness not only from the suggestion that whatever the authority considers good must be good, but also from the mistaken assumption that a person who is an expert in one field is neces-

sarily an expert in others. Whenever the opinion of an authority is presented as an argument, therefore, one ought always to ask himself what competence the person has concerning the point at issue. For competence in one field is no guarantee whatsoever of competence in another.

4. *Testimonials.* The testimonial is a favorite device of advertisers. Distinguished people or just plain citizens of no particular distinction are quoted in advertisements as using, preferring, or recommending the product being advertised. The person is frequently selected to fit specific attitudes. Athletes are selected to endorse razor blades; drunkards are never selected to endorse alcoholic beverages.

This device of persuasion overlaps misuse of authority, for frequently the person giving a testimonial is an authority in some field, or at least a person who has prestige and whose name is well known. But frequently, too, the testimonial is a statement by an "average" citizen. This kind of testimonial is used to suggest that people "just like yourself" have found the particular brand of soap, or insurance, or headache pills to be "best."

3. Repeated Assertion

Both attitude fitting and meaning from association are frequently used in conjunction with *repeated assertion.* Advertisers and propagandists repeat their messages over and over again, on the theory that the public will believe anything it hears often enough. Even though most of us realize that repeating a statement does not make it true, we succumb to this device all too often. Repeated assertion is used in the "technique of the big lie," in which propagandists persuade their victims to believe falsehoods merely by repeating them over and over again. The effectiveness of slogans is due not only to the immediate response that the slogan urges, but also to the delayed re-sponse that comes from suggestion as repetition fixes the slogan in one's mind. We unconsciously permit repetition to influence our beliefs.

4. Confident Manner

Repeated assertion is often reinforced by a device called *confident manner, i.e.,* the use of words, gestures, and intonations that suggest certainty. In radio and television commercials the voices of the announcers ooze confidence, on the theory that the listeners will assume that the announcer must be right because he sounds so certain. The advertising agency knows that on the battlefield, in the public forum, in sports, and in many other circumstances a show of confidence is so persuasive that it frequently carries everything before it.

A candidate for public office uses the confident manner when he says, "I can tell you what's going to happen in November. The fine, honorable people of this district are going to the polls and they are going to send me to the legislature to represent *their* interests — not the interests of the lobbyists — that's what is going to happen." Such a display of confidence often convinces voters who are eager to be on the winning side. People who know often show confidence, but those who show confidence do not always know. Careful observation will demonstrate that people who know the least are frequently those who make the most confident and convincing statements, especially about complex and difficult matters.

5. Argumentum ad Misericordiam

If a person appeals to sympathy or to pity instead of presenting relevant evidence, he is employing the device of persuasion called *argumentum ad misericordiam.* This kind of argument is frequently heard in courtroom trials, when an attorney for the defense ignores the relevant facts and tries to elicit favorable consideration for his client by playing upon the sympathy of the jury.

Although evaluative words may play an important part in *argumentum ad misericordiam,* they are not essential; a play on sympathy can be achieved without the use of words. The attorney for the defense may, for example, bring into the courtroom the poorly-dressed wife of the defendant, surrounded by pathetic children in rags, and thus say in effect to the jury, "If you send my client to the electric chair, you make a widow of this poor woman and orphans of these innocent children. What have they done to deserve this?"

Argumentum ad misericordiam is by no means confined to the courtroom. The beggar on the street emphasizes his appeal for money by prominently displaying his blind eyes or twisted limbs to the passers-by. A student's mother says to a faculty member, "How can you fail my boy, Professor Flunkmore? You have always been a good friend of the family, and you know the financial difficulties we have in sending him to college."

While sympathy is a noble human emotion, and should motivate many of our actions, we should not allow it to obscure the relevant facts. When we base a decision on sympathy we should at least be aware that we are doing so.

6. Misuse of Analogy

We noted in our study of creative thinking that analogies are invaluable as sources of new ideas. Concrete analogies are also useful in promoting understanding of abstract ideas. You will find a number of analogies so used in this book.

Invaluable to effective thinking as they are, analogies can be *misused.* They are misused when they are offered as proof. Consider this advertisement. "Your television set is a delicate and complicated mechanism. You should select your service-man with the same care you would select your doctor." This advertisement argues, in effect, that since the human body and a television set are alike in that both are delicate and complex, they must also be alike in that both require professional care. The weakness in this argument is that two objects, ideas, or actions, though alike in some respects, can be significantly different in others. The following exaggerated analogy should make this point clear.

> The human body and an automobile engine are alike in many respects: both must operate within certain temperature limits, both last longer if cared for, both consume fuel. Since adding tetraethyl lead to the gasoline makes an automobile engine run better, you should put tetraethyl lead in your coffee.

Analogies are frequently misused by advertisers and propagandists because they can combine the persuasiveness of attitude fitting with meaning from association. Consider an advertisement by an association of electric power companies. The upper part of the page shows a picture of an unusual football scene. An official is carrying the ball; another official is blocking for him. The caption, in large letters, asks "What's going on here?" The text below the picture then asks these questions: "Would you let the officials referee and play too? Then why let the government compete with private electric power companies and regulate them too?" The analogy to a football game encourages transferring to the government the American attitude of anger at such unfairness.

To protect ourselves against misusing analogy, we must remember that two things may be alike in many ways and yet be different in others. It is possible to neutralize the effect of analogy by posing a counteranalogy. An opponent of capital punishment may say, "The execution of a human being for a crime is useless. It is like locking the barn door after the horse has been stolen." To this, an advocate of capital punishment may respond, "But we are not locking a barn door. We are destroying a rabid animal before he does further damage." It should be recognized, however, that both the analogy and the counteranalogy are inadequate and misleading as arguments. Neither throws light on the disputed subject. A counteranalogy is not adequate evidence, but it may point up the inadequacy of the original analogy by suggesting other possible comparisons.

EXERCISE 34

Using the key list below, identify the principal device of persuasion in each of the following arguments.

KEY LIST

1. *Attitude fitting*	4. *Confident manner*
2. *Meaning from association*	5. *Argumentum ad misericordiam*
3. *Repeated assertion*	6. *Misuse of analogy*

1. *Incumbent:* "You wouldn't change surgeons in the middle of an operation. Why change governors in these days of constant crises?"

   _____

2. *Political speaker:* "His hobbies show what a regular guy our candidate is. A lot of people have expensive hobbies, but his are simple and down to earth. He likes to go into the kitchen and cook up a tasty meal for his friends. Even the things he cooks are a clue to the kind of man he is. Nothing fancy — just good, plain American food."

   _____

3. "Well," said the kind-hearted professor, "this student has not done the work of the course, but he has had a hard time. He has been ill a large part of the semester, and he has also had financial worries. In consideration of all these circumstances, I suppose I should give him a passing grade."

   _____

4. *Child about to be punished:* "I'm sorry I broke your vase, Mother. I feel very bad about it. See how I cut my hand on the broken glass. Gee, but it hurts! Can't you fix it? It feels terrible."

   _____

5. *Saleswoman to customer:* "This face cream is used by eight out of every ten women stars in Hollywood."

   _____

6. A full-page advertisement pictures an automobile in front of a luxurious hotel, with a very handsome young man assisting a beautiful, mink-coated girl to alight. In the upper left-hand corner the brand name of the vehicle is written in elaborate gold letters.

   _____

7. *Student:* "A practicing physician very often looks up a case in his medical books. Students therefore should be given their textbooks when they have a difficult examination."

   _____

8. On August 26, 1939, Adolf Hitler reassured worried Hermann Goering that although Britain and France were Germany's enemies, "Our enemies are little worms. They cannot fight, so they are paralyzed with the fear of a world war. They will certainly not interfere with our Polish invasion."

_____

9. *Advertisement:* "Our Gassmizer helps your car get more miles per gallon. Lowered gasoline consumption saves you money. Fewer stops to fill that tank make travelling a pleasure. Buy Gassmizer today."

_____

10. In an interview for a position with a small corporation, Smythe, who hasn't really given much thought to the matter, assures the interviewer that he believes the large corporation is a danger to the American way of life and the small corporation a living monument to the principles of American business.

_____

11. *Famous lacrosse player:* "Tri-edge stainless blades are the best friends your beard ever had. I use 'em, why don't you?"

_____

12. *Lecturer:* "The little red schoolhouse represents the soundest type of education for the country. Our modern ills stem from the so-called improvements in education, from the frills and fads of 'progressive' philosophies and from luxurious school plants and equipment. People have become soft and have forgotten the old-time virtues."

_____

13. *Student:* "A college curriculum should depend entirely on what interests the students. After all, teaching is like selling. The teacher is the seller; the student is the buyer. If nothing is learned, then nothing is taught; just as if nothing is bought, then nothing is sold. Buyers determine what is sold; so the students should determine what is taught."

_____

14. Lake's Face Lotion will make your wrinkles disappear. Youthful beauty is yours after a month with Lake's. Lake's is the lotion that laves the loveliest women of all. Buy Lake's at any fine cosmetics counter.

_____

15. *Advertisement:* "Mr. Igo Swiftli, an employee of the Submerged Log Company for more than ten years, takes Ridofills regularly. He says he never has that run-down feeling. Buy the large economy size of Ridofills today."

_____

16. *President of firm to personnel manager:* "I have decided to raise Smythe's salary $2,000 this year because of his tragic family problems."

_____

35 Refining Value Systems

Let us now apply the procedures we have been studying to perhaps the most important of all areas of thinking — refining one's value system. If you are beset by chronic anxiety or excessive emotional tension, the basic cause may lie in your value system. Even if you are not troubled by anxiety or tension, an effort to refine your value system is worthwhile for a number of reasons. In the first place, as we noted in Chapter 14 (a review of which is now in order), value judgments are involved in nearly every important decision you make.

In the second place, value premises are a major factor in shaping both the frame of reference and the self-concept. Thus the value premises you follow are a major factor in making you what you are. It seems reasonable to assume, therefore, that if you wish to guide your own development, instead of leaving it to chance or to the forces to which you are constantly exposed, you yourself must select the value premises by which you live.

In the third place, it is highly probable that you are now basing some of your decisions on value premises you would reject if you examined them critically. Many of the value premises you now follow were accepted uncritically from your parents and from your culture. While most of them are doubtless sound, there are probably a few that should be modified or discarded.

Finally, even assuming that every one of your value premises was sound when you adopted it, which is highly unlikely, some modification would probably be desirable. The value premises that were suitable when you were six years old are not altogether suitable for a college student, and the value premises that are suitable for you now will not be altogether suitable twenty years from now.

Thus a critical assessment of your value premises from time to time would seem essential. The five-phase cycle of decision making will apply with appropriate modifications to values as well as it does to other areas. For Phase 1, let us define the problem: to examine your value system and to make appropriate modifications in it in order that you may become more nearly the person you wish to be.

1. Discovering Value Premises

The objective of Phase 2 is to reveal the content of your system. In the first stages of your analysis a representative sample of the premises in your system is sufficient. Even if you could bring to light your entire system in all of its detail, which is highly doubtful, the mass would be so great that you would need a computer to analyze it. It is important, however, that the sample be reasonably representative. You can begin to accumulate such a sample merely by writing down the premises that come to mind. Accumulating a representative sample, however, is not as easy as you might suppose. First, you habitually behave in certain ways in certain situations without thinking about the value premises involved. For example, conscientious students do not, as a rule, debate with themselves every day whether they should prepare their assignments: they habitually do their work without giving much thought to the matter. The premises underlying habitual actions are not easily recalled.

Second, many of your value premises form chain syllogisms, such as the one below.

Activities that promote efficiency are good.
Activities that promote health promote efficiency.
Fun-type exercise promotes health.
Playing tennis is fun-type exercise.
Playing tennis is good.

Doubtless you have many times decided to engage in some activity without being consciously aware of the fundamental value premises that lie behind those you consciously used in making the decision. Even when you take the trouble to trace your reasoning back several links in the chain, there may be other links that you have not thought about.

Third, it is easy to deceive yourself into believing that you follow a given premise when actually your practice is quite different. In some instances you may have changed your practice so gradually that you fail to realize that you are no longer following the original premise. Consider, for example, the tired businessman who takes up golf to improve his health. At first he plays a few holes at a time and walks for the exercise. Gradually, however, he becomes more interested in golf and less interested in exercise. In order to play more holes he buys a golf cart and confines his walking to the distance from the cart to his ball and back. Then he begins to find pleasure in defeating his friends. To improve his game he takes lessons. To add spice he begins to wager a dollar on the outcome of each hole. Eventually he "plays" golf as seriously as he works at his business. If he continues to believe that he plays golf for exercise and recreation, he has changed his value premise without realizing it.

Finally, we hide our real value premises from ourselves in order to protect our self-concepts. Consider, for example, the case of Mrs. Prosser. When Jim, her only son, announced that he intended to marry a divorcée, Mrs. Prosser objected strongly. When Jim refused to renounce the girl, Mrs. Prosser, who was wealthy, threatened to disinherit him. When Jim married the girl, Mrs. Prosser carried out her threat. Although she could have afforded to give Jim the capital to start a business of his own, he had to struggle along without her assistance. The value premise Mrs. Prosser claimed to be following was that her religion prohibited divorce. But it is doubtful that she was actually following this value premise, since she was not particularly devout in other respects. It is more likely that her real premise was that she wanted her son for herself. If this was really the case, it is easy to understand why she would have been ashamed of this premise and would have concealed it from herself. The premises we conceal from ourselves are the ones most likely to cause us trouble. It is important, therefore, that they be brought to light. A procedure for discovering concealed premises was discussed in Chapter 14.

2. Criteria

When the five-phase cycle is used to assess and refine a value system, the objective of Phase 3 is to form the criteria for assessing the system. You can derive your criteria in part by applying the techniques of forming and testing causal theories discussed in Chapters 11 and 12. You can find others in the accumulated wisdom of the human race as expressed in literature and philosophy. A number of criteria from which you may choose are stated below. Since the ultimate goal is to choose your own premises, and since the criteria you choose will presumably influence your evaluations and hence your choices, you should add criteria of your own to the list.

1. *A value system should include a premise that states major goals in life in terms of your concept of life's meaning and purpose.* Some people argue that, since we cannot prove in any scientific sense that life has either purpose or meaning, there must not be any purpose or meaning in life. You will recognize that this argument is based on *argumentum ad ignorantiam.* This particular *argumentum ad ignorantiam* is pernicious. The literature of psychoanalysis, psychiatry, and psychology provides strong support for the hypothesis that inability to find meaning and purpose in life is a common cause of excessive anxiety and of neuroses.

Even if we assume that life has no extrinsic meaning or purpose — an assumption that cannot be proved — it is still possible to give life an intrinsic meaning and purpose in the same way that an artist creates a meaningful picture from meaningless canvas and meaningless pigments.

2. *A value system should provide a basis for decision making in all areas of life.* You make so many decisions every day that you do not have time to examine all the values involved. If you do not have a body of mutually compatible value premises to draw upon, you will inevitably fall victim to decision by indecision or be forced to make decisions without considering the values involved.

3. *A value system should provide for reasonably balanced need satisfaction.* To do so, the system should be compatible with man's nature as a biological being living in a physical and social universe. As a biological being man has desires and emotions. But he is not free to satisfy his desires or express his emotions without restraint; man is also a social creature living in a social universe, and he strives to develop and maintain a satisfactory self-concept. Since this self-concept must be developed in relation to other people, the manner in which he satisfies his desires and expresses his emotions affects his self-concept. Hence he cannot avoid holding himself responsible for the effect of his actions on other people. Any value premise that gives man free rein with his fellows must be judged incompatible with man's nature. Similarly, a value system is inadequate unless it includes premises that guide man in meeting his biological needs in socially acceptable ways.

4. *A value system should include a strong code of ethics.* This criterion follows in part from the one above. Moreover, in order to develop a satisfactory self-concept, man must inevitably compete with his fellows to some extent. If men were not guided by ethical codes, life would be as chaotic as a football game without rules. In life, as in football, of course, there are people who appear to be unrestrained by ethics. On the surface these people may seem to be happy. There is no real evidence, however, that they have succeeded in developing and maintaining satisfactory self-concepts. On the contrary, there is much evidence that these people suffer from feelings of guilt, insecurity, and general or specific inadequacy.

5. *The premises in a value system should be compatible with each other.* In a manner of speaking, values are forces. Any given value tends to make you move in a certain direction. Figuratively speaking, two values of equal strength which push you north and east, respectively, will combine to move you northeast with greater force than either value alone. But two values of equal strength pushing you north and south, respectively, cancel each other.

The closer your values come to pushing you in the same direction, the more efficiently you can use your energy and abilities. Consider, for example, the law student whose long-term goal is to achieve a record for statesmanship in high public office. One of his short-term goals is to be the best poker player in law school. His short-term and long-term goals are incompatible in several respects. Playing serious poker creates tension and therefore is not likely to provide the relaxation from intellectual labors that a law student needs. Furthermore, serious poker is in conflict with the ethics of statesmanship. The objective of a statesman is to serve other people; the objective of a serious poker player is to take something away from other people. Thus this student's short-term and long-term goals may pull him in opposite directions and hinder his progress. A more compatible form of recreation for this law student might be a relaxing type of physical exercise, which would help rather than hinder the achievement of his long-term goal.

6. *Your values should be realistic in terms of both your own abilities and the world in which you live.* This criterion can be treated as a matter of definition. If your aptitude for college is average and you define success in college as having the highest grade-point average, the probability of success is extremely low. If you define success in these terms, you are likely either to fail or to sacrifice other important values, or both. The same principle applies to judging other people. If you define goodness as perfection and badness as any degree short of perfection, you commit the black-or-white fallacy.

3. Classifying Value Premises

The objective of Phase 4 of the cycle is to test your system as a whole, as well as the individual premises in it, by applying the criteria you have selected. Suppose the sample of premises you have listed includes the following.

1. One should always follow the golden rule.
2. A broad and deep understanding of man is an essential part of a good education.
3. Happiness is the prestige of having lots of money, two cars, and a big house.
4. The primary objective in life is the accumulation of material wealth.
5. Knowing the truth is preferable to ignorance or self-deception.
6. The ultimate purpose of human life is to serve God.
7. The most important objective in college is high grades.
8. The best careers are those that pay the highest salaries.
9. T. S. Eliot's poetry is better than Browning's.
10. The major goal in life is the balanced satisfaction of needs.
11. The best way to serve God is to be a medical missionary.
12. The end justifies the means.

The basic procedure for testing individual value premises was described in Chapter 13. The only necessary modification of this procedure is to use the premise in question as a proposal for action and then predict consequences in terms of the criteria you have tentatively adopted. An incomplete test of Premise 8, using this procedure, is shown below.

Advantages

I follow the premise ⊃ the career I choose will
that the best probably satisfy my
careers are those need for prestige.
that pay the
highest salaries

Disadvantages

my career may not
satisfy my need to
contribute to the
welfare of others.

I may undertake a
career that is unrealistic
in terms of my abilities
and interests.

Testing individual premises is not enough, however. To assume that a value system is satisfactory merely because the individual premises in it are satisfactory is to commit the fallacy of composition. A thorough assessment of your value system must include an examination of the interrelationships among the premises. The best way to see these interrelationships is to classify them. Since your purpose is to understand your system as thoroughly as possible, you should follow the procedures for forming and testing explanatory classifications which were discussed in Chapter 19. Premises 1–12 above, which are listed in random order, are shown below in a classification.

I. *Major goals in life*

  A. The ultimate purpose of human life is to serve God.

  B. Happiness is the prestige of having lots of money, two cars, and a big house.

  C. The primary objective in life is the accumulation of material wealth.

  D. The major goal in life is the balanced satisfaction of needs.

II. *Areas of decision making*

  A. Career goals

    1. The best way to serve God is to be a medical missionary.

    2. The best careers are those that pay the highest salaries.

  B. Educational goals

    1. The most important objective in college is high grades.

    2. Knowing the truth is preferable to ignorance or self-deception.

    3. A broad and deep understanding of man is an essential part of a good education.

  C. Ethics

    1. The end justifies the means.

    2. One should always follow the golden rule.

  D. Aesthetics

    1. T. S. Eliot's poetry is better than Browning's.

When the premises in a value system are properly classified, the flaws in the system are much easier to find. The classification above makes it clear that the list does not constitute a complete system, for many important areas of decision making are not covered at all. The entries under ethics, for example, are far from adequate. The two career goals are incompatible with each other and with one or more of the major goals. As any college student knows, the first premise classified under educational goals is incompatible with the other two. The two premises classified under ethics are also incompatible. A person who tried to follow all of these premises would have to move in three or four directions at once.

4. Modifying Value Systems

When the decision-making cycle is being used to assess and refine your value system, the objective of Phase 5 is to decide what changes should be made. Although some of your value premises doubtless need modification, the modifications should be made with caution. Quick and radical changes of important premises should be avoided: since the premises in a system are interrelated, a radical and ill-considered change in any one of them may disrupt the entire system.

A classification of a sample of your value premises will probably reveal gaps. Trying to fill in these gaps will not only help you find some of your hidden value premises but also indicate areas needing further creative and critical thinking.

5. Conflicts

Unless you are most unusual, a thorough analysis and classification of your value premises will also reveal conflicting propositions. Unresolved conflicts between important values can be the starting point of a vicious cycle of emotional tension. During the period of indecision some need is not being satisfied. As a result, emotional tension is generated. But while you are trying to decide what to do, you usually do nothing — and so the emotional tension is not released through action. Your very indecision, too, is damaging to your concept of yourself as an individual able to cope with reality and make decisions. The resulting distress stimulates still greater emotional tension. And, as we have noted, when emotional tension becomes strong enough, it interferes with your ability to think. The result may be either decision by indecision or a rash and impulsive act designed to break the indecision. Conflicts that are allowed to continue unresolved may eventually pose a serious threat to mental health.

Conflicts do not necessarily indicate a need to change your values. Many conflicts result from competition for time, space, energy, and money rather than from faults in the value system. If you elect a course in psychology, you may have to omit some other course. If you go out for varsity football, you will probably not have the time or energy to earn high grades in a difficult curriculum. If you marry, you may have to give up college, or reduce your standard of living, or require more time to graduate. Whichever choice you make, you have to give up something you value. The more nearly equal the choices seem, the more trouble they cause. When you have only a mild interest in zymology, as against a strong interest in chemistry, you will experience little conflict in sacrificing the former subject to the latter. But when you have a strong desire to marry and, at the same time, a strong ambition to finish college, you will have trouble unless you can find a way to do both.

Perhaps the worst way to deal with this kind of conflict is to treat it as a dilemma. Suppose your conflict is between marriage and completing your college degree. If you treat your problem as a dilemma, you will feel that you have been stuck by the consequent of whichever alternative you choose. You will then be tempted to ease the pain with some form of self-deception. If, for example, you decide to drop out of college and get a job in order to get married, you might make the consequent more bearable by using the sour-grapes device — you can persuade yourself to believe that college is unimportant, that twenty years hence you will be as far ahead as if you had graduated. But this method of self-deception is likely to aggravate the problem. Assuming that you really wanted to finish college, you will have to keep deceiving yourself for many years. And this deception will become increasingly difficult to maintain as you see others of less ability go ahead of you because they hold college degrees. You may even turn your resentment against your wife and find yourself in a divorce court. At best, you will always experience some tension from your thwarted ambition.

A better procedure is described in Chapter 13. Your first step should be to put your creative skills to work to find a proposal for action that will enable you to achieve both goals. Failure to find such a proposal for action does not necessarily mean that you must sacrifice one of your goals forever. Doors that are closed today may be open tomorrow. The next step, therefore, is to decide which value can be better postponed while you continue to seek a means of achieving it. It is far better to satisfy one and postpone the other than to remain in a state of indecision, thereby accomplishing nothing. Having to postpone a goal is not necessarily a disadvantage. For example, a study of college records shows that many students who had to interrupt their college educations for military service made much better academic records after returning to college. Many of these students returned to college with more definite goals and with a clearer understanding of the value of a college education.

Another and more difficult type of conflict is the fundamental one involved in the satisfaction of certain needs. For example, when we try to satisfy some of our biological needs we are likely to find ourselves hemmed in by the manners, customs, and moral codes established by society for its own preservation. These rules and our needs seem to be the horns of a continuing series of dilemmas. If we fail to satisfy our needs, we experience unpleasant and unrelieved inner tensions, and that is bad; if we satisfy these needs in a certain way, we are punished by society, or by conscience, or both, and that is bad.

Conflicts between our needs and the rules are intensified by the competitiveness of our culture. We measure prestige and achievement not by absolute but by relative standards, that is, in terms of what others are doing. Furthermore, our culture awards prestige not for actual merit but for competitive position. We must outstrip our brothers, but we must also be our brother's keeper. We must get ahead, but we must not be too aggressive. We must climb to the top, but not by climbing over others.

Many people attempt to solve such conflicts by cheating on the rules. But such a course is fraught with danger, for when you start to cheat you begin a vicious cycle of erosion in your ethical code. To ease your conscience you are likely to resort to psychological aspirin. The next time a similar situation appears it will be harder to keep yourself from cheating again because you have already justified your previous behavior to yourself. The more often you use psychological aspirin, the more distorted your view of your own conduct becomes. The tension generated is likely to spread and lead you into even more questionable behavior in the future. Many a promising and useful career has been ruined in this way. The cashier convicted of embezzling $50,000 of the bank's funds probably started by borrowing a few cents, and never expected to take more or to get caught.

A better way to deal with conflicts between society's rules and the satisfaction of needs is to examine carefully both the need and the method by which you propose to satisfy it. Have you exaggerated your need? Will its satisfaction place demands on you which you cannot meet? Would a more modest degree of success be more rewarding in the long run? When you have determined your minimum need, the chances are that you can find a way of satisfying it without violating the rules of society or conscience. If you cannot achieve a particular goal, perhaps you can find a substitute goal which will satisfy the need. For example, if your need is prestige, and you lack the ability to graduate from college, you can change your goal to succeeding in some vocation that does not require a college degree. You should beware of fixing on one particular method of satisfying a need, for there are many ways of satisfying most needs.

But even if we concentrate on abiding by the rules, we seem to get into dilemmas because the rules themselves are often in conflict. What do you do when you see a fellow student cheating on an examination? If you report him to the proper authorities, you violate the code which prohibits squealing; if you let him get away with cheating, you violate the code which prescribes your duties as a citizen. Either way, you lose.

When analysis reveals that the conflict lies between two rules of conduct, the next step is to examine the conflicting rules. Perhaps you are committing the error of oversimplification. Helping one's neighbor is a rule of Christian ethics, but interpreting it to mean helping your neighbor pass his examination by showing him your paper is oversimplifying the matter. You can seldom solve problems of conduct by rigid rules because each problem has its own complex context.

To assume that you must necessarily abandon one value premise completely because it is in conflict with another is to commit the black-or-white fallacy. Consider Premises C and D listed above under the category of major goals in life. As stated they certainly conflict: the primary objective in life cannot be both the accumulation of material wealth and the balanced satisfaction of needs. Usually, however, seemingly incompatible premises like these two can be reconciled without abandoning either completely. This pair can be made compatible by subordinating the goal of accumulating wealth to the larger goal of a balanced satisfaction of needs. If accumulating a *reasonable* amount of wealth is made a means of satisfying some needs instead of a primary goal, most, if not all, of the conflict is removed. You also commit the black-or-white fallacy if, because you have sometimes failed to follow a given value premise, you assume that you can never follow it.

Many college students become disturbed when they find that their seemingly "old-fashioned" moral codes are in conflict with so-called "modern" codes. Before discarding these "old-fashioned" moral premises, it is well to remember that many of these are backed by long experience; "modern" ones

are not. If you assume that traditional values are at fault merely because they have not produced a Utopia, you are committing the *post hoc* fallacy. The faults in our society could be due to our failure to follow these premises rather than to flaws in the premises themselves.

If an analysis of conflicting premises reveals no error in your interpretation or application of the rules, test them by Kant's rule of conscience: "Act as though the maxim of your action were by your will to become a universal law of nature." What would happen if everyone followed the rules in question? What course of conduct would you approve for someone else in the same situation? It will often happen that one of the two conflicting rules will fail to meet this test, and you can revise it accordingly. But beware of rationalizing. You cannot make an exception of yourself on the ground that your intentions are good.

A thoughtful assessment and modification of your value system is not easy, but wisdom and happiness may be the rewards. It is the only way to be or become the person *you* choose to be.

EXERCISE 35A

1–4. *These items refer to the following set of values recommended by Polonius to his son Laertes, who is about to depart for France* (Hamlet, *Act I, Scene 3*).

A.   Give thy thoughts no tongue,
Nor any unproportion'd thought his act.

B.   Be thou familiar, but by no means vulgar.

C.   Those friends thou hast, and their adoption tried,
Grapple them to thy soul with hoops of steel;

D.   But do not dull thy palm with entertainment
Of each new-hatch'd, unfledg'd comrade.

E.   Beware
Of entrance to a quarrel; but being in,
Bear 't that the opposed may beware of thee.

F.   Give every man thy ear, but few thy voice;

G.   Take each man's censure, but reserve thy judgment.

H.   Costly thy habit as thy purse can buy,
But not expressed in fancy; rich, not gaudy;
For the apparel oft proclaims the man.

.   .   .   .

I.   Neither a borrower nor a lender be;
For loan oft loses both itself and friend,
And borrowing dulls the edge of husbandry.

J.   This above all: to thine own self be true,
And it must follow, as the night the day,
Thou canst not then be false to any man.

1. Classify these value premises by writing the appropriate letter in the outline below. A premise may be entered in more than one category.

   I.   *Major goals in life* (in terms of meaning and purpose)

   _____

   II. *Career goals*

   _____

   III. *Educational goals*

   _____

   IV. *Ethics*

   _____

V. *Aesthetics*

_____

VI. *Procedures of thinking*

_____

VII. *Premises for success*

_____

2. Are the premises above compatible with man's nature? If not, explain why.

_____

_____

3. Are the premises above mutually compatible? If not, explain why.

_____

_____

4. What is your evaluation of the above premises as a value system?

_____

_____

5–6. *These items refer to the value premises below.*

K. "The vocation of every man and woman is to serve other people."

L. N. TOLSTOI

L. Power and wealth: these alone are worth the striving.

M. "Fear God, and keep His commandments: for this is the whole duty of man."

ECCLESIASTES

N. "Man's highest blessedness,
In wisdom chiefly stands."

SOPHOCLES

O. ". . . that best portion of a good man's life,
His little, nameless, unremembered acts
Of kindness and of love."

WILLIAM WORDSWORTH

P.   ". . . any man's death diminishes me, because I am involved in man-kind; and therefore never send to know for whom the bell tolls; it tolls for thee."

JOHN DONNE

Q.   "A thing of beauty is a joy forever."

JOHN KEATS

R.   "One ought to seek out virtue for its own sake, without being in-fluenced by fear or hope, or by any external influence. Moreover, in that does happiness consist."

DIOGENES LAERTIUS

S.   "Act as though the maxim of your action were by your will to become a universal law of nature."

IMMANUEL KANT

T.   "So act as to treat humanity, whether in thine own person or in that of another, always as an end, never as a means."

IMMANUEL KANT

5. Which, if any, of the value premises above are mutually incompatible?

_____

_____

6. If you followed Premise L, what needs would be unsatisfied?

_____

_____

7–10. _These items refer to Value Premises A-J as well as K-T._

7. Classify Value Premises A-T by writing the appropriate letter in the outline below. A premise may be entered in more than one category.

   I.   _Major goals in life_

_____

  II. _Career goals_

_____

 III. _Educational goals_

_____

IV. *Ethics*

_____

V. *Aesthetics*

_____

VI. *Procedures of thinking*

_____

VII. *Premises for success*

_____

8. What is your evaluation of the premises classified above as a value system?

_____

_____

9. List below the letters from any of the premises that you believe should be omitted.

_____

10. Write below a premise you believe should be added to the system.

_____

EXERCISE 35B

1. Write below a representative sample of the value premises you believe you live by.

A. _____

B. _____

C. _____

D. _____

E. _____

F. _____

G. _____

H. _____

I. _____

J. _____

2. In the space below marked *Conclusion,* state in propositional form a decision you have made recently. In the space marked *Minor Premise,* state in propositional form the immediate situation that led to the decision. Then derive the value premise necessary to make the conclusion valid.

Major Premise: _____

Minor Premise: _____

Conclusion: _____

3. On the basis of this evidence, what is the probability that you actually follow this premise?

_____

4. In the space below, state the categories you would use in classifying your own value premises (all lines need not be used).

I. _____   _____

II. _____   _____

III. _____   _____

IV. _____   _____

V. _____   _____

VI. _____   _____

VII. _____   _____

VIII. _____   _____

IX. _____   _____

X. _____   _____

5. Classify the premises you listed in Item 1 by writing the letter for each premise after the appropriate category above.

6. Evaluate the premises so classified as a value system.

_____

_____

_____

7. What premises would you omit or modify to make these premises an ideal value system?

_____

_____

_____

8. What premises would you add?

_____

_____

_____

Index